AFTER COMMUNISM

VOLUME 1 IN THE FULBRIGHT INSTITUTE SERIES ON INTERNATIONAL AFFAIRS

After
COMMUNISM

PERSPECTIVES ON DEMOCRACY

Edited by Donald R. Kelley

The University of Arkansas Press
Fayetteville • 2003

07   06   05   04   03   5   4   3   2   1

Text design by Ellen Beeler

⊖ The paper used in this publication meets the minimum requirements of the
American National Standard for Permanence of Paper for Printed Library
Materials Z39.48-1984.

LIBRARY OF CONGRESS CATALOGING-IN-PUBLICATION DATA
After communism : perspectives on democracy / edited by Donald R.Kelley.
   p. cm.   (The Fulbright Institute series on internationalaffairs ; v. 1)
Includes bibliographical references and index.
   ISBN 1-55728-746-5 (pbk. : alk. paper)
   1. Democracy—Former Soviet republics—Congresses. 2. Former Soviet
republics—Politics and government—Congresses. 3. Post-communism—Former
Soviet republics—Congresses. I. Kelley, Donald R., 1943– II. Series.
JN6531 .A33 2003
320.947—dc21

                                                              2003000202

To Quinn Meiying

Contents

CHAPTER ONE

What Is to Be Done?

DONALD R. KELLEY

Who We Are, and What We Do . . .

The Fulbright Institute of International Relations at the University of Arkansas is dedicated to the scholarly examination of important international issues. Created to honor the memory of J. William Fulbright, who served both as the president of the university and later, with greater national and global impact, as the chair of the Senate Foreign Relations Committee, the Fulbright Institute attempts to mirror the senator's dual commitment to serious and unbiased scholarship and to a timely examination of important issues that define America's place in a tumultuous world. His tenure as committee chair was marked by a curious and unresolved tension; on the one hand, Fulbright shared with virtually all Americans a distaste for communism as embodied in the Soviet Union and, after World War II, in the new communist regimes in China and Eastern Europe. But on the other hand, his dislike for the philosophies and oppressive institutions of these nations did not obviate either his willingness to engage them in productive international dialogue or his insistence that we learn as much as possible about nations hostile to the United States as well as about traditional allies more congenial to our philosophy and way of life. That commitment was embodied not only in his sponsorship of the Fulbright exchange programs but also in his often-controversial efforts to examine America's policies toward both allies and enemies.

It is this commitment to an unflinching and scholarly examination of the premises and practices of America's foreign policy and to an insistence on the rigorous scholarly examination of controversial topics that the Fulbright Institute intends to bring to its activities. The Institute hosts an annual conference dedicated to the examination of some important international topic, bringing to campus experts from around the nation and the world. The first volume of this series focuses on the fate of democracy in the nations that overthrew communist rule in the late 1980s and early 1990s. In one sense, this is an appropriate point of departure for a series undertaken in the name of Senator Fulbright, whose emergence on the world stage occurred at a time when the basic tenets of the cold war were defined at the end of World War II and whose continuing commitment to seeing "new realities" instead of "old myths" would have lent itself to an examination of the nature of the post–cold war world. The second volume, now in preparation as this work goes to press, is the result of the collaboration between the Fulbright Institute and the Diane D. Blair Institute of Southern Politics and Society. *Vantage Points: Perspectives on the Clinton Presidency* will offer the first scholarly assessment of the Clinton years. In 2004, the Fulbright Institute and the King Fahd Center for Middle East and Islamic Studies will collaborate with the Institute of Oriental Studies of St. Petersburg State University in Russia on a joint study of Central Asia, with the proceedings to be published in both English and Russian.

What Is to Be Done . . .
and Not Done, at Least for Now

Although the regime Lenin created has not survived the test of time and voter approval, he (and Chernyshevsky, from whom he borrowed the phrase) has offered us a useful injunction to state at the beginning of a project the current tasks before us. Our purpose is to provide an assessment of the fate of democratic reforms that occurred in Russia and Eastern Europe a decade ago. That is an ambitious undertaking by any standard, and both modesty and intellectual honesty dictate that a number of caveats be set forth at the beginning.

We acknowledge that no definitive judgment can yet be offered. As the conclusion indicates, some things are certain, but for many of the key questions about whether democracy will "stick" or even why the democratic project(s) took place in the manner in which they unfolded the jury is still out. That said, as "experts"—and as academics—we cannot resist the temptation to offer a preliminary judgment, with all of its strengths and weaknesses. Those judgments must be tempered by certain admissions concerning the limitations of the current study as well as the state of the art—a new art called "consolidology" by many.

Much of the modesty about our conclusions stems from the time frame. As Richard Rose observes, only one-half of a generation—that is, ten of twenty years—has passed since the fall of what were thought to be firmly entrenched communist regimes. For some aspects of democratization, even ten years is adequate for judgment. New constitutions can be assessed; new institutions can be held up to comparative standards of successful democracies elsewhere in the world; and even the more intangible dimensions of democratic political life such as the formation of viable political parties or secondary associations can be examined. But for other aspects, especially those tied to the emergence of a democratic political culture and the development of favorable attitudes toward the new democratic institutions and market economies, ten years may not be an adequate time frame. For the next generation on whose commitment to democracy so much has been staked, a decade probably is adequate to chart attitudes and behavior patterns; not having lived under the old order, this new generation has not been compelled to "unlearn" the patterns of the past. For those who have prospered under the new democratic regimes and market economies a decade also may be sufficient, regardless of their age. For the former communist *apparatchiki* turned democrats who have succeeded in the new electoral milieu and the *nomenklatura* capitalists who have enriched themselves during marketization, the new order is as acceptable as the old, assuming that they would have prospered to some degree in either. But what about those who are not young, not rich, or not elected to public office—that is, the vast majority of those living in the new democracies? About them, the judgment is more difficult, and a longer time frame may be required to assess the depth and breadth of their commitment to post-communist reforms.

The incredible diversity of the post-communist experience also instills a sense of modesty in those who would offer sweeping conclusions. In all, twenty-seven nations emerged from the fall of the communist regimes in the former Soviet Union and Eastern Europe. Only two of the contributions attempt to deal comprehensively with the entire experience of democratization —my largely theoretical essay on democratization itself, and Valerie Bunce's historical overview of the process of democratization and its implications for the post-communist experience. Both accept that the initial diversity among these nations and their varied experiences in the transition to post-communist rule confirm that, as Bunce says, "history matters." Some of these twenty-seven nations had centuries-long identity as nations, while others had been crafted as a part of the empire-building tendencies of monarchs or commissars. None had any long-standing experience with democracy. With the exception of Czechoslovakia, the Wilsonian democracies of post–World War I Eastern Europe failed to weather the political and economic storms of the 1930s. It is therefore not surprising that there are as many variations on post-communist democracy as there are nations themselves. Some clearly have negotiated the transition with considerable success; Bunce puts the number of likely-to-survive democracies at one-quarter of the total, while I more optimistically put the figure at around one-third. The proportions are about the same for those nations that are democracies in name only. It is the middle portion for which there is the least consensus, and therefore the greatest debate about both the theoretical meaning of democratic consolidation and the likely trajectory of democracy in these nations, which include key states such as the Russian Federation and Ukraine.

In addition, the twenty-seven post-communist nations evidence an incredible cultural and economic diversity. Whatever putative unity had been created through their professed devotion to the philosophy of Karl Marx or their propensity to apply (admittedly, with considerable variation) the Leninist organizational model, at root these nations ranged from the former Catholic and Protestant monarchies of central Europe, through the Orthodox regimes of Russia and Ukraine, to the Moslem emirates of Central Asia. Neither the seventy-four years of communism in the former Soviet Union nor the less extensive post–World War II experience of socialist rule in Eastern Europe could erase that diversity.

No less important was the economic diversity of these nations. They ranged from the industrialized states of north-central Europe through to the still essentially agricultural states of Central Asia. Some had "made it" as industrial nations long before the advent of communist rule, while others had barely emerged from third world status even under the economic tutelage of the Soviet Union. More importantly for our purposes, even under communism they presented many different faces to the world. While in the Soviet Union the worst vestiges of central planning were preserved virtually until the end, in Eastern Europe wide-ranging experimentation had occurred. Moreover, most nations had several "economies"—that is, the "official" economy administered by the state, which existed simultaneously and symbiotically with creative variations of an unofficial "gray" economy that increasingly compensated for the state's failings. To varying degrees, these nations had engaged Western capitalist economies, either as producers or consumers. Some, especially in Eastern Europe, found further engagement in the post-communist world an easy task, while others faltered in their attempts to encourage outside investment or to escape their status as raw materials suppliers, especially in the energy sector. Not surprisingly, that diversity continued over the first decade of post-communist rule, resulting in the creation of many variations of market economies.

We are also properly modest about how much we can resolve the long and spirited theoretical debate about the processes of democratization and consolidation. To be sure, that debate began even before the communist regimes began to topple in connection with the so-called third wave of democratization in south Europe, Latin America, and Asia. In its most recent incarnation, it has filled the pages of the *Slavic Review* and the *Journal of Democracy* with discourse on what should or should not be regarded as a consolidated democracy or what factors are most critical in its emergence. It is not our purpose, however, to take sides in that dispute or to offer a systematic and exhaustive test of the multifaceted theory of consolidation. Much of our reticence stems from our earlier acknowledgment that a decade may not be a sufficient time frame within which to make this call. Thus our approach is eclectic, at least to the extent that the Kelley and Bunce essays, which together constitute a theoretical and historical overview of democratization, take the broader perspective, and to the degree that the other contributors focus on a particular part of that consolidation process—Jack Bielesiak, for example, who looks at party structures and electoral processes, or Richard Rose, who deals with public opinion—or at a particular region—Gregory Gleason, for example, who deals exclusively with Central Asia.

Modesty Aside ...

Modesty and our *samokritika* (self-criticism, an old soviet tradition) aside, how much can we claim for this admittedly eclectic examination of the post-communist experience? At the least, the contributors have labored productively in their respective vineyards and produced a fine yield of individual studies, most focusing on a particular aspect of the process of consolidation or on a particular region or country. Taken in toto, they provide instructive snapshots of the successes, failures, and unresolved struggles that make up the process of democratic consolidation. While they do not yield a comprehensive and integrated study of all aspects of democratization or a test of the theory of consolidation, they certainly point to the most prominent examples of when fledgling democrats got it right, when they abjectly failed, and when their efforts have not yet produced clear results.

What, then, should the reader expect to take away from his or her reading of this collective effort? The answer can best be expressed in terms of our relative levels of certainty about what constitutes a successful transition to democracy. As the concluding chapter, which terms democratization a "work in progress," argues, we are more certain of some things than of others. For example, our studies suggest that the sort of "reverse waves" that Samuel Huntington described are unlikely to occur. To be sure, even those states which began the democratic transition with the best of intentions may slip backward from time to time. But it is unlikely that such setbacks will take the form of military coups or the return of Leninist-style dictatorships. There is also substantial evidence that market reforms are now irreversible, which is not to argue that considerable disagreement will not occur over the level of state intervention or the role of powerful oligarchies in otherwise free markets. There is also widespread agreement that a democratic transition requires the creation of a strong state, which in virtually all cases implies strong executive power. But it is far less clear how such strong states and executives should relate to legislatures, parties, and the myriad private institutions that make up a viable democracy. In the broader perspective, there is consensus that eventually fully empowered and institutionalized civil societies must arise if democracy is to survive, even though there is little agreement about how to assess the thresholds of viability. And so it goes, at least at this early stage of our understanding about both the theory and practice of democratic consolidation. Each truth we discover—that democracies require competent states to sustain the democratic process itself, for example—confronts us with new questions: how much strength is needed, and how much is too much? It is simply too early to be certain that we have fully understood the pertinent questions, much less discovered the answers.

CHAPTER TWO

The Complexity of Democratic Consolidation

DONALD R. KELLEY

An assessment of the consolidation of democracy in those nations that over-threw communist rule a decade ago must begin with some understanding of what consolidation means. That is no easy task. A new subdiscipline of "con-solidology" has been born, and the scholar who coined the term has described the idea of consolidation as an "unclear, inconsistent, and unbounded concept."[1] Juan Linz and Alfred Stepan have offered a complex and multifaceted "working definition":

> *Behaviorally,* a democratic regime in a territory is consolidated when no significant national, social, economic, political, or institutions spend significant resources attempting to achieve their objectives by creating a nondemocratic regime or by seceding from the state. *Attitudinally,* a democratic regime is consolidated when a strong majority of public opinion . . . holds the belief that democratic procedures and institutions are the most appropriate way to govern collective life. . . . *Constitutionally,* a democratic regime is consolidated when government and nongovern-mental forces alike become subject to, and habituated to, the resolution of conflict within the bounds of the specific laws, procedures, and insti-tutions sanctioned by the new democratic process.[2]

Much of the ambiguity of the term results from imprecision about what the term "democracy" itself means, and no analysis of consolidation can ever hope to sort out completely this debate. One study has identified more than 550 different definitions and notes that most discussions are about what it terms "democracy with adjectives," that is, "liberal democracy," "authoritarian democracy," and so on, suggesting that it makes little sense in the real world to discuss a perfect prototype.[3]

The need for such adjectives stems from two fundamental definitional ambiguities: first, are we to describe democracy in terms of *process* or *outcome;* and second, are we to think of it in terms of *institutional* or *cultural forms?* The former distinction addresses the fundamental question of *means vs. ends.* Is democracy defined merely by the way its citizens reach collective decisions, or does it require certain characteristics that go beyond process to address either the outcomes of governmental action or the nature of the society itself? Emphasis on process alone results in a minimalist definition similar to that offered by Joseph Schumpeter, who argues that the term democracy should be applied to any system "for arriving at political decisions in which individuals acquire the power to decide by means of a competitive struggle for the people's votes."[4] In the terms of the current discussion, democratization therefore has been consolidated when the process of democracy has become "the only game in town."

A more demanding emphasis on outcomes goes well beyond a minimalist definition. In the context of Western democratic theory, it brings us to Robert Dahl's concept of *polyarchy,* in which democracy is defined in terms of the broader pattern of structured interaction within the community and the requirement that society sustain both a high level of pluralism and personal freedom.[5] In the now discredited Marxist context, it resulted in a definition of democracy in which economic outcomes became more significant than participational criteria in legitimating the political order. In both, democracy was not just about the process of reaching public decisions; it also involved an assessment of the sort of society that the democratic process was destined to create and ultimately upon which its survival depended.

The inclusion of institutional and cultural factors also complicates the definition of democracy. The weight of history and no small dose of European and American cultural ethnocentrism have created the impression that "proper" democracies are more likely to be formed in and, more importantly, to take lasting root in societies that have shared cultural, religious, and historical experiences. "Proper" democracies resemble their European predecessors in institutional and structural terms, mirroring the presidential or parliamentary models of the world's older democracies and creating ancillary structures such as parties and interest groups from the same mold.

Perhaps because of these ambiguities, the notion of consolidation has broadened over the last two decades as scholars first turned their attention to the birth of democracies in Latin America, Asia, and Southern Europe and later to the democratization of former communist nations. Initially consolidation seemed to mean little beyond protecting the fledgling democracies from authoritarian regression, from what Samuel Huntington termed "reverse waves," which seemed inevitable given earlier experiences with democratization.[6] But as Andreas Schedler has observed:

> Now the concept has been expanded to include popular legitimation, diffusion of democratic values, neutralization of anti-system actors, civilian supremacy over the military, elimination of authoritarian enclaves, party building, organization of functional interests, stabilization of electoral rules, routinization of politics, decentralization of state power, introduction of direct democracy, judicial reform, alleviation of poverty, and economic stabilization.[7]

Larry Diamond offers an even longer list of requirements for the consolidation of a "liberal democracy," including

- regular, free, and fair electoral competition, universal suffrage, and the expectation that regime change will be a regular occurrence;
- the absence of reserved domains for the military and other social groups that are not directly accountable to the electorate;
- both the "vertical accountability" of officials to the electorate and their "horizontal accountability" to one another within the constitutional structure;
- restraints on executive power set forth by a constitution;
- the rule of law;
- provisions for political and civic pluralism; and
- individual and group freedoms.[8]

As the list continues to grow, an important caveat seems in order. Any assessment of the consolidation of the democracies that have emerged in former communist states must accept the reality that there are vast differences among these nations. Some have come close to the establishment of advanced liberal democracies, some have adopted the formal rules of the game of democracy but have remained essentially authoritarian states, while the vast majority seem to have fallen somewhere between the two extremes. Accepting this diversity compels us to acknowledge that no single model of consolidation is appropriate. To be sure, an artificial standard may be created, with the criteria set low to label virtually all nations with democratic procedures in place as consolidated democracies (the argument of the minimalists) or set high to exclude all nations that have not established the full array of social, cultural, and economic features associated with our Eurocentric notion of liberal democracies. But such an approach would seem to miss the nuances both of the processes of democratization (assuming that those processes include cultural, social, and economic as well as political changes, and that these changes may occur differently in various nations) and of the substance of the current political order (further assuming that there may be different institutional forms and behaviors that, at least from the perspective of common sense, qualify as democratic).

Civic Culture and Democratic Consolidation

The full consolidation of democracy unquestionably requires the eventual creation of a democratic civic culture appropriate to the level of democratization. Representative institutions cannot function viably in a society whose values are hostile or indifferent to their preservation. Yet the formation of civic cultures supportive of democracy is the most intangible and subjective aspect of consolidation. Such cultures exist not as institutions, constitutions, or codes of law, although their values are embodied in them. They exist in the minds and in the habituated behaviors of the citizens of newly democratized nations, and they are as complex and potentially self-contradictory as the multitude of citizens themselves.

The idea of civic cultures is rooted in the concept of *political culture,* which emerged over three decades ago. It focused on the attitudes and perceptions of citizens and sought to explain both political behavior and to characterize regime types. Political cultures were labeled *subject, participant,* or *parochial* with references to citizens' level of meaningful involvement in politics and their attitudes toward the regime.[9] Political culture focused attention on what the citizen thought about the regime under which he or she lived and used these findings to explain political behavior. Analysts examined "attitudes toward the political system and its various parts, and attitudes toward the role of the self in the system" as well as "cognitions, feelings, and evaluations" that informed citizens' understanding of the political process, their approval or disapproval, and their perception of its effectiveness.[10] Taken together, such attitudes and perceptions produced "orientations toward political action," that is, they disposed citizens toward certain forms of behavior: active and meaningful involvement in a participant political culture, quiescent obedience in a subject political culture, and avoidance of political life in a parochial political culture.

From these studies emerged an assumption: if they were to survive, political systems had to have political cultures that were in synchronization with their essential nature. Authoritarian regimes required the presence of a subject political culture in which citizens accepted their limited role in public life, and democratic regimes demanded the presence of participant cultures that encouraged meaningful involvement in public life and certain values such as tolerance and a sense of fair play that would facilitate the operation of democratic institutions. The problem was that no one was quite sure of how to deal with change; no one doubted that democratic institutions could be created in nations that lacked or had incomplete participant cultures, but no one knew how completely a formerly subject civic culture had to be transformed before democracy could hope to survive.

Three caveats are in order before we attempt to spell out what a democratic civic culture means. First, all political cultures are, and perhaps need to be, a mixture of participant, subject, and parochial elements. The need for such symbiotic union will be examined in greater detail below as a part of the discussion of congruence, but for the present it is sufficient to note that it is the balance of the three elements that permits society to manage the inherent tension between the need for some form of political contestation (which may not necessarily mean democracy) and the simultaneous need for the preservation of social order and cohesion. In democratic systems, of course, the participant features are dominant, but the other elements must also be present in some acceptable mix.

The second caveat is about the sequence of events in creating and consolidating democracy. The formation of a democratic civic culture may either lead or follow the creation of formal democratic institutions. The first scenario is consistent with the argument that certain social and cultural traditions are necessary for or may facilitate the creation of democracies; when the right "preconditions" have been met, democracies will emerge virtually spontaneously. The latter scenario is more consistent with the "crafting" school of democratization argued most forcefully by Giuseppe DiPalma; in this version, democratic institutions emerge because leaders create (or "craft") them, and their long-term survival then depends upon the willingness of political elites to play by the rules of the game and the ability to develop a supportive political culture.[11]

The third caveat speaks to the contradictions that exist within any society. The sort of changes that must occur during the creation of a democratic civic culture may occur at different rates for different elements of the society. Political and economic elites, for example, may embrace the new values, some for philosophical reasons or some because they see the democratic process as the key to the retention or attainment of political or economic power. Other elements of the same society—elites incapable of benefiting from the transition, the middle class whose economic or social status are challenged, or workers and farmers who share the same concerns—may accept the new democratic values more reluctantly, if at all. Moreover, different elements of the society may simultaneously move in different directions; political elites who have learned to play the new democratic game to their advantage may increase their commitment to the new order, while other once supportive elements which have lost economic or social standing may decrease their commitment.

The Elements of a Democratic Civic Culture

The literature on democratic civic cultures offers a long list of characteristics that supposedly must be present for democracy to survive. Some authors mechanistically stress the acceptance of democratic procedures or the rule of law, while others emphasize characteristics such as tolerance of other points of view, perceptions of empowerment on the part of the voters, or the efficacy of governmental institutions themselves. As "consolidology" has developed, the list has tended to grow longer and more demanding; a consensus has emerged that *creating* democracies may be a much simpler task than *consolidating* them even.

What follows is a list of the many elements that have been offered as important parts of a democratic civic culture:

- widespread agreement that a *community* exists—conventionally defined as a "nation" rooted in a "state"—linking all of the elements of the society together despite their ethnic or religious differences, or the creation of power-sharing arrangements that acceptably manage such diversity
- widespread acceptance of the *procedural rules* of democracy, both written and informal, including universal franchise, majority rule (with possible provisions for the protection of minority rights), freedom of assembly and association, acceptance of the concept of "bounded uncertainty" (that is, no one knows who will win the next election, but all agree to accept the outcome, at least until the next election)
- widespread acceptance of the *form of government*, that is, a parliamentary, presidential, or mixed system, or a willingness to pursue change only through constitutionally sanctioned channels
- widespread perception of the *effectiveness of government*, that is, its ability actually to reach binding decisions and avoid institutional gridlock (*deci-*

sional efficacy), to mobilize public resources and collect taxes (*support efficacy*), and to enforce its decisions throughout the nation (*administrative efficacy*)

- widespread perception of the political efficacy of the individual citizen, that is, voters perceive themselves as "empowered," that they possess a meaningful political "self" as mediated through parties and associations, that their actions make a difference, and that they are offered meaningful choices; even among voluntary nonvoters, a strong sense of latent efficacy exists
- widespread tolerance of political and social diversity, and acceptance of the institutionalization of such differences within the community
- widespread acceptance of the rule of law
- widespread presence of what Harry Eckstein has termed "congruence" of democratic values, that is, that other social institutions manifest internal procedures and sustain social milieu that are essentially (although not necessarily completely) democratic, lending support to the creation of a democratic civic culture[12]

Congruence and Democratic Political Culture

The last point concerning congruence bears special consideration. As Harry Eckstein and others have noted, governments perform well and evidence a higher level of stability "to the extent that their authority patterns are congruent with the authority patterns of other units of the society."[13] In other words, democratic political institutions are most likely to prosper within societies in which other social units—economic organizations, professional or interest-oriented associations, social organizations, and, to some degree, even primary units such as the family—also evidence at least some degree of participatory and democratic values. In such a setting, political and other social units are mutually supportive, especially to the extent that nonpolitical units act as "schools of democracy." In established democracies, the congruence of political and nonpolitical units is simultaneous; both political and other social institutions have long adhered to democratic norms. But in newly democratized nations, the democratization of political and nonpolitical units may be out of synchronization. Especially in those nations in which democratic institutions have been created overnight as a consequence of the fall of authoritarian and/or communist systems, nonpolitical institutions are likely to be less extensively democratized than the formal political institutions themselves.

The lack of synchronization creates several dilemmas. On the one hand, there are pressures to opt for the most rapid democratization of nonpolitical institutions and to create open and responsive intermediate organizations such as political parties and interest groups. But on the other hand, political realism and the limited malleability of any society suggest that such transformations should be undertaken with caution. Especially in nations in which democratic institutions are crafted by elites who may themselves be less than fully steeped in democratic values, care must be taken to combine elements of the new democratic culture with systems of belief and patterns of social interaction that are rooted in the old order. Speaking of the problems facing new democracies, Eckstein notes that "congruence theory implies that new institutions must be designed in a way that does not dramatically violate the congruence condition—in other words, that adapts, in some degree, to the preestablished order."[14] The inevitable result is the coexistence of democratic and predemocratic elements within the same society. In established and stable democracies, such differences reach the level of "balanced disparities" in which democratic and authoritarian elements are combined to provide for the simultaneous existence of meaningful participation and social and institutional stability. But in new democracies, the "balance" may be difficult to achieve and to maintain.

Civil Society and the Consolidation of Democracy

The creation of a viable civil society also is essential for the consolidation of democracy. Civil society is an intermediate link between the individual and what below will be termed "political society." It is made up of autonomous groups and associations that structure and define the political identity of citizens as well as provide intermediate mechanisms that link them to more explicitly political institutions. In most societies, such groups and associations include labor unions, churches, economic or functional associations, cultural or ethnic groups, or special issue groups. Diamond describes them as "the realm of organized social life that is voluntary, self-generating, (largely) self-supporting, autonomous from the state, and bound by a legal order or a set of shared values."[15]

Civil society performs a number of necessary functions in a democracy. Most important, it organizes and gives form to the myriad demands that compete for the attention of political institutions. Membership in groups and associations provides individuals with a sense of political identity; in psychological terms, perceived affinity with or direct membership in such associations defines one as a lawyer or a blue-collar worker, as a consumer or a producer, as a Baptist or a Catholic, as an advocate of gun control or a member of the National Rifle Association, and the like. As a consequence, such groups structure at least a part of citizens' political involvement, especially to the extent that political parties (which belong in the "political society" examined below) are broader coalitions of diverse interests.

Just as important, a broadly pluralistic civil society that interacts well with explicitly political entities such as parties, legislatures, and the bureaucracy contributes to the emergence of consensus within society. To the extent that such associations stress compromise and consensus building within the broader political process, and to the extent that the average citizen is a member (or potentially could be a member) of multiple and conflicting groups that produce cross-pressures, civil society moderates the intensity of political conflict.

In addition, civil society supplements parties in promoting participation; develops democratic attitudes, especially to the degree that the values of the associations and groups are congruent with the broader democratic society; creates alternative and multiple channels for articulating interests; contributes to the emergence of countervailing power, that is, the existence of articulate groups on both sides of any given issue; helps to train and recruit political activists and future leaders; and increases the amount of information available to ordinary citizens.

The existence of a viable civil society is of particular importance in restraining the authoritarian tendencies of government, especially in recently formed democracies with little tradition of constitutionalism and the rule of law. As Diamond argues,

> Civil society is a vital instrument for containing the power of democratic governments, checking their potential abuses and violations of the law, and subjecting them to public scrutiny. *A vibrant civil society is probably more essential for consolidating and maintaining democracy than for initiating it.*[16] (emphasis added)

The formation of civil society is particularly difficult in former communist nations, where the party-state abolished almost all remnants of independent social organization and replaced them with approved associations that functioned under party control. Under state corporatism, as this arrangement has been called, associations never reached the level of true autonomy, and their participation in the political process always was at the sufferance of higher authorities. Particular care must be taken in the creation of post-communist civil societies to avoid the de facto recreation of such a state corporatist model; while newly formed democratic governments can facilitate the creation of truly independent groups and associations and establish the legal framework required for their operation, they must eschew the temptation to create civil societies from the top down. However difficult and initially disorderly the process, civil societies must emerge from the grassroots level.

A final caveat is in order concerning the relationship between civil and political societies. Under ideal circumstances, the two operate symbiotically; each benefits from the viable functioning of the other, civil society gaining focus and finding its appropriate institutional targets within the political society, and the political society itself benefiting from the mediating role of civil society. But a warning is still in order: neither can substitute for the other. As Diamond has noted:

> Interest groups cannot substitute for coherent political parties with broad and relatively enduring bases of popular support. [They] cannot aggregate interests as broadly across social groups and political issues as parties can. Nor can they provide the discipline necessary to form and maintain governments and pass legislation.[17]

In the context of post-communist democracies, this warning has particular relevance. Under these circumstances, both civil and political societies must emerge simultaneously, and it may be difficult to strike a balance between the two. After decades of repression and control, new civil societies may burst forth with exceptional force, organizing every interest, pressing every demand, and seeking confrontation in the understandable if divisive desire to emphasize the representational and participational features of democracy. Conversely, it is probable that the formal institutions of political society will stress the need for order and discipline to compensate for the increasing pluralism and disorder of society. Finding a balance that will sustain an open but still governable society may be difficult.

Market Reforms and the Consolidation of Democracy

The relationship between democracy and market economies has provoked endless debate. Two issues are involved: first, whether the creation of market economies leads to the emergence of democratic regimes (and implicitly, whether they can be created in their absence), and second, whether market economies are required for the consolidation of fledgling democracies. The first issue is virtually moot in the case of the former communist regimes under study; whatever the merits of the theoretical argument that under normal evolutionary processes market economies lead to the creation of democracies, such clearly was not the case with the fall of communism. At best, a few of the more reform-minded of the communist states had experimented with mixed economies or had scaled back on the level of direct state control by the mid-1980s. But in most cases, political and economic change occurred simultaneously, and the formal democratization of the political system was completed, at least in institutional terms, long before market reforms had fully taken root.

In virtually all cases, market reforms and the other changes that marked the end of centrally planned economies were imposed from the top down. To be sure, not all nations started from the same point. Especially in Eastern Europe, reform had begun in some nations long before the communist regimes were in any danger; in Yugoslavia, they dated back to the break with the Soviet Union in 1948 and had created a genuinely mixed economy, while in Hungary or Poland, reforms were more modest, creating a sort of "consumer communism" or doing away with specific features of the soviet model such as the collectivization of agriculture. Even the Soviet Union had attempted limited reforms under Nikita Khrushchev and Leonid Brezhnev, although they were intended more to fine-tune the planning mechanism and provide for greater consumer welfare rather than to offer fundamental structural change.

These early beginnings aside, the real economic transformation came in the late 1980s and early 1990s. It is important not to lose sight of the complexity of these transformations and to understand that they proceeded at different paces in different nations. They included

- the economically selective privatization of formerly state-owned resources, including not only the manufacturing and agricultural sectors but also the service sector;
- the creation of market mechanisms for both producer and consumer goods to replace the state-controlled planning process;
- the creation of a new pricing system to replace government-set prices;
- the creation of new management structures at the corporate and enterprise level;
- the creation of a stock market and other appropriate markets for agricultural commodities and raw materials;
- the creation of a banking system and other financial institutions needed to administer a market economy;

- the creation of a legal framework appropriate to the functioning of a market economy;
- the creation of governmental regulatory mechanisms; and
- the creation of a wide assortment of groups and associations based in the private sector that represent its interests to political authorities.

Several caveats are in order regarding these changes. Given the complexity of the transformation, it is hardly surprising that not all changes have occurred simultaneously or at the same pace in all post-communist nations. Privatization of state-held resources and the creation of (frequently unstable) stock markets and banking systems usually occurred first, while agricultural reform or the creation of a stable legal environment for business lagged behind. In many post-communist nations, the state has continued to intervene in the economy in pursuit of both economic and political goals.

The creation of a market economy also required a psychological change on the part of producers and consumers alike. Whatever their failures, the socialist economies had provided a degree of predictability and security; workers could be sure that their jobs were safe and consumers could be reasonably certain that at least the bare necessities would be available to them at acceptable prices. The harsh realities of the new market economies changed all that. Managers were no longer told what to produce, workers had to learn that uncertainty was a part of any market economy, and investors had to learn that opportunity also meant risk. Factories could and with increasing frequency did close; unemployment became widespread; inflation soared, especially in the early years, wiping out savings and outdistancing wage and salary increases; the state-supported safety net of social services vanished; stock markets rose to create overnight riches and just as quickly crashed to erase yesterday's gains; and corruption was everywhere. The new economy quickly produced striking inequalities between rich and poor. As the relative few who had profited from the transfer of state resources into private hands grew richer, the vast majority suffered—or perceived that they suffered, at least in the short term—from market reforms.

Market Economies and the Consolidation of Democracy

If we accept the reality that in the unique case of the former Soviet Union and Eastern Europe political change led to market reforms, we must now pose a somewhat different question: is the creation of a successful market economy necessary for the consolidation of these fledgling democracies? When the issue is redefined in these terms, it seems apparent that the transition to a market economy sets in motion a number of factors that contribute to the consolidation of democracy. But a warning is in order: such consolidation ultimately depends on far more than merely the transformation of the economy. It is therefore by argument that the creation of a successful market economy is a *necessary but not sufficient condition* for the consolidation of democracy.

As Peter Berger has pointed out, no viable democracy has survived over time without a reasonably successful market economy.[18] One important element in that connection is the symbiotic relationship between a market economy and the creation of an active civil society. Market economies depend on the operation of a viable civil society, and an activist civil society in turn supports the consolidation of democracy. A market economy fosters social pluralism, which is more than just the creation of a middle class. It also involves the formation of independent associations and social groups whose activities articulate and aggregate the demands of the citizens/consumers, place restrictions on the role of government, and contribute to the formation of a democratic civic culture.

As our choice of the adjective "successful" implies, the mere presence of the formal structure of a market economy may not be sufficient. Such economies must perform—and must be seen as performing—at a level that satisfies the expectations of both the new democratic elites and the general public. A recent study by Adam Przeworski and colleagues argues that the survival of new democracies depends upon affluence, economic growth with moderate inflation, and declining inequality.[19] Once a nation has created democratic institutions, the probability that they will survive is related to the overall level of economic development. The lower the per capita income, the more likely that the democracy will fail. Seymour Martin Lipset argues that higher levels of affluence reduce the importance of distributional conflicts, especially if the newly democratized political system is perceived as reducing inequalities.[20]

Under certain conditions, democracies also can survive in poorer nations to the extent that the new market economies generate economic growth accompanied by a moderate rate of inflation.[21] Growth is especially important in the nations, which emerged from communist rule, where by the late 1980s the economies had stagnated. Such growth is a critical element in restoring faith in the future, especially when democracy is equated in the popular mind with prosperity. Just as important is a moderate rate of inflation, guaranteeing that economic gains will not be outstripped by rising prices.[22] Both are important elements in avoiding economic crises or prolonged hardship that might fuel antidemocratic forces.

It is also important that the nation's new economic elites perceive that they have an important stake in the maintenance of democracy. To be sure, in many cases these new elites are drawn from the political elite of the communist era, the so-called nomenklatura capitalists who survived the transition not only by professing to accept democracy but also by arranging for the privatization of state-owned resources into their own hands, or from among a new class of entrepreneurs who pieced together vast holdings as the old order collapsed. However cynically we may judge these market "reforms," the reality remains that these important elements of the new political order will accept democracy only so long as it works to their advantage. They will therefore judge that new market economy and democracy by two standards: how well they provide for prosperity sufficient enough to meet their own (usually incredibly greedy) economic demands, and how well they provide them with access to and control over political authorities and, in a broader context, political parties and the media needed to defend their interests. In a sense, these new economic elites should be regarded as important "stakeholders" in the new democracy, especially in the short run until acceptance of democratic rule is instilled more deeply within the population as a whole.

It is also critical that the general public perceive that it has some stake in the future of a market economy. Whatever the dislocations of the transition itself, at some point the average citizen must begin to see the light at the end of the tunnel in terms of his or her own survival and well-being. Short-term privations can be borne stoically by a population that expects the future to be brighter.

In the long term, the survival of a market economy also will depend on the ability of new democratic states to create a supportive legal and institutional framework for business. The hodgepodge of laws and institutions cobbled together in the early phase of the transition ultimately must yield to systematic legislation creating a legal environment suitable for a market economy, a stable banking system, a viable equity market, and effective regulatory mechanisms. Paradoxically, these developments in most cases require the creation of a strong state possessing the political will to see reforms through to their conclusion and the ability to enforce its will on vested economic interests. Indeed, much of the recent scholarly commentary on market reform has focused on this latter implementation phase, eschewing earlier debates over the relationship between economic and political reforms and emphasizing the nitty-gritty details of creating viable institutions.

Political Society and the Consolidation of Democracy

Political society encompasses the expressly political institutions of the society: the formal institutions of government at all levels and political parties. As in any modern nation, the state performs the formal functions of governance. It makes legally binding decisions for the society, enforces them through some executive structure and its attendant bureaucracy, and adjudicates disputes both among citizens and between the citizen and the state. It is government in the sense that citizens most directly experience it. How its officials are chosen, and how they are held accountable to the people is the very essence of democratization, and the consolidation of new democracies can be measured in terms of the durability and effectiveness of these institutions and how well they bring to life the goal of popular rule.

Political society also includes the party system, even though it technically lies outside the formal structure of government. In modern democracies, parties are the most significant force in structuring the competition for political power. This is not to suggest that party systems need be orderly or stable to play such a role, and it certainly is not to argue that the governments that emerge from their activity must meet similar criteria. But it is to argue that parties typically play two important and expressly political roles. First, they structure the competition for formal office; they nominate candidates, conduct campaigns, and structure the governments that emerge. In this they are different from lobbies and other secondary associations that do not offer their own candidates for office. Second, parties mediate between individuals and groups and the formal political institutions. In their efforts to reach (and frequently to create) constituencies, parties aggregate the interests of individuals and groups within the society, thereby fundamentally organizing and simplifying the way in which citizens interact with the state.

How do we assess political society's role in the consolidation of democracy? Two caveats are in order. First, consolidation is about the survival of democratic rule, not about the durability of particular institutions. A nation that shifted from a presidential to a parliamentary system or vice versa would remain democratic if both provided for popular involvement and competition among aspirants to power. While stability may be a political virtue under normal circumstances, it is not the litmus test of the consolidation.

The second caveat reminds us that formal organizations never tell the whole story. No detailed reading of the post-communist constitutions, no examination of the formal legislative, executive, and judicial institutions, and no analysis of the formal structure of party systems reveal the informal side of formal institutions. Every formal organization has an informal organization nested within it. Formal role structures and the behaviors that they define are vested with human meaning by the individuals who, literally, flesh out the formal organizations, creating informal networks of patron-client relationships and, in some cases, replicating patterns of informal behavior that date back to the era of communist rule.

Executive Leadership and Consolidation

Most of the nations emerging from communist rule chose mixed presidential/ parliamentary systems in which directly elected presidents share responsibility with prime ministers and cabinets. Of the twenty-seven states that survived the Marxist experiment, eighteen initially chose such mixed systems. Yugoslavia and Slovakia opted for direct presidential election nearly a decade after democratization, and in July 2000, Moldova shifted from direct election to selection by the legislature. At present, nineteen chief executives are directly elected, constituting 70 percent of post-communist systems.

The exact division of powers among the presidency, the prime minister, and the legislature is highly idiosyncratic. From the beginning, some directly elected presidencies were intended to be figureheads, a pattern which prevails most strikingly in Slovenia, where Milan Kucan, an independent, won election in 1997 with 56 percent of the vote. At the other extreme, the creation of some presidencies represented little more than a change of job title for former communist-era leaders. In four of the five Central Asian republics of the former Soviet Union, incumbents remained in power, and in others such as the Russian Federation, Azerbaijan, and Georgia, high-ranking former communists quickly won top office.

Assessing the strength of these presidencies is highly situational, depending as much on the authoritarian style of the incumbent or the circumstances of his rise to power as on the formal institutional arrangements. In Croatia, for example, a relatively authoritarian leader chosen just after the fall of communism eventually yielded power to a more democratic successor, while in Belarus, the second round of presidential elections brought a more authoritarian figure to office. Authoritarian leadership also sometimes came from prime ministers or subnational leaders. In Slovakia, Prime Minister Vladimir Meciar temporarily amassed nearly dictatorial power, and in Yugoslavia, a regional post—the Serbian presidency under Slobodan Milosevic—de facto controlled the fate of the nation for most of the post-communist period.

Despite the diversity, the relative strength of these presidencies may be assessed in terms of (1) the constitutionally established powers of the office, including the ability to name and dismiss prime ministers, to dissolve the legislature and call for new elections, to issue presidential decrees with the force of law, and to call for national referenda (although as Thomas Remington's chapter establishes for the Boris Yeltsin presidency, such formal powers can be hedged by a host of de facto political realities); (2) the margin of victory at the polls and/or the leader's longevity in office; and (3) the president's de facto control over the legislature, established either through the dominant role of a presidential party or coalition (even if cobbled together for each election) and/or through the quiescence or disorganization of opposition forces.

Assessed in these terms, the twelve states with the strongest directly elected presidents are Armenia, Azerbaijan, Belarus, Croatia, Georgia, Kazakhstan, Kyrgyzstan, Russia, Tajikistan, Turkmenistan, Ukraine, and Uzbekistan. To some degree, predictable similarities emerge: the list includes all of the Central Asian republics, all three Slavic republics, and all three Caucasian republics of the former Soviet Union. Indeed, the initial inclusion of Croatia under Franjo Tudjman is no longer justified since his death in December 1999. That said, it is also striking that a strong presidency does not necessarily imply that incumbents will remain in power. In seven cases—Azerbaijan, Kazakhstan, Kyrgyzstan, Tajikistan, Turkmenistan, Uzbekistan, and, for most of the post-communist period, Georgia—the leaders who rose to power in the immediate aftermath of the fall of communism remain in power. But in the other five nations—Armenia, Belarus, Croatia, Russia, and Ukraine—the current incumbent was elected well after the fall of the old regime (although in the case of Russia, Vladimir Putin clearly was Yeltsin's handpicked successor).

Less powerful, although directly elected presidencies initially were created in seven other post-communist nations. These include Bulgaria, Lithuania, Macedonia, Moldova, Poland, Romania, and Slovakia. In at least two cases—Poland under Lech Walesa and Lithuania under Vitautas Landisbergis—the anticommunist credentials of the incumbent initially strengthened the office, although both leaders eventually fell from favor and were removed from office by a disgruntled electorate. In no case has the first chief executive retained power throughout the entire post-communist period. In Bosnia and Herzegovenia a weak three-member collective presidency was created (one Bosnian, one Croat, and one Serb, each directly elected by his or her own constituency, with the chairmanship rotating every eight months).

Six post-communist nations have created systems closer to the parliamentary model in which the chief executive is chosen by the legislature. This pattern exists in Albania, the Czech Republic, Estonia, Hungary, Latvia, and after 2000, in Moldova. In half, the successful candidate must win a weighted majority (Albania requires a three-fifths' vote of the 140-member legislature, Estonia a two-thirds' victory, and the Czech Republic that the winner achieve majorities in both houses of the legislature). On the whole, these chief executives have remained relatively weak. Even Vaclav Havel, whose anticommunist credentials and prominent role in the liberation of his nation were beyond question, found that his prestige did little to strengthen the office, and his bid for reelection for a second term was closely contested.

Slovakia and Yugoslavia shifted from indirect to direct election of the presidency relatively late in their brief post-communist experience. Slovakia's president initially was chosen by the legislature, and the real power remained in the hands of its authoritarian prime minister, Vladimir Meciar. In the first direct presidential election held in January 1999, Meciar was defeated by the more democratically inclined Rudolf Schuster, whose tenure in office has done little to strengthen the inherent powers of the presidency.

Not surprisingly, the Yugoslav pattern was even more complex. Serbia and Montenegro each directly elect its own president, and the federal president—at first a relatively weak office, especially compared to the Serbian presidency—initially was chosen by the federal legislature. When Slobodan Milosevic constitutionally was denied the right to run for reelection to the Serbian top office, he engineered his election to the federal presidency by the Serbian-dominated federal legislature and subsequently amended the federal constitution in 2000 to provide for the direct election to that office, which had grown in power vis-à-vis its regional counterparts. In a bitterly contested election months later, Milosevic was defeated by Vojislav Kostunica, who has begun to disassemble the more authoritarian aspects of Milosevic's rule.

Another way to assess the democratic credentials of the new presidencies is to apply the criterion of *contestation,* that is, whether there has been real competition for the top post. To be sure, most of these nations have experienced only two presidential elections, making the determination of the level of competition idiosyncratic to each situation. That said, it is still possible to paint a preliminary picture. In those nations that directly elect a chief executive, the presidency will be judged to be competitive in the most recent presidential election (1) if an incumbent seeking reelection was defeated; (2) if the victor, whether incumbent or challenger, was forced into a runoff election; and/or (3) if the victor received fewer than 60 percent of the vote in the first round of balloting. In those cases in which the legislature makes the choice, the election will be judged to be competitive if a serious challenge were mounted against the eventual winner.

Applying these criteria, seventeen of the twenty-seven nations under study may be said to have competitive presidencies. Included are Armenia, Bulgaria, Croatia, the Czech Republic, Estonia, Hungary, Latvia, Lithuania, Macedonia, Moldova, Poland, Romania, Russia, Slovakia, Slovenia, Ukraine, and Yugoslavia. Direct presidential elections occur in eleven of the sixteen. Nine are from among the former socialist states of Eastern Europe, and seven were created from the breakup of the Soviet Union. Only four—Croatia, Russia, Ukraine, and Yugoslavia—were earlier classified as strong presidencies for at least a portion of the post-communist period.

Noncompetitive presidencies occur in eight of these nations, including Azerbaijan, Belarus, Georgia, Kazakhstan, Kyrgyzstan, Tajikistan, Turkmenistan, and Uzbekistan. In Belarus, Kazakhstan, Uzbekistan, and Turkmenistan, presidential terms were extended for several years by referendum (only in Kyrgyzstan was such an effort thwarted). In all, incumbents have won reelection by overwhelming margins (Alexander Lukashenka in Belarus with 76 percent of the vote; Nursultan Nazarbaev in Kazakhstan with 82 percent; Islam Karimov in Uzbekistan with 92 percent; Askar Akaev in Kyrgyzstan with 75 percent; and Imomali Rakhmonov in Tajikistan with 97 percent). In Turkmenistan, a ninety nine percent victory in a referendum extended the term of Sapamurad Niyazov "indefinitely."

With caveats attached, Albania and Bosnia and Herzegovenia should be added to this list. The Albanian president is chosen by a single-party-dominated legislature. The collective presidency of Bosnia and Herzegovenia evidences mixed results; while the popular election of the Serbian president was competitive, the elections of his Bosnian and Croatian counterparts were virtually uncontested.

Presidents, Parties, and Legislatures

Ultimately the consolidation of democracy will depend not only upon the performance of presidents and prime ministers but also on the productive interaction of executive leadership, legislatures, and party systems. As with all other post-communist experiences, there is remarkable diversity in the patterns that have emerged. In eighteen nations, multiparty legislatures have been created, and in the remaining nine the legislature has been dominated by a single party (sometimes affiliated with handpicked "independents" whose combined presence constitutes majority control). The multiparty systems include Armenia, Bosnia and Herzegovenia, Bulgaria, Croatia, the Czech Republic, Estonia, Hungary, Latvia, Lithuania, Macedonia, Moldova, Poland,

Slovakia, Slovenia, Romania, Russia, Ukraine, and Yugoslavia. Not surprisingly, multiparty systems are more common where the president is chosen by the legislature and/or where a relatively weak presidency exists. Only four from this list—Armenia, Russia, Croatia, and Yugoslavia—created strong presidencies for all or a part of the post-communist period, and the latter two have moved down the list of strong executives with the passage of the Tudjman and Milosevic regimes. Single-party dominant systems exist in nine post-communist nations: Albania, Azerbaijan, Belarus, Georgia, Kazakhstan, Kyrgyzstan, Tajikistan, Turkmenistan, and Uzbekistan. Eight of the nine also possess strong presidencies.

Viewed from a different perspective, ten of twelve nations of Eastern Europe have created successful multiparty systems, while only seven of the fifteen republics of the former Soviet Union reflect such diversity. If the Baltic states of Latvia, Lithuania, and Estonia are regarded as a special case because of their earlier (if brief-lived) experience with democracy and their relatively short tenure as soviet republics, the results are all the more striking; only four of the non-Baltic republics of the former Soviet Union have created successful multiparty systems: Russia, Ukraine, Moldova, and Armenia.

That said, it is also important to recognize that parties remain the weakest link in the consolidation of democracy. As Jack Bielasiak argues below, the institutionalization of a viable party system is far more precarious in the post-communist setting than in earlier episodes of the transition from authoritarianism to democracy, creating a pattern similar to such experiences in the Latin American context than in Western and Southern Europe.

What can be said of the long-term prospects for the consolidation of democracy in light of these institutional choices, especially in terms of the interplay of executive leadership, legislatures, and party systems? A study of mixed presidential/parliamentary systems indicates that they enjoyed the highest survival level in comparison with purely parliamentary or presidential arrangements; of the eight cases available for study for the period from 1950 to 1990, only one had succumbed to antidemocratic pressures.[23] In contrast, 76 percent of presidential democracies created from 1950 to 1990 fell victim to authoritarian rule, while roughly a third of purely parliamentary systems suffered the same fate.[24]

Perhaps the key to understanding the operation—and in many ways, the relatively high survival rate—of such mixed presidential/parliamentary systems is to comprehend that they operate in two separate modes. In one sense, they are not "mixed" systems as much as they are "alternate" systems. As Ezra Suleiman has pointed out, they are unlikely to operate on a prolonged basis with their presidential and parliamentary elements in equal balance.[25] At certain times, they will operate essentially as presidential systems, with the chief executive dominant either because of the strength of his or her electoral mandate, because overwhelming problems face the nation, or because the legislature is in disarray. In its most benign configuration, this mode will reflect a genuine consensus linking a dominant president with a like-minded majority in the legislature, either through the strength of a presidential party or a stable coalition of parties that supports the chief executive. In this mode, there will be few if any real limitations on the power of the president. To be sure, such executive strength does not necessarily signal a stable presidency, but merely an activist one. Political crises may be frequent and, from the president's perspective, conducive to the maintenance of his or her own power. Indeed, the president may be the source of such crises, dismissing prime ministers with little predictability, interfering in or outright ignoring the operations of the legislature, challenging the positions and sometimes the very legality of opposition parties, picking fights with the nation's neighbors or ethnic minorities at home, or provoking both the rumor and sometimes the reality of unconstitutional actions to maintain the dominant role of the presidency.

At other times, mixed presidential/parliamentary systems will operate essentially in the parliamentary mode, reflecting the relative weakness of the presidency vis-à-vis a strong prime minister and/or an assertive legislature. In formal terms, it is not necessary for the prime minister to lead one of the more powerful parties; mere acceptance by the dominant party or a coalition of parties strengthens the prime minister both against the president (who undoubtedly chose individuals in recognition of uncontestable political realities) and against the legislature itself (which has a vested interest in maintaining in office a strong prime minister over whom they have some control). To be sure, such "cohabitation," as the French have termed this relationship in the post-Gaullist period, has short-term drawbacks and long-term dangers. In the short term, the need to maintain the delicate three-way balance among the president, the prime minister, and the legislature leads to a sort of "minimalist" government; stability and perhaps even survival may be more important than making difficult decisions, leading such governments to be politically correct but overcautious. In the long term, the three-way balance always is fragile. As the French have learned, at least in terms of politics, cohabitation usually is a bumpy road. Presidents grow jealous of the power of "their" prime ministers and sack them sometimes seemingly just to demonstrate that they have the power to do so. Prime ministers grow ambitious and overly assertive, or they just exhaust whatever credit they had with the legislature. And legislatures, especially if there is no dominant presidential party, find it difficult to maintain long-term support for even the most compliant prime ministers.

What factors determine whether a mixed system operates in a presidential or parliamentary mode? One of the more obvious in the immediate post-communist years is the role played by dominant leaders identified with the fall of communism. The initial role played by leaders such as Boris Yeltsin, Lech Walesa, or Vaclav Havel underscores the significance of such purely personal concerns, although the growing opposition to all three signals how transitory such influence may be once a genuinely competitive political system has taken root. In these cases, their preeminent status as a leader of the opposition to communist rule undoubtedly contributed to the strength as presidents, winning them the support of wide segments of the population who otherwise were suspicious of "politicians" per se.

The strength of the presidential component of mixed system also is highly issue-specific. Perhaps understandably, presidents have benefited from—and have purposely exploited or even created—economic crises, civil wars or other domestic disturbances, ethnic or religious tensions, and external threats, or have fanned the flames of nationalist sentiment to strengthen their hand. But such issues also are a double-edged sword. Just as some presidents have used crises to augment their power, so too do they face the prospect that the legislature and the public will lay responsibility for failure at their door. With little ability to shift the blame elsewhere, presidents soon discover the truth of Harry Truman's dictum that "the buck stops here."

The relationship of the executive and legislative elements is deeply affected by the party system. As Suleiman has noted in his discussion of the Gaullist presidency, the dominance of that office came as much from the role of the Gaullist party in the legislature as it did from the formal powers of the presidency itself. The presence or absence of a presidential party plays an important role in shaping the de facto powers of the office, especially if such a party has a continuing identity and is not merely cobbled together in different form for each election. To the extent that it emerges as a bona fide nationwide political force, it can affect not only elections to the national legislature but also have impact on regional politics. Control of the legislature virtually guarantees the confirmation of the president's choice of prime minister and the passage of his or her legislative agenda, assuming that a degree of internal party discipline is present. To be sure, presidential parties suffer from the same weaknesses in mixed systems as they do in purely presidential ones. Regional party leaders look to their own interests, and ambitious aspirants to the highest office divide the party as they maneuver for position.

Conversely, the absence of a coherent presidential party limits the powers of the office. Even the strongest public mandate secured in the presidential race will not guarantee a working majority within the legislature. If the legislature is controlled by opposition parties, the president faces a difficult choice in the selection of a prime minister. He or she has three imperfect options: first, to select an apolitical technocrat whose administrative skills may win respect from the legislature but will not necessarily increase the likelihood that the president's legislative proposals will receive respectful attention; second, to choose a prime minister from within his or her own party (if such exists), guaranteeing conflict with the legislature; or third, choosing a prime minister from one of the opposition parties, creating the sort of uneasy cohabitation described above.

The relative weight of the presidential and legislative components also may turn on how well the opposition is organized. Presidents may emerge as the dominant force virtually by default if opposition forces are disunited. The rush to create new political parties after the fall of communist rule has led to unstable and undisciplined multiparty systems in many nations. To the extent that divisions among these parties makes it difficult or even impossible to form a viable opposition, the president will maintain a strong position vis-à-vis a divided legislature. Temporary coalitions that form within the legislature to oppose the president's legislation are likely to disintegrate during legislative or presidential elections, when it is every party and every would-be presidential candidate for him or herself, or when attention shifts to a different issue.

CHAPTER THREE

Comparative Democratization

Lessons from the Post-Socialist Experience

VALERIE BUNCE

Introduction

During the past twenty-five years, we have witnessed a global wave of democratization.[1] This process began in Southern Europe in the late 1960s with the collapse of the Antonio de Oliveira Salazar regime in Portugal (in 1968), followed soon thereafter by the death of Francisco Franco in Spain (in 1975). In both countries, though in very different ways, long-standing dictatorships gave way to democratic orders. Since that time, a number of regimes in Latin America, East Asia, Africa, and the European communist world have emulated the precedent set by Southern Europe.

While many of these new democracies have been fragile, if not fleeting, the fact remains that publics around the world today have a greater chance than they have ever had of living in a democratic order. There have been other waves of democratization—for example, after the First and Second World Wars, when such factors as mass conscription, the rise of new international norms, decolonization, and the creation of new states converged to launch experiments in democratic politics. However, neither of these prior rounds of democratization demonstrated the geographical reach of the most recent expansion of democratic governance.

The Puzzles of Post-Socialism

Perhaps the most remarkable chapter in this already remarkable story has been the transition from dictatorship to democracy in east-central Europe and the former Soviet Union. I use the term *remarkable* advisedly. Unlike the Southern European and Latin American cases, where democratization is more appropriately termed re-democratization, the eastern half of Europe is a region having little prior experience with democratic politics. For example, Russia has no historical precedent for democracy—though one might argue that the Aleksandr Kerensky government of 1917 made some steps, albeit ambivalent and brief, in that direction. Indeed, whatever one's theoretical perspective, Russian historical evolution provides a virtual textbook case of how a country can avoid acquiring those economic, political, and social characteristics that facilitate the rise of democracy.[2] It could be countered, of course, that the Russian case is exceptional. After all, there were democratic experiments in east-central Europe during the interwar period. However, except for Czechoslovakia, these flirtations with democracy were short-lived, lasting at most ten years. Moreover, even in Czechoslovakia, but especially in the other countries of the region, the term *democracy* obscured the reality of a social structure and political dynamics both at odds with democratic politics.[3]

What also rendered the communist world a highly unlikely candidate for democratic politics was the nature of state socialism—a distinctive form of dictatorship that combined state ownership of the means of production, central planning, and isolation from the global economy with such equally unusual political features as rule by a single, Leninist party and an ideology committed to rapid transformation of the economy and the society. This system was, in short, an unusually ambitious, invasive, and despotic dictatorship. It was also long in place, strongly committed to building nations and states (though not anticipating either nationalism or state dissolution), and, as noted above, the heir to a long dictatorial tradition. What all this meant was that state socialism was fundamentally antidemocratic and anticapitalist in its ideology, institutional design, and everyday practices. As a result, state socialism was unusually inhospitable to the development of those institutions central to a liberal order—for example, rule of law, private property, political competition, or civil society. In contrast to other regions of the world, then, the new democracies in the post-communist world had to contend with a past that made democratization unlikely and, if by chance attempted, unusually burdened from the start.

Just as debilitating for democratic governance were two more legacies of the state socialist past: severe economic problems and the rise of new states in the wake of regime collapse. While the former made the transition to capitalism, already difficult and dislocating, all the more painful and politically divisive, the latter forced a majority of the new regimes in the region to combine the "uncombinable"; that is, the spatial consolidation of political authority (a necessarily violent process) with the construction of accountable government. Historical precedents for either situation—that is, joining democratization with a transition to capitalism and adding to this state building—were nonexistent.

Perhaps the most surprising aspect of transitions to democracy in the world, however, has been the results. In a mere ten years, one-quarter of these new regimes—or seven out of twenty-seven countries—have, arguably, become consolidated democratic orders; that is, polities where elections are free, fair, and regular, where politicians are fully accountable, and where civil liberties and political rights are extensive and guaranteed by law. Thus, one can safely predict that ten years from now, Latvia, Lithuania, Estonia, Poland, Hungary, the Czech Republic, and Slovenia will still be in the democratic column. Given recent developments, this list could even expand in the near future to include Slovakia, Croatia, and Bulgaria, with some other countries, such as Romania, Moldova, and Russia, possible candidates as well. Such a record is astonishing, even from the unrealistic vantage point of the extraordinary optimism surrounding the collapse of communist regimes in 1989. This record is also far better than the one registered in Africa, another region of the world that was widely viewed as hostile to democratic governance for some of the very same reasons that cautioned skepticism in the context; that is, the absence of a democratic tradition and poor correspondence between national and state boundaries.[4]

The purpose of this chapter is to survey the political and economic landscape of east-central Europe and the former Soviet Union with one overarching question in mind. What have developments during the first decade of post-socialism taught us about democratization? I will draw four lessons based upon the experiences thus far of the twenty-seven countries that make up the region. These lessons, in turn, will be put to good theoretical use by using them to rethink prevalent understandings of the origins and the sustainability of new democracies. This chapter, therefore, constructs a dialogue, with the patterns of post-socialism representing one interlocutor and theoretical arguments about democratization the other.

Lesson One: The Diversity of Post-Communism

Perhaps the most noticeable characteristic of post-communism is the economic and political diversity of the regimes that comprise this region of the world. Once isolated, once identical in form, and once constituting an alternative world system, the region has become in the brief span of one decade a microcosm—albeit a sizable one, given the sheer geographical span of this region—of the larger and quite heterogeneous world within which it is now embedded.[5] Let us turn, first, to the economic side of the ledger. Here, I will merely highlight some extremes, since the primary focus of this chapter is political, not economic trends.

We can begin by noting dramatic differences in the size of these economies. Slovenia's gross national product per capita at purchasing power parity was eight times that of Azerbaijan in 1999. Thus, while Azerbaijan was ninety-sixth out of the one hundred and twenty-two countries that the World Bank ranked on this measure, Slovenia's position was twenty-sixth. Dramatic differences are also apparent if we focus on the degree to which these countries have shifted from a socialist to a capitalist economy. To take one indicator: the private sector share of the economy in the region ranges from about 15 percent in Azerbaijan, Tajikistan, and Turkmenistan to around 70 percent in the Czech Republic, Estonia, Poland, Hungary, and Croatia.

These countries also vary enormously in a third measure, economic performance—though *all* the countries in this region registered a substantial contraction in the size of their economies in at least the first few years of post-socialism.[6] The Polish economy, the best performer in the region over the past decade, was about 20 percent larger in 1999 than in 1989, whereas the Georgian and Bosnian economies in the same year (reflecting the costs of war and, because of that, based on rough estimates) were slightly more than one-third of their size when the Soviet and Yugoslav states, respectively, dissolved in 1991. Indeed, Russia—a country widely acknowledged to be in economic freefall (though robust oil prices have recently countered the trend)—sits at the very center of the region's distribution with respect to economic performance. From that perspective, it becomes all the more disturbing to note the following: if the Russian economy were to grow by 5 percent a year over the next fifteen years, it would only be at the end of that time—or 2015—that Russia would return to the economic size it was at the beginning of the transformation.[7]

Political Variations

Political variations in post-socialism are equally pronounced.[8] One important aspect of politics in this region is the age of the state. Combining the measures of sovereignty, juridical statehood, and continuity of existing borders, the oldest states in the region are Albania and Bulgaria, both of which date from the Balkan Wars. At the other extreme are the newest states: the twenty-two countries that emerged from the dissolution of Yugoslavia, Czechoslovakia, and the Soviet Union from 1991 to 1992—though the Baltic states, taking advantage of the disarray surrounding the Bolshevik revolution, had functioned as sovereign entities during the interwar years and Serbia had been an independent state from the final quarter of the nineteenth century until it joined the new Yugoslav state after World War I.

All of this highlights a larger point. After 1989, regime transition went hand in hand with transition in political boundaries—a relationship with obvious historical resonance, once we remember the rise of new states, border shifts, and regime change in the eastern half of Europe following the First and Second World Wars. However, it is important to remember at the same time that the boundaries of these new states have proven thus far to be, contrary to most expectations, durable—though not without contestation, as territorial disputes within the Russian Federation, Georgia, Bosnia, and rump Yugoslavia, as well as between Armenia and Azerbaijan, all remind us.

A second political consideration is stability—a very hard term to define, despite its centrality to ongoing debates within political science. Political stability is the capacity of the regime (or the organization of political power) and the state (or the spatially bounded projection of political authority) to provide political order. It implies such characteristics as relatively constant rules of the political game that are recognized by all and inform the behavior of all; the existence of a hegemonic regime (as opposed to competitive regimes); governments that function effectively; and physical boundaries that are clearly defined and uncontested. Instability, therefore, is indicated by high levels of social disorder, secessionist pressures, contestation over preferred regime forms, high rates of governmental turnover, the failure of public officials to be *the* source of public policy, and governments that cannot decide, or, if deciding, cannot implement. Instability, in short, testifies to the failure of a regime and/or a state to be hegemonic—without ideological or spatial competitors—and to function effectively. It is a question of both regime and state capacity, with the two spheres of political activity often interactive and, thereby, either mutually supportive or mutually subversive—points that we will explore in greater detail later in this chapter.

The various indicators of political stability suggest, once again, considerable variations across the area. The stability of, say, Slovenia and Hungary is in sharp contrast to the virtual states of Albania, Bosnia, Georgia, and rump Yugoslavia. To this second group must be added the Russian Federation, given the incapacity of that state to harmonize its legal system across space, establish a single economic or political regime within its borders, collect taxes, or meet its domestic and international financial obligations. By any measure, however, a majority of the regimes and states within this region are unstable. Moreover, whether a state is new or old does not predict stability perfectly—as the Slovenian versus Albanian examples, cited earlier, suggest.

The final aspect of politics—and the one that has received the lion's share of scholarly attention—is regime type, or the simple contrast between democracy and dictatorship. Since I will be addressing this issue in greater detail later, suffice to note here that democracy, even according to minimal standards, constitutes the regional exception. This is evident, for example, if we take Freedom House rankings, which target the provision of civil liberties and political rights. By their measures, about one-third of the region is fully democratic, about one-third fully authoritarian, and about one-third falling between these two regime stools.[9] Other measures that emphasize the inclusiveness of the electorate, while producing different democratic "scores" for some countries, nonetheless end up with the same conclusion: a minority of the countries in the region can be judged to be democratic.[10]

Theoretical Implications

The economic and political evidence, therefore, points to one conclusion. The post-communist experience is better termed post-communist experiences. The question then becomes: what implications might we draw about democratization from the variability of post-communist pathways? The most obvious one is methodological. The varieties of post-communism, combined with some built-in limitations on the range of causal factors as a consequence of the homogenizing effects of the state socialist past, remind us of the value of sampling on the independent variable—advantages less fully available to scholars working on Latin American and Southern European democratization (though recent developments in, say, Venezuela, Peru, and Argentina have been helpful in this regard). Put simply, we are more likely to derive robust explanations of why democracy develops, sustains itself, or fails when we focus our analytical attention on variable regime trajectories. It is only under such circumstances that we can distinguish sufficient from necessary conditions.[11] This is particularly so when, as in the context, the number of cases is large and the timing of transition so similar.

These observations have not been lost on specialists in the field of post-communist studies. Thus, we have a number of comparative studies of this region that have developed compelling explanations of why democracies do or do not arise;[12] why some democracies succeed and others break down;[13] why democratization and economic reform vary together;[14] when nationalist movements form;[15] why some states end and why state dissolution is violent versus peaceful.[16]

Another implication focuses on the questions we pose and their consequences for approaches taken and concepts used. The global wave of democratization, in combination with the increasing popularity of democracy as the focus of study in comparative politics, has produced three pronounced and problematic tendencies: to ignore authoritarian forms of government as objects of study; to presume that each state has a regime and that the regime is necessarily coterminous with the state; and to assume that a weakening of authoritarian rule is necessarily followed by the collapse of the system and a transition to democracy. As our brief survey of the region suggests, all of these assumptions seem to be suspect. Only a minority of the countries meet democratic standards; the "collapse" of state socialism was in fact highly uneven across space and, for that matter, political and economic arenas within states; most of the regimes within the region are contested, not settled formations; and most of the region's states fail to monopolize the exercise of coercion or carry out in effective fashion the tasks of defining and defending borders, collecting taxes and distributing revenues, and, most generally, commanding popular compliance. What we see, in short, is that democracy is the exception, not the rule, and that state socialism was interrupted, disrupted, and amended, not necessarily destroyed. When viewed from the perspective of the regime or the state, then, politics in the area resembles less a tablecloth constructed from one bolt of fabric than a patchwork quilt, dizzy with patterns and fraying at its many seams.

These observations sensitize us, in turn, to several other important considerations, all of which counsel a rethinking of how we have understood democracy and democratization. One is that democratization is, like most political dynamics, a spatial process. As such, it can be highly uneven—not just over time, as is commonly noted, but also and just as importantly, over space. Note, for example, the microregimes nested within Russia, Albania, Bosnia, Georgia, and rump Yugoslavia. Democracy, it seems, is not the only game in Russian towns.

At the same time, we can begin to question the thick line drawn between dictatorship and democracy—a line that has the unfortunate effects of treating all regimes as an either-or proposition and thereby preventing these two types of regimes from inhabiting the same political space at the same time. In practice, as the experience reminds us, regimes in transition from dictatorship to democracy often combine elements of each system, and dictatorship and democracy define the ends of a regime continuum, with most "new" regimes falling between these two poles. Indeed, even the very concept of regime exists on a continuum. If there are degrees of stateness, as many have argued, then there are also degrees of "regime-ness." Regime implies spatial hegemony of a particular ideology and set of political arrangements, and different types of regimes have different standards, which they must meet to be given the title of choice. Most regimes in the post-socialist world, however, fail to meet either standard, and they are not, as a result, regimes, let alone dictatorships or democracies. Instead, they are melded formations, combining in haphazard fashion elements of dictatorship and democracy and thereby lacking the ideological, spatial, and procedural consistency and constraints that together define regimes, whether democratic or authoritarian.[17]

Lesson Two: The Durability and the Appeals of Democracy

The political diversity of the region, however, should not obscure two pronounced patterns. One is that democracy tends to be sticky. This is obvious if we note two trends. First, very few countries in the region have witnessed a breakdown in democracy. Thus, Belarus, Armenia, Georgia, Slovakia, and Croatia are, by the standards of the past ten years, exceptional. This is despite such powerful threats to new democracies, well represented not just in these cases but throughout the entire region (and threats absent, it must be emphasized, from the Latin American, Southern Europe, and East Asian contexts) as, say, war, secessionist pressures, economic collapse, and illiberal nationalism. However, it is also the case that *all* the democracies that have broken down in the region were flawed from the start—not unlike the story of interwar European experiments with democracy. At the same time, if we focus on those countries that had strong democratic credentials from the first election onward, we find a clear trend. Every one of the early robust democracies has endured. Democracy, therefore, while far from the regional norm, has demonstrated nonetheless a certain "stubbornness."

If democracy seems to be sticky, it also seems to be seductive. For example, of the six countries listed as having experienced democratic breakdowns over the past decade, two—Slovakia and Croatia—have recently moved from a democratic "downturn" to a democratic "upturn." Indeed, there are good reasons to assume that these two states are likely to maintain their political momentum. In addition, thanks largely to pressures from the European Union, both Latvia and Estonia have been moving from a more restrictive to a more expansive definition of citizenship. The European Union, plus institutionalization of competition, has also strengthened the Bulgarian and Romanian democratic projects. All of this leads to two conclusions. The list of democracies in the region has grown over time. Second, for the east-central European states at least, the European Union has played a key role in providing incentives for democratization—which it is likely to continue doing in the cases of Slovakia and Croatia.

Implications for the Study of Democratization

We can now step back from these trends and, combining them with the earlier discussion of diversity, address several key issues in the literature on democratization. One is identifying factors that seem to account for variations in political trajectories. Several plausible causal variables stand out. The first is the outcome of the first or founding election. Here, the pattern is quite clear. Where the opposition forces won handily, democratization followed and proved to be a sustainable project.

Indeed, this is even the case where the ex-communists won the second election—for example, Hungary, Poland, and Lithuania. One can argue for these cases that the victory of the former ruling party (albeit renamed) was itself an investment in democracy. This is because democratization in all settings involves three seemingly irreconcilable tasks: breaking with the authoritarian past, building democratic institutions, and yet at the same time finding ways to attach the political losers in the transition to the new order.[18] It is precisely because of these tasks, for example, that specialists in Southern Europe have been so approving of both pacted transitions to democracy and founding elections that incorporate leaders from the authoritarian past into the winner's circle.[19] When combined with progress on the procedural side of democracy, these compromises with the old order stabilize its political successor.

In the setting, however, the solution to the dilemma of constructing a democracy, yet co-opting those who might oppose it was quite different. By having lost, then won, the ex-communists were eliminated from decisions involving the design of democratic institutions, but were subsequently given, nonetheless, powerful incentives to participate in the democratic process. Just as electoral loss by the left liberated the liberal opposition, so electoral success in the next round co-opted the left, with the result that both sides—and the constituencies they courted—became partners to the democratic project.

This leaves two other outcomes of founding elections, both of which predicted quite well what followed in the region. In the cases of Belarus, Serbia, and much of Central Asia, the ex-communists—often maintaining their original names—won the first elections. What followed was authoritarian rule. The third category is where the first election produced a division of power between the opposition and the communists—for example, within the legislature or between the legislature and the presidency. It is precisely here where we see the melded regimes combining dictatorial with democratic elements. This is, for example, the Russian, Ukrainian, Romanian, and Bulgarian stories.

These variations in electoral competition and political outcomes, however, should not obscure the central point: the outcome of the first election seems to have powerful effects on the political dynamics that follow. This conclusion is all the more persuasive, once we note that in the Slovak and Croatian cases—that is, where de-democratization has been followed by re-democratization—the opposition forces did in fact win the first election. However, these opposition forces were different from their counterparts elsewhere in the region in that they combined a nationalist agenda with an illiberal ideological agenda, therefore constituting a threat to democratic politics. Another critical distinction was that the victorious parties in both Croatia and Slovakia had within their ranks a substantial number of communists turned nationalists. What I am suggesting, therefore, is that the experiences of Croatia and Slovakia seem to confirm the importance of opposition victories, with the proviso that the capacity of those victories to translate into a sustained commitment to democracy was slower to materialize. In these contexts, "the cult of culture" had to be worked through for the cult of democracy to take its place.[20]

It could be countered that founding elections constitute a problematic causal factor in two ways. In the ideal world, causal variables should be close enough to the outcome of interest that their influence is above challenge, yet removed enough from the outcome that they do not constitute a part of the outcome itself.[21] To put the matter succinctly: were founding elections causes, or were they simply part of the democratic project itself? At the same time, how parties fare in founding elections would seem to be a function of what precedes these elections and how those dynamics shape the development of political parties and partisan preferences. From this perspective, founding elections as an explanation of democratic development could be said to beg the question.

My response to these concerns is to argue the following. First, there is a rich literature on the importance of founding elections for democratization. Second, many of the very elections that seemed to predict robust democracy were held when democratic institutions had not yet been defined. In this sense, the elections can be interpreted as having produced a map charting future political directions. Just as important in this regard is that political leaders in these contexts seemed to have interpreted the elections that way. Third, electoral outcomes often took citizens, party leaders, and analysts by surprise. Thus, they did set a political agenda by altering the definition of what was considered politically feasible.

Finally and most importantly, there are two factors that are removed in temporal terms from the democratic experience and that predict the outcome of these elections quite well. The first is quite distant from the elections themselves; that is, long-term patterns of historical development within the region. As Andrew Janos has recently argued, it was not just that Eastern Europe and the Soviet Union were on the periphery of Europe, but also that their peripheral location translated, for example, into "later" and "different" capitalism, along with authoritarian orders that were, again by the standards of Western Europe, unusually entrenched and unusually resistant to liberalization.[22] What is striking about this argument is its predictive capacity. Thus, the corridor most proximate to Western developments is precisely the corridor that has the strongest contemporary claims to democratic politics (and, for that matter, capitalist economics). This point has not been lost on analysts who have noted a powerful correlation between geographical proximity to the West and recent political trajectories.[23]

Just as supportive is another observation. Very few longtime analysts of the region have been surprised by the political patterns of post-socialism. For example, we expected that Poland and Hungary would be "ahead" of, say, Bulgaria and Romania, in the race to democracy and capitalism, and that these two countries in turn would be ahead of, say, Turkmenistan and Azerbaijan. This expectation was based upon our sense of history and what that suggested about the preferences of publics and the power of opposition forces. But history, it must be noted, is helped along by more contemporary considerations—for example, the capacity of the European Union to pick and choose the region's[24] winners and losers.

But these arguments, while accounting for electoral outcomes, seem to be too far removed and too vague to explain the "cause of the cause." It is precisely here where another factor, more proximate to founding elections and just as analytically robust, enters the picture. This factor is patterns of protest during the state socialist period. In those countries where protests were substantial and took anticommunist forms, the founding elections after 1989 produced a significant victory for the opposition forces. The examples in point are Poland, Hungary, Czechoslovakia, Slovenia, and the Baltic states. What I am suggesting, therefore, is that the communist experience, for a variety of reasons too detailed to mention here, produced in some instances popular preferences in support of a liberal order and an opposition that was ready to mobilize substantial support, once the constraints of the dictatorial order were lifted.

Thus, "founding elections" can be understood as a surrogate measure for a longer-term process involving the development of the opposition and popular support for democratic politics. Founding elections, therefore, summarize developments over the course of the socialist experience. This does not deny their importance, but, rather, recognizes their complex origins and their efficiency as a summary of complex historical developments. Indeed, this is hardly an unusual role to ask of explanatory factors. After all, this is precisely what happens when social scientists, for example, rely on such factors as, say, gender, generation, class, and urban-rural distinctions to explain political behavior.

Quality and Sustainability

This leads to another issue of equal theoretical importance. As already suggested, the political trajectories of the countries testify to the importance of developments early in the transition—most notably, founding elections. However, some other "early" factors fail to have explanatory purchase—for example, the contrast, so central to theorizing about the "southern" transitions, between pacted transitions—where deals were struck between authoritarians and democrats—and transitions that began in response to mass mobilization.[25] Here, the experiences of the world suggest that neither approach to leaving dictatorship necessarily favors a democratic outcome. Pacted transitions, therefore, are no better at delivering stable and sustainable democracy than transitions involving mass mobilization.

Indeed, the most successful transitions in the world are the product of what can be termed "breakage," not bridging between the old and the new order. This is evident if we note, for example, the variable already mentioned; that is, the contributions to democratic governance of substantial victories gained by the opposition and the thorough-going elimination of the communists from governing positions. In fact, it is precisely those cases where the old and the new order are combined—that is, where electoral mandates were divided between the two—where we see the greatest problems with building and sustaining a democratic order in the context. In this sense, the Russian experience resembles Spain—to combine two cases of bridging that nonetheless anchor the extremes of a continuum defining the least and the most successful transitions to democracy. Thus, while breaking with the old order seems to be the approach generating the highest payoffs in the context, bridging appears to be preferable in the contexts of Latin America and Southern Europe. Regional effects, therefore, are sometimes important in shaping the causal dynamics of democratization.[26]

The Russian case, moreover, asks us to reconsider another argument central to the comparative study of democratization; that is, the presumption that the quality of democracy correlates highly with its sustainability. That correlation is often understood to verge on the tautological and is, therefore, rarely discussed in any systematic fashion. At the same time, scholars have used democratic deficiencies to account for democratic breakdowns—for example, flawed institutional design, polarized publics, and deficits in civil and political society—just as they have treated these conditions as setting the standard for democratic consolidation.[27] In all of these cases, however, the message is the same. The quality of democracy has powerful consequences for the sustainability of the democratic project.

However, we can think of the relationship between these two factors in a different way—and one which forces us to rethink some fundamental assumptions underlying both the study of democratization and the conclusions we draw from comparisons among cases. First, there are good theoretical reasons to argue that the probability of democratic governance in year two is higher when some—as opposed to no—aspects of democratic politics are in place. Put simply, it is harder to move from authoritarian to democratic politics than from thin to robust democracy. Second, there is empirical support for this proposition. Here, we can note the striking durability of democracy, especially at higher levels of economic development—a conclusion shared by some unlikely bedfellows, including Robert Dahl,[28] Adam Przeworski and Fernando Limongi,[29] and the current president of the Russian Federation, Vladimir Putin.[30] The region, moreover, provides support for this proposition. For example, without exception the democracies we see in that region today began the era as either full-scale or partial democratic orders. There are no cases of a midstream shift from dictatorship to democracy.

We can now take these arguments to the Russian context and suggest the following. It can be argued that the uneven quality of Russian democracy may be the very factor that helps sustain that democratic order. To elaborate: if Yeltsin had moved against powerful figures from the old order rather than attempted to co-opt them, those figures might have brought democracy down. The costs of compliance, in short, may have risen to a level that produced a concerted reaction against the nascent democratic order. Instead, what we see in Russia is a compromise: certain democratic norms are met, but at the price of limiting rule of law, undermining the economic and territorial integrity of the state, and maintaining the political influence of unelected officials behind the scenes. Thus, rather than bemoan the deficiencies of Russian democracy and presume that these deficiencies lower the probability of democratic sustainability, we might argue, instead, that it is precisely these deficiencies—the costs of political rent seeking—that allow Russian democracy to continue.

A parallel with the economic side of the equation can also be drawn. Joel Hellman has argued that tolerance of rent seeking has undermined Russia's transition to capitalism, and that the winners in this process, not the losers, are responsible for a stalled and costly transition to capitalism.[31] However, it could be countered that it is precisely the power of the winners that sustains (as well as distorts) the capitalist experiment. Put simply, as with the democratic side of the equation, the costs of compromises with the old order and, more generally, rent seeking, can also be construed as the benefits—an argument that rests on the assumptions that the new system cannot continue without vested interests, that the alternative to "wild capitalism" may be no capitalism at all, and that capitalism in year two is more likely to exist if there are elements of a capitalist economy in year one.

If it is plausible that the low quality of democracy may be under some circumstances an investment, not a disinvestment in democratic sustainability, then we need to reconsider the lessons we have drawn from comparisons among the cases. To take one example: it has been commonly argued on the basis of comparisons between the Polish and Russian experiences that the Polish approach to the transition is preferable to the Russian approach, given the sharp contrasts between these two cases with respect to shock therapy and economic performance, democratization and the quality of democratic governance. However, is the issue that there are optimal and sub-optimal approaches, with decision makers responsible for each, or is the issue one of different political and economic contexts producing a different list of politically feasible choices? The first interpretation has been the dominant one, largely because of the assumption central to the literature on both democratization and economic reform that the central factor shaping reform trajectories are political leaders and the choices they make. However, as all political scientists know, choices are made within political parameters, and those parameters—not ideal circumstances—define what constitutes more and less preferable choices, given competing opportunity costs.[32] From that perspective, the issue is not why Russia fails to be Poland, or why Russian elites decided to go in directions that diverged from the Polish path. Rather, the issue is whether the Russian approach to transition maximized within the constraints imposed by that particular context both democratization and the transition to capitalism.

Just as important for thinking along these lines is recognizing the extraordinary politics, as Leszek Balcerowicz has put it,[33] of the Polish situation in the aftermath of 1989—a popular consensus supporting the transitions to democracy and capitalism; a large governing mandate that was derived through legitimate elections; Polish nationalism that lengthened the time horizons of publics, expanded their tolerance of economic stress, and strengthened state capacity; consensus among elites regarding the advisability of shock therapy; and substantial international support for democratization and economic reform, given the considerable engagement of the European Union, the World Bank, and the International Monetary Fund (IMF). Put succinctly, this was a rare and unusually enabling moment for democratic politics: the combination of political power, public tolerance, and a radical agenda. In this sense, the common assumption of democratization and economic reform as a series of key decisions that resourceful elites make is an accurate one when applied to the Polish case. Polish leaders were free to experiment. But the Russian context was quite different, because it combined ordinary politics with an extraordinary agenda. As a result, Yeltsin's choices were constrained and the question was not how can one ideally build capitalism and democracy, but, rather, how one might build either system at all. Rent seeking was a necessity, not an either/or proposition, and the overarching question was not between high- and low-quality democracy and capitalism, but, rather, between some of each versus neither.

The Russian case, therefore, challenges the argument—indeed, assumption—that there is a necessary trade-off between the quality and the sustainability of democracy. Rather, compromises in the first case can invest in the second. If the assumption about the relationship between the quality and the sustainability of democracy is problematic, then so is a second assumption: that elites make choices and that democracy, as a result, can be crafted.[34] This assumption grew out of two considerations: a strong reaction against the focus in the literature on democratization in the West on structural conditions, with political elites bystanders in the process, and the accumulating evidence drawn from the most recent wave of democratization that democracy could in fact be constructed quickly.[35] While I am sympathetic to these arguments, I am also mindful of one important consideration: in some contexts, democratization can proceed quickly and thereby be analyzed fruitfully through the transitological approach. However, for other contexts, where politics is neither so consensual nor so pliable, the older emphasis on constrained choice would seem to be advisable. Different contexts, in short, may dictate different theoretical approaches.

Lesson Three: The Centrality of the State

Specialists in comparative democratization, influenced by the Latin American and Southern European cases, have argued in virtual unison that the biggest threat to democracy is the military. This observation has strong empirical support. For example, one can point to the long history of military interventions in Latin American politics, all testifying to how states were built in that context, and most of which terminated democratic politics, though some oversaw a return to democracy. In either role, a signal was sent: the capacity of the military to make or break regimes. There is also the attempted military coup d'état in Spain in 1982, which constituted by all accounts the biggest threat to democracy in the post-Franco era. A final indicator is the power and political legitimacy accorded the military in many Latin American constitutions —even in this most recent democratic political interlude.[36]

In the world, by contrast, the dominant threat to democracy is a weak state.[37] Before I elaborate, some definitions are in order. By the state, I refer to a political entity that combines two monopolies: a spatial monopoly and a monopoly over the legitimate exercise of coercion.[38] What distinguishes a state from other political constructs, therefore, is the existence of spatially bounded political authority—or what was defined at Westphalia in the seventeenth century as the geographically bounded maintenance of political order. States vary, of course, in the degree of contestation over boundaries and over the exercise of political authority within those boundaries. In weak states, contestation is high; in strong states, a monopoly is in place. Put more concretely, weak states feature such characteristics as permeable boundaries (as a result of secessionist pressures and/or repeated international interventions); conflicts over the definition of and thus membership in the political community; the privatization of coercion (in the place of a state monopoly); limited capacity of the state to extract popular compliance; and state failure to collect revenues and meet financial obligations.

It is precisely these deficiencies that describe many states in the region, with rump Yugoslavia, Albania, Bosnia, Georgia, Tajikistan, and the Russian Federation providing the extreme cases. For example, as a number of studies have demonstrated, the Russian state lacks spatial harmonization of its laws, such that local laws are in repeated conflict with the laws of the center.[39] This means in practice that the Russian state incorporates a number of micro-states, resembling in this way the German principalities prior to German unification in the final third of the nineteenth century. These microstates are sufficiently well defined, moreover, so that political boundaries translate into economic boundaries, thereby promoting conjoined political and economic protectionism; publics tend to define their political allegiances in terms of local political units; and local officials take as their mandate the administration of local laws and resistance to interference from the center. The Russian state, in short, lacks consistency across space, which in turn compromises the capacity of the state to extract compliance.

If internal political and legal boundaries within Russia are "too strong," then the external boundaries of the Russian state are "too weak." Public agreement on the boundaries of the state is lacking, and the boundaries are, as a result, an object of conflict. This is evidenced most dramatically by the ongoing wars in Chechnya—one of several secessionist regions in Russia, but the only one that has shifted from a position of bargaining with the state to becoming a target of state violence.[40] Russia, therefore, exhibits a pattern precisely opposite to that of strong states, where internal boundaries are soft and external boundaries hard. Finally, there is the economic crisis that has engulfed Russia. There are many factors that have contributed to this crisis, but one of the most important—as identified in cross-national studies of economic performance within the region—seems to be the weakness of the Russian state.[41] This is a state that lacks a geographically consistent commercial code, that cannot collect taxes, pay its bills, deliver energy, or provide public order, and, finally, that leaks significant capital abroad. While the Russian economy is no more corrupt than a host of other economies that are judged, nonetheless, to be effective (for example, China), corruption in Russia becomes a serious problem because it is joined with all the deficiencies already noted. It is far from accidental, therefore, that President Putin has defined as his major goal a strengthening of the Russian state.

This leaves us with two questions. First, why are the Russian state and so many other states in the region so weak? Here, I will be brief, since the answer takes us somewhat afield from the concern of this chapter. We can begin to explain why many states are weak by noting the obvious: the newness of these states. After all, Russia, like twenty-six other states in this region, is only a decade old—though its borders today are similar to those of the Russian Empire in the seventeenth century. At first glance, this is a persuasive argument. We know from the Western European experience that building state capacity takes time. We also know that a violent process is usually required to establish a coercive monopoly—hardly the stuff of democratization. Indeed, that is why state building and democratization are usually understood to be necessarily sequential processes. Finally, the weakest states in the region do tend to be the new states—though the Albanian case provides an exception.

At the same time, however, many of the new states in the region seem to have succeeded in very short time in establishing well-defined and widely accepted borders, an inclusive definition of the nation, consistent exercise of political authority within the boundaries of the state, and high levels of public compliance. What is important to recognize here—and what will be addressed in greater detail below—is that all of the successful new states fall into the categories of either full-scale democracies or full-scale dictatorships. This seems to suggest that the strength of the regime—that is, whether it is accepted or contested—has powerful consequences for state capacity. The weakness of these states, then, speaks to the weakness of regimes. This observation in turn suggests that we need to return to the state socialist past—in particular, whether developments during state socialism produced a consensus regarding the definition of the nation, the boundaries of the state, and the preferred character of the successor regime. Where they did, new as well as older states were empowered—as we see, for example, in the Hungarian and Polish cases in the first instance and the Czech, Slovenian, and Baltic cases in the second. Thus, in some contexts state socialism—largely by accident—functioned as a nation-building, state-building, and counter regime-building project. How far this project went and how much consensus there was surrounding this project tells us a great deal about subsequent state and regime trajectories.

The second question flows from these considerations and is more central to our interests. What is the relationship between the strength of the state and democracy? After all, the state refers to the spatial projection of political authority, whereas a regime refers to quite another set of issues—in particular, the organization of political power, or, in the democratic case, to the specific condition of accountable political power as a consequence of combining civil liberties, political rights, and competition for political office. We can begin to assess the relationship between the state and democracy by recognizing the more general point: the close interdependence between states and regimes. To be effective, regimes of whatever type must function as an ideological monopoly across space. Thus, within the borders of the state, there must be one regime. If regimes are contested, they are by definition weak and less likely to be sustainable. Regimes, therefore, depend upon the state to specify and defend their borders, to provide ideological consistency within those borders, to define the nation that then constitutes the subjects as well as the objects of the regime, and to give the regime the spatial reach and the compliance it requires to govern effectively and reproduce itself. Weak states, in short, are necessarily associated with weak regimes, whether the regime in question is democratic or authoritarian. Just as the deregulation of the regime's ideological monopoly can deregulate the state's spatial monopoly, so a decline in the state's capacity to project authority across space usually has the effect of creating patchwork politics within the state.

It is, therefore, far from accidental that revolutions tend to combine spatial with ideological fragmentation; that is, secessionist movements, the collapse of the state's coercive capacity, and the multiplication of regimes. Note, for example, the Bolshevik revolution, with its signifying indicators of dual power and leakage of the Polish and Baltic parts of the Russian empire (which revolutionary leaders of Ukraine attempted to emulate, but without success). It is also not accidental that the weakening of authoritarian regimes is often accompanied, especially in multinational contexts where minorities are geographically concentrated, by growing demands for regional autonomy at the least and at the most independent statehood. Here, the Spanish and Mexican cases are instructive; so, most obviously, are the cases of the Soviet Union, Yugoslavia, and Czechoslovakia during the last decade of authoritarian rule. Just as instructive, regarding the final three cases, was the perfect correlation between secessionist demands by nations and their status as the titular nations within the republics of these three federations and, in addition, between the boundaries of those republics that constituted the federation and the subsequent boundaries of the states that formed in the wake of regime and state dissolution.

The theoretical boundaries that political scientists have erected to differentiate the domain of the state from the domain of the regime—boundaries that are in practice often discarded with state and regime used interchangeably —are in an empirical sense highly porous. Deficits in one arena usually carry with them deficits in the other. Put differently: the ideological and the spatial sides of politics—or the provinces of the regime versus the state—tend to be infectious, with liabilities transferable across political arenas. The same holds for assets. Strong regimes can build strong states. By strong regimes, I

refer to regimes that are based upon a widespread public consensus about—
and elite compliance with—the rules of the political game. With such a consensus, even newly formed states can be strong. In this sense, states can
borrow power from the regime. The Indian experience provides one good
example. One important consequence of the Indian Nationalist Movement
was the creation of a political consensus regarding three issues: an expansive
definition of the nation, independent statehood, and the formation of a
democratic political order.[42] Thus, despite the "leakage" of Pakistan (which
spoke in part to competition among elites within the independence movement) and despite the many difficulties India faced as a new, poor, and
extraordinarily multinational democracy, the Indian state survived decolonization, drawing support in part from the strength of its national and
democratic orders.

A more recent case, drawn from the world, is Slovenia—a new state that
formed in 1991 as a result of the disintegration of Yugoslavia. We can understand the strength of the Slovene state by noting its origins; that is, as a
republic, located within a highly decentralized federal system, that was well
endowed with its own institutions and distinctive in its political and economic profile.[43] During the last years of Yugoslavia, Slovenes began to converge around two principles: that a liberal economic and political order was
preferable to the alternatives, and that independent statehood represented the
best chance for establishing such a system. This consensus was remarkable,
because it came to embrace both a large opposition movement and the
Slovene League of Communists. As a result, both the new state and democracy were empowered—a process helped, no doubt, by the homogeneity of
the Slovene population and by the small size of the state. It was precisely the
absence of such assets that made the Russian Federation's transition to independence and democracy so difficult. In that context, as in much of Africa,
the difficulties involved in defining a common nation and governing a vast
and thinly populated territory constituted a sure recipe for a problematic
interaction between state building and democratization.

Thus far, we have focused on the interdependent relationship between the
regime and the state. However, we can also think about this question in more
concrete terms; that is, how the state itself shapes the democratic project in
particular. Here, we need to return to the definition of democracy; that is, following the procedural and parsimonious proclivities of the discipline, a system of government that combines liberties, rights, and competition. Absent
from this definition, therefore, is any recognition of the role of the state. Does
this mean that the state is irrelevant or that a capable state is assumed? I think

it is the latter. This follows from the following considerations. Can there be civil liberties and political rights in the absence of rule of law? To meet the democratic standard, civil liberties and political rights must be expansive, guaranteed, and consistently applied across individuals, circumstances, and space. It is precisely the state that provides these necessary conditions.

At the same time, can political competition function effectively in a weak state? Again, the answer is no—in four ways. First, competition itself must take place through elections that are free, fair, and regular. In the absence of the standard operating procedures that the state provides, these guarantees would ring hollow. Second, the rules governing competition for political office must be democratic, irrespective of where and when they take place. Put differently, the internal borders of the state—that is, the administrative subunits that make up the whole—can diversify the electoral context, but not in ways that violate democratic standards. Again, the key issue is spatial hegemony, legal consistency, and compliance. Third, competition rests upon political parties. However, if there are political-economic boundaries within the state that prevent the development of a statewide party system, then competition lacks the spatial consistency and the degree of institutionalization necessary for parties to play their democratic role; that is, to structure the electorate, to generate and then encourage choice among competing programs, and to connect government and governed. Finally, if those exercising power are not elected officials and if elected officials cannot access the resources necessary to meet public expectations and implement the decisions they make, then the relationship between competitive elections and political accountability—a relationship assumed by most definitions of democracy— is necessarily severed.

What I am suggesting, therefore, is that the attributes commonly used to define democracy are best understood as necessary, but not sufficient conditions. They recognize the forms of democracy, but ignore their foundations. Thus, in a weak state context, the attributes of democracy do not have the same meaning, nor do they have the desired—and assumed—effects. The importance of a capable state to the democratic project was easy to overlook in cases where the state could be taken for granted; that is, where the state-building project, preceding and foundational for democracy, had produced a conjoined coercive, spatial, legal, and administrative monopoly. Without well-defined borders, consolidated political authority, and legal and administrative procedures that transform the state into a "cage of reason,"[44] the acquisition of democratic traits in the West could not have translated into genuinely democratic politics.

Incorporating the State

There are two theoretical implications that follow from this discussion. One is that state building and democratization are not necessarily hostile processes. Whether they are or not depends upon the extent to which authoritarian regimes had built a capable state and a consensus around a liberal political project. If so, state building and democratization can go hand in hand—as can, for example, state building and economic reform. This generalization even works for brand-new states. Here, I am referring to the new states that formed in the wreckage of the Soviet Union, Yugoslavia, and Czechoslovakia. In these cases, the national-federal form of the state during the communist era had the effects of building nations and states within the state. Just as this led to state dissolution along republican lines when the regime weakened, so this provided the new states that formed with important resources—-for example, well-defined boundaries, a stable of political leaders, many of the institutions of statehood, and national identities. Moreover, where a consensus emerged around a liberal project and the definition of the nation was inclusive, both of which produced large victories for the opposition forces, strong regimes translated into strong states. In this sense, the dissolution of these three states could be said in the cases that met these stipulations to have invested in both a viable state and a democratic regime. Indeed, liberal regime trajectories were less likely if, say, Slovenia and Macedonia, Russia and the Baltic states, or the Czech Republic had remained within their respective federations. The less liberal parts of these federations would have sabotaged democratic politics and, for that matter, the transition to capitalism. In these ways, state dissolution is not necessarily a bad idea for the creation of viable states or viable democracies.

The other implication is definitional. If we give the state its due, does this mean that we need to give up on the idea of a parsimonious definition of democracy? I think that we can recognize the importance of the state to the democratic project by treating democracy as a two-part proposition; that is, as a combination of uncertain outcomes and certain procedures.[45] This has an additional advantage. If we construct a two-by-two table with certain and uncertain procedures on the X axis and certain and uncertain outcomes on the Y axis, we can capture the variable forms that both democracy and dictatorship have taken. We can also highlight on such a table the problem, already noted, of hybrid regimes. In the region, a common situation is one that combines uncertain outcomes with uncertain procedures; that is, political competition, but in the absence of standard operating procedures and, more generally, rule of law.

This definition, moreover, as much of the discussion that preceded it, has relevance for understanding capitalism as well. Just as with the transition from authoritarianism to democracy, so the study of the transition from socialism to capitalism has emphasized the necessity of what can be termed "state subtraction." This is central to neoliberal economic orthodoxy; it has also been central to concerns about limiting the state in a political order moving from dictatorship to democracy. However, in both the political and economic realms, a distinction needs to be drawn between what Michael Mann has termed *penetration versus despotism,* with the former a necessary condition for state effectiveness in the modern era and the latter a question of the goals of the state.[46]

We also need to recognize the difference between desirable and undesirable forms of state intervention. If by intervention we mean, for example, rule of law, standard operating procedures, and the consistent projection of political authority across space, then such interventions are necessary conditions for democratic governance. By the same token, capitalism cannot have efficient outcomes in the absence of property rights and spatially integrated markets, both of which are the responsibility of the state and its laws and its projection of political authority. Thus, certain procedures and uncertain outcomes seem to capture the essence of both capitalism and democracy. Absent the procedural certainty, neither functions well; that is, democracy fails to provide accountability and capitalism, minus the incentives provided by property rights and minus the free movement of labor and capital provided by an integrated domestic market, fails to yield efficient economic outcomes.

Lesson Four: The Nation, Nationalism, and Democratization

If the state is critical to democratization, so is the nation. Once again, a definitional aside is necessary. The nation can be defined as a shared understanding among a group of people that they have a common cultural identity that distinguishes them from other groups. That identity comes about through shared historical experiences that have produced common cultural symbols and common institutions. A shared language, religion or ethnicity is neither a necessary nor a sufficient condition for the formation of a nation—though these considerations have often been influential in nation building since the final quarter of the nineteenth century, when the idea of the nation diffused from Western Europe, where it was invented and states were in place, to other parts of Europe, Asia, and Latin America, where empires had been the norm and where this different approach to encasing populations produced different definitions of the nation and different consequences for the relationship between nation and state building. Moreover, there is no necessary correlation between the boundaries of the state and the boundaries of the nation. States can have many nations; nations do not necessary have states; and nations can straddle many states. Finally, nations are not objective formations; rather, they are inter-subjective. But their inter-subjectivity is premised upon an unusual principle: commonality not just among those who know each other and interact repeatedly, but also among strangers who are presumed in theory to share the same identity. In this way, the nation is a product of three factors: interaction, political design, and imagination.

Nationalism enters the scene when the nation, or at least political leaders claiming to speak on behalf of the nation, define a political project that demands expanded sovereignty on behalf of the political community. In practice, these demands take variable forms. They can involve calling for greater autonomy of the nation within an existing state or the creation of a new state. Nationalism, therefore, uses politics to legitimate difference, to expand autonomy, and to define or redefine the boundaries of political authority. Nationalism is a political project that can be embraced by minorities or majorities. Nationalism, however, should not be understood as an ideology. Ideologies are expressed preferences about types of regimes and, within a single regime project, about public policies and preferred governments. By contrast, nationalism is concerned with the reach of political authority. This is a critical distinction, often missed. From an ideological perspective, then, nationalism is wanton. It can couple with any manner of political ideologies, liberal and illiberal, leftist and rightist.[47]

Since the end of the Cold War, we have come to think of the nation and nationalism as a problem for democracy. Witness, for example, the title of Michael Hechter's newest book: *Containing Nationalism.*[48] This conclusion rests upon a view that nationalism is divisive at best and the purveyor of violence at the worst. Central to this assumption are three observations: that democracy is more difficult in multinational contexts, that the breakdown of democracy often occurs as a result of nationalist mobilization on the part of minorities, and that the major source of conflict in the world has shifted from fights between states to fights among nations within states. Inter-state conflict, in short, has been replaced by "inter-national" conflict.

Alongside these arguments, however, must be placed some other considerations. First, violent conflicts among nations are the exception in the region, not the rule. Indeed, such conflicts have declined over time. Nationalism, it seems, has come to run its course—not unlike the familiar cycles of social movements, of which nationalism is one type.[49] Second, nationalism was, we must remember, a powerful force for democracy in the West. One lesson of the French revolution, for example, was that nations do not just demand states; they also provide a powerful platform for demanding rights. Thus, the nation can play a critical role in undermining authoritarian regimes. Third, it was precisely this role that it played in the communist context. As Charles King has summarized, communists have always been nation builders—even if they did not realize the costs of their political strategy.[50] It is hardly accidental, therefore, that the end of state socialism was preceded and accompanied by nationalist mobilization.[51] Finally, if nationalism undermined communist regimes, it also undermined communist states—particularly those states that had been organized along national-federal lines. In some instances, as previously suggested, the dissolution of these federal states opened up for some republics at least the possibility of democratic governance—a possibility far more remote if these republics had remained part of a larger state. More generally, however, nationalism functioned not just as an anticommunist project; it also functioned as a pro-democracy project. By rejecting communism, nationalist movements in much of the socialist world ended up embracing communism's opposite: liberal democracy. To echo an earlier point: instead of uncertain procedures and certain outcomes, nationalist movements demanded certain outcomes and uncertain procedures.

The best example of this role for nationalism is Poland. The Polish nation did not just reject Soviet hegemony and thereby embrace state sovereignty, and the Polish nation did not just reject communism and thereby embrace liberal democracy. In being the first country where communism collapsed, Poland also set a remarkable precedent for its neighbors—which lowered the costs of protest against state socialism and soviet hegemony and thereby provided the spark for a region-wide collapse of state socialism and the soviet bloc. In this way, Polish nationalism was a powerful domestic and international force—not unlike French nationalism two hundred years before 1989. Indeed, the closest equivalent in historical terms to 1989 was 1848—a pan-European revolution that was founded in nationalism and that was strongly influenced by the French revolution.

In dissolving states within the communist region, moreover, nationalist movements also opened up the possibility, considered unimaginable at the time, that democratic governance could fall within the realm of political choice. Because of substantial conflicts over the regime and the state taking place among the republics making up the communist federations, continuation of the state at a time of regime collapse would have led at best to soft authoritarianism and at worst to war. Precisely because of nationalism and its role in dissolving the state and multiplying regimes, the political options of the Baltic countries, Russia, the Czech Republic, and Slovenia expanded considerably. These new states had been liberated from the confines of a repressive political order. While full-scale democracy was not always the outcome of state dissolution, the possibility of democracy for at least some of the successor states increased substantially.

Finally, in the context, nationalism even invested in the transition to capitalism—a key point once we remember that every democracy has had a capitalist economy. Again, the Polish case is instructive. As elsewhere in the region, economic stabilization in combination with the transition to capitalism produced a dramatic downturn in economic growth. In Poland, however, this process was strongly influenced in positive ways by Polish nationalism. First, nationalism gave policymakers after the formation of the Solidarity-led government in August, 1989 the luxury, rare in democratic politics, of not just a political consensus, but also one converging around radical change. Just as unusual was the widespread understanding that the political honeymoon would be a long one. To borrow from a common observation: if the collapse of communism in Poland took ten years, then the transition to capitalism might take some time as well. As a result, politicians in Poland felt that they had the political capital necessary to introduce shock therapy—and historically unprecedented, radical and rapid move in the direction of macroeconomic stabilization, microeconomic liberalization, privatization and integration with the global economy. At the same time, these policymakers learned quickly that their assumptions about Polish publics were well founded (even in the face of a more severe and prolonged economic downturn than expected). Polish nationalism lengthened the political horizons of the public, thereby enhancing the willingness of Poles to tolerate sustained economic difficulties. This, in turn, had three salutary effects: policymakers stayed the difficult economic course, the return to economic growth was sooner in Poland than elsewhere, and Poland has registered, as a result, the strongest economic performance in the region. Russia provides a sharp contrast in all three respects. Thus, central to the Polish story has been the political and therefore economic benefits of nationalism.

Also central to this story is a point easily forgotten. Majorities can be nationalists, not just minorities. This is not to suggest, however, that nationalism, whether of majorities or minorities, is always a plus insofar as democracy is concerned. If nationalism means contestation over existing boundaries that demarcate states, then it can challenge and sometimes end the democratic experiment. This is especially the case, if the central leadership, representing the dominant nation, uses contestation over boundaries to suspend the democratic rules of the game or to deploy the violent tools at their disposal to maintain those boundaries. This is the story in a nutshell of the early politics of Georgia, Russia, and rump Yugoslavia. Second, if the nation is defined in ways that exclude other long-term residents within those boundaries, democracy will also suffer. This is because the definition of the nation creates a hierarchy of civil liberties and political rights. Until the interventions of the European Union, for example, this was a problem in both Latvia and Estonia. Until nationalism had run its course, moreover, it was also the major problem in both Croatia and Slovakia. Finally, if the nation rejects the democratic rules of the game in pressing for its rights, then democracy will cease to be the only or even the dominant political game in town. This is one interpretation, for example, of the breakdown of democracy in Armenia—where it was less the nation than leaders presuming to speak on their behalf that ended democratic politics in this state. A similar argument can be made for Croatia, Slovakia, and Serbia, where citizens have recently rejected those politicians and those parties that used nationalism to divide and subvert the liberal political opposition.

The problem with nationalism, therefore, is when it combines with an illiberal political project. Indeed, this is what many fear is happening in the Russian Federation, especially given the weakness of Russian nationalism— or the failure of Russians to agree upon and embrace a common identity— and the terrible human costs of that transition. At present, nationalism in Russia has become the preserve of political extremists, who attract a lot of attention and some support, but who have failed to generate a nationalist movement of any size. Nationalism in this context undermines democracy, but is too fragmented and variable to consolidate authoritarian rule.[52] This is one blessing of the weakness of the Russian state: democrats as well as authoritiarians are divided.

Implications for the Study of Democracy

Several implications follow from this discussion. One combines the earlier comments on the state with these observations about nationalism. More than thirty years ago, Dankwart Rustow argued that democracy cannot enter into the zone of political choice until the national and state questions are resolved.[53] What this discussion suggests is that Rustow was right. Liberties, rights, and competition can only translate into a democracy when the state is well defined and widely accepted and when the nation—as defined by political authorities and as recognized by the public—is coterminous with the state.

Second, we must recognize that nationalism in and of itself cannot be a force either for or against democracy. Rather, what matters in authoritarian settings is a series of historical factors that shape whether national identity is well developed and whether there is a strong liberal opposition. When both are in place and regimes are in flux, nationalism supports democracy and, if the state is in flux as well, generates a positive interaction among nationalism, state building, and democratization. While Poland is an example of the former, Slovenia provides an example of the latter. However, where nationalism is weak (Russia), where it is used by leaders to divide the liberal opposition (Serbia), and where it is strong, but in a context where vulnerable authoritarian elites confront a weak opposition (as in Croatia), nationalism cannot contribute to democratization and may in fact undermine it.

Conclusions

There are four generalizations, therefore, that we can draw on the basis of the first decade of post-socialism. The first highlights the tremendous diversity of this region, whether we focus on economic indicators, such as progress in the transition to capitalism and economic performance, or political indicators, such as stability, the age of the state, or regime type. The variance in the region, reflecting the complex effects of state and regime dissolution, historical legacies, and policy decisions, carries with it several lessons—that this region is more varied than it has ever been; that this region constitutes from a social science perspective an ideal comparative laboratory; that democracy is the exception not the rule after communism; and that the "collapse" of communism is a highly misleading phrase that obscures what has been in most cases varying and often considerable continuities with the state socialist past.

The second generalization concentrated on democracy as both a sticky and a seductive form of government. Here, I noted, for example, the durability of those new democracies, which from nearly the beginning of the transition met democratic standards; the few cases of de-democratization; and the growing number of regimes over time that can be placed with confidence in the democratic column. Perhaps the three most important implications to be drawn here are the following: that democracy seems to be appealing in its own right, that authoritarian systems seem to be less capable of reproducing themselves than democracies, and that developments early in the transition —for example, the outcome of founding elections—seem to play a powerful role in structuring the political trajectories that follow.

The next generalization focused on the importance of the state for democratization. Put simply, weak states undermine democracy in several ways. First, if a state fails to establish a spatial and coercive monopoly, then the regime—of whatever type—within that state cannot establish an ideological monopoly. The end result is a state subject to contestation over its borders and over political authority, and a regime that lacks ideological consistency over space, that cannot extract compliance, and that fails, as a result, to govern effectively. By the same token, strong states empower regimes—and vice versa. Thus, the fate of the regime and the state are mutually interdependent. Second, in the particular case of democracy, a weak state deprives the democratic order of meeting required standards; that is, of guaranteeing expansive rights and liberties irrespective of time, place and circumstances and of converting political competition into accountable government. All this implies that definitions of democracy cannot assume a capable state. Rather, what is preferable is that equal emphasis be placed upon what can be termed uncertain results—or competition—and certain procedures—or rule of law. This definition, moreover, applies as well to capitalism, which requires spatially integrated markets and property rights—its equivalent of certain procedures—in order to function efficiently.

If the state is critical for democratization, so is the nation. Here, I argued that nationalism can be a force for or against democracy, depending upon whether the definition of the nation is inclusive, whether publics within a state share a national identity, and whether nationalism—a force for expanding the reach and depth of political authority—is joined with an ideological commitment to liberal politics. When those conditions are met, then nationalism contributes to democracy—as it did long ago in France and as it has, more recently, in, say, Poland, the Baltic states, and Slovenia. Here, one important implication is that at least some of the nationalist movements that arose in the wreckage of the Soviet, Yugoslav, and Czechoslovak regimes and states were responsible not just for the creation of new states, but also for democratic political orders.

We cannot now use these four generalizations to produce a fifth and final one: the power of the authoritarian past. Central too many analyses of recent democratization has been a pronounced tendency to prefer proximate over distal influences on the founding and course of democratization; that is, to privilege in a causal sense influences immediate to the transitional experience, such as the power and preferences of elites and the subsequent costs and benefits of the institutions they select. Moreover, if the authoritarian past is acknowledged, it is usually understood to be harmful to the democratic project. What we have discovered in our discussion, however, is that the authoritarian past is both a powerful predictor of what follows and quite variable in its effects. Can we, for example, understand the diversity of post socialism, the stickiness of democracy, or the role of the nation and state in democratization without looking back at the design and impact of communist-era federations and the power and political and economic agenda of opposition movements during the state socialist era? The point here is not just that the authoritarian experience is still influential in both positive and negative ways. It is also that what is often understood to be proximate is in fact historical—for instance, the ways in which protests during state socialism shaped the power of the opposition and the willingness of the communists to compromise with that opposition, which in turn shaped the outcome of the elections that founded the new political order.

CHAPTER FOUR

A Decade of Change but Not Much Progress

How Russians Are Coping

RICHARD ROSE

Since 1992, Richard Rose has explored a new dimension of Russian politics through the New Russia Barometer, which regularly surveys public opinion and yields important insights into the development of a democratic civic culture and civil society. As with many aspects of post-communist politics, the poll paints a picture of a society still in flux. It does, however, permit us to explore in ways not before possible the critically important question of the creation of a civil society. On this issue, its findings are at best ambiguous. On the one hand, it reveals that Russians now grudgingly accept the new political and economic order. According to Rose, the turning point came in the summer of 2001 when poll results first indicated that more respondents offered a favorable evaluation of the changes that had occurred since 1991; 47 percent responded favorably, while 37 percent were negative. But on the other hand, this "lukewarm readiness to comply with the existing regime" came about more from a revolution of declining expectations than from improved government performance. While poll results indicate that the average citizen perceives that he or she has benefited materially from market reforms and feels a greater sense of personal freedom, they do not yet fully establish a firm commitment to democratic norms that guarantee the further consolidation of Russian democracy. As Rose notes, it is perhaps too early to expect a complete transformation in a society that initially had virtually no commitment to democracy or a market economy.

A decade ago Russians experienced a treble discontinuity in the institutions governing their lives. The Soviet Union broke up; a regime that had maintained a one-party communist state for almost three-quarters of a century disappeared; and a centrally planned socialist economy in which bureaucratic commands rather than market prices determined supply and demand imploded. The simultaneous collapse of the state, the regime, and the economy was not the start of a steady transition toward a known and agreed destination. It was the start of the transformation of society in unknown ways. As Mikhail Gorbachev aptly said eight months before his world collapsed, "We are making such a large turn that it is beyond anyone's dreams. No other people have experienced what has happened to us."[1]

The advice offered to Russians by Westerners often draws on the experience of living in a modern state with a democratic political system and a market economy. This is true of institutions promoting the market, such as the World Bank and the International Monetary Fund, offering loans and grants to the Russian government on nonmarket terms, and economists and bankers advising on the privatization of major industries in the absence of a private sector. It has also been true of political scientists accustomed to studying elections and public opinion in established democracies where the rule of law prevails. If it was noted that Western institutions were absent, a convenient response was to prescribe their immediate introduction in the belief or hope that this would make Russia another country "just like us."

But to those familiar with Russian history, the country has never been like its European neighbors. For the past two centuries Russian intellectuals have debated whether or not Russia ought to emulate Europe or turn its back on the West and create a society in keeping with its Orthodox traditions.[2] The country's tsars favored a regime that gave them despotic powers. The 1917 Russian revolution created a communist regime that offered a Marxist-Leninist ideal as an alternative to the American way of life. Virtually every Russian adult today experienced political socialization in that system. As Vladimir Putin said, in explaining his ambition to join the KGB, "I didn't think about the Stalin-era purges. I was a pure and utterly successful product of Soviet patriotic education."[3] The system that created Putin's outlook has collapsed, but its legacy remains in the minds of Russia's people.

There are great changes from the 1980s. Western goods are sold in shops, cities formerly closed by order of the Ministry of Defence are now open to would-be Western investors, and public opinion polls are published showing how little Russians trust their government. However, signs of change are not proof of progress; they can be milestones on the road to nowhere.

It is now commonplace to say that it will take a generation to deal with the changes triggered by the collapse of the communist system. Today, we are half a generation from the launch of the federation, and by implication, halfway along the road to inter-generational change. With the retirement of President Boris Yeltsin at the end of 1999, Russians are now living with the legacy of the Yeltsin era as well as of the soviet era.

How are Russians coping with upheavals far more pervasive and disturbing than the swing of the electoral pendulum in an established democracy or business cycles in a market economy? As Nikolai Gogol reminds us, even when there is agitated movement, the direction of change can be very unclear. Instead of drawing on anecdotal observations or deductions from abstract theories, for evidence of what Russian people are doing and thinking this paper draws on the New Russia Barometer (NRB), a series of representative sample surveys of the Russian population organized by the Centre for the Study of Public Policy, University of Strathclyde. The initial NRB survey was launched in January 1992, the first month of the fledgling Russian Federation; the tenth survey was conducted in June/July 2001, almost two years after Vladimir Putin appeared on the national political scene.

Time Past, Present, and Future

The study of a society in transformation must focus on three different points in time: the starting point a decade or more ago; the present; and the future. At the unprecedented foundation of the Russian Federation, any judgment about the future was necessarily speculative. At the end of 1991, what we now describe as the present was the future. The only thing that was certain then was that, because of the upheavals under Mikhail Gorbachev, the future could not reproduce the past. Today, the past is recalled and reconstructed selectively, for there is a plenitude of pasts, from the days of the tsars to the days of the revolution, of Stalin, of Brezhnev, of Gorbachev, and of Boris Yeltsin too. The present is an elusive concept; it can refer to today's events or to the whole set of experiences that characterize a decade of life in the Russian Federation. The continuity of stable societies results in the future that is, next year or five years hence, tending to be a projection of the present. Russia lacks that continuity.

The past is the logical starting point for any dynamic model of change, but there is no agreement about which past is important. In the soviet era, historians were ready to treat folkways from the days of Ivan the Terrible or before as relevant to understanding the communist system established by

Josef Stalin.[4] Today, many social scientists argue that post-soviet Russia cannot be understood independently of its origin in the last decades of the
Soviet Union.[5] The point has special relevance when studying public opinion, since most adults have lived more of their lives in the Soviet Union than
in the Russian Federation. Yet to project soviet life into the twenty-first century is insufficient, since the regime of Mikhail Gorbachev as well as that of
Ivan the Terrible is now part of the status quo ante—and cannot tell us where
we are today.

Many studies of democratization focus on a defining moment in the
transition between regimes, especially the negotiation between departing
rulers and their opponents of a pact setting out the terms by which new
rulers will govern.[6] The logic is that of path determination: the rules of the
game established at the start of the new regime offer incentives and impose
constraints that determine what the new governors, their opponents, and
their successors can and cannot do.[7] However, there was no pact between
Gorbachev and Yeltsin; instead, there was a confrontation in which Yeltsin's
charismatic appeals encouraged the destruction of the Soviet Union and the
emergence of post-soviet regimes on an ad hoc basis. Defining moments in
the first years of the Russian Federation were based on vlast, that is, raw
power: the failure of the communist coup of August 1991 and the successful
armed assault by President Yeltsin's troops on the Duma in October 1993.
These events decided who would not govern but did not define the terms on
which Russia is governed today.

The present is the starting point in any dynamic model of change. It measures the extent to which what happened yesterday is a good guide to what is
happening today. This has been inadvertently demonstrated by political scientists who use survey studies of party identification at one point in time to
argue that Russians have stable partisan commitments. However, so fast do
Russian politicians abandon parties that by the time their articles are published half or more of the parties studied have disappeared.[8] Journalists writing against a daily deadline avoid the academic risk of assuming that data
several years old is still current in Russia. The occupational hazard of journalists is assuming that the Kremlin's newest decision will annul all that went
before, or that a flying visit by an American or international dignitary will
leave an imprint on Russian politics after the visitor's plane has taken off.
Moreover, since many media stories are statements of intent or speculations
of politicians, it is open whether or not what is written up will ever be realized.

Our current understanding of the future consists of expectations that
may or may not come to pass. Amidst the upheavals at the end of the Soviet
Union, nothing seemed certain and almost anything seemed possible. A

decade later Russians have firmer grounds to expect that the lives they lead tomorrow will be much like the lives they lead today and that next year will be much like this year. Insofar as people are concerned with coping in the minimal sense—for example a pensioner wanting to meet monthly needs or a politician wanting to survive in office—the future continuance of present circumstances is acceptable. But insofar as today's life is unsatisfactory or Russia's system of government is grossly deficient in maintaining the rule of law and other democratic features, then the future persistence of current conditions is the denial of progress.

From the beginning of the Russian Federation the New Russia Barometer has asked people practical questions about how they are coping at present: Do you often have to go without food? Do you have to borrow money or spend savings to get by? How do you evaluate the current system of government? It also asks people to compare their current circumstances with how they lived before transformation: Is the material living standard of your family better, worse, or the same? Do you feel freer to say what you think than under the former regime? Questions are also asked about hopes and fears for the future. The questionnaire for the initial NRB survey was drafted in Moscow in conditions of extreme uncertainty between the failure of the August 1991 coup and the implosion of the Soviet Union, and some major trend indicators were only developed in subsequent surveys. Hence, trends in the tables and graphics that follow sometimes report the result of ten NRB surveys and sometimes report evidence from a lesser time span. The timing of particular surveys was influenced by election hence, two surveys were conducted in 1996, one in January after the Duma election and another in summer, after the presidential election; the same pattern was followed in 2000. No survey was conducted in calender 1997 or 1999 (for details, see Appendix; www.cspp.strath.ac.uk; for subsequent updates, see www.RussiaVotes.org).

How Good Were the Good Old Days?

In retrospect, many Russians see Leonid Brezhnev's years as soviet leader, 1964–1982, as a golden era. When the New Russia Barometer asks people to evaluate the soviet system of government on a "heaven/hell" scale running from plus 100 to minus 100, a substantial majority gives the old Soviet regime a positive rating (see figure 1). Moreover, the proportion giving a positive rating has been rising; in 1992 only 50 percent were positive, but by 1996 the proportion had risen to 60 percent and those positive about the pre-perestroika regime have consistently been above 70 percent since 1998.

Figure 1. In Retrospect the Soviet Regime Looks Increasingly Good

Q. Here is a scale for evaluating the political system. The top, plus 100, is the best; the bottom, minus 100, is the worst. Where on this scale would you put the political system we had before perestroyka?

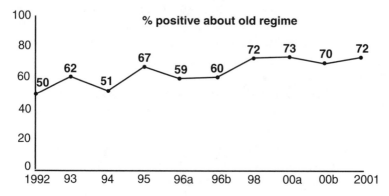

SOURCE: New Russia Barometer 1-X, 1992–2001. For details, see Appendix.

However, a historical review of what actually happened under Brezhnev shows that the era also had its drawbacks. In the words of Archie Brown:

> For the party-state, the Brezhnev era was one of unprecedented calm. They did not have to fear for their lives, as in Stalin's time, or even for their jobs, as in Khrushchev's. Security of tenure in high office led to the entire party and government leadership growing old together. At the beginning of 1982, the last year of Brezhnev's life, the average age of the Politburo was over seventy. Patron-client relationships, which had always been a feature of Soviet political life, flourished as never before, while corruption grew in response to the lessening of the fear of retribution and to the loss of belief in the ultimate goals of the system. If the Brezhnev era was both politically and socially the most stable of all periods of Soviet history, it was also the most cynical.[9]

For a Russian who wanted to see progress (and Mikhail Gorbachev was one example), the stagnation that characterized the Brezhnev era was a source of frustration. Moreover, the political hardening of the arteries that characterized the era stored up troubles that contributed to the subsequent collapse of the soviet regime.[10]

Evidence about the actual living conditions of the Russian people in the Brezhnev era is bedeviled by multiple deficiencies in soviet statistical data, ranging from nonreporting (no data is published about many years); through misleading reporting (the measure of output in the soviet economy, Net Material Product, was not intended to be nor was it the same as Gross Domestic Product); to false reporting ("retouching" statistics to give a better historical impression than reality justified, for example, underreporting infant mortality).

While Russians led a quieter life in the Brezhnev era, they did not live a longer life (see figure 2). Official Russian statistics showed that shortly after Brezhnev arrived in office, the average Russian man could expect to live 64.3 years, and the average Russian woman 73.4 years. By 1981–82, when the geriatric Brezhnev died in office, the best (*sic*) that official statistics could report was that Russian male life expectancy had fallen by 2.3 years, and that of Russian women had risen by only one-tenth of a year.[11]

Comparing trends in Russian life expectancy in Brezhnev's time with advanced capitalist societies shows the cost in human life of Russian stagnation. In 1965 there was a difference of 3.8 years between the life expectancy of Russian males against the average in eight major advanced capitalist societies, including the United States, Germany, Japan, and Sweden. By 1970 the gap had widened to 5.5 years because Russian life expectancy had fallen by more than a year while it had risen in advanced capitalist societies. By 1975 the gap had widened to 7.4 years, because Western countries were becoming healthier while Russia was stagnating. Further drops in male life expectancy in Russia meant that by the time Brezhnev was carried from office the average Russian man was living two years less than when Nikita Khrushchev had exited more than a decade and one-half earlier. Concurrently, men in advanced capitalist countries were living more than three years longer. Thus, during the Brezhnev era the East/West gap in male life expectancy widened to 9.5 years for men. For women the gap increased from less than half a year to four years.

Even when Russians were making progress, as in the case of the rise in car ownership, Russians were falling behind neighboring countries in the communist bloc as well as falling behind West European countries.[12] In 1960 there were 81 cars per thousand persons in the Federal Republic of Germany as against 4 per thousand in Poland. By 1970, car ownership in Poland had increased to 15 per thousand, but in West Germany it had increased to 223 cars per thousand people. Although car ownership in Russia had undoubtedly risen too, by 1980, car ownership stood at only 30 per thousand, less than half the level of Poland, and one-twelfth that of Germany. Between 1980 and 1990, car ownership continued to progress, reaching 58 per thousand in Russia. But because material living standards were so much lower, it fell further behind West Germany, where car ownership was 412 per thousand (see figure 3).

Figure 2. Russian Male Life Expectancy in the Brezhnev Era

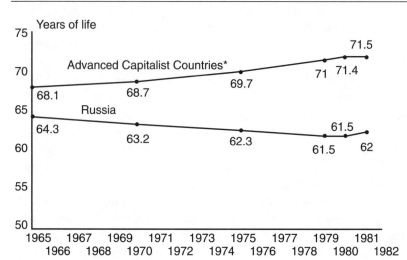

* Mean for USA, Britain, Canada, France, Germany, Italy, Japan and Sweden.

SOURCE: Boutenko and Razlogov, *Recent Social Trends in Russia, 1960–1995*. Montreal: McGill-Queen's University Press, 1997, p. 9. *OECD Health Systems: Facts and Trends, 1960–1991*. Paris: OECD Health Policy Studies No. 3 vol. 1, 1993, Table 3.1.2. Because of inconsistencies in years in reporting OECD data, the nearest year is taken when compiling averages.

Statistics of material progress in soviet times exaggerate the extent of progress, for comparing cars on the basis of a simple count of engines and wheels assumes that a soviet-era Lada car is the equivalent of a German Volkswagen or Mercedes, an assumption that rich Russians rejected after 1991, when car ownership not only rose but also included the purchase of second-hand or new Western cars by those who could afford to do so.

Changes of world importance in the political system of Russia that most concern policymakers, such as the end of the cold war or the introduction of free elections, are not immediately relevant to the everyday lives of Russians. However, Russians socialized politically in the Brezhnev era by parents and teachers who had learned how to survive under Stalinism do notice changes in what they can say and do free from interference by the state. In communist times, Russians did not enjoy freedoms from the state—for example, the right to choose one's own religion or join an organization of your choice—taken for granted in established democracies.[13] Membership in communist political organizations such as Komsomol was virtually compulsory for youths who wanted a career, and refusal to join party-sponsored organization could dam-

Figure 3. Car Ownership: Making Progress and Falling Behind

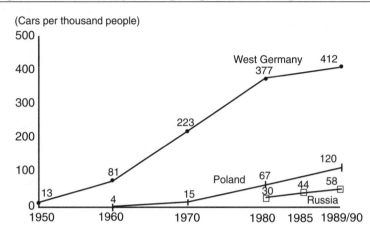

(Cars per thousand people)

SOURCE: For West Germany and Poland, *United Nations Demographic Yearbook* (various years). Final year for West Germany is 1993. For Russia, Boutenko and Razlogov, *Recent Social Trends in Russia 1960–1995*, Montreal: McGill-Queen's University Press, 1997, pp. 7 and 230.

age one's prospects in almost all walks of life. The collapse of the communist party's control of patronage no longer makes this necessary. Hence, the New Russia Barometer has developed a consumer index of freedom, asking people to compare what they can do in the new regime as compared to the old.

The replacement of the soviet party-state by a weak new regime has given ordinary Russians much greater freedom from the state (see table 1). In every NRB survey an absolute majority of Russians say they feel freer now than before in making decisions about religion, saying what they think, joining organizations, and deciding for themselves whether or not to take an interest in politics. Moreover, the Russians' sense of being freer today than in the old days has increased over time. In 1993, when the question was first asked, an average of 64 percent said they felt freer under the new regime than before; by 2001 the proportion feeling freer averaged 82 percent. Whereas Anglo-American theorists see political participation as a civic virtue,[14] Russians are enjoying freedom from compulsory participation in politics.[15]

A Random Walk

A chronicle of Russia in the past decade is full of shock events affecting everyday life, such as the collapse of the nonmarket economy in the autumn of 1991

Table 1. Freedom from the State—Then and Now

Q. Compared to our system of government before perestroika, would you say that our current system is better, much the same, or not so good as the old system in allowing people to:

	1993	94	96	96	98	00	00	01	Change
Everybody has freedom of choice in religious matters									
Better	71	83	80	80	79	83	84	88	17
Much the same	29	15	17	16	16	14	14	11	-18
Worse	6	2	3	4	5	2	2	1	-5
Everybody has a right to say what they think									
Better	65	73	74	76	73	79	81	78	13
Much the same	27	18	21	20	21	15	13	16	-11
Worse	8	8	6	4	6	5	6	6	-2
One can join any organization one likes									
Better	63	77	82	79	75	77	76	81	18
Much the same	28	18	14	15	18	16	17	15	-13
Worse	9	5	3	5	7	6	6	4	-5
Everyone can decide individually whether or not to take an interest in politics									
Better	57	62	69	63	66	70	73	81	24
Much the same	39	33	27	32	27	23	23	16	-23
Worse	4	5	4	4	7	6	4	3	-1

SOURCE: New Russia Barometer II–X, 1993–2001.

and the collapse of the ruble in foreign exchange markets in August 1998. A sequence of unexpected shocks encourages the conclusion that Russian politics is simply one damned thing after another. Yet in statistical terms, any sequence of events over ten years, 120 months, or 3,653 days is bound to form some sort of pattern, even if it is simply a set of uncorrelated responses that statisticians characterize as a random walk, an apt metaphor for many pillar-to-post lurches of Russian government under President Boris Yeltsin.

Theories of incremental change explain step-by-step movements in different directions as the consequence of policymakers responding to difficult problems on an ad hoc trial-and-error basis until the problem goes away of its own accord or political satisfaction is achieved.[16] The cumulative result is progress if there are more hits than misses, for example, over a decade the economy will grow significantly if there are more years of growth than contraction. Even if growth rates cycle up and down, cumulative growth will result as long as low growth is still positive growth. However, incremental change can also follow a downhill path. In the 1990s the Russian economy was declining at a rate that implied, were it to continue, the disappearance of all industry.

In a short-term perspective, a random walk has no apparent pattern, for each shock appears independent of what went before. But cumulatively, a pattern does appear: it is going nowhere. Instead of Russian conditions getting better over a decade, there is an absence of progress. The churning of resources in response to multiple shocks can be interpreted as showing that Russians are coping; instead of conditions steadily deteriorating, people are no worse off than before, and even if some people are worse off than before others are better off. From the "under all" perspective of the ordinary Russian, going nowhere is preferable to becoming destitute.

Russians Respond to Shocks

When political difficulties threaten conflict in Moscow, many Russians prefer to absent themselves. Ordinary Russians want to cope, that is, have enough to live on from day to day and even have enough for something extra on Sunday, a birthday, a holiday, or another special event. However, the fallout from the implosion of the nonmarket economy could not be avoided.

When living standards are under pressure, many people must temporarily do without everyday goods, but that does not make them destitute. Destitution is a matter of duration, the consequence of often doing without basic necessities. Since 1993 the New Russia Barometer has measured the extent to which Russians have been threatened with destitution by asking the frequency with which people have gone without food, clothing, and heating and electricity. There are big differences in what Russians do without. People are most likely to do without clothes that are really needed, less likely to do without food, and very unlikely to do without heating (see table 2). Russians are rarely without heating because the domestic price of energy is kept well below world market levels because privatized energy companies are still closely linked with the Kremlin, and energy is often provided communally.

Notwithstanding the ups and downs of the macroeconomy, there is much consistency in the extent to which Russians in aggregate are doing without necessities. For all the rows in Table 2, the average change over eight years is only five percentage points. Most Russians report that they sometimes do without clothes that they really need; sometimes or rarely go without needed food; and never or hardly ever go without heating. Those who have been immune from the shocks of transition, never doing without necessities, are a minority—but so too are those often doing without necessities. In the 2001 NRB survey, only 6 percent said that they often had to do without two or three necessities, and 14 percent said that they never went without necessities. Four-fifths are sometimes or rarely doing without things.

When waves of difficulties flood a society, the ideal is to keep your head above water. Since this is not always possible, the second-best solution is: If your head goes under water, be sure to come back up. Ordinary Russians have three alternatives: to adapt, to bounce back from adversity, or to become destitute.[17] *Adaptation* occurs when people find new ways to make sure that their household does not go short of basic necessities during the year, whether by adapting old connections to new purposes or making money in the market. If this is not possible, then Russians must be resilient, operating on "mend and make do" principles. If there is no money in the house to buy new clothes, then old clothes are patched until something better can be obtained. If you do not have enough money to buy something for the weekend, then make a meal of vegetables grown at one's *dacha*. Resilience is a means of coping by getting out of the difficulties that have arisen with transformation. Destitution is the result of often doing without basic necessities. The uncertainties and shortages of the soviet command economy gave Russians many opportunities to learn how to adapt or be resilient.[18]

Combining the frequency with which Russians do or do not go without basic necessities shows that a majority are resilient (see figure 4). In the 2001 NRB survey, 34 percent had already adapted to transformation, of whom nearly half never lacked any necessities. In addition 60 percent were resilient, finding ways to get things they needed after a limited period of doing without. Only 6 percent appear destitute, often doing without at least two necessities, typically food and clothing. While the conditions of such Russians are debilitating, often doing without necessities only becomes life-threatening if it continues from one year to the next. Analysis of Hungarian panel data indicates that a big majority of people who are often without necessities over a period of twelve months find means of bouncing back within eighteen months.

The secret of Russian resilience and adaptation is that the overwhelming majority of Russians do not rely solely on the official economy. In soviet

Table 2. Destitution Scale

Q. Sometimes people have to do without things that people usually have. In the past 12 months, has your household had to do without:

	1993	94	95	96a	96b	98	00a	00b	01	Change
Food										
Often	29	22	30	33	39	19	28	31	24	-5
Sometimes	31	n.a.	29	28	23	28	30	25	25	-6
Rarely	20	35	20	19	19	24	18	18	19	-1
Never	20	43	21	19	19	29	24	26	33	13
Heating, electricity										
Often	3	2	12	14	16	5*	8*	5*	6*	3
Sometimes	8	n.a.	18	21	18	9	13	10	12	4
Rarely	10	6	18	19	19	12	16	15	12	2
Never	78	91	52	46	46	74	24	70	71	-7

* 1998, 2000, and 2001 questions refer to heating. Electricity asked separately.

	1993	94	95	96a	96b	98	00a	00b	01	Change
Clothes that were really needed										
Often	30	34	43	44	43	32	49	44	40	10
Sometimes	29	n.a.	26	26	24	27	25	26	28	-1
Rarely	21	37	17	18	18	19	13	16	15	-6
Never	20	22	15	12	15	21	13	14	18	-2

SOURCE: New Russia Barometer II–X, 1993–2001.

times, Russians learned to have a portfolio of "second" or "rainbow colored" economies, some monetized and others nonmonetized, some legal and others illegal, in order to secure what they needed and wanted.[19] Since the regime change, Russian people have continued to rely on multiple economies, and the New Russia Barometer has monitored the portfolios used to adapt or be resilient in the face of adversity.[20]

In response to gross economic pathologies of soviet times, most Russians have a defensive strategy, augmenting a money wage or pension with goods and services produced in a nonmoney social economy, for example, growing food and exchanging help with friends and relatives. In 1992, 51 percent of Russians were trying to cope with economic difficulties with a defensive portfolio of economic activities; in 2001, 56 percent were defensive. Russians who rely on one nonmoney as well as one monetized economy are not worse off materially; their households are just as likely as the average Russian household to have durable consumer goods costing a substantial amount of money.

Figure 4. Responses to Shock: Adaptation, Resilience or Destitution

Frequency of doing without food, clothes, or heating

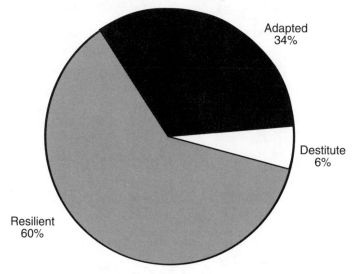

Adaptable = Never or rarely doing without food, clothing and heat.
Resilient = Rarely or sometimes doing without food, clothing and heat.
Destitute = Often having to do without food, clothing or heat, or two of these.

SOURCE: New Russia Barometer X, 2001.

Journalistic accounts of Russian coping often focus on opportunities to earn money in unofficial economies, whether as a street vendor or taxi driver or producing goods "on the side" in a factory. But for this to happen, there must be effective demand, that is, lots of people ready to put cash in the hands of people seeking a second job. In 1992 a total of 21 percent of Russians were enterprising, having one income from their regular job and one from the unofficial economy. In 2001, the proportion had fallen slightly; 18 percent were enterprising. Russians who rely solely on the official economy that produces poverty statistics quoted by the International Monetary Fund and the World Bank are best described as vulnerable, since they have nothing to fall back on when things go wrong. At the start of transformation in 1992, 35 percent were vulnerable. By 1995 those vulnerable because relying solely on the official economy had shrunk to 11 percent. In 2001, 18 percent relied solely on the official economy, most of whom were worse off materially than the average Russian. The smallest group, 8 percent in 2001, are marginal, a residual category describing Russians whose strategies for coping are so idiosyncratic that they would be distorted by forcing them into a logical conceptual framework.

Figure 5. Portfolio for Coping

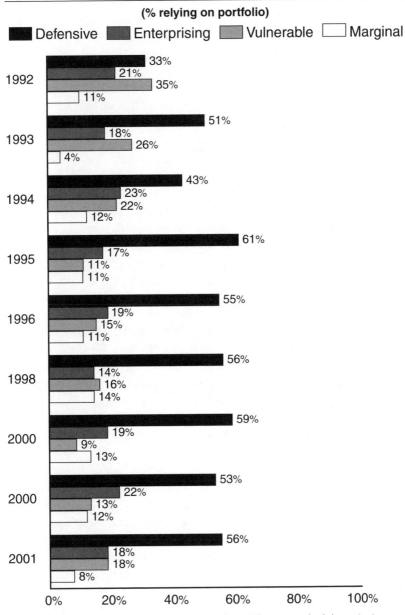

(% relying on portfolio)

■ Defensive ▨ Enterprising ▨ Vulnerable ☐ Marginal

1992
33%
21%
35%
11%

1993
51%
18%
26%
4%

1994
43%
23%
22%
12%

1995
61%
17%
11%
11%

1996
55%
19%
15%
11%

1998
56%
14%
16%
14%

2000
59%
19%
9%
13%

2000
53%
22%
13%
12%

2001
56%
18%
18%
8%

0%   20%   40%   60%   80%   100%

Defensive: Earnings from official economy AND social economy both important
Enterprising: Uncivil economy one of two most important economies
Vulnerable: Earnings from official economy only important economy
Marginal: Only social economies or don't know

SOURCE: New Russia Barometer 1-X, 1992–2001.

Incremental Changes, Benign and Otherwise

To regard annual changes as all that matters is to commit what Aristotle described as the sophist fallacy, "If each is little, then all are little." Russians who have lived through the past decade would agree with Aristotle that it is the cumulative impact of annual rates of change that is critical in determining the impact of transformation. Economic indicators can show little change, changes for the better, for the worse, or for both better and worse depending on the indicator selected.

Consumption Improving

Notwithstanding shocks imposed on Russians by transformation, most Russians have experienced material progress by purchasing durable consumer goods. When the first New Russia Barometer asked about car ownership, 20 percent of Russians had a car; by 2001 the proportion of Russian households with a car had increased by almost half to 29 percent. A second indicator is having a video cassette recorder (VCR), a consumer durable only introduced to Russia after the collapse of the old system. A VCR will cost several months' wages or more and must be paid for in cash; it cannot be obtained through connections, as may be done with hospital treatment, nor can it be grown at one's *dacha*. In the July 1996 NRB survey, 27 percent reported their home had purchased a VCR. Five years later ownership of a video cassette recorder had risen to 42 percent of Russian households. Possession of a VCR or other consumer durables is a reminder that Russians who sometimes do without necessities are sometimes able to buy goods they want to improve their standard of living.

Money Deteriorating

Inflation is a pervasive concern of everyone who lives in a money economy, whether employed, unemployed, or a pensioner, and it is a bigger worry for Russians than is unemployment.[21] Policymakers and journalists want to know what impact their actions and events of the past few months have had on prices. Hence, the inflation figure usually quoted in headline news is the latest rate, and it is compared with the rate for the previous month, quarter, or year. If the latest figure is lower than before, this is interpreted as progress, and if higher, as a sign of deterioration. But producing an "annualized" inflation rate from monthly figures assumes that the next eleven months will be like the most recent for which data is available, an assumption that is not tenable in an economy as turbulent as Russia.

If annual inflation rates are compared, the pattern from 1992 to the present appears to show continuing progress.[22] From a dramatic high of 2,500 percent inflation in 1992, when market prices were first introduced, the annual inflation rate fell by two-thirds in the following year and three-quarters in 1994. The annual rate halved in 1995, and in 1996 fell by more than four-fifths. Since then, the annual inflation rate, albeit still in double figures, has gone down more often than it has risen, and relative steadiness since the upheavals of 1998 is sometimes interpreted as evidence that the Russian government has inflation under control or even that it should strive to attain low inflation rates of established market economies.

However, ordinary Russians are more likely to focus on the cumulative inflation rate. Whatever date Russians choose as their base year in calculating cumulative price increases, the pattern is the same. Prices keep going up, since inflation is cumulative, and this is true whether the annual inflation rate rises or falls (see figure 6). Furthermore, a reduced rate of inflation applied to a higher price level can even lead to an increase in the absolute level of price increases. For example, the big drop in the official inflation rate from 1992 to 1993 was accompanied by an eightfold rise in prices, and the drop the following year was accompanied by an additional trebling of prices. Altogether, this produced a cumulative rise in prices of more than 2,400 percent in two years. From the beginning of 1998 until the end of the year 2000, the com-

Figure 6. Cumulative Price Inflation, 1992–2000

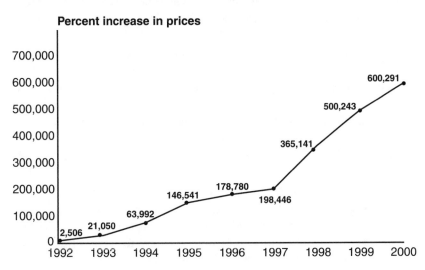

SOURCE: European Bank for Reconstruction and Development, *Transition 2000* (London), p. 205.

pounding of fluctuating inflation rates of 84, 37, and 20 percent has had the cumulative effect of trebling prices in the run up to and aftermath of the latest Russian elections.

Reversals

The logic of the dismal science of economics is that benefits are accompanied by costs—and the costs usually come first. This implies that trends in Russian society should deteriorate and then improve. More than half a century ago Joseph Schumpeter coined the phrase "creative destruction" to describe the process by which some firms supplant others in the course of economic development.[23] The phrase aptly describes how, after a decade of painful rebuilding, the German economy rose from the ruins of World War II to become the most dynamic economy in Europe.

The payment of wages, a fundamental feature of any market economy, was less important in soviet days because controlled prices led to a shortage of goods in the shops and a "ruble overhang," as Russians accumulated cash savings in default of goods that they could buy, and the acquisition of shortage goods often depended on who you knew rather than what you paid. The movement of the Russian economy to the market has been erratic, and this is evident in the substitution of barter for cash payment in exchanges between enterprises and the extraction of "forced savings" from employees by the late payment of wages. Employees most likely to suffer from the late or nonpayment of wages are those working for state-owned enterprises or in public sector institutions such as hospitals or schools. Nonpayment has also been substantial among new private enterprises, which have been so undercapitalized that cash flow problems result in what are nominally market enterprises being unable to pay workers on time or at all (see figure 7).

When the New Russia Barometer began measuring problems with wage payments in 1995, only 48 percent of those in work were receiving their wages regularly. Even though the following year was an election year, incremental increases in the "feel bad" factor continued. By summer 1996 only 22 percent of Russians in work were being paid on time, including an increasing number who would never receive what they had earned. Since then, the pattern has reversed: there are now incremental improvements in the payment of wages. By the last elections, half of Russians were being paid regularly, and in 2001 the New Russia Barometer reported more than half of Russians are now paid on time. Relatively speaking, the reversal is positive evidence of progress. But the fact that Russians have experienced a decade or more of uncertainty about whether they will be paid for the work they do is

Figure 7. Wages Paid on Time

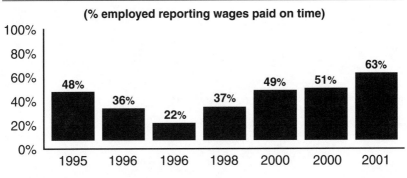

SOURCE: New Russia Barometer IV–X, 1995–2001.

indicative of the distance that Russia still is from achieving a modern market economy.

Stabilization and Stagnation

When living conditions are falling as a consequence of the initial shock of transformation, then ending a deteriorating situation is an improvement. (Also known as "the law of holes," propounded by Denis Healey, a former British economics minister: "When you are in a hole, the first thing to do is to stop digging.") But if a reversal of fortunes does not follow, then stabilization is the prelude to stagnation.

Throughout the post-communist world, the collapse of the command economy caused a decline in the officially measured gross domestic product. The first difference between countries was the depth of the decline. In Poland, for example, "shock therapy" stopped the rapid decline in its economy before the end of 1992 and in the Czech Republic and Hungary in 1994. A comparison between Russia and Estonia, both integral parts of the Soviet Union until the end of 1991, shows that ex-soviet republics can register economic reversals (see figure 8).

The contraction of the official Russian economy was particularly sharp; by the beginning of 1995 official statistics indicated that it had contracted by a third. So great was the contraction that it left limited scope for further contraction. This did not happen. Instead, the economy showed signs of stabilizing. Since then official figures have resembled a random walk, insofar as the economy contracted again in 1998 and then recovered a little in the next two years. Whereas Estonia was on the same steep downward path as Russia in its

Figure 8. Two Patterns of Economic Change: Russia and Estonia

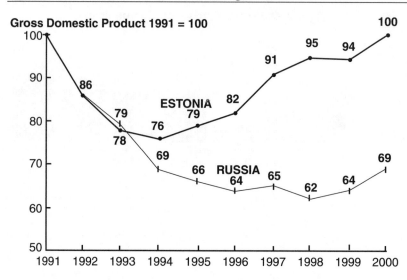

Gross Domestic Product 1991 = 100

SOURCE: EBRD *Transition Report Update, April 2001* (London), p. 15.

first two years, deterioration slowed down in 1994. While the Russian economy continued to contract, the Estonian economy started its upswing in 1995. By the year 2000 the official Estonian economy had not only recovered but also, on the Europena Bank for Reconstruction and Development (EBRD) statistics, was two-fifths more prosperous than Russia.

The best proof of coping with a turbulent economy is that people can sustain themselves indefinitely with the resources that they have. When the New Russia Barometer asks people whether they have been able to get by during the past year without borrowing money or spending savings, the pattern shows great stability (see table 3). While very few manage to save money, an absolute majority is able to get by, if only just. At the start of transformation in 1992, 62 percent said they were getting by; in mid-2001, the proportion was only 1 percent higher. In the interim, the proportion getting by fluctuated up and down; the result of this random walk was nil progress.

Stagnation in aggregate, combined with very little destitution, indicates the extent to which Russians are resilient, in some years not needing to borrow money or even loaning money to friends, while in other years borrowing money or, if they have them, spending savings. When without regular employment or pay, Russians can use the time gained to raise food, do odd jobs to help friends, or work in a cash-in-hand second economy. If none of these activities

Table 3. Getting By

Q. In the past year, has your household been able to:

	92	93	94	95	96a	96b	98	00a	00b	01	Change
						(percent)					
Save money	13	11	8	18	6	10	10	5	5	8	-5
Just get by	49	64	69	48	48	50	53	58	52	55	6
Borrow money	10	12	*	23	35	27	30	22	15	19	9
Spend savings	27	13	*	4	5	6	3	9	19	13	-14
Spend and borrow	-	-	*	6	5	7	4	5	8	5	-1

*Replies not strictly comparable

SOURCE: New Russia Barometer I–X, 1992–2001.

is possible, then 78 percent of Russians reckon that they could borrow as much as a week's wages or pension from friends or relatives, seven times more than believe they could borrow money from a bank. Surveys in Britain and Austria show that in a market economy up to a fifth of adults borrow money or spend savings at some point during the year. The difference between a market economy and Russia is that in a market economy the four-fifths who get by do so on earnings in the official economy rather than by planting potatoes and cucumbers or on insecure earnings in unofficial economies.

Settling Down to What?

In a society in transformation the first few years are the most uncertain, for everything—the system of government, the value of money, and even the very boundaries of the state—is up for grabs. This period is now over. After a decade, the probability that next year will be similar to this year is far higher than that next year will see a return to the upheavals of the early 1990s. The constitutional hand over of the presidency from Boris Yeltsin to Vladimir Putin on the last day of the last millennium is a sign that things are settling down.

Settling down can be interpreted in several ways—no more change, stopping a deteriorating situation, or a random walk leading nowhere—and each alternative can apply to different aspects of contemporary Russian life. Decisions about the constitution and the economy made in the early 1990s have set the country on a path that cannot be reversed. Political inertia makes incremental change more likely than the Kremlin inducing radical change. It is misleading to describe the new Russian regime as "consolidating," for that word is associated with the consolidation of democracies.[24] The priorities of President Putin are not determined by Anglo-American theories of democratization. As he said in his millennium address to the Russian people:

> Russia will not become a second edition of, say, the U.S. or Britain, where liberal values have deep historic traditions. Our state and its institutions and structures have always played an exceptionally important role in the life of the country and its people. For Russians, a strong state is not an anomaly to be got rid of. Quite the contrary, it is a source of order and main driving force of any change.[25]

The state that Vladimir Putin now heads is at best an incomplete democracy.[26] Even though competitive elections have now been institutionalized, the government is not accountable to the populace because there is a lack of institutions of civil society and a floating rather than a stable party system. The weakness of the rule of law—Russia ranks among the most corrupt governments in the world on the Transparency International Corruption Index (www.transparency.org)—is bad for government and discourages investment in the economy. In Russia today, settling down can mean a lowering of expectations leading to an acceptance of an increasingly stable but far from satisfactory status quo.

The economic hopes that Vladimir Putin held out in his millennium address were inconsistent with past performance and directed at the very distant future. He said that his advisors forecast that if Russia were to sustain a rate of economic growth of 8 percent per annum for fifteen years (cf. figure 8), then by the year 2015 it might attain the standard of living in Portugal in the year 1999! Checking the calculations of Putin's advisors against World Bank data alters the picture: At best, Russia would reach Portugal's 1999 standard of living in the year 2020.

Putin's landslide victory in the March 2000 presidential race and his consistent post-election approval by three-quarters or more of Russians show he is a popular politician. But popularity is insufficient to overcome the force of political inertia. The tenth New Russia Barometer asked whether Russians thought President Putin had achieved changes for the better, the worse, or not at all in major areas of public policy (see table 4). The replies emphasized stability. In four areas—maintaining order in society, enforcing the rule of law, reducing crime, and keeping prices from rising—the largest bloc of Russians saw no change. Consistent with pension increases and more people being paid wages on time, a majority saw social protection of the poor as improving. Any president is at risk from unwanted shocks, whether another Chernobyl civil nuclear disaster or a second Chechen-style rebellion occurring elsewhere in the Russian Federation. While not many NRB respondents think such disasters are likely, in view of past events, fewer still hold the view that "it can't happen here."

Although a majority of Russians are prepared to voice endorsement of one or more undemocratic alternatives—a return to communist times, government by a tough dictator, or the dismissal of the Duma and suspension of elections—there is no agreement about which undemocratic alternative is best. The idea of returning to the communist system of governance is a dream, not a practical possibility, given all that has happened since 1990. The Duma too appears secure. Even though 51 percent told the tenth New Russia Barometer that they would welcome the suspension of the Duma, more than half of this group are frustrated authoritarians who would like to see the Duma suspended but do not think it will happen.

Revolution of Falling Expectations

Events of the past decade have tested the patience of Russians and shown that it is great. Yet many social scientists predicted that if the social security network of soviet times was not maintained or reinforced, then protests in the streets and factories would lead to the fall of the new Yeltsin regime.[27] In January 1992, the NRB survey found that 93 percent of Russians said they thought mass demonstrations were likely in protest against inflation, 81 percent thought demonstrations likely against the political situation, and 76 percent thought demonstrations likely against rising unemployment. When asked if they would participate in demonstrations if they were held, 57 percent said they would definitely or probably demonstrate against inflation; 44

Table 4. Russia Settling Down under President Putin

Q. After the election of Vladimir Putin as President of Russia, how much has the situation of the country changed compared to that of his predecessor?

	Improved	Same (percent)	Worse
Social protection of the poor	55	35	10
Order in society	46	46	8
Everyone, including public officials, equally obeys the law	37	56	7
Keeping prices from rising	25	46	29
Reduction in crime	20	63	17

SOURCE: New Russia Barometer X, 2001.

percent would demonstrate against unemployment; and 37 percent would definitely or possibly demonstrate against the political situation if demonstrations were organized.

Throughout the 1990s inflation, unemployment, and political turbulence gave Russians cause to demonstrate. Even though the confrontation between the Duma and the president in early autumn 1993 was of profound importance for the future course of Russian governance, Muscovites avoided demonstrating on one side or the other. Through the decade Russians preferred to sit on the sidelines or tend to their potatoes rather than go into the streets waving political banners.

The longer the Russian Federation persists, the more people are settling down to accept it (see figure 9). In the first NRB survey in 1992, only 14 percent of Russians positively endorsed the new political regime; 12 percent were neutral and a massive 74 percent gave a negative assessment. Subsequently, the proportion positive rose, then fell, then rose again in response to events, and those giving a negative rating were a plurality or an absolute majority. A line was crossed in the tenth NRB survey, when 47 percent expressed a positive evaluation of the current system of government, while 37 percent were negative.

Political change thereafter is expected to consolidate democracy. While elections have decided who governs the Russian Federation, in the absence of a modern state it is premature to predict that Russia's rulers are seeking to move from an electoral democracy to a complete democracy. It is also premature to say that the Russian people are strongly committed to democratic rule. The tenth New Russia Barometer found that when Russians were asked to evaluate the idea of democracy on a 10-point scale, most Russians responded positively to this symbol, giving it a mean rating of 7.0. However, when asked to evaluate how democratic the current system of government is, the mean rating fell to 5.5, almost equidistant between being completely undemocratic or completely democratic. Moreover, when Russians were asked how suitable they believe democracy is for Russia in its current condition, the mean rating, 5.6, is similarly halfway between believing democracy is completely suitable or unsuitable for the country.

The big shift in Russian opinion has been from a reactionary nostalgia for the communist regime to a lukewarm readiness to comply with the present regime. In 1992, 44 percent of Russians were reactionaries, approving the old regime and disapproving the new. The second-largest group were skeptics, negative about both old and new regimes. By 2001, even though the percentage in favor of the old regime had risen substantially, the proportion of reactionaries had fallen to 39 percent. This did not reflect a big increase in

Figure 9: Disapproval of the New Regime Falling

Q. Here is a scale for evaluating the political system. The top, plus 100, is the best; the bottom, minus 100, is the worst. Where on this scale would you put our current political system?

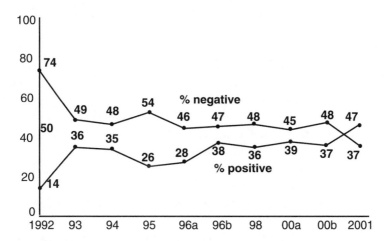

SOURCE: New Russia Barometer I–X, 1992–2001.

Russians positively favoring the new regime against the old; in 1992 a total of 8 percent was unequivocally in favor of the new against the old regime, and in 2001 it was 13 percent. The big change is in the proportion of compliant Russians, people who give a positive evaluation of both the old and the new regimes. In 1992 only 7 percent were in this category; by 2001, compliant Russians were the second-largest group, 30 percent of the total.

Meanwhile, Patient Endurance

Russian time horizons differ greatly from the instant gratification of mass consumption societies or carefully calculated investment schedules of medical students borrowing money to finance their education. Russians have a long tradition of patient endurance, suffering difficulties without protest and without expecting that difficulties will necessarily be overcome in their lifetime. Revolutionaries such as Lenin were patient, requiring more than a quarter-century before they could see some fruits of their efforts. The power of the communist party-state taught other Europeans patience too. In soviet days, a popular joke was about a person discussing with the telephone company when a phone could be connected in their home. The date offered was

17 March—five years hence. The clerk was asked anxiously, "Morning or afternoon?" and replied with a shrug of his shoulders, "Who knows. Does it matter?" The irate customer replied, "Certainly. I'm due to collect my new car that afternoon."

A decade of life in the Russian Federation has encouraged patience in the face of uncertainties about when or whether individual hopes and expectations will ever be met. When the New Russia Barometer asked people in 1993 when they expected to be satisfied with their standard of living, half said they didn't know; a quarter were optimists, believing that they would be economically content within ten years; and a quarter were pessimists, fearing they would never be content. By the time of the tenth NRB survey the optimists, expecting to be content within the next ten years, had risen to 36 percent and the same proportion didn't know whether they would ever be content. This left 28 percent feeling they would never be content. When Russian hopes of becoming economically content are not realized, as has been the case for many Russians in the past decade, people simply push their expectations back to the year 2010—or to the more distant future.

Experiences of the past decade have shown how ill-founded were the hopes of "market Bolsheviks" in the rapid transformation of Russia into a market economy and the hopes of "democratic Bolsheviks" in quickly achieving a complete democracy. In his farewell speech, President Yeltsin apologized to the Russian people that the costs of transforming society had been so great and that more benefits had not come sooner. In his initial address to the Russian people, President Vladimir Putin cautioned against expecting dramatic changes overnight.

However, Russian people have not given up hope. When the tenth New Russia Barometer asked how long people thought it would take before there were positive benefits for those who had suffered hardship during transformation, few were complete pessimists, believing that positive results would never come (see figure 10). Respondents did differ in the amount of patience they thought necessary. Very few thought that positive results would be evident within five years, and one-fifth expressed the hope that positive results would be evident in a decade, that is, by 2011. A majority showed the patience of Chekhov's *Three Sisters*, hoping that positive results would eventually come.

Russians do not aspire to an ideological goal; the journey to and from socialism has shown how great are the costs of relentlessly pursuing an impossible ideal. Instead, Russians aspire to a normal life, not in terms of what was *normalno* under Leonid Brezhnev or Boris Yeltsin, but conditions that are also thought normal by Americans and Europeans. When the tenth NRB survey asked Russians what they think are the chief elements of a nor-

Figure 10. Patience—With or Without Much Hope

Q. Do you think that the big changes since Soviet times, which have imposed so many hardships, will bring positive results to the majority of people of this country sooner or later?

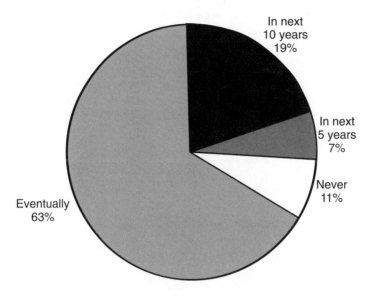

In next 10 years 19%

In next 5 years 7%

Never 11%

Eventually 63%

SOURCE: New Russia Barometer X, 2001.

mal society, overwhelming majorities said it was one in which people are free to go about their everyday lives without government interfering, government officials treat people fairly, there is little fear of crime, there are opportunities for you and your children to improve living conditions, money does not lose its value because of inflation, everyone who wants work can find a job, and welfare services will help if things go wrong.

The context in which Russians aspire to a normal life is, however, radically different from the United States. It is also substantially different from the way in which post-communist countries of Central and Eastern Europe have developed. Mikhail Gorbachev saw *perestroika* as creating a new and enlarged bloc of countries, with Russia inside what he called the "common house of Europe." In half a generation since the fall of the Berlin Wall, East Central European governments formerly under Moscow's domination have made progress toward becoming complete democracies and are now approaching integration with established democracies in the European Union.[28]

Russia is settling down differently. In tsarist and then in soviet times, many Russian leaders endorsed a civilization that rejected Western values.

When Vladimir Putin argues that the Russian state should be the "main driving force of any change" he is true to that history. History has taught Russians how to cope with both stagnation and shocks. The Russian people have accepted that there is no turning back to the past, but also recognized that any road to progress stretches a long way into the future.

Appendix: New Russia Barometer Surveys

	Date	Number respondents
I	1992: 26 January–25 February	2,106
II	1993: 26 June–22 July	1,975
III	1994: 15 March–9 April	3,535
IV	1995: 31 March–19 April	1,998
V	1996: 12–31 January	2,426
VI	1996: 25 July–2 August	1,599
VII	1998: 6 March–13 April	2,002
VIII	2000: 13–29 January	2,003
IX	2000: 14–18 April	1,600
X	2001: 17 June–3 July	2,000

Each survey is a multistage stratified random sample covering the whole of the Russian Federation, except 1992, when the universe for the sample omitted rural areas. All the surveys, except for 1994, have been conducted by VCIOM, the oldest survey organization in Russia. For more details, see Richard Rose, *A Decade of New Russia Barometer Surveys* (Glasgow: University of Strathclyde Studies in Public Policy, 2001).

CHAPTER FIVE

Taming *Vlast*

Institutional Development in Post-Communist Russia

THOMAS F. REMINGTON

Thomas Remington raises the critically important question of the limitation of executive authority in democratic systems. Noting the Russian propensity to conceptualize authority as "vlast"—dominance by the state, with a virtually unquestioning acceptance of strong, paternalistic leadership—he explores whether either the institutional structures or the political realities of the new Russian democracy impose effective checks on the power of the office of president created by the 1993 constitution. He further poses question of the relationship between the empowerment of an effective government and accountability to the electorate. What level of checks and balances is consistent with the need to preserve a level of contestation that maintains a viable democracy, and what level of authority is needed to create a competent state capable of regulating the society and sustaining the very rules of democratic competition? Remington suggests that these aspects of political society may be more completely developed than one might expect given the low level of development of civil society. He concludes that the institutional structures of the new system and the political realities have led both Yeltsin and Putin to seek significant compromises with the Duma, and both have agreed to observe the written and unwritten rules of the game. Moreover, the interaction of the president and the Duma has produced a reasonably clearly understood political calculus on the part of both the executive

branch and the legislature in which each can assess its relative strength and opti-
mum position on most policy issues, further lending structure and predictability
to day-to-day political life.

The Problem

At the conclusion of their book, *How Russia Votes,* Stephen White, Richard
Rose, and Ian McAllister contrast Russia and the United States with a comment on the relation between law and power. In the United States, political
actors behave as if power is constituted through law and invoke the constitution as authority for their actions. In a dispute—such as the proper scope of
authority for a state supreme court to dictate standards for counting ballots
in a contested election—rival camps turn to the Supreme Court for adjudication. How much the Supreme Court, in deciding such cases, is guided by its
members' policy preferences and how much by reliance on judicial precedent,
"plain meaning," or other politically neutral cues, is of course another matter.[1] In Russia, however, the situation is different. As the authors comment,
"the word for political power, *vlast,* refers to domination by the powers that
be. Yet democracy is not a system of domination; it is about taming power. In
Russia, there is a need to tame *vlast* on a continental scale."[2] My goal in this
chapter is to assess the experience of the last decade in Russia and to see how
well the constitution adopted in 1993 has managed to tame *vlast* within a
framework of institutions.

In Russian usage, *vlast* means more than raw political power; it refers in
fact to a quite specific domain of political power, that of the state, where the
state is understood in the most traditional way as hierarchical, unitary, and
patrimonial. When sophisticated political actors say that *vlast* wants this or
does not approve of that, they are referring to the current policy line of the
Kremlin, the focused, coordinated strategy of the authorities who embody
and hence exercise the totality of state power. The continued use of the term
in this sense implies that power today has not been divided among the constitutionally separated branches of government, but is still unitary, as if it
were an extension of the sovereign's will. This conception of power is analogous to the way in which Byzantine architecture embodied the principle of
hierarchical order and repeating forms descending from heaven to earth.
Does this mean that Russians continue to belong to a predemocratic, even
premodern, political culture? Or does the continued use of the term *vlast* to
refer to state power simply reflect a pragmatic grasp of the way power realities operate in Russia? Either this way of speaking about *vlast* tells us that

popular conceptions of the political system are lagging well behind the newer forms of constitutional democracy and rationalized bureaucracy, or that today's constitutional democracy is simply another façade, similar to the fictions of soviet-era constitutionalism, by which autocratic vice pays a comforting tribute to democratic virtue. Our question, therefore, is this: are the institutional arrangements created under the 1993 constitution another façade behind which patrimonial rulers at the center, in the regions, and in other sectors, continue to claim absolute authority over their subjects, or has constitutional democracy in fact begun to tame *vlast?*

Scholarly attention to the regime changes in post-communist Europe over the last decade has proceeded through several stages. The great wave of communist regime breakdowns in 1989–1990 stimulated a burst of efforts to apply models of political transition developed in the contest of Southern Europe and Latin America to the changeovers to constitutional democracy in Eastern Europe and parts of the former Soviet Union. This quickly led to analyses of the politics of the design of new constitutional and electoral arrangements, including the balance of legislative and presidential power and the rules of the electoral game. More recently, scholars have begun to explore the effects of post-communist states' early institutional commitments on the character of policymaking and the performance of government.[3] Observers and policymakers recognize that a nationally democratic framework can allow appalling poor administrative performance and deeply corrupted state structures to flourish for long periods, as public cynicism and mistrust, and high institutional barriers to collective action, keep the system in equilibrium.[4] In such systems, democratic governance is undermined by self-fulfilling public and official expectations of poor government. The implementation of even the best policies will be distorted to benefit the strong or the corrupt if the quality of administration is low. And of course, policy is unlikely to be optimal in the first place, having been compromised by the concessions made to powerful organized interests such as the *nomenklatura,* regional bosses, or oligarchs in order to buy their consent to the reform programs. Pseudo-partisan electoral competition will not supply either responsiveness or accountability if instead of delivering broad public policies, winners parcel out particularistic benefits to their clients.[5] Intractable pathologies such as bureaucratic inefficiency and corruption, rent seeking by the powerful, and low social capital are less readily subject to measurement and explanation than are the mechanics of institutional structure. Yet they are of fundamental importance in determining long-term system performance.

The rise of this third-generation concern with problems of institutional performance coincides with the emergence of the post-Washington consensus appreciation for the importance of sound working institutions in ensuring the success of economic reform. Just as stable democratic institutions regulate the struggle for power in the political arena, sound public institutions help ensure that a market-oriented economy produces good economic performance. The new attention to the quality of government was marked by the World Bank's 1997 *World Development Report,* which laid out the case for strengthening state capacities for enforcing open and competitive markets.[6] Fortunately, there has been a high-quality and fast-accumulating literature dealing with the impact of early institutional decisions on the nature of policy and performance in the post-communist world.[7] The dismal economic performance of the post-soviet states has made observers acutely sensitive to the importance of political and legal guarantees of property rights and an effective and transparent system of economic regulatory institutions, macroeconomic stability, and social protection.[8] Without them, the incentives embedded in a market system are likely to produce outcomes that are both economically and socially perverse: widening inequality blocked capital and social mobility, economic instability, massive rent extraction, and low growth. Where *vlast* is intertwined with control over the productive assets of society—as in the case in Russia's patrimonial heritage—sound public institutions protect both economic and political competition in ways which promote public welfare and limit the opportunities for the strong to exploit the weak.

In this chapter I attempt to assess the degree to which Russia's constitutional rules and procedures regulate the exercise of executive and legislative power or are themselves simply instruments in the hands of the powerful. Do constitutional provisions in fact constrain actors in any meaningful way? I assume that politicians are strategic maximizers of political self-interest, whatever the mixture of policy and power goals may be that they pursue, and that they are locked in competition such that their success in realizing their goals depends on their joint efforts. Do such politicians have an interest in complying with rules that regulate their competition? One answer is that they do to the extent that they judge that their rivals are constrained by such institutions, that is, their willingness to obey the rules is contingent on their estimates of the probability that other politicians will do so as well. Take electoral law as an example. Without electoral rules, as we know from generations of study of ostensibly closed political systems such as that of the USSR, competition among ambitious politicians is not eliminated, but takes on forms which become destructive both for the individual actors and for the larger political system. The absence of open and regulated competition among political forces leads to the negative externalities with which we are only too familiar: corruption, policy paralysis, repression, and ultimately system failure stemming from the regime's inability to adapt to the competitive pressures from the outside world.[9] We can take it for granted that competition for power is inevitable due to the inextinguishable flame of politicians' ambition, and that by regulating and channeling the efforts politicians make to satisfy their ambition, political institutions such as parties solve collective dilemmas for both politicians and society, including accountability of policymakers to the public.[10] Therefore a system of institutions that can tame *vlast* must provide opportunities for ambition to be satisfied through agreed-upon rules of competition. We can suppose that even in tenuous post-communist democracies, politicians stand to gain from a system of electoral competition that limits the downside risk of losing out in a power struggle (they do not fear losing everything if they run and lose) and offers the new upside benefit of a prestigious electoral mandate if they win. Therefore, as Adam Przeworski has shown, if the present value of the stream of future benefits from anticipated electoral victories under democratic (and hence uncertainty-generating) rules is not discounted too heavily by the probability that there will be no electoral victories in the future, rivals would prefer electoral competition under democratic rules that they cannot directly control to competition of the unrestrained, winner-take-all-and-shoot-the-opposition kind.[11]

Advantageous though they are to politicians, democratic electoral rules, like other institutions that reconcile political competition with cooperation in preservation of a constitutional democracy, provide valuable positive externalities to society. Electoral institutions create means for the accountability of elected officials to the citizens. In the simple modes of democracy sketched by Joseph Schumpeter, politicians are given considerable discretion to enact policies as they choose, but are subject to the power of voters to punish them at the next election; the competition among them is the sole means for checking the tendency to abuse power and to keep the actions of the politicians more or less consonant with the preferences of the voters. More recent models of democratic accountability have distinguished between two subtly different accountability links through the electoral nexus: ex post facto sanctioning by the voters of politicians by denying them reelection, and ex ante selection of politicians whose conduct in office is predicted to be consistent with the voters' preferences.[12] Even in fully democratic systems, the electoral process is a noisy and inefficient mechanism for producing accountability of officials to citizens, because it may exaggerate, stifle, or utterly confuse the process by which citizens use sanctions or selection to bring about accountability and through it, representation.[13] Moreover, politicians who, after an election, carry out policies quite contradictory to those that they committed themselves to during the campaign may still in some meaningful sense be "representing" their voters.[14] Yet generations of democratic theory have convincingly demonstrated that in the absence of an electoral nexus, no other institutional arrangement can ensure that there is at least a possibility of meaningful accountability of political leaders to the public; the electoral institution can be considered a necessary, if not sufficient, condition for accountability.[15] It may also be the case that there are other institutions necessary to democratic accountability as well, among them a system of criminal law and enforcement which ensures that abuses of power are also subject to criminal penalty, as well as a system for disseminating adequate information about the actions of politicians to the general public.[16] But at a minimum we would probably agree that the electoral system is an indispensable element in any democratic framework for taming *vlast*.

Recently Guillermo O'Donnell has proposed conceptualizing accountability in two dimensions, vertical and horizontal.[17] Vertical refers to the electoral process by which voters grant or deny an electoral mandate to politicians. Horizontal accountability refers to the checks on officials' use of power exercised by legal and other agencies that preserve basic constitutional rights, as well as the constraints wielded by less formal centers of power. We might suppose these to include the checks and balances contained in a system of separated powers, as well as the scrutiny to which politically alert journalists and interest groups subject politicians. The two kinds of accountability are quite different. The checks and balances of a system of separated powers do not require that policymakers be responsive or representative. This "horizontal" dimension of accountability is not based in principal-agent relation. It is closer in some respects to the partisan mutual control mechanism identified by Robert Dahl as a critical component of pluralist theory.[18] Nevertheless, the independence of the judiciary and institutional means for allowing the public to monitor the actions of political leaders are clearly necessary conditions for accountability to operate. Where a president enjoys an electoral mandate but is not in fact accountable horizontally, O'Donnell has proposed, we can speak of democracy only in a very conditional sense: O'Donnell has suggested calling such a system "delegative democracy."

The larger implications of electoral competition in transitional politics have been well exposed in the literature. In this chapter I attempt to demonstrate that politicians may also find it advantageous to comply with constitutional rules in the realm of executive-legislative bargaining over policy. How otherwise can we explain the fact that even though the Russian president has awesome constitutional and extra-constitutional resources, he often accepts second-best alternatives? Since the Russian president can issue decrees with the force of law, what would prevent him from ruling by decree? The only conceivable answer is that laws have greater political value than decrees, something that would only be possible if interested third parties—such as citizens, investors, banks, and overseas governments and financial organizations—value the rules of constitutional democracy, under which laws are approved by majority vote of an assembly of democratically elected representatives. If Russia's constitutional regime has evolved to the point where it creates strategic incentives for presidential self-restraint, then we should find that the president would actually prefer to reach agreement with parliament on a statute (*zakon*) than to enact his own preferred policy in the form of an edict (*ukaz*), so long as the net value of the law is higher than that of the decree. The same logic dictates that the president would expend political resources on bargaining to bring legislation closer to his preferences. Certainly if he can get a law reasonably close to his ideal point, he prefers it to a decree. And if he is constitutionally unable to act by decree on the issue, his choice is to sign or veto; if the veto is sustained, policy reverts to the status quo.[19]

Parliament faces similar choices in using its constitutionally given legislative powers. It must decide how far to go to accommodate the president's preferences in passing laws. It must define the point at which it prefers to allow the legislation to die rather than to approve a bill it dislikes. We will use simple spatial depictions of the strategic situation of president and parliament to test our predictions about where the outcomes of the policymaking process will fall depending on the locations of the status quo and the preferences of parliament and president, as well as the formal constraints on legislative action set by the constitution.

The evidence is that Yeltsin, Putin, and parliaments have engaged in continuous bargaining to pass a large volume of legislation, and that the use of decree power has declined sharply since the early 1900s. Our task is to determine whether the use of legislative powers by president and parliament is consistent with our hypothesis. Ideally, to do so, we would need to know the president's ideal point, parliament's ideal point, the location of the status quo, and the constitutional constraints on the use of decree, for every policy; then we would be able to predict the legislative strategies of both president and parliament. If we judge that both sides are behaving as the theory predicts, we could conclude that the constitutional rules of the game are taming *vlast*. Here I do not claim to offer a systematic test of the theory. Rather, I attempt to illustrate it with a series of legislative case histories taken from Russia under Presidents Yeltsin and Putin.

Executive-Legislative Relations since 1993

Article 10 of the 1993 Constitution of the Russian Federation refers to separation of powers as the core principle of the organization of Russian state
power.[20] In this respect, as in its federal character, Russia's constitution differs
from that of France, although otherwise there are a number of similarities
between them in the way parliamentary and presidential forms of government are combined. But the Russian Federation explicitly divides power at
the federal level between executive, legislative, and judicial branches. The
president is "guarantor of the constitution," but the head of government is
the chief executive, who must be confirmed by parliament and must enjoy
the confidence of parliament.

On the other hand, the Russian system gives the executive considerable
independence of the legislative branch in the way it is formed and in its survival, as in the United States. And, as in the United States, but not France,
Russia's constitution explicitly separates a domain of federal power from
domains of power, which are jointly exercised by federal and regional levels,
and further designates areas, which are in the exclusive domain of the
regions. Moreover, the upper chamber represents the country's federal territorial units equally, as in the United States.

In some respects, Russia's system departs from either semipresidentialism
or separation of powers. Russia's system gives the president an exceptionally
wide range of powers, including appointment of government, dismissal of
parliament, initiation of legislation, veto of legislation, and decree. Timothy
Frye shows that Russia's president has eighteen of twenty-seven possible
direct powers as well as wide residual powers, reflecting the combination of
high bargaining power and low uncertainty about who the leading candidate
for president was that characterized the Russian referendum in 1993.[21] The
president has both "proactive" and "reactive" powers, to use the terminology
of Matthew Shugart and Stephan Haggard, meaning that he can introduce
legislation or even enact it directly through edicts, and can veto laws. In their
comparative survey of presidential policymaking power, they note that Russia
has one of the most powerful presidencies in the world.[22]

The asymmetry in the distribution of powers has led some observers
(and most Russians)[23] to dismiss the other institutions in the constitutional
system as being of marginal significance.[24] On the other hand, some argue
that parliament, courts, and regional executives have constrained presidential power.[25] To be sure, the constitution is not a particularly informative
guide to the actual exercise of power, given the personalized nature of
authority relations, the vast domain of discretion given to administrative and

police agencies, and the willingness of principals—notably Yeltsin—to consider actions abrogating the constitution itself. Quite apart from the September 1993 decrees dissolving parliament and calling new elections and a national vote for a new constitution, a case in point under Yeltsin's own constitution is the moment in March 1996 when Yeltsin seriously considered simply canceling, or indefinitely postponing, the 1996 elections, outlawing the communist party, and dissolving parliament. According to his own testimony, he was barely dissuaded from the course when Anatolii Chubais strenuously objected on strategic grounds, arguing that in contrast to 1993, now whoever stepped outside the constitution first would lose.[26] Generally, as George Breslauer shows, Yeltsin consistently manifested a predilection for holding unlimited personal power, both as president and earlier in his career, and was unwilling to promote the institutionalization of rules and procedures in policymaking. Instead, he tended to put political relations on a personal, even familistic basis.[27] Certainly Yeltsin used his unpredictability as a tactical weapon, catching both opponents and friends off-guard with his moves. But Yeltsin's leadership style was far from the only source of uncertainty, and his political advisors have written that the real problem with Russia's constitution was not that the president's powers were excessive, but that there was so much uncertainty hovering over the system as a result of the weakness of institutions regulating political competition and the immaturity of civil society.[28]

Still, because Russia's president has such wide powers, if the constraints and incentives built into its constitutional framework can be shown to constrain executive behavior in its relations with parliament, we could say that Russia's post-1993 institutions have made some progress in taming *vlast*. Untamed *vlast* might let the president set policy in either of two ways. First, he might "rule by decree," rather than having to negotiate with parliament or making concessions to it for the sake of obtaining legislation. Alternately, if the president so dominates the parliament through his control of carrots and sticks that he can obtain the laws he wants at little cost, then he should need to make very few concessions to the Duma over legislation, and veto bargaining should not matter.[29] But if there is effective separation of powers in lawmaking, the president would be restrained from using decree power where the constitution calls for a law or where political considerations dictate that relying on decree would be less effective than acting through law.

Let us look more closely at the way in which the 1993 constitution distributes decision making, agenda setting, and veto power between president and parliament.[30]

Agenda and Decree Power

The president can put issues into the parliamentary hopper by submitting legislation and he can add force to his proposal by issuing or threatening to issue a decree making policy on the same issue.[31] In a number of domains, the constitution specifies that policy must be made by federal law, that is, not by decree. However, the Constitutional Court has ruled that the president can issue decrees in advance of legislation even on subjects where the constitution requires legislation to "fill gaps" in existing legislation.[32] Therefore the president can sometimes threaten to issue a decree to "fill a gap" in legislation and therefore spur the Duma to move more quickly than it would otherwise do. The president is free to enact decrees that do not violate or contradict existing law. By the same token, however, in areas where there is standing legislation, the president may not use decree power to alter or supersede the legislation.

In fact, the president uses the threat of decree as a club to force the Duma's hand rather rarely. Threatening to issue decrees as a way of pressuring parliament to pass the president's desired legislation was much more frequent in the early 1990s than later. An example of heavy-handed decree threat tactics after the 1993 constitution entered force occurred in summer 1994. Chubais demanded that the Duma pass a law, which would regulate the privatization of state and municipal enterprises after the voucher program; if the deputies failed "to show a sufficient level of even an elementary understanding of their role in the state machine of power," he threatened, the president would launch the next phase of privatization by decree.[33] The president also threatened to issue decrees on tax reform and regulation of the securities markets and of stock companies in the summer of 1994 in order to spur the Duma to pass his proposed package of legislation on these issues.[34] Intensive negotiations between Chubais and the Duma produced a bill on privatization, which was acceptable to Chubais and to the privatization committee and several factions in the Duma. It failed on the floor, however, by thirteen votes. According to the head of the Duma's privatization committee, the failure of the legislation was not absolute: a number of the provisions that had been agreed on in the defeated legislation were incorporated into the president's decree.[35] Moreover, from Chubais's point of view, the outcome was more than satisfactory: he had made a public display of the executive's willingness to bargain with the Duma over a contentious legislative issue, putting the onus of failure on the Duma; he moved the Duma closer to the president's position; and the president remained free to act by decree. Indeed, according to Yeltsin's own political advisors, Chubais never really wanted a law in the first place, preferring to leave the president's hands untied after making a show of seriousness about seeking a compromise agreement with the Duma.[36]

Gradually, however, the threat of using decrees to substitute for stalled legislation became hollow. For example, in the summer of 1997, the government threatened the Duma with decrees and even dissolution if it failed to pass its proposed laws cutting budget spending, restructuring social benefits, and changing the Tax Code. Chubais (then first vice-premier) announced in June 1997 that the government was dissatisfied that the Duma had failed to pass these urgently needed laws; he called the Duma irresponsible and promised that "all decisions on these issues will be made by the president." When asked if the president would dissolve the Duma, Chubais remarked cryptically that "extreme steps must be taken only in extreme cases"; meantime, on the same day, the first deputy premier noted that while negotiations over the social policy bills between parliament and government should resume in the fall, the president might be required to enact them for now by decree.[37]

However, by the time it recessed for summer, the Duma had rejected nearly all of the proposed social policy legislation, refused to approve the proposed budget cuts, and only passed the new Tax Code in first reading, but neither decree nor dissolution followed. Moreover, the Duma mobilized its own defenses with efforts to pass a no confidence motion in the government, passed a privatization law so that the president could not act unilaterally by decree, and began to work on a law re-nationalizing some of the previously privatized enterprises. In interviews, many deputies called the threat of presidential decrees idle because most of the issues in dispute were currently regulated by law rather than decree, so could only be changed by law.

In the case of the budget, the president and government—we can treat government and president as identical for those purposes; there is a division of labor among them but the two institutions make a serious effort to avoid working at cross-purposes—have another way of pressuring the Duma to pass a budget acceptable to the government: if the budget law is not enacted by the start of the new fiscal year, the government will put a continuation budget into effect. The government has the right to continue spending and collecting taxes month by month at exactly the same level as the prior year if there is no budget in place. The reversionary policy—that is, the situation to which policy reverts in the event that legislation fails—is the continuing budget, in other words, not, as in the United States, the end of legal authority to spend and a government shutdown. So if the Duma wants to change spending levels or tax rates, it must compromise with the government. It might seem that this rule favors the executive. But since the executive, too, usually wants to change the levels and structure of the budget, the rule that policy reverts to a continuation budget also leads the government to prefer a bad budget law rather than no law at all.[38]

A growing body of evidence suggests that in addition to the constitutional limitations on the president's decree power—that a decree not violate standing federal law or the constitution, and that some areas of policy can only be decided by legislation—there are also well-understood political limitations.[39] A decree simply has less credibility in the eyes of third parties than a law. Everyone understands that it can be reversed more easily, whether by another decree, by a court decision, or by a law which supersedes the decree. Private actors, such as banks deciding whether to make loans secured by property which has been privatized through a decree rather than through a law, make judgments about the credibility of a decree. An important example is ownership of land. Until July 2001, there was no federal law permitting private transactions involving the sale or purchase of land, although the constitution declares that "the land and other natural resources can be in private, state, municipal or other forms of ownership" (Article 9, paragraph 2) and that "Citizens and their associations are entitled to hold land in private ownership" (Article 36, paragraph 1). But it also specifies that: "The conditions and procedure for the use of land are defined on the basis of federal law" (Article 36, paragraph 3). Therefore land transactions have been in legal limbo, without a secure legal foundation. President Yeltsin tried to use decree power to put the right to land ownership into effect in March 1996. The parliament quickly countered with a law "clarifying" the implementation of the decree, which nullified the impact of the decree. Since then the basis for the growing volume of land transactions has been a patchwork of local laws and presidential decrees. Buyers cannot be confident of the security of their title. Experts and market actors agree that only legislation will have sufficient credibility to assure lenders and buyers that the title is safe.[40]

Government officials also must calculate whether to take action on the strength of a decree if the action is risky or costly. Under Yeltsin, no government official was ever fired for ignoring a presidential decree.[41] And bureaucrats were adept at deciding how assiduously to carry out decrees. A conspicuous case in point was Yeltsin's August 1996 decree nullifying fifty decrees issued during the spring when Yeltsin was campaigning for reelection. Private sector and government actors know that laws, on the other hand, are subjected to extensive deliberation in the Duma by a broad spectrum of political forces and, once passed, are harder to reverse; third-party actors might also consider them to be more legitimate as well. Most decrees are carefully vetted within the presidential administration and government before being issued, but, even so, very few are used as substitutes for legislation, even to "fill gaps" in advance of anticipated legislation.

A decree has definite political attractions. Quite apart from the likelihood that he will have to make concessions to parliament in order to win passage of a law, a decree can be enacted far more quickly, even allowing for the normal "clearance" (*soglasovanie* procedures). When the president believes that executive action is needed urgently, he can respond swiftly with a decree. Likewise, if he can alter the status quo in such a way as to make its reversal politically costly, he may make it difficult or impossible for the parliament to pass a law superseding the decree. Yeltsin's decrees privatizing a number of state assets were used in exactly this way. For instance, in 1991 Yeltsin issued a *ukaz* turning all the assets of the second all-USSR television channel to a new RSFSR television company; at Boris Berezovsky's behest, he issued a *ukaz* creating the ORT television company as a stock company, in such a way as the notorious oligarch acquired effective control over it; and in 1998, he issued a *ukaz* giving Vladimir Gusinsky's NTV channel the status of an "all-Russian television company," enabling it to purchase airtime from the state at low prices.[42] Like presidential executive orders in the United States, decrees can give the president a "first mover" advantage when they create new rights and rents that are subsequently very costly to rescind.[43] One final benefit of presidential decrees is their value as signals of presidential policy: they indicate to observers in Russia and overseas what the president's position is on an issue and that he is paying attention to it. The president's decree power was also useful in the early years of bargaining with the IMF when the president could complain about the left-leaning Duma. Later, of course, this game proved self-defeating when it became apparent that undermining the normal democratic give-and-take of executive-legislative relations was harmful to Russia's political consolidation and also that decrees were not especially effective instruments of policy.[44]

Beyond the rough calculation of these advantages and disadvantages in using his decree power, however, the president must also take into consideration the state of existing law on an issue. If no law exists that regulates the particular question, the president is free to act by decree, so long as he is not constitutionally barred from doing so. (He could not enact a new tax of budget law by decree, for instance.) But all observers agree that as the volume of legislation passed in the 1990s has grown, the range of discretion left to decree has narrowed. For instance, once the parliament passed a law on privatization, the president could not ignore it and set privatization policy by decree. Gradually, therefore, the president's ability to use decree power as a substitute for law has diminished.[45] The president (both Yeltsin and Putin) has continued to use decree power to organize the executive branch. In this sense, decrees have become increasingly similar to U.S. presidential executive orders; acts directing the U.S. executive branch to enforce affirmative action in hiring are equivalent in importance to a decree by the Russian president creating a powerful federal commission to set the rates charged for utilities services throughout the country.[46] The point is not that the president is weak; it is that the domain of his power has shrunk as more policy is set by law.

Although both government and president have the right to introduce legislation, neither can force an item into the Duma's calendar for floor consideration or demand an immediate vote; they cannot force a vote on a take-it-or-leave-it offer (by example, by using a French-style "package vote" or British-style guillotine). These limitations are softened by the fact that since 1994 the Duma has followed an informal rule of giving precedence to executive branch initiatives, perhaps in order to avoid being blamed for obstructing the lawmaking process. Nevertheless, the Duma's prerogatives in deciding its own agenda make the Russian system features closer to a separation of powers model than to the French semipresidential model (the French constitution has no provision for separation of powers).

In short, the president and government do have considerable agenda and decision power over policy, but their power is not unlimited. They can submit legislation to parliament, and their bills have (informal) priority over other bills. The president can act by decree in some areas, bypassing the legislative process or at least "filling gaps" until legislation is enacted. Therefore the president's decree power can have some effect on the Duma in forcing the pace and shaping the content of legislation. But the use of decree to make policy decisions faces both constitutional and political limitations. The constitution provides that some issues may *only* be addressed through legislation, that any matters for which prior legislation exists can only be addressed by new legislation, and that presidential decrees may not contradict federal law or constitution. Politically, a decree lacks the credibility of a law because it is easier to reverse and lacks the legitimacy of a law. Thus presidential decree power may allow the president to extract more concessions from the Federal Assembly than it could otherwise, but cannot force total capitulation. And empirically, the president has used decree power rather sparingly since 1993.[47]

Veto Power

The president's veto power, combined with his agenda and decision-making powers, gives him significant bargaining leverage in dealing with parliament. The president can veto a bill or can send it back with proposals for altering it. The Duma decides whether to modify the bill in accordance with the president's preferences or to try to override the veto. If the Duma agrees with the president's proposed changes, a simple majority suffices to pass the revised version, and then the standard legislative process resumes. If the Duma seeks to override the veto, a two-thirds' majority is required, as is likewise a two-thirds' majority in the Federation Council. In that case the president is given no choice but to sign the bill.[48] The strategic logic of the veto power is therefore comparable to that found in the United States.[49] Decree power undoubtedly adds to the president's ability to extract concessions from parliament in this game, but, as we have seen, the threat of its use is not always credible. Moreover, the president cannot veto a portion of a bill he dislikes (there is no "item veto"); he must sign or reject the entire bill. Yeltsin tested these limits, to be sure. He devised a novel procedure called "returning without consideration" (which the Constitutional Court ruled constitutional) under which he would neither sign nor veto a bill; rather, he declared that the procedure used in its passage had been illegal or unconstitutional and therefore that he was returning it to the Duma so that the irregularities could be corrected. In effect this was a soft veto, intended to induce the Duma to make modifications to the bill without resorting to a direct confrontation. But in one famous instance —the Law on the Government in 1997—the president changed his mind after "returning without considering" the bill and signed it after winning minor concessions from the Duma. Below we will also recount another precedent-setting case, when Yeltsin initially refused to sign a law after the parliament had overridden his veto, but was ultimately forced to sign it when the Constitutional Court ruled against him. The Russian president's veto power thus faces the same limitations as that of the American president: he cannot veto particular portions of a bill, and he must sign a bill when his veto has been overridden by two-thirds' majorities in both chambers.

Dissolution Power

The president's right to dissolve the Duma further increases the president's leverage in bargaining over legislation, but, again, the threat of its use faces real limits. The president may dissolve the Duma if a confidence vote fails or if a no-confidence vote passes twice within three months, and he must dissolve in the event that his nominee for prime minister is not confirmed three times. This power can lead to high-stakes games of brinkmanship. The Duma must estimate the credibility of the president's threat of dissolution. Certainly members of parliament must anticipate paying a high price at the polls if a crisis culminates in dissolution. In contrast to the brinkmanship game played over a presidential veto threat, the threat of dissolution introduces the element of immediate electoral costs into the equation for deputies. The president's opponents may find it costly in terms of policy to move toward the president's position on an issue, but if the president raises the specter of dissolution, the deputies must calculate the probability that they will fail to be reelected. In that case, the electoral costs of defying the president may outweigh the policy costs of compromising with him, and the deputies submit to the president's blackmail.[50]

But the president faces costs and risks from dissolution as well. He must estimate the probability that elections will return a friendlier Duma as opposed to a worse Duma, with which he will have to coexist for at least a year; presumably this inhibits the president's freedom of action. Moreover, as in France, the president cannot dissolve twice within a year, and cannot dissolve if parliament has passed a motion of impeachment. Note also that there is no direct way for the president or government to pledge its confidence on a bill. Thus this power does not confer agenda power on the executive, in contrast to France. Indeed, there is some debate, in fact, about how the president could engineer a political crisis, which would entitle him to dissolve the Duma.[51] Presumably his government could try to force the Duma to vote on a motion of confidence, which, once it failed, would allow the president to dissolve the Duma and call new elections. But the Duma has protected itself from such blackmail by providing in its rules that before voting on a motion of confidence, it can vote on a motion of *no* confidence. This of course it can arrange to allow to fail, thus forestalling the need to vote on the electorally more painful vote of confidence. Thus the Duma has apparently insulated itself from ever being blackmailed into dissolution. Note also that the president cannot force the Duma's hand by threatening to put an issue to a national referendum.

Thus, notwithstanding the considerable power which Russia's constitution does confer on the president, therefore, it also imposes some of the limitations on the autonomy of the executive that are found in parliamentary systems as well as some of those found in separation of powers systems. As in a parliamentary system, the president's government must command the parliament's confidence, and as in a separation of powers system, he may face a parliament with an opposing political majority. Both sets of limitations contribute to the president's incentives to resolve differences with the parliament through bargaining.

Forming Majorities in the Duma

As in a separation of powers system, but not a French-style semipresidential system, the parliament controls its own agenda. But in contrast to the strongly majoritarian two-party U.S. House, no majority party controls the

Duma's agenda. Rather, partly because of a strong proportional component of the parliamentary election law that Yeltsin enacted, the Duma's governing institutions employ an all-parties power-sharing rule to reach decisions about the agenda.[52] Not only does the Duma employ the parity rule of representation in forming the Council of the Duma, it also follows it on all legislative commissions that are created to hammer out compromise language on contentious issues, a practice it has followed consistently since 1994. It is the Council of the Duma, as the joint creature of all the faction leaders, which collectively sets the agenda. The Council can keep legislation from reaching the floor if it calculates that the median member prefers the status quo to a proposal. Because no committee has the power to prevent amendments on the floor, once an item reaches the floor, an open rule for debate and low centralization let the floor median dictate outcomes, subject to the Federation Council's and the president's actions. To be sure, there is some committee gatekeeping power, which may shift outcomes slightly to the committee median on some bills. Committees are usually successful in winning approval for the packages of amendments they propose to the floor, which include one set of amendments recommended for rejection and another proposed for acceptance.[53] However, committees go to great lengths to accommodate the preferences of deputies in preparing the legislation for the second reading, so that the packages they report out already anticipate the preferences of the majority.

Factions have some levers with which to induce disciplined voting from members. The Duma's faction-centered governance structure gives carrots and sticks to faction leaders over members; the carrots include patronage and career benefits and electoral support. The sticks include the threat of exclusion from the faction for chronic violations of faction discipline. In turn, the *intra-factional* coordination of voting positions factions allows leaders to reach negotiated *intra-factional* agreements that will command a majority of votes on the floor. The Duma's capacity to reach stable agreement on policy issues means that the upper house and president must take the Duma's median member's (or pivotal faction's) position into account in choosing whether to support or oppose Duma-passed legislation. In contrast to the Gorbachev-era USSR parliament and the interim Russian parliament, the Duma has been unwilling to abdicate its legislative powers by delegating decree power to the president. It is less susceptible to agenda manipulation by its chairman and is less vulnerable to deadlock, instability, and cycling.[54]

To be sure, majorities are formed of ad hoc multifactional coalitions. Issues are often multidimensional due to the contests over the distribution of power between center and regions and between president and parliament.

Often issues related to economic reform are implicated in disputes over the proper locus of control (executive or legislative, center or regions). As a result, the Duma does deadlock internally on some issues; some issues remain stuck for years because the sponsors cannot find a stable majority agreement for any particular version of the legislation. Thus, the Duma's non-majoritarian governance and weak agenda control allow lawmaking on some issues to get stuck, that is, when there is no single majority-preferred policy point over the status quo. Voting alignments differ significantly according to the nature of the issue dimension. Federalism matters bring together a different set of alliance partners than do market and property issues.

Since no one leader, faction, committee, or majority agent possesses strong gate-keeping or agenda power, the pivotal faction is in an advantageous position. The pivotal faction is the faction without which a majority cannot form. Its pivotal status is due to the combination of the fact that it includes or is close to the median member of the chamber, and its ability to command cohesive voting from its members (if it can induce disciplined voting, it has the ability to strike and keep bargains with other factions). A disciplined faction is therefore more attractive to other factions as a coalition partner, particularly if its cohesiveness is accompanied by flexibility in its policy positions.[55] The lack of strong agenda-setting power (and of restrictive rules on floor debate) means that the Duma cannot commit itself in advance to any position other than the position of the pivotal faction. But the faction's support, while necessary to the passage of nearly all legislation, is not sufficient to ensure passage. Majorities must be constructed individually for every piece of legislation, but the building blocks of majorities are factions, not individual deputies.

The fundamental constitutional fact is that without the Duma's approval, a bill cannot be enacted into law. So long as legislation is the desired, or constitutionally mandated, form for a policy decision, the Duma's consent to its passage is essential. This simple point cannot be made about either the Federation Council *or* the president—the Duma can pass a law with *either* the Federation Council's approval *or* the president's, or both; but neither the Federation Council nor the president can pass a law without the Duma's approval. Whether Russia's system of separation of powers works in practice, as opposed to reverting to some sort of "delegative democracy," therefore, depends on whether the Duma can form a stable collective will on important policy issues, so that it can exercise those constitutional prerogatives in lawmaking that it *does* possess. This point is formally equivalent to the argument found in some of the literature on presidential systems in Latin America and elsewhere, to wit, that a situation of a hypertrophied presidency facing a marginalized parliament—a "delegative democracy"—may reflect less a president's illegitimate *usurpation* of power than the conscious or tacit delegation of power to the president by a fragmented legislature.[56] That is, what we might otherwise take to be an exogenous attribute of a "system" is instead the product of an assembly's inability to overcome its collective dilemmas.[57]

Let us consider six types of situations to see how president and parliament have used their lawmaking powers in several different areas of policy.

Case 1: Duma Deadlock

Lacking a standing party majority, the Duma must find majorities separately for each piece of legislation. On some issues, distances between right and left are too great or too many dimensions are involved to let the inter-factional bargaining process reach an agreement on any version of a bill. For instance, for many years the Land Code, parts 2 and 3 of the Tax Code (all the substantive issues!), the law on parties, the law on lawyers (*advokaty*), and the code of administrative law were all deadlocked in the Duma.

In practice, we can ignore the possibility that conflict between Duma and Federation Council blocks legislation. If the Duma can muster a two-thirds' majority, it can override a Federation Council veto. More commonly, Federation Council opposition to an item is usually resolved through an agreement commission. So long as the president and the Duma can agree on a policy position, Federation Council objections can be overruled or accommodated.

Case 2: Inter-branch Deadlock

In this instance, an impasse occurs when president and median member (or pivotal faction) of the parliament stand on opposite sides of the status quo, and there are no decree or dissolution powers available to the president. Likewise, there are no other policy dimensions in which the sides can bundle together a multidimensional package. There are a number of examples from the 1994–1999 period.

a. Separation of Powers

Under Yeltsin, the Duma wanted to restrict the rights and powers of the president, for instance, through constitutional changes to give the Duma more rights over naming ministers removing the president. Yeltsin resisted. Under the constitution, the president cannot make constitutional changes by decree, but he can use his decree powers to reorganize the executive branch. Therefore, Yeltsin preferred the status quo to any policy which parliament may have passed. Note that the law on government passed with a veto-proof constitutional majority of three hundred votes and moved closer to the president's position in order to win the support of the veto pivot deputy.[58]

b. International Relations

Under Yeltsin, the Duma wanted a less pro-Western alliance policy, while Yeltsin wanted a free hand and a pro-Western policy. This affected bills such as the trophy art law and ratification of some treaties, such as START-II, the Comprehensive Test Ban, and some symbolic bills concerning Russian support for Yugoslavia.

c. Privatization

As noted above, the Duma and executive could not agree on a privatization law in 1994–1996, which left the executive branch free to formulate the privatization program by decree. After the Duma passed and the president signed legislation on privatization in 1997, the government was obliged to obtain the Duma's approval for plans to privatize large enterprises. Privatization slowed considerably as a result. The government fought to win back the right to privatize, but the Duma fought to retain this power even after the 1999 election. Finally in June 2001 the government won passage of a new bill on privatization giving it the right to decide which enterprises to privatize, but only in first reading.

Case 3: Legislative Agreement

An election can move the Duma to the same side of the status quo as the president, giving the president an incentive to find common ground with parliament. In some areas, such as tax and spending policy, the president cannot make policy by decree and must reach agreement with parliament. Therefore in a number of policy areas, the president and parliament do find agreement somewhere between their idea outcomes, with the parliament typically moving a greater distance toward the president's position than the president moves. Many examples can be cited, some from the Yeltsin period, and more since 1999.

a. Federal Relations

Generally speaking, Duma and president have tended to agree on the desirability of establishing uniform legal norms throughout the federation in matters concerning election law, law enforcement, economic regulation, and fiscal relations. This has been true both under Yeltsin and Putin, even though Yeltsin was more willing to make concessions to regional interests than Putin. The constitution specifies that legislation is required to regulate federal relations, not decree.[59] So, for example, in October 1999 the Duma passed (and overrode a Federation Council veto) and President Yeltsin signed a bill restricting regional governors to two terms and specifying other limitations on regional autonomy.[60] A dramatic example is from the summer of 2000, when the Duma agreed with the president over the Federation Council's strenuous objections, and passed a law establishing a new principle for forming the upper house. The Duma also passed a law providing a narrowly defined right for the president to dismiss governors, and another giving the governors a similarly restricted right to dismiss mayors. All three bills passed in modified form. The law on dismissing governors required a Duma override of a Federation Council veto.

b. Tax Code

The Duma and the president both want a uniform federal tax code to increase uniformity of tax policy throughout the country, but the president has tended to want a more business-friendly tax code than has the Duma.[61] Under Yeltsin, tax policy was deadlocked because the Duma could not find a veto-proof policy position. In effect, the Duma and the president stood on opposite sides of the status quo, as in case 2. After the 1999 elections, the Duma median shifted substantially to the right of the status quo, closer to the president's preferences, and tax reform passed. For instance, the income tax was set to a flat 13 percent rate. A new law unified social contributions into a single social tax, despite wide Duma opposition. However, the executive branch had to move closer to the Duma on issues such as the excise and turnover taxes, for example retaining a 1 percent turnover tax rather than scrapping it entirely, as the government had wanted to do. The Duma and government agreed on a major change in taxation of business profits: the Duma dropped its insistence on preserving a number of investment-related deductions in return for an across-the-board cut in the tax rate of 24 percent. These reforms were the result of intense bargaining, with concessions made on both sides, but were possible because both legislative and executive branches wanted to move tax policy a considerable distance toward simplifying and reducing the tax burden for business.

c. Budget

As noted above, the federal budget cannot be enacted by decree, although a continuation budget is possible. Both sides have consistently bargained and compromised to win the passage of budget before the start of the new year. The 2001 budget law includes a provision strongly opposed by the government, which prohibits government action to privatize any large-scale industrial enterprises. The government also made concessions to the SPS faction on issues in the Code of Administrative Violations in order to win its votes on the budget.

d. Code of Administrative Violations

The first two Dumas were unable to find agreement on a new version of the administrative code, which provides a system of administrative sanctions for minor offenses, including traffic offenses and business code violations. However, the 2000 Duma managed to pass this large, unwieldy law. The Federation Council rejected it, but the Duma overrode the veto. Then President Putin vetoed it, on the grounds that the law allowed the regions too much discretion. Presently the Duma and the president are negotiating to resolve their differences.

e. Judicial Reform

The constitution requires that legislation, not decree, regulate the structure of the judicial system.[62] All the provisions in the constitution establishing the powers and structure of the judicial system provide that federal law sets the procedures for the exercise of judicial authority. Under both Yeltsin and Putin, substantial agreement was in fact reached between executive and legislative branches. Examples are the Constitutional Court law, the criminal code, and the criminal corrections code, all enacted under Yeltsin. In summer 2001 the Duma passed in first reading new judicial reform legislation introduced by Putin that would improve working conditions for judges but also subject them to stricter accountability.

A critical case of negotiated compromise in this area in the Yeltsin era was the constitutional law on the federal judiciary in 1996. The left was reluctant to grant Yeltsin the right to appoint federal judges, but did so on the grounds that it was even more important to establish the principle that all courts of general jurisdiction are federal courts, and federal law applied. Yeltsin in turn had to accept a minor limitation on his right of appointment, in that he had to choose from among locally certified candidates.

Case 4: Veto and Override

The president's representative to parliament participates directly and extensively in Duma debate. He regularly intervenes to signal the president's position on an issue. On occasion he declares that the president will veto a particular bill if it passes in its present form or demand that a particular provision be removed. More often, he offers an appraisal of the merits or defects of a measure under discussion without directly committing the president to a particular course of action. Depending on the credibility of a veto threat and the Duma's foreknowledge of the president's positions, the Duma may accept a proposal closer to the president's position than it would otherwise.[63] But whether the Duma can pass a veto-proof law depends not only on the location of its own veto-pivot deputy (the deputy whose position stands to the left of one-third or the right of two-thirds), but also on the position of the equivalent member of the Federation Council. If the median deputy is not willing to accept the position of the veto pivot, the veto is sustained. But if the veto pivot in each chamber stands at least as far from the president as does the median member, the veto is overridden.

An example is the trophy art law claiming Russian ownership of all artwork and cultural artifacts seized by the soviet army in WWII. In 1997 Yeltsin vetoed the law that had been passed by both chambers, and both chambers overrode his veto two months later. He still refused to sign the law, citing constitutional and procedural objections. In 1998 the Constitutional Court upheld the parliament's position that he had to sign the bill notwithstanding his opposition to it. Yeltsin complied, but immediately sought a ruling from the court on the law's constitutionality.[64] The case illustrates the point that *both* chambers have to pass a bill in its original version with a two-thirds' vote in order to override a presidential veto, which empirically has proven to be rare. Yet when it has occurred, the president has gone along.

Case 5: Law or Decree?
In these cases, the president and the Duma are on the same side of the status quo, but the president can issue a decree. The president has less incentive to move toward the Duma than the Duma has to move toward the president's position, but the Duma can also allow the decree to stand if it is too costly in policy or reputation to accept the president's proposal. The Duma cannot claim credit for the policy, but lets the decree stand until it can pass legislation that the president will sign or that can override a presidential veto.

a. Crime and Corruption
Many issues concerning law enforcement are subject to either law or decree: law, because only legislation can regulate criminal law, criminal procedural law, and criminal corrections; decree, because the president has wide powers to organize the work of the executive branch, under all the law enforcement bodies fall. The Duma and president both want to claim credit for fighting crime and corruption. Eager to demonstrate zeal in the fight against organized crime, the president issued a draconian (and certainly unconstitutional) decree in 1994 authorizing police to detain individuals suspected of participation in organized crime for up to thirty days, but he formally rescinded it in June 1997. The Duma has been trying to pass legislation directed against

corruption and organized crime since 1993, but all of its bills have either failed in the Duma or been vetoed by the president.

b. Rights of Regional Executives

The president can use decree power to suspend action of a regional chief executive; Putin used decree to establish seven federal super-districts and appoint representatives to them. But he did not use his decree power as a bludgeon to pressure the Duma into passing legislation. He used his decree power to create the State Council as a consolation prize for governors displaced by his reform of the Federation Council. These actions are consistent with law and practice: a reform of the manner of forming the Council of the Federation requires legislation, but the formation of advisory and supervisory structures in the executive branch are within the purview of presidential executive power. The Duma has not attempted to supersede, either to confirm or countermand, Putin's creation of the seven federal districts, although a few deputies called for putting this structure on a legislative foundation.

c. Pensions and Other Social Benefits

President and parliament compete to increase social benefits, but the president usually wants to hold the line on budget-busting measures more than the Duma. In this area the president has used the combination one-two punch of veto and decree vigorously. Both Yeltsin and Putin used decree power liberally to provide one-time benefits to selected groups of beneficiaries (e.g., WWII veterans) as well as to raise base benefits for other categories, and both opposed pension bills that they argued could not be financed from the budget. The result is a characteristic dilemma for legislators: as one Duma deputy put it during floor debate: "No matter what, you and I are in an unpleasant situation. Look how the situation develops: as soon as it is necessary to index or increase the size of pensions, a presidential decree appears, while at the same time any time a bill comes out of the Duma, it never finds support from the government of the president."[65]

In addition to decreeing a number of pension benefits increases into effect (including decrees increasing benefits for pensioners in January, July, October, and November 2000, and again in February, April, and August 2001), President Putin also issued a major decree in September 2000 depriving regional governments of the right to pay out pensions: they must instead turn that function over to the regional branches of the Pension Fund. The Duma contested the constitutionality of this decree on the grounds that it contradicted existing law, but the Constitutional Court ruled that the decree was legal, arguing that where existing federal laws, rules, and regulations form a contradictory or confusing whole, the president has the right to issue a decree "in advance" of legislation codifying policy on the matter.[66]

d. Privatization

As we have seen, privatization has been handled both by law and decree at different times. Yeltsin enacted most of the privatization program of 1992–1993 by decree. After 1993, the Duma wanted a more restrictive property rights regime than existed, and Yeltsin wanted a less restrictive regime, although both sides wanted more uniform federal regulation. In 1994, Chubais demanded that the Duma pass a law on privatization and threatened to issue a decree if it failed to do so. Chubais and the Duma negotiated intensively, moving toward each other's positions and reaching a compromise agreement, which almost carried a majority on the floor, failing by thirteen votes. The president then issued a decree regulating privatization. But reportedly a number of the provisions that had been agreed on in the defeated legislation were incorporated into the president's decree. Finally, in 1997, the Duma passed a law on privatization, so that the president could no longer act by decree. And, as we have seen, even the present Duma, sympathetic though it is to Putin and his government, refused to give the government the right to privatize without Duma consent through 2000 and the first half of 2001.

The president's decree threat in 1994 was credible, given the history of decrees on privatization in 1992 and 1993. The bill's narrow margin of defeat in the Duma indicates that the median deputy would probably have preferred to sustain the president's veto (and allow a decree) than to have moved the position of the bill to a point where it could have overridden a veto. Passage of the 1997 law on privatization, which Yeltsin signed in July 1997, meant that the president could not use (or threaten to use) decree power to adopt a blanket privatization program. The law required the government to submit a list of large enterprises to be nationalized as part of each year's annual budget law, prohibited "loans for shares" arrangements, and gave the state the right to renationalize enterprises if the new owners failed to carry out their obligations. The government has continued to carry out privatizations of smaller enterprises, but has found the restrictions onerous and has tried to persuade the Duma to lift them.

e. State Symbols

On 8 December 2000, the Duma passed a law submitted by Putin making the Stalin-era soviet national anthem—the music, that is, not the words—the anthem of the Russian Federation, passing the bill in all three readings immediately. The Duma did not, however, approve a set of lyrics for the anthem. Impatient to put a text in place that could be used for New Year's ceremonies, Putin issued a decree on 30 December making a revised version of the old Mikhalkov wording official, but inviting at the same time the Duma to supersede the decree and pass the corresponding constitutional law. The president was consciously acting in anticipation of the Duma, confident he would get the law that he wanted, and confident as well that the deputies would agree with his rationale. The Duma duly went along, and passed the law on 7 March, in all three readings at once, with a margin of 353 affirmative votes. Putin's action may have not been constitutional, but it certainly was not in defiance of parliament.

f. Rights for Former Presidents

In another case of legislation in this category, the Duma's automatic agreement to the president's policy could not be taken for granted. This concerned the law on benefits for former presidents. The law was prompted by President Putin's decree issued immediately after Yeltsin's resignation and was no doubt part of a prior understanding between them. Putin's decree, it will be recalled, granted Yeltsin and members of his family full immunity from all criminal liability, along with other material benefits. The communists objected strenuously to the decree and tried unsuccessfully to appeal it to the Constitutional Court. The law that the Duma subsequently considered was then the object of a conflict between those wanting to grant an unconditional right of immunity to former presidents and those wanting to build in exceptions so that presidents would be threatened by the possibility of future prosecution. On 24 January 2001, the Duma passed in second reading a bill on presidential guarantees which provides that a former president is liable for criminal prosecution only in the event that the general procurator finds that the president committed "serious crimes" while in office, with the Duma's consent, and the Federation Council agrees to strip him of his legal immunity.[67] The president was willing to accept this provision and signed the bill on 13 February 2001.

Case 6: Policy in Two Dimensions

Elsewhere I have argued that it is only possible to explain both the difficulty with which Yeltsin won approval of his new constitution and the stability of the constitution once it was adopted by understanding that it had to resolve conflicts over power competition in two cross-cutting dimensions.[68] These axes of police conflict were partitioned through the Duma's party-oriented structure and the separation of a federal chamber from the popular lower chamber. The same difficulty continues to affect legislation on matters that lie in both dimensions. Land legislation is a good case in point. The question of private ownership and markets in land has been one of the most controversial policy issues in Russia. It is a defining issue separating left from right, but it is important to recognize that there is also a second dimension affecting positions on the issue. Under Yeltsin, the president and the Duma lay on opposite sides of the status quo in one dimension—the left-right dimension of market reform versus state socialism—but were on the same side in the federalism dimension. Currently, Duma and president are on the same side of the status quo on the left-right dimension, but the president and governors are on opposite sides of the federalism dimension.

Legislation on property in land has a long history. In 1996 the Duma passed a Land Code but the Federation Council rejected it. In 1997 the Duma passed a new version which passed the Federation Council, but was vetoed by the president. The Duma overrode the president's veto but the Federation Council sustained it in 1998. The Duma and the Federation Council then worked out a version, which both chambers could agree on, but this version was again vetoed by the president. Then the Duma debated a version acceptable to the president, but failed to find 226 votes for it (at one point it received 225). This legislation would have allowed some market transactions in land under highly limited conditions, thus tightening federal control over land policy and bringing president and Duma closer to each other on the market dimension. When this version failed on 16 July 1998, action largely lapsed until the end of the Duma's term in December 2000. The president's strategy, supported by many of the liberals in the Duma, was to allow regions to enact their own, more liberal, land legislation, rather than to hold land legislation hostage to the powerful communist-agrarian lobby in the Duma. In effect, land legislation involved two dimensions, market reform and federalism, and the president and the liberals were willing to trade off some otherwise undesirable autonomy to the regions for the sake of winning gains on the private property dimension. Note that compromise between Duma and president was nearly available when leftists were willing to give up some ground on private property in land in return for greater central control over the rules on land transactions. But ultimately, neither the president nor the left was willing to compromise enough on the left-right dimension to make an agreement possible. And no version which could have overridden a presidential veto (and been acceptable to the upper house) would have been preferable to the status quo to the median deputy.

The shift in the position of the Duma pivot following the 1999 election broke the impasse in this area. Now the liberals—apparently with the Kremlin's blessing—tried repeatedly to pass legislation that would unblock Chapter 17 of the Civil Code, which provided a legal basis for private transactions in land.[69] Three efforts by the SPS to unblock the action of that chapter failed in the course of 2000. However, the Duma voted by a narrow margin to approve the right of borrowers to secure debt with land. Then, on 26 January

2001, the Duma voted in first reading to pass a law that puts in force Chapter 17 of the Civil Code. The law passed by the narrow margin of 229 votes. On 21 March, the Duma then passed the legislation in second and third readings by wider margins of 254 and 252 affirmative votes, respectively. However, the general lifting of the legal prohibition on the free sale of land still does not affect agricultural land, which will be subject to regulation by the Land Code.

The Land Code, meantime, remains the object of intense struggle between central and regional interests. President Putin finally committed himself to a liberal position and instructed the government to prepare a new draft land code by 1 May, for submission to the Duma. His allies in the Duma then engineered a small procedural coup by transferring jurisdiction over the bill from the anti-reform agriculture committee to the pro-reform property committee. Thereafter, the bill—from which the provisions governing transactions in agricultural land were dropped—succeeded in passing in first and second readings in June and July 2001, although during the first reading the floor deliberations disintegrated into fistfights and shouts, as opposition deputies tried to prevent the bill's sponsors from speaking or moving to the podium. Afterward, Chairman Gennadi Seleznev had to be rushed to the hospital with heart problems.

Figure 1 illustrates the location of the ideal points of Yeltsin and the Duma on this issue in 1997–1998 and the narrow winset (indicated by the petal marking the region in which a compromise between Yeltsin and his opponents might have been reached) that was available for an agreement. The status quo had drifted to a point that was unacceptable both to the left and to some democrats (such as Yabloko) in the Duma with respect to the center-regions axis, because regional governors had begun enacting their own regional land regimes and the federal government was losing its ability to set uniform rules. Yeltsin was willing to tolerate this situation as long as it was closer to his ideal point that legislation that a left-dominated parliament might pass. A majority in the Duma was very nearly available for a policy that would have established some uniform federal standards for land transactions, with restrictions that did not go far enough to satisfy the communists fully, but were too onerous to suit the liberals. In the end, there were not the votes for a policy that would have satisfied both a Duma majority and the president simultaneously. Deadlock has prevailed ever since, although the Duma median has now moved toward the right (i.e., president's) side of the status quo along the horizontal axis. Compromise with the Federation Council will probably mean that the bill will need to move upward on the vertical axis to accommodate the demands of regional interests for discretion in regulating their own regional land markets.

Figure 1. Yeltsin and Duma Ideal Points on Land Code Legislation

Status quo is shifted in favor of regional autonomy in land law. Duma is willing to compromise with Yeltsin to pass a land code with some market elements for the sake of centralizing policy. Yeltsin is willing to allow restrictions on land market for the sake of getting federal legislation. But the zone in which compromise is available is very small. Deadlock results. Policy reverts to status quo.

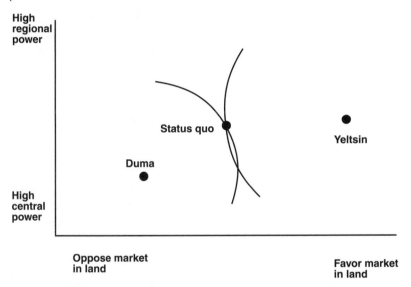

Conclusions

We asked whether the 1993 constitution, which was so favorable to the president's power despite the principle of separation of powers, induced any strategically motivated self-restraint by the president. The cases reviewed suggest that the president often did prefer to negotiate and compromise with the legislature, rather than to rule by decree. We found that the president was willing to move closer to the parliament's preferred position on a wide range of issues, but not all. On some, deadlock resulted until the 1999 elections brought to office a new set of deputies where the location of the median voter (in fact, the pivotal faction) was much closer to the president, and even then, agreement between legislative and executive branches proved difficult to reach in some cases. Moreover, it is clear that the Duma cannot be bullied or sweet-talked into supporting the president's demands for legislation; a substantial amount of bargaining goes on between the branches in which both sides make concessions for the sake of obtaining laws. As we would have predicted, the change in the composition of the Duma brought about a marked change in the ability of the two branches to agree on contentious policy issues, including tax legislation, administrative law, and relations with the West. The president's prerogatives—decree power, veto power, dissolution power, and the right to introduce legislation—had some impact on the president's bargaining power. But in almost no case did they give the president the ability to bypass the legislature. The fact that the Russian president cannot rule by decree—notwithstanding the frequently repeated claim that he does so—is due both to constitutional and political considerations which limit his ability to use decree as an alternative to law. For this reason, in an expanding sphere of policy areas, decisions are made either in the form of new legislation or not at all. Still, we noted that there are occasions when deputies may prefer to allow the president to act by decree. On many occasions, though, the executive was forced to make concessions to the legislature for the sake of passing desired legislation.

An often-overlooked feature of a separation of powers system is that the legislature cannot use the government as a steering or executive committee, as it does in a parliamentary system. Thus it is weakly suited to the task of forming stable majorities for legislation unless it has a well-disciplined majority party. The Duma uses an unusual all-parties governing arrangement, which succeeds in forming majorities in most policy areas, but not in all. The Federation Council only has to *react* to the Duma, so its need for institutional solutions to such collective choice problems is easier to meet. A necessary condition for a constitutional framework of separation of powers to work to tame *vlast* is that the legislature overcome its own collective choice problems sufficiently to be able to bargain coherently with the executive branch over policy issues. It is noteworthy, that, unlike its two predecessor parliaments, the Federal Assembly has retained its lawmaking powers, rather than delegating sweeping extraordinary power to the president. How often the branches have reached agreement, therefore, has depended both on parliament's own internal deliberation processes in enabling it to reach stable, majority-supported agreement, and on the distance separating executive from legislature in policy space. Judging from the evidence considered here, it is clear that both the president and his parliamentary opponents have been willing to observe the constitutional restraints on their power put in place in 1993 in lawmaking even when they had to settle for second-best alternatives.

CHAPTER SIX

Social Relations and Political Practices in Post-Communist Russia

MICHAEL URBAN

Michael Urban points to the importance of informal networks as a part of civil society. As in any society, there is a necessary interface between the formalized and institutionalized patterns of interaction that take place in the realm of political society and the less formalized networks that form as a part of civil society. In stable democracies, the relationship is mutually supportive; formal institutions are assisted by but not replaced by such informal networks, and informal networks interact productively with but do not take the place of formal institutions. Yet in the Russian experience, the balance tips in favor of the dominance of informal ties. This reality has been a mixed blessing for the formation of Russian democracy. On the one hand, it has eased the transition in many ways, providing mechanisms for what Richard Rose has described as "coping" behavior. But on the other hand, it has retarded the emergence of a more institutionalized civil and political society. As Jack Bielasiak points out in his conclusion, parties systems are not yet adequately developed as formal mediating mechanisms between civil society and political institutions in large measure because of the role of such networks, and several contributors note that reliance on such informal networks at the highest levels have tended to personalize the relationship between leaders and followers or to perpetuate the power of oligarchies based on what Urban describes as "networks of trust."

Western scholarship on post-communist politics has been absorbed by the project of establishing liberal democracies and market economies across that ample geographic space formerly under the dominion of communist party-states. Among political scientists—both former soviet specialists as well as those new to this area of study—particular attention has been focused on institutions and processes thought to be essential to the development of democracy anywhere: public elections; legislative, executive, and judicial institutions; public opinion and its import for democratic practices, and so forth. This orientation is both understandable and valid in its own right. On one hand, communism's collapse against the background of sizable popular mobilizations marching under the banner of democracy represented epochal phenomena that captured the attention, imagination, and hopes of scholars and publics alike. History, as it were, seemed to inscribe itself on our research agendas. On the other hand, valid scholarly purposes recommended themselves immediately. Here was the chance to apply theories and frameworks already current in the field of political science to a relatively virgin area. Most of these societies were now sufficiently open to empirical investigation to enable researchers to replace informed conjectures with hard facts, systematically gathered and analyzed. In short, the opportunity to study a world-historic phenomenon, coupled with the chance to employ the conventional techniques of political science to an area of the world in which they had been little used represented something of a gravitational force pulling scholars toward the study of newly inaugurated institutions and practices identified with democracy.

The downside of our preoccupation with the new democratic forms emerging in the post-communist world has been a relative neglect of established patterns of social relations. Indeed, these have often occupied a place in our research designs comparable to the one that official communist doctrine had reserved for actual behaviors that deviated from the designs of authority. Whether their "habits of the past" impeding the progress of communism or our "communist legacies" obstructing the development of liberal democracy, the implication has been that while certain ways of thinking and acting remain that are not conducive to realizing formally established social goals, these are of far less import than are the putative engines of social transformation leading to those goals. Moreover, the "habits" or "legacies" can be expected to grow weaker with time and will ultimately be overcome by the forward march of history. Katherine Verdery has exposed these tendencies in Western thinking by calling attention to metaphors evident in professional parlance during the initial years of the post-communist transition that encouraged disregard or de-valuation of the actual societies that we study. One of them, "the big bang," had invited us to imagine the advent of an altogether new world of liberal democracies and market economies emerging, as it were, out of nothingness. Another, "shock therapy," had encouraged observers to think in medical terms and likened societies emerging from communism to mentally ill people whose health can only by restored by administering the proper policy/medicine.[1] These tropes suggest something of the background understandings that have informed many scholarly agendas during the first decade or so of post-communist studies.

This study aims to retrieve something from the sovietological past and to apply it to post-soviet Russia: specifically, the linking of social relations to political practices as conceptualized in the late-communist period by scholars who studied clientelism and patronage networks in the USSR.[2] Analysts concerned with patronage networks developed a perspective on soviet state and society that differed fundamentally from other models in vogue at the time. Instead of a unified party-state hierarchy in which instructions and tasks flowed downward to performing agents who executed them, these scholars proffered a far more complex image according to which the machinery of state was animated by various patronage groups that had appropriated it for their own purposes. This problematization of the formal hierarchy of offices emphasized the personalistic basis of collective action over the institutional one and focused on actual policy outcomes as opposed to policies on paper. The insertion of social relations and their attendant practices into our picture of soviet government enabled analysis to treat more systematically those phenomena which both communism's official explanations and most Western sovietologists had been at a loss to explain: Why do so many of the official policies of the communist state remain unimplemented? In brief, the patronage approach argued that power, which in this system formally belonged to state and party offices, was increasingly unable to overcome the resistance offered by informal networks of actors—embedded in personal dependencies and reciprocal exchanges of favors—who used their offices to thwart or to drastically modify the policy prescriptions issuing from above. The perspective thereby opened on the party-state indicated that the repressive features of the soviet order could no longer be mistaken for power *per se.* When it came to shaping actual practices, this state was exceptionally weak.[3]

To be sure, the influence of interpersonal networks in social and political life is a ubiquitous phenomenon. To illustrate, consider a common instance in which a contractor colludes with a client to perform some home repairs for cash. In so doing, the parties enter into a personalized relation that bypasses the formal rules of the tax code in order to reap mutual benefit— lower costs to the client, a better return for the contractor—at the expense of the state. This episode would represent an example of social relations initiating collective action outside and against the established rules concerning tax paying, construction codes, and so forth. From the vantage offered by Norbert Elias in his study of the forms of social relations prevalent in modern society, it is evident that our contractor and client are engaged in an exchange rooted in a natural economy as yet not fully extirpated by the "civilizing process."[4] Their choice to reject the rules is also a refusal to enact the roles that those rules define. Importantly for our purposes, those rules and roles can be characterized as impersonal. In principle, conformity to the rules would entitle any person to enact any social role. Thus the structure of institutionally based collective action is designed to mediate relations among actors who appear in such cases as interchangeable strangers. However, with respect to the contractor and client in our example, we encounter another pattern of collective action that overcomes institutional constraints. In this instance, we observe a personalized relation among intimates in which not formal rules but informal relations of reciprocity obtain.

Analytically, the relation between these two modes of collective action can be depicted as zero-sum: the more that institutions structure and control collective action, the less that action is governed by personalistic considerations and informal norms—and, so, conversely. This consideration necessarily impinges on the study of any specific society. Are its institutions of sufficient strength in organizing collective action that the residue of personalistic practices can be safely ignored? Or is it the case that these practices are so widespread as to require systematic investigation themselves? In this respect, we might imagine some tipping point at which one or the other pattern prevails. Take the matter of corruption. As Susan Rose-Ackerman has remarked in her study of this problem, "*some* level of corruption will be associated with every mix of market and democratic mechanisms."[5] Distinguishing, then, a corrupt regime involves an empirical determination that the relevant tipping point has been reached or exceeded. When that has occurred, it would make little sense to take at face value the outward appearances of society's institutions. Not only have they been subverted by corrupt practices, but prevailing norms of trust and reciprocity become redirected *against* formal institutions, sanctioning instead the unauthorized pursuits of parties in personalized relations. Although these practices may be themselves illicit, their ubiquity tends to extinguish the normative understanding that they are, in fact, corrupt. For most, if not all, members of society they have become "normal" ways of acting.[6]

For contemporary Russia, my argument is that the balance between institutionalized and personalized forms of collective action tilts toward the latter. Hence, the investigation of political practices remains incomplete without reference to the particular social relations in which they are embedded. Moreover, by including social relations into the framework of political study we are obliged to assume a culturalist perspective that rejects methodological individualism and the objectification of formal institutions. Rather, the focus falls on the culturally mediated forms of social interaction, informed by available behavioral repertoires and their normative components.[7] For example, the office of president is simultaneously both a formal institution and a cultural construct. In concrete instances, action might be tipped in either direction; that is, according to the specifications of impersonal norms or along the lines of shared cultural practices operating independently of those norms. Locating that office within the coordinates supplied by Russian culture reveals something of consequence for the relations between the officeholder and relevant others: namely, that the president's actions may violate their institutional basis yet remain perfectly acceptable. That acceptability is provided by familiar patterns of behavior anchored in broadly based cultural understandings of paternalistic rule within which license must be afforded to the "father" in order for him to secure the welfare of the family (nation).[8] George Breslauer has shown the relevance of this cultural paradigm in shaping the presidency of Boris Yeltsin,[9] while at regional level Georgi Derluguian has called attention to the same phenomenon in the instance of Krasnodar governor Nikolai "Father" Kondratenko.[10] In either case—and, doubtless, in many more—we observe how informal cultural practices and understandings override the formal requirements of institutions. Indeed, the formal institution would remain an abstraction were we to neglect culture's constitutive role.

The organization of this chapter is designed to illustrate this thesis concerning the dominance of personalized associations and loyalties by, first, considering the character of the contemporary Russian state. Here, a distinction is introduced between the material and symbolic aspects of the state, drawing particular attention to the latter as, in principle, the product of a collective imagination—reinforced by extant practices—that construe the state as a continuously acting, impersonal power standing apart from society and enforcing on its members the rules by which they must live. In the Russian case, both the material and symbolic sides of the state appear to be remarkably weak, a condition reflected in the operation of power networks within it, the subject of the following section. Thence, the discussion turns to the "gray zone," that ample area of informal practices which, although technically illegal, have become common features of Russian life as a consequence of the state's weakness. The following section aims to complete the sketch of social relations and political practices by examining the ways in which ordinary people organize their collective lives. Here, particularistic networks of trust prove salient, enabling individuals—through regularized exchanges of favors and loyalties—to cooperate, even while they inhibit the formation of a civil society and a public consciousness. In the concluding portion, a few words are ventured about Vladimir Putin's experience as president and the likely shape of things to come. These comments steer clear of current controversies concerning such things as the future of press freedom and the (reduced) opportunities available for mounting political opposition to the authorities. While these things are important in themselves and are not unrelated to the topic at hand, they merit a more extended discussion than space allows.

The Russian State

The state represents the premier institution in any modern society. This proposition is axiomatic. As numerous studies have pointed out, the advent of the modern state has been coextensive with social modernization inasmuch as state building has directly involved the renovation of social relations according to abstract categories that the state supplies.[11] In James Scott's formulation, the state surveys, assesses, enumerates, and enjoins from its vantage of the whole. It deploys its resources to reward and punish, thus helping to bring its abstract categories to life.[12] More than that, the state colonizes the interiors of its respective population. Especially through the school system, the mental structures of its subjects are molded according to state criteria that are routinely reproduced in social action. The relative correspondence between social action and the mental construct of the state brings the state to life in public consciousness. Indeed, it is that very correspondence in our own thinking—and its violation in a given case—that underlies our example, above, of contractor and client. Were they behaving according to the state's scheme of things, then their activity would be merely an illustration of the quotidian. It only becomes noteworthy in this case because the state's objectified manifestations—which we ordinarily perceive as "natural" and "right" —do not correspond to the mental structures and resulting behavior of the parties to the transaction.[13]

"The 'present-day state' is . . . a fiction," counseled Karl Marx.[14] He was not, of course, referring to those corporeal agents who frequently disrupted his personal life as well as his political visions, but to the fact that, above all, the state represents a shared mental construct of an entity and force standing outside of society. As Timothy Mitchell has argued, the "phenomenon we name 'the state' arises from techniques that enable mundane material practices to take on the appearance of an abstract, nonmaterial form."[15] This transformation can be likened to the one postulated by Michel Foucault in his study of modern "disciplines," according to which all manner of human activity in what we call modern societies has been subsumed under abstract codes specifying the precise manner in which given activities are to be performed.[16] Just as Foucault's disciplines lead two lives—they both inform human activity and simultaneously stand outside of it as measuring rods and guides to action—so Mitchell observes a comparable phenomenon in the case of the state. In the institutions of modern government:

> the precise specification of space and function . . . the coordination of these functions into hierarchical arrangements, the organization of supervision and surveillance, the marking out of time into schedules and programs, all contribute to constructing a world that appears to consist not of a complex of social practices but of a binary order: on the one hand individuals and their activities, on the other an inert "structure" that somehow stands apart from the individuals, precedes them, and contains and gives a framework to their lives. Indeed the very notion of an institution, as an abstract framework separate from the particular practices it enframes, can be seen as a product of these techniques.[17]

As such, the secret of the state's power resides in the particular "effect" of these techniques, engendering in social consciousness the apprehension of the state as a freestanding, autonomous actor rather than as merely a particular terrain on which social power is enacted.[18]

This "state effect" is, at best, weakly reflected in the everyday consciousness of Russians, who regularly refer to their state in concrete, personal terms such as "them," "the powers" [*vlasti*].[19] This orientation appears to correspond to the presence of personalistic, and often corrupt, practices that riddle the state's machinery from top to bottom, subverting any appreciation of the state as an autonomous entity standing apart from society. A measure of the invasive presence of social power within the state apparatus is provided by Mikhail Afanas'ev's 1995 survey of upper-level administrators studying at the Russian Academy of State Services. Afanas'ev found that only 20 percent of these officials regarded the formal regulations specifying their duties as coincident with their actual work, while some two-thirds viewed the formal rules as only remotely related to their actual practices and another one-fourth claimed that these rules had no significance whatsoever. Moreover, respondents identified informal patterns of personal loyalty and patronage as, by far, the most important factors impinging on their workplace activities and as the decisive considerations in career advancement.[20] The infiltration of personalized relations into the state apparatus has been symptomatic of the decline of the Russian state, the erosion of its material capacities to perform as an institution. This is readily apparent with respect to its relative incapacity to discharge those two functions widely regarded as definitive of the state itself.

The first concerns the ability of the state to finance its activities by raising revenue. Modern states accomplish this task in part by establishing an exclusive national currency in which economic transactions are denominated, thus rationalizing economic relations as well. In Russia, however, the state has been unable to establish a monopoly on the accepted means of payment. Rather than the official currency serving as the universal equivalent in the economy, as much as 50 percent of the GDP has involved either barter or the use of monetary surrogates issued by banks and subnational governments.[21] In addition to depriving the national government of revenues, this condition plays havoc with the state as a fiscal entity, destroys the possibility for public accountability in the budget process, and encourages the partitioning of the national economy into those separate fiefdoms that we meet, below, in our discussion of regional power groups.

The state's second surrender of a vital function concerns its loss of a monopoly on violence. Unable to protect its citizens and to enforce contracts, the Russian state has effectively ceded the bulk of these responsibilities to a private protection industry rooted in the criminal world. Individuals and firms either prefer or are compelled to enlist the services of violence-wielding organizations to which they pay "taxes" that otherwise might have reached the state's coffers.[22] Private protection, moreover, also includes many tens of thousands of former and current state officials who profit from this privatization of essential state functions. Those working or moonlighting in private protection agencies maintain influential and lucrative contacts with state officials that are used for the particular benefit of their clients—say, to escape taxes or to ensure the success of client firms by seeing to it that the local fire department responds tardily to instances of arson visited on competitors —thus undermining further the state's diminished ability to appear and to act as an impersonal guarantor of public security and the rule of law.

Considerations of this order appear to condition Neil Robinson's recent remark that following the violent dissolution of the first republic in 1993, "Russia [has] had a government, but not a state."[23] The truth encoded in this exaggeration refers to the particular political-governmental order installed in the wake of Yelstin's seizure of power in October 1993. The president's decrees dissolved sitting legislatures at all levels, thus removing the principal restraint on executive power. Although legislative institutions were reconstituted in the following months, their constitutionally diminished authority, combined with the use of executive power to shape election outcomes, has conduced to the near-complete emancipation of executive agencies from the control of autonomous legislatures. Thus, executive power—represented, above all by the "superpresidency" enshrined in the 1993 constitution—has altered radically the rhythms of public life, consigning political parties and public associations to the role of bit players in the political drama whose leading roles are enacted by top officials in the executive and their confederates in the business and financial sectors.[24] As the public forms available for the satisfaction of particular interests have atrophied, personalistic ties between the executive and associates in the private sector have flourished. An indication of the importance of the interplay between these strategic groups appears in the surveys of experts published monthly by the newspaper, *Nezavisimaya Gazeta.* Under the heading of leading lobbyists in the country, one will find mainly the names of high governmental officials, just as surveys of leading politicians disclose the names of major bankers and industrialists who hold neither public nor party positions. Under these conditions in which personalistic ties among governmental officials and their partners from the worlds of business and finance overshadow the importance of institutions, the Russian state more resembles a particularistic *regime* than a state *per se.*[25] Accordingly, the study of politics is directed toward an investigation of that regime and of the personalistic networks that comprise it.

Networks of Power

Nicolas Hayoz and Victor Sergeyev have recently introduced a distinction between what they term "networks of power" and "networks of trust" in Russia. The former tend to be vertically structured groups functioning under the patronage of one or more occupants of high governmental office; the latter are more horizontal in structure and amount to informal but regularized relations of mutual aid.[26] Although the distinction is an analytic one that by no means precludes the possibility that networks of trust might operate in high governmental circles and that networks of both types might interact, it nonetheless denotes a situation in which power networks are organized within and under the formal institutions of the state while trust networks are more prevalent in society. In this section, then, we examine power networks, deferring for the moment a discussion of their counterparts.

In two important respects, the origins of the power networks functioning in today's Russia are readily traceable to the soviet past. On one hand, we find that established and emerging networks were well positioned to avail themselves of the opportunities to seize state assets presented by Russia's economic transformation.[27] Although new players would join these networks and in some instances create their own, the bulk of Russia's new government/business groups represented old elites adapting themselves to new conditions. On the other, these power networks brought to the new conditions a set of practices modified only by the opportunities presented by the economic transformation itself. It is important to emphasize in this respect that Russia's economic reform provided impetus for, rather than constraint on, the growth of power networks that would privatize not only economic firms but the state apparatus itself. As the state receded from the economy, it neglected to erect that institutional scaffolding on which market relations depend—signaled fatally by the simple fact that a "market" was installed in the complete absence of trained accountants in Russia, never mind adequate legislation in the fields of contracts, torts, property assessment, bankruptcy, and so forth—and thus initiated a situation in which personalistic associations with relevant state officials, rather than the discipline of a legally regulated market, would be the decisive factor in organizing behavior.[28] Accordingly, the pattern examined by Michael Burawoy and Kathryn Hendley in the late-soviet period—whereby colluding actors in the first flush of money-making opportunities appropriated their respective institutions, turning them into so many shells manipulable in the new game of private extraction[29]—would be reflected on a far grander scale throughout the national economy. Here, David Stark's concept of "recombinant property" is particularly germane. Stark has shown that relations of ownership in post-communist systems tend less to fix individual rights and obligations than they do to establish conditions in which networks composed of state and private actors utilize the formal entitlements of office and ownership to engineer interlocking and mutually beneficial economic complexes operating under the governance of these networks themselves.[30] Russia's size and resource potential has meant that the need to attract foreign capital (and, therefore, to institute impersonal rules for economic activity) has been less pressing than it has been elsewhere in the post-communist world, enabling established networks to continue operating in established ways.[31]

Although some newcomers have proven themselves more than adequate to the task of mastering the ways of Russia's power networks,[32] the point worth emphasizing is not the talents or proclivities of individuals but the social practices in which they are engaged. These are readily revealed in the language of the actors themselves. Along these lines, Caroline Humphrey has observed that, "present trading activities developed from an illegal pursuit, without a vocabulary of its own legitimacy."[33] This binary opposition between social relations and their attendant practices, on the one hand, and the available public discourse for representing those relations and practices, on the other, has continued in the current period. Language functions in this regard in ways analogous to the opposition that we have noted between formal institutions and the welter of informal practices occurring within them. Just as those ongoing practices are concealed and sustained by formal institutions—functioning in this respect as a *krysha* (roof) protecting those under it—so the language through which practices are represented exhibits a comparable split. One plane of reality is occupied by instrumental language particular to the practices themselves, another by available discourses for representing those practices publicly. The first tends toward anomie, as moral standards are either weak or nonexistent on this plane; the second, where moral discourses prevail, becomes nonreferential, unable to name and to thematize that which it purportedly claims to address.[34] The coexistence of these separate planes conduces to a situation in which those in control of state offices and, thus, of available public representations, can utilize that control to dominate others and exact tribute from them. As Alexei Yurchak has observed:

> Because state officials are aware that most businesses have to practice heteronymous shift [i.e., concealing actual practices under the *krysha* of authorized public discourse] in their business, they often use this knowledge to blackmail entrepreneurs into "subscribing" to additional heteronymous services [roughly speaking, bribes] that these state agencies themselves offer today. If a firm refuses to comply with such demands imposed by a state organ, it can be punished through official methods. Basically, if a firm refuses to violate the *practical* meaning of the state law it may be punished by means of this very law.[35]

It would be mistaken, however, to regard the chaotic nature of Russia's institutional order as symptomatic of generalized chaos. Order, there is—"grounded squarely in customary ways of getting things done."[36] Above all, "getting things done" continues to depend on personalistic ties to relevant others, a phenomenon that appears to have increased in scope and intensity in the post-communist period.[37] At the top of the social order, power networks are arrayed along continual stretching from state institutions to criminal organizations with all manner of semi-state and private bodies lodged in between. As the concept of recombinant property suggests, it is the networks themselves—rather than the particular individuals or units comprising them—that count as the real actors. As such, it appears that exchanges within these networks—say, charters, licenses and tax breaks for stock options, *dachas* and jobs for relatives—constitute the actual substance of collective action.[38] Legal relations formally pertaining to these exchanges amount to open frames whose actual content is supplied by power networks.[39]

To be sure, these networks enjoy no public existence, nor do they seek one. Rather like our consideration of language, they live "heteronymous" lives. In addition to penetrating state agencies, power networks function within formally constituted political parties as groups whose control of resources relevant to electoral competition is sufficient to supplant formal party rules and programs.[40] Likewise, they are inchoately present in business associations whose members have little if any interest in undertaking some collective action associated with their formal affiliations—promoting, say, the interests in realtors or agricultural suppliers—and have instead joined these associations in order to seek out ties to others who might advance their individual fortunes.[41]

At regional level, situations vary, of course, but the results seem to be rather uniform: the dominion of power networks enjoying the patronage of their respective governors or presidents.[42] The first in-depth analysis of a contemporary Russian provincial elite has conclusively confirmed the existence of this network pattern.[43] Although Russia is formally a federation, network interactions tend to render institutional questions—such as centralization versus decentralization—as secondary to the main concern: the struggle for power in which competitive networks comprised of government agencies, economic enterprises, banks, and others battle over "jurisdiction and prerogatives."[44] In the same way that in its day the soviet enterprise had congealed as a unit solely out of the interests of its members to present a united front against the unwanted interventions of the central authorities,[45] so regional networks are solidified by a common interest in protection against a predatory center consisting of power networks ensconced at the national level.[46] The failure of the Russian state to institute a monopoly on the means of payment can be regarded as both cause and consequence of the rupture in the federal system in which regions have come to resemble self-contained economies. The scramble to sustain at least minimal levels of productive activity—and, along with it, the existence of entire cities and towns—in the wake of the devastating economic reforms has led to the creation of those barter chains and local currencies on which we have commented above. These arrangements have been improvisational, relying on informal chains of trust and mutual understanding to organize collective action. Regularized over time, these personalized patterns of activity function as networks that constitute the informal infrastructures of their respective political economies.

The fact that the linchpin of a regional network is an elected governor or president appears to introduce an element of instability into the mix. Could not others band together to unseat the existing power networks in the next public election? The answer to this question comes in two varieties of "no." On one hand, through network associations, governors control resources sufficient in most instances to ensure their reelection or that of a designated successor. Even when sizable financial resources are pumped into their opponents' campaigns—or when the president himself calls on his subnational plenipotentiaries "to take full control of the elections," as Vladimir Putin did in fall 2000—regional power networks usually manage to secure the reelection of their respective patrons, as was true in about two-thirds of the thirty-five gubernatorial races held in Russia during fall and winter 2000–2001.[47] However, when an incumbent governor or his designated successor does suffer defeat at the polls, would not this amount to an unseating of the region's power networks? In this instance, we encounter the second variety of "no." Just as Mary McAuley discovered a switch of allegiances from Supreme Soviet to the president affected by regional elites once Boris Yeltsin had vanquished his opponents in 1991 and 1993,[48] so regional power networks seem simply to embrace the new victors as their own.[49] Moreover, as Marie Mendras points out, "an individual who is a direct product of the local system will usually stay in the system even if he has been defeated [in an election] by one of his peers. He remains a member of the ruling group."[50]

Formal institutions find little to sustain themselves in such a world. As Grigorii Golosov has shown, the influence of political parties is either nonexistent or particularly weak in Russia's regions. Tellingly, even attempts by some of Russia's powerful governors to organize parties have invariably failed. Golosov attributes this to the fact that parties are not relevant to a governor's principal task—negotiating favorable relations with Moscow—because there are effectively no party organizations present in either the State Duma or the government that could render assistance to him. Because governors dispose of sufficient resources to field their own electoral organizations, they tend to eschew any affiliation with political parties out of fear that their symbolic and programmatic baggage would injure rather than aid the candidate's chances for success. Even in those instances in which a party's candidate has defeated an incumbent, the influence of party is, at most, minimal. In the same way that the unseated governor remains a member of the ruling group, so his replacement will be co-opted into it, and his previous ties to his party and its program will be cut.[51] This pattern represents another instance of deinstitutionalization that has been observed at all levels of government: namely, when party leaders assume positions in the executive, rather than enhancing the status of their party they, by effectively leaving, diminish it.[52]

These practices illustrate the inverse relation obtaining between institutions and informal social relations as alternative methods for structuring action. The state's weakness and the influence of power networks feed off one another. In this respect, Steven Fish is right in calling attention to the fact that "the origins of most institutions, institutional development, and institutional innovation are found in *competition for the right to rule,* rather than in the process of ruling itself."[53] Russia's political institutions have been and remain weak in large part because the right to rule has not been established by an institution-building process of formal accommodation of competing forces leading to consensus on the rules of the game, but by the force displayed in Yeltsin's October 1993 coup d'état. With the opposition physically vanquished, the need to craft state institutions, in which the right to rule would be impersonally specified, disappeared. Because the ruler is already known to everyone—whether Yeltsin or Putin, the formality of an election notwithstanding—the organization of an opposition, in the accepted sense of that term, would represent an exercise in futility. Instead, the path to influence and access to state resources would be paved by association with power networks capable of controlling state offices that can be used to dispense desired benefactions. These networks come to resemble so many nits infesting the institutional fabric of the ruler's creations, steadily devouring it from within.[54]

The Gray Zone

The concept of gray zone generally refers to arenas in the social world in which practices are neither unconditionally permitted nor proscribed. Accordingly, collective action in the gray zone depends upon a high degree of trust and shared values nourished by extended interactions through mutual-aid networks shielded from the gaze of outsiders.[55] Such gray zones appear to exist in all modern societies, but their circumferences are usually relatively narrow. However, in post-communist Russia, the gray zone, while difficult to measure, seems to be especially large. By official estimates, it accounted for some 45 percent of the GDP in 1997.[56] The size of the gray zone is conditioned by the fact that in actual practice—rather than on paper—the state has failed to draw firm lines separating permitted from proscribed behaviors. Consider, for instance, the reply of Russia's then Minister of the Interior, Vladimir Rushailo, to a reporter's comment that some 70 percent of Russian officialdom is suspected of being corrupt. Rushailo retorted that the figure was vastly exaggerated because it included bribe-taking as a form of corruption, when, in fact, "only those who have links with organized crime can be regarded as corrupt officials . . . Do not mistake bribe-taking for corruption."[57] Formal rules against bribery and extortion notwithstanding, the country's top law enforcement official gives voice to the fact that these practices are not necessarily illegal. Criminality is determined in practice not by actions *per se*, but by the wrong associations.

Apart from the particular instances in which particular officials invoke the law to sanction certain others, the boundaries of the gray zone become impossible to determine. The categories "criminal" and "corrupt" seem to denote very little in themselves. Conditioned over time by these circumstances, social consciousness adapts itself to its surroundings. For instance, whereas in the early 1990s the word "scandal" enjoyed a lively prominence in public discourse, by the end of the decade it had effectively disappeared. Yet, according to outside observers, it was precisely during these years that Russia had taken its place among the most corrupt countries in the world.[58] Habituated to these circumstances, that which had been scandalous ceases to be remarkable. If anything, it has become the norm.

In today's Russia, what then counts as "criminal" or "corrupt"? We can address this question by adopting the perspective employed by Vadim Volkov in his study of violent entrepreneurs and the private protection industry in Russia. On the field of providing security to those engaged in economic pursuits, Volkov encountered criminal fraternities formed in soviet prisons, Afghan war veterans, Cossacks, newly constituted gangs of racketeers, licensed security firms, and segments of the state's coercive agencies—all engaged in the same activities, all looking (except for the state uniforms and the Cossack regalia) and sounding remarkably alike. Consequently, Volkov bracketed the notion that offering security in return for a tax was an activity peculiar to the state (especially because its officials were often interchangeable with some of the other groups that in many instances covertly operated hand in hand with state agencies) and, instead, adopted the idea that the formation of the state itself was presently represented in desultory fashion by all of the groups—official, licensed by government, or illegal—operating on this particular field.[59] From the perspective suggested by his account, crime and corruption are not so much categories informing the practices of the actors as they are matters of judgment rendered by outside observers. In terms directly comparable to the gray exchanges (*blat*) of the soviet period analyzed by Alena Ledeneva, corruption—once it has become widespread and pervasive—tends not to be recognized as such by those trafficking in illicit practices.[60]

Although corruption and criminality often involve the exchange of non-monetary considerations—say, the award of housing to state officials or their relatives in return for a favorable determination in matters of licensing or taxation—by creating a convertible currency, Russia's economic reforms have enormously raised the importance of money in these transactions. In consequence, the banking sector has become something of a hub for corrupt and otherwise criminal practices. Indeed moneymaking in this sector usually has nothing to do with the functions commonly associated with banking—raising capital from deposits and lending it for a profit—but with a number of activities designed to bilk state and society, often for massive sums. Certain large banks have superintended the transfer of funds involved with domestic spending and arms sales to foreign countries, skimming substantial portions of the money for themselves; at sham auctions they have purchased profitable firms for a pittance; and, until the financial collapse of August 1998, select banks were the beneficiaries of a government scheme to prop up the national currency, purchasing state bonds with a maturation period as short as six months that offered returns of 100 percent and more.[61]

Money laundering has become a particularly lucrative activity for a number of Russia's banks. Given the clandestine nature of these operations, the sums channeled through the banks and into off-shore accounts are difficult to determine precisely, but informed estimates suggest that they are colossal: Transparency International has calculated that the yearly volume has been as high as $25–$30 billion;[62] Pino Arlacchi, head of the UN Office of Drug Control and Crime Prevention, has claimed that as much as $100 billion was laundered through Russia between June 2000 and June 2001;[63] the Russian weekly, *Argument i fakty,* has calculated that by the end of the 1990s, the country's twenty top individual money launderers had moved at least $40 billion to their overseas accounts, a sum roughly equivalent to twice the national government's annual budget.[64] These achievements by private individuals notwithstanding, however, the government's Central Bank appears to own the distinction of being the country's largest money laundry.[65]

These practices by Russia's leading financial institutions help to explain the prolonged economic contraction in the country who's GDP has been nearly halved since soviet time.[66] Depriving the treasury of tax revenue, they also have figured decisively in the state's contraction. According to Mikhail Fradkov, Russia's director of the Federal Service of Tax Police, tax avoidance is not only widespread—currently, some 1.5 million registered firms out of a total of 3.5 million render no accounts of their operations and pay no taxes—but is often inseparably connected to chains of organizations engaged in money laundering and the export of capital to the West.[67] These activities have been supported by the bridges built by power networks that span state institutions and private sector organizations. On one side of the institutional divide, banks are officially commissioned to serve as agents of the state's tax inspectorate, encharged with supervising the financial transactions of those firms that maintain accounts with them, providing relevant information to state officials, and even participating in raids conducted by authorities on enterprise accounts.[68] Little imagination is required to appreciate the possibilities for corruption contained in such a relationship: banks are formally expected to reduce liquidity in the economic system by assisting the state in extracting capital from depositors. As Eva Busse has concluded, the rules and procedures of the tax system appear to have been designed to enable the authorities and the taxpayers to collude in personalized arrangements promoting tax evasion.[69] On the other side of the divide, power networks systematically insert their agents into such institutions as the Central Bank, the Tax Police,[70] the Presidential Administration, and relevant government ministries where they can, with the authority of state office, render direct assistance to their patrons.[71]

The theft of state assets has thus reached staggering proportions, with sums equivalent to many billions of dollars disappearing from the federal budget without a trace. Of the $3 billion appropriated for reconstruction after the first Chechen war, for example, only $150 million actually reached Chechnya, making not only war but, in this case, peace a very profitable undertaking for some.[72] The surfeit of crime has been made possible by a corresponding dearth of punishment as "not a single one of the thousands of highly placed politicians, generals, and businessmen on whom the police have lengthy dossiers has been sentenced and jailed: and even figures of lower rank have met this fate only in a few cases."[73] The single significant case to the contrary would confirm the rule. When the government of Evgeny Primakov commissioned its prosecutor general, Yurii Skuratov, to pursue criminal cases against members of the country's top power network ensconced in the Kremlin (the president's "family"), the Federal Security Services under the leadership of Putin arranged for a compromising video featuring Skuratov (or someone resembling him) engaged in sexual activity with two women to be broadcast on state television. Yeltsin then initiated the removal of his prosecutor general from office.[74]

Networks of Trust

By the close of the communist era, civil society and its anticipated (re)emergence in post-communist states had become prominent issues on the research agendas of many Western scholars.[75] Heartened by the decay of communist party-states—a process in part signaled by the formation of social and political groups acting outside of the control of their respective regimes—a number of specialists forecasted that shortly a vibrant public sphere, anchored in autonomous civic associations, would replace that orchestrated sterility that had passed for public life under communism. This development was broadly considered as essential to securing democracy in the post-communist world, supplying the meat and muscle of civic initiative, as it were, to the bare bones of democratic institutions.

Experience has not confirmed these expectations. Across the post-communist expanse—and even in those countries that have been most successful in instituting liberal democracy and a market economy, such as Poland, the Czech Republic, and Hungary—civil society has receded. In place of the desideratum of civic associations contending and cooperating in public fora, we observe a general depoliticization of social relations and a concomitant retreat of citizens into personalized forms of needs satisfaction.[76] Why has this happened?

Without attempting an exhaustive explanation for this phenomenon generally, we can introduce two related considerations that bear especially heavily on the Russian case. The first would be the social dislocation engendered by economic reforms. The magnitude of this problem and the levels of deprivation that it has occasioned would be difficult to fathom. Social spending has nose-dived; inflation and monetary reform have wiped out the savings of most people; wages and pensions, often ridiculously low to begin with, have been delayed in innumerable instances for many months; uncertainty about what tomorrow will bring casts a long shadow over the very prospects of survival for the majority of the population. While leading figures in the country's power networks have been amassing fortunes and shipping the money abroad—amounting to a combined sum of $300 billion by one estimate— over 70 percent of Russians have been "brutally impoverished,"[77] with as many as 40 percent of the population living below an official poverty line calculated on the basis of the world's poorest countries.[78] The exigencies of everyday struggles to keep bodies, souls, and families together would appear to leave little time or energy for associational activities in civic organizations.

A recent investigation of social relations among Russians has revealed that, in the turbulent period following independence, Russians have roundly abandoned the public sphere as an arena for pursuing collective interests. They display few traces of interest and involvement in that associational life characteristic of civil societies. Rather, individuals have diverted their attention and energies elsewhere; namely, toward those informal, face-to-face networks of trust that had been prevalent under communism in the form of gray exchange (*blat*).[79] This pattern represents the second consideration bearing on the disappearance of civil society in communism's aftermath. Faced with the challenges of survival in a new and uncertain world, individuals have turned to those forms of collective action to which they had already become accustomed; forms that are incongruent with that set of social relations on which civil society, a market economy, and a democratic state are predicated.

Ironically, it seems that the resilience of these social relations has ensured relative levels of political stability in the post-communist world. In his comparative study of this subject, Bela Greskovits has inquired into the divergent social responses registered in Latin America in the 1980s and in East Europe in the 1990s to the onset of austerity mandated by international financial institutions and enacted by governments as neo-liberal economic reform. In the former, country after country erupted in massive public protests, often leading to riots; in the latter, very little, if any, public protests have occurred. The difference, according to Greskovits, can be explained primarily by the fact that in post-communist countries people exercised the option of "going informal"—that is, retreating from civic life and securing their private/communal existences by means of exchanges of favors in networks of trust composed of family and friends.[80] The political costs of Russia's reforms have thus not been measured in organized protests and overt unrest that topples governments, but in the retrenchment of those patterns of social and economic activity that the reforms sought to destroy.[81]

The retrenchment in social relations has taken, broadly speaking, two general forms: private economic activity undertaken by families and close friends, usually in the home, and informal redistributive practices centered around the workplace collective. With respect to the former, the fieldwork conducted by Michael Burawoy and his associates has led them to the conclusion that

> A new type of society is appearing in Russia that statistical data cannot disclose. It is a network society that is both resilient and quiescent, that adapts without mobilization. . . . [When] industrial production began to lose its centrality in everyday life . . . for many of Russia's workers the fulcrum of economic activity has moved from workplace to family.[82]

For many individuals, social relations since communism have been reduced to small, dense networks composed of kin and other intimates,[83] acting collectively as small economic units that produce (usually) in the home and sell their wares in primitive public markets under the paid protection of those agencies providing security in the gray zone.

An alternative pattern is visible in shadow labor markets where individuals are employed for a wage. Although practices here remain completely outside the law, they evince a certain orderliness and predictability issuing from the informal norms and expectations that surround them. Employers and employees do not encounter one another as strangers. Rather, potential employees enter these shadow markets on the basis of personalized ties connecting their own trust networks to potential employers. Although employees under these circumstances are severely exploited and dispose of no actual rights, the personalistic ties of loyalty operating in their respective networks of trust that secured for them their jobs tend to be transferred over time to their employer/patrons.[84] In sum, whether we are considering kin-based production in the home or informal labor exchange at, say, the construction site, the social and, indeed, physical existence of tens of millions seems to be predicated on ties of personal loyalty rather than on the impersonal relations characteristic of the market.[85]

With respect to trust networks operating in and through workplace collectives, we observe the remarkable recrudescence of soviet-era institutions. Under communism, the collective had been installed throughout Russian society as the modal form of social organization. Effectively every individual belonged to one, and participation in the affairs of the collective—although coerced—was critical to the individual's social existence, both ensuring the provision of material things (food, health care, vacation opportunities, and so on) and molding the personalities of its members.[86] The impact of the economic reforms undertaken after communism actually strengthened the collectives in certain respects. Impoverished workers facing the prospects of imminent unemployment as the economy collapsed around them could rely on the paternal benevolence of enterprise directors[87] to procure for their respective workplace collectives at least the minimal provision of life's necessities organized by means of barter chains and other informal arrangements orchestrated through regional power networks.[88] Although the lack of actual work to be performed at the workplace has redirected much economic activity to the home and the public market, workplace collectives remain as sites for redistribution, for enabling economic activity (leasing shops for private production) and for maintaining social solidarities.[89]

A particularly revealing study of this matter has compared patterns of social interaction among schoolteachers in Helsinki and St. Petersburg. In the former, the teachers exhibit a pattern of associations common in Western countries and congruent with the concept of civil society: a "horizontal" network of ties among similarly situated individuals—in this case, the teachers—that spans the entire city. In St. Petersburg, however, the situation is fundamentally different. There, teachers in a given school have few if any associations with their counterparts working in the same locality; rather, they maintain rather strong ties to administrators, students, parents, and staff in the schools in which they work, thus creating a dense network pattern that the researchers describe with the term "school as community."[90] This community would represent the intersection of the types of networks that we have discussed: horizontal networks of trust based on face-to-face relations and the exchange of favors that are connected by workplace associations to vertical networks of power, personified in this instance by school principals whose associations with city officials and others emplaced in relevant offices can be used to ensure the survival of their schools.

This intersection appears to be emblematic of social relations in post-communist Russia. It can be regarded as the set of political practices coextensive with weak institutions and the attendant deficit of mobilizing structures in society—say, autonomous labor unions, civic associations, or effective political parties—that might otherwise formulate social interests and press the state for their satisfaction. It is reflected in social consciousness as an effective absence of ideology, for a world composed of personalistic networks is a world bounded by its particular participants whose practical concerns leave no room for considerations of a public and its welfare. "In that world," Yuliya Shevchenko explains:

> Things and events seem simple and intelligible. Within [their] networks, individuals have the concrete knowledge that they need to navigate in their worlds and this knowledge has the networks' imprimatur on it already. There is no common interest standing outside the relations of this knowledge. Hence, there are no programs or ideologies in elections —rather, all depends on the resonance of the communicative style projected by the candidates—can he pass for one of us?[91]

It may be that the social relations and political practices that we have surveyed would provide some clues to the otherwise improbably accession of Vladimir Putin to the Russian presidency. How was it that an individual— who had never run for or held elected public office, who was proffered as a candidate by an outgoing president (himself both broadly despised and ridiculed), who eschewed the need actually to campaign for office and who had no platform whatsoever—was elected by a substantial margin? Was it the fact that on the basis of a well-crafted set of images projected daily to the Russian public by the country's mass media that he was able "to pass for one of us"? Or might it be that the tele-mediated Putin personified to a network society its idealized patron?

Perspectives

Russia retains the formal institutions of democratic government and, accordingly, the potential for a democratic political practice. In itself, this is an accomplishment worth noting. At the same time, however, our survey of social relations would warn against reading too much into it. Along these lines, it is important to mention that knowledgeable Russians themselves withhold the adjective "democratic" when referring to their political institutions. For instance, Anna Temkina and Vitalii Grigorev, who surveyed some three hundred books and articles published in Russia on political topics during the period 1985–1997, found that not a single one regarded the existing regime as democratic.[92] Rather, Russian students of the subject tend to conceive of the animating forces in politics as being of the personalistic variety,[93] rendered, here, as power networks.

At this writing, Putin's presidency retains an aura of determination and energy devoted to the purpose of building a strong Russian state that would bring order to society. Were this actually to come about, then a necessary condition for democratic government—namely, a strong state—would be put in place. However, the indications to date suggest that the president's project interprets the idea of state strength to be entrancing the government's coordinated capacity for repression rather than constructing impersonal public institutions that constrain the behaviors of citizens and officials alike. The perspective, then, for the building of a democratic state in Russia is not particularly encouraging. We conclude with a few words on some of its dimensions.

First, although catapulted into the country's highest office by the corrupt Yeltsin "family," Putin has drawn on his own ties with *siloviki* (those in the repressive organs) to install a number of his clients in important positions in the government. One observer has interpreted this as part of Putin's struggle to emancipate himself from the patronage of those who had propelled his career to the very top of the hierarchy and to establish his own network of supporters positioned to deliver the strong state that he has promised.[94] Some of the early outcomes of this endeavor, however, indicate that presidential directives may not be sufficient to control the activities of state security personnel dispatched to bring order to the affairs of certain government enterprises. Once in place, the *siloviki* con the state and pocket the proceeds in much the same manner as had those whom they have replaced.[95]

Second, Putin's reform of the federal system, which has diminished the power of the governors considerably, appears to be designed to extend the operational reach of his office into regions and localities.[96] His plenipotentiaries in the country's seven new super-regions formally serve as direct extensions of presidential authority. But the institutional basis under which these new agents of the center carry out their functions is extremely thin. As one specialist on federal affairs has observed:

> What is crucial to this transformation is not only the weakening of all independent players, but the weakening of legal institutions as such. The president's already enormous power is growing, while legal institutions are increasingly replaced by new, opaque ones with poorly defined powers: the Security Council instead of the government and the presidential administration; the State Council instead of the Federation Council; the presidential representatives in federal districts and chief federal inspectors instead of the former presidential representatives in regions; and the Audit Chamber as a kind of law enforcement agency. What is this, if not growing authoritarianism? The emergence of less legally legitimate structures parallel to existing state bodies represents the construction of an entirely new political machine that will work for a while in parallel with Yeltsin's old one, and soon replace it entirely.[97]

It would thus seem that despite the many formal administrative changes, which have altered the balance of power between the center and the regions, the organization and composition of the state's apparatus continue to display the marks of personalism, making "the major instrument of administration in the country the re-assignment of cadres . . . and not the juridical force of law."[98]

Finally, while Putin's dispatching of *siloviki* to strategic positions in government and economy appears intended to strengthen the Russian state, it may well have the opposite effect. Already a merger of state and hitherto criminal organizations—facilitated by state licensing regulations—is well under way in the protection industry.[99] Inasmuch as this is occurring under the aegis of the state, an institutional process might be at work, rationalizing this critical sector, reducing levels of violence, and introducing a measure of stability and predictability in the interactions among private firms and government agencies. However, even as some of the signs of institutionalization seem to be growing here, this merger of state and private force-wielding agents presents a considerable problem for the state's autonomy. It is important to recall, in this respect, the many service operations undertaken by organizations providing protection: surveillance and intelligence gathering on competitors and clients, contract enforcement and the informal resolution of disputes, the enlistment of official bodies to solve the problems of client firms, and so forth. In brief, the protection industry has grown into a

massive complex on which business activity in Russia depends. As state officials are drawn more into the workings of this complex, the question arises
as to the direction of their loyalties. Is it to the state as represented by formal
law and regulations or to their partners in business? Does the current trend
represent a process of institutionalization *per se,* or can it more accurately be
described as an enlargement of the gray zone and the normalization of relations within it? This instance would count as a salient example of what one
observer refers to as rule by a bureaucratic bourgeoisie, a power structure
reminiscent of tsarism and one toward which, after some seventy-four years
of communism, Russia seems again headed.[100] From the perspective developed here, a certain stability based on a low-level equilibrium obtaining
between state and society is apparent. The state, an arena for the interplay of
power networks, appears to be incapable of mounting public projects, just as
society, fragmented into innumerable personalistic networks of trust, seems
unable to be mobilized either for or against them.

CHAPTER SEVEN

Russia in the Middle

State Building and the Rule of Law

ROBERT SHARLET

*Robert Sharlet speaks to the interface between political society—the formal insti-
tutions of government and the constitutions and laws that give them form—and
the broader civil society within which they operate. He describes contemporary
Russia as a "melded" society in which long-standing authoritarian patterns of
behavior are intertwined with democratic practices. The further consolidation of
democracy depends upon the completion of both aspects of the relationship
between social practices and former institutions. The formal institutions themselves must be further grounded in the rule of law, which entails the creation of
a competent and law-governed state and an expansion of the corpus of law in
critical areas such as criminal behavior and commercial activities. In addition,
the civil society must change its perception of the nature of power, shifting from
"networks of trust," as Michael Urban terms them, to more formalized and con-
tractual relationships between government and the citizenry and among citizens
themselves. Only on this basis can the balance between empowering the state
and sustainable controls over government be established.*

This is a study of how Russia has survived its turbulent transformation
from an authoritarian polity and centrally planned economy to a developing
democracy and emerging market society. Understanding post-soviet Russia's
first decade entails examining the costs of the transition incurred under Boris

Yeltsin, in particular state weakness and poor legal discipline, as well as evaluating Vladimir Putin's policy responses to this legacy as an effort to meet the challenges of further democratization and the development of the Rule of Law.

Presently, Russia is at mid-passage in its transformative project, with a hybrid or "melded" political system[1] still retaining familiar authoritarian habits entwined with new democratic practices. A major Western theory of democracy argues that democratic governments in fact perform best when they combine democratic and nondemocratic traits, but Russia has not yet reached the theorist's equilibrium point of "balanced disparities."[2] Further progress toward democracy in Russia will require more effective state building framed and articulated through accelerated rule-of-law development.

At the ten-year mark, Russia stands in the middle. Internationally, the country is at midpoint in a spectrum between consolidated or advanced consolidating democracies in East Central Europe and the Baltics, and an array of patriarchal regimes, "guided" democracies, and even garrison states among other former Soviet republics in the Near Abroad. Similarly, on the domestic front, although Russia may have passed the point of irreversibility, the journey from its authoritarian past to a more fully realized democratic future continues.

State building has progressed, but in an uneven fashion.[3] Only of late has the Russian state begun to significantly strengthen its *extractive capacity,* especially in the crucial area of collecting tax revenues for public purposes. The state's *regulative capacity* has been a continual work in progress as more and more essential legislation has been enacted to effectively regulate relations between citizens, as well as between citizens and the state.[4] However, while the process of erecting a necessary regulatory framework for society has been underway, Russia's *administrative capability* has been foundering.[5]

The governmental bureaucracy which is tasked with administering much of the regulatory legislation is still often afflicted with the old soviet mindset and work style to which now can be added massive corruption. All of this seriously burdens the policy implementation process. Finally, the state's *adjudicative capacity* presents a mixed picture. While the Constitutional Court began to function more effectively and accrue public respect in the latter half of the 1990s and the commercial courts have worked reasonably well to resolve business disputes, the main general court system has lagged behind in the institution-building process. The latter includes the courts that preside over the criminal justice system as well as the vast majority of civil suits. The judicial system's substantial personnel, funding, physical plant, and enforcement problems were largely treated as deferred maintenance during the Yeltsin era. Only in the past few years has this important dimension of state building begun to be systematically addressed.[6]

As is the case in democratic systems, law is the fundamental medium of state building in Russia. Just as an effective and efficient state is essential to building a democratic polity and a viable market, law is the indispensable ingredient in the construction of the all-encompassing state and its four major capabilities or functions. Hence, my focus in this study will include the ongoing development of the rule of law in Russia. Evaluation according to three criteria will guide us in this sector. Is the law contributing to stability and hence predictability to facilitate individuals, corporations, and government agencies in formulating and carrying out their respective agendas? Is the law becoming more transparent so that all who are subject to its regulatory oversight and administrative programs can know and understand the relevant rules either directly or through proxy of an attorney? Finally, is the law progressively ensuring equity and fairness between contracting parties, citizen and state, and those who approach, as well as those who are brought to the bar of justice?

Critical Tests of Russia's Transitional Political System

In its first decade, Russia's young polity managed to survive five critical moments in its difficult transition, any one of which might have derailed the democratic transformation process or even doomed it altogether. These included (1) the collapse of the First Post-Soviet Russian Republic in 1993; (2) internal war—the first Chechen conflict, 1994–1996; (3) the economic crisis of August 1998; (4) the first transfer of power, 1999–2000; and (5) the challenge of growing a constitutional culture during the first decade, 1992–2002.

Surviving the Collapse of the First Republic

The Russian Federation survived the profound constitutional crisis between president and parliament of 1992–1993 followed by the ensuing collapse of the First Post-Soviet Russian Republic in the fall of 1993. The constitutional collision was a consequence of the heavily amended 1978 soviet Russian Constitution under which the First Republic was governed. A patchwork document pending completion of a new constitution, it incompatibly included an executive presidency endowed with strong powers grafted on to a constitution proclaiming parliamentary supremacy, a constitutional fiction of the soviet period. Yes, Yeltsin resorted to extra-constitutional means in September to overcome the deadlock, and ultimately in response to parliamentary violence, shut the institution down with tanks in October. Three months later, however, at the end of a brief interregnum in early December, generally free and fair elections for a new parliament were held simultaneously with a referendum on the draft post-soviet Russian constitution. Indeed, Yeltsin had ensured that the draft charter favored a strong executive, and the turnout numbers required for a legal referendum were apparently fudged, but, contrary to dire predictions, there was no return to authoritarianism.[7]

Conversely, Yeltsin accepted the limits of the new constitution, which initiated the Second Republic. As early as February 1994, although not without considerable grumbling, the president acceded to the new State Duma's exercise of its constitutional power of amnesty, which effected release of his erstwhile major opponents of the late First Republic then under investigation for resorting to violence during the final confrontation of October 1993. In addition, in spite of the constitution's centrist bias, not long after the Duma's amnesty, Yeltsin agreed to a bilateral treaty with the restless Republic of Tatarstan, thereby beginning the longer-term process of negotiating power-sharing treaties with federation subjects. The result over the next several years was a substantial devolution of the central government's powers.[8]

Surviving Internal War—
The First Chechen Conflict

The Russian-Chechen conflict had it roots in the nineteenth century, but its twentieth-century reincarnation first arose during the fall of 1991. The Soviet Union was disintegrating as the union republics moved toward the exits, declaring not only their sovereignty but also independence. The Chechen minority, who lived in a small administrative enclave within the Russian Republic, seeing in the moment an opportunity to free themselves of Russian domination, declared their independence. Yeltsin and the Russian leadership, embroiled in their final face-off with President Mikhail Gorbachev of the USSR, denounced the Chechen declaration, but had neither the resources nor political will to undertake action against the secessionist Chechens at that time. During the fractious First Republic, Russia's Chechen problem was relegated to the political back burner, but by December 1994 of the Second

Republic, Yeltsin's generals persuaded him the Chechens could easily be brought to heel through a brief show of force.[9]

Thus was launched the first Chechen war which, in spite of confident assurances to the contrary, raged on for nearly two years with terrible human losses. The internal war, in which the greatly outnumbered and outgunned Chechens bravely and often effectively took on the Russian armed forces against all odds, was not without its political costs for the still relatively new polity under construction from the constitutional blueprint of the Second Republic. Paradoxically, the fledgling post-soviet Russian constitutional system not only withstood the strains of internal war, but elite opposition to the conflict contributed to strengthening the separation of powers doctrine and the embryonic system of checks and balances.[10]

Negative fallout for Russia from the Chechen war included the demonization of the Kremlin's critics; ethnic scapegoating of the Chechen minority, especially those living outside the republic; and the sidetracking of an important piece of pending legislation, the draft Federal Constitutional Law on the ombudsman or commissioner of human rights.[11]At the same time, however, the unrelenting military conflict had the surprising effect of accelerating state building. Elite opposition in the Duma, the lower house, brought forth the first attempt, albeit an abortive one, to amend the 1993 constitution. Opposition to the president's war policy also encouraged deputies to become more assertive toward the executive, and it was a factor in the first no-confidence vote in the government during summer of 1995. A few years later, the Chechen war became a key issue in a major attempt to impeach the president. Although the required reconfirmation of the Duma's no-confidence vote failed, and the impeachment drive eventually fell short, both moves signaled greater parliamentary activism in challenging executive power.

Political opposition to the Chechen fighting also sped up reemergence of the Constitutional Court, which had been suspended during the final crisis of the First Republic in 1993. A new statute for the court had been passed and signed into law during the summer of 1994, but then months went by before the upper house, the Federation Council, and the president could agree on his judicial nominees to fill the six vacancies in the enlarged nineteen-member court. The infighting over judicial selection between Yeltsin and the senators had been so intense that in a few instances the president had even defiantly resubmitted nominees already resoundingly rejected, only to see advise and consent withheld once again. Political gridlock over the makeup of the court was looming when Russian forces invaded the Republic of Chechnya.

In addition to the proposed constitutional amendments to limit the executive, the outbreak of fighting provoked parliamentary petitions to the forthcoming second Constitutional Court to review the constitutionality of the executive decrees on the basis of which Russian armed forces had been dispatched "to restore constitutional order" in breakaway Chechnya. The catch, however, was that the court could not convene until the last remaining seat was filled. Under the circumstances, the Federation Council quickly confirmed the president's final nominee, thereby completing the rehabilitation of the Constitutional Court as the principal component of the third branch under the new constitution's separation of powers doctrine. That several months later, the court reviewed the parliamentary petitions and essentially affirmed the Kremlin's Chechen policy, did not nonetheless diminish the tragic irony that the war had indirectly contributed to democratic state building in Russia.[12]

Surviving the August Economic Crisis

Russia's endemic economic crisis reached catastrophic proportions in August 1998, bringing the political institutions of the country and those who ran them to a level of public disrepute unknown to that time in the Second Republic. Yeltsin's approval rating fell to the statistically nebulous zone of 3 to 5 percent, signaling the nadir of his presidency. Yet, in spite of the economic calamity and the most severe political perturbations, the Russian polity not only weathered the August crisis, but due to Yeltsin's acute political weakness, parliament at last gained traction to exercise some leverage over the all-powerful executive branch. Although the political advantage eventually eroded, the crisis did establish a new benchmark for the developing legislative-executive culture within the constitutional framework.

Russia's economic problems had deep roots, but the train of events leading to the August crisis began in the spring of 1998. Yeltsin dismissed his longtime prime minister, Viktor Chernomyrdin, and asked the Duma to give its advice and consent to a relatively unknown, politically inexperienced replacement. The opposition-dominated lower house balked, rejecting the nomination twice before, under threat of constitutional dissolution, the deputies confirmed Sergei Kiriyenko as the new prime minister. It was, however, a pyrrhic victory for the president since his new head of government could not push through the parliament an austerity package promised as quid pro quo for an international financial bailout to stabilize the shaky ruble during the summer. In this environment, Russia devalued the ruble and defaulted on its foreign and domestic debt, bringing about the collapse of its stock market as well as many banks and plunging the population to new depths of despair.[13]

Predictably, the president again fired his prime minister. Yeltsin then desperately sought to restore political stability and some economic credibility by asking Chernomyrdin to return as head of the government. The veteran politician, however, set conditions. Chernomyrdin insisted on more authority to choose his ministers, and more autonomy for the government within the executive branch. The president, with little choice, conceded these conditions and sent Chernomyrdin's name to the Duma, which promptly rejected him by an embarrassingly large margin. Now in face of an emboldened lower house unintimidated by the threat of dissolution, Yeltsin was forced to negotiate to secure his prime ministerial choice. Parliament's negotiators demanded and the president conceded his support for long-sought constitutional reforms that would rebalance legislative-executive relations, by giving the two houses a degree of authority and control over the government, its personnel, and its policies. However, the major opposition faction pulled out at the eleventh hour, causing the deal to collapse, and Chernomyrdin was resoundingly rejected for a second time. At that point, the president, acknowledging political reality, put forward an acceptable compromise candidate who quickly won confirmation. Although Yeltsin was no longer obliged to support constitutional reforms, he did permit Prime Minister Evgeny Primakov to carry out some of the prospective changes on a de facto basis. Russia was again severely tested, but in the wake of the August events, the shaken polity emerged with its resilience tempered by crisis.[14]

Surviving the Transfer of Power

Democratic theorists argue that the first transfer of power is a crucial success indicator in the transition to democracy. During late 1999 and early 2000, Russia successfully passed this test. While the passage was not pretty, a peaceful transfer of power from the country's first elected chief executive to his successor was accomplished. Although the transfer was unorthodox, it did take place within the prevailing constitutional and legal frameworks for presidential successions, or to paraphrase a prominent American politician, within "controlling legal authority." In effect, Yeltsin was within his constitutional authority in resigning pre-term at the end of 1999 which automatically conferred on his preferred successor, Prime Minister Vladimir Putin, the title of Acting President pending a mandated special presidential election. Yes,

Yeltsin's surprise resignation and the ensuing abrupt and brief election campaign favored incumbent Putin, and some ballot fraud was detected. But, no
one, not even the distant runner-up, Gennady Zyuganov, the communist
party candidate, argued that Putin would not have easily won a runoff election if he had not polled the requisite 50 percent of the first-round vote.[15]

Learning to Play by the Rules of the New Game

In the course of any one of the preceding transitional crises, Russia could well
have slid from the path of democratic development. Negative models
abounded in the Near Abroad. For instance, in fall 1993 after shutting down
parliament and suspending the Constitutional Court, Yeltsin enjoyed unlimited powers and might have governed indefinitely by means of executive
decree, but he chose not to. Instead, he decreed new parliamentary elections,
the outcome of which, as it turned out, backfired on him politically, and promoted the ratification of Russia's first post-soviet constitution to bring an
end to the deadly constitutional stalemate of its soviet-era predecessor.

Likewise, in the first Chechen war, the Russian Federation could have
fought on indefinitely at full bore, in contrast to the present lower intensity
Chechen conflict. In the summer of 1995, a majority of the Constitutional
Court had given its blessings to the president's authority to wage war to curtail Chechnya's defiance of the constitution. Instead, Yeltsin began to wind
the war down during the spring of 1996, in a process driven by his desire for
reelection. True, he considered canceling the election when he thought his
chances of a second term hopeless, but he was persuaded to play by the election rules and went on to win a decisive runoff victory despite debilitating
illness. Similarly, the 1998 financial collapse presented a classic situation
ready made for backsliding to familiar authoritarian solutions, but the
Russian political class instead skillfully navigated a safe passage through
troubled waters, using the constitution as a rudder and as an arena for discourse, compromise, and the peaceful resolution of conflict. Finally, the initial transfer of political power in a transitional polity is always potentially
fraught with dangers: An incumbent might invoke emergency powers or
change the rules, frustrated power seekers could attempt a coup, or putative
successors might irreparably divide society through a divisive, no-holds-
barred election campaign. Russia, fortunately, did not fall prey to any of
these dangerous possibilities.

Thanks in particular to strategic incentives built into the constitution,
which induce presidential self-restraint, the chief executive, as well as the

major parties, factions, institutional actors, and individual players have consistently stayed within the parameters of the new constitutional rules of the game.[16] Within the Russian political class, it might be said, a democratic constitutional culture has been steadily evolving in the course of the Second Republic. Although occasional flirtations with extra-constitutional measures have occurred, ultimately all major actors have acquiesced in the electoral outcomes and played by the rules of the new, democratic political game.[17]

Constitutional Politics in the Second Russian Republic

While Russia was learning to live within constitutional constraints during its first post-soviet decade, a theme of political disquiet was apparent within the growing constitutional culture. In three of the four most acute tests of survival, a clear subtext was parliament's unease about its relationship with the executive. The clash of interests between the two power branches had of course been sharpest during the First Republic because of the contradictions in the then-extant constitution. The political deadlock came to an end with the ratification of the successor constitution of 1993, which gave the executive ascendancy over the legislative branch within an imbalanced separation of powers doctrine.

The power resolution proved to be short-lived in the Second Republic. Within a year, the Chechen crisis provoked parliamentary demands for more leverage over the presidency and the government, as well as, later, the more extreme step of impeachment proceedings against the president. In the August economic crisis, parliamentary demands for redressing the imbalance in legislative-executive relations resurfaced in the context of the political negotiations and constitutional bargaining with the president over his prime ministerial nominee. Some de facto progress in the relationship did occur, but de jure changes have yet to be realized, a significant issue which bears implications for Russia's future democratization.

Within the Russian political system, the thrust of these attempts to strengthen the legislature's position at the expense of the executive branch was predicated on the image of a dominant presidency, hence the calls for constitutional reform. The several constitutional reform attempts during the Second Republic, none of which were successful, tended to conflate Yeltsin's immense constitutional authority with his actual power in political reality. Consequently, the reform efforts from 1995 to 1999 for which there developed an increasingly stronger consensus across the parliament's factional lines, focused primarily on revising the separation of powers doctrine. In contrast, the issue of the constitutional division of powers, which was usually characterized by dissensus between central and provincial elites, was generally given less attention.

The paradox of the proposed constitutional reforms of the 1990s was that Yeltsin in reality was never as strong as he appeared to be. The weaknesses of his presidency contributed significantly to a weak state and lagging law reform and, derivatively, to an eventual division of powers crisis.[18] Much of the perception of an all-powerful president arose from the way the 1993 constitution came into being. Contrary to appearances at the time, however, the new constitution was not imposed in the manner of the MacArthur Constitution for Japan. The Russian Constitution represented the resolution and synthesis of three years of constitutional drafting and contained elements of both parliamentary and presidential drafts. The final version that went before the voters in the constitutional referendum reflected collective memory of the chronic instability of the First Republic and the then-prevailing correlation of political forces during the 1993 interregnum; hence, the constitution's strong tilt toward executive power and a unitarian state.[19]

Aside from misperceptions of the president's actual power versus his textual authority, parliamentarians had a legitimate grievance about their constitutionally inferior status vis-à-vis the executive branch. Thus, during the latter half of the 1990s, in spite of the daunting, American-style procedures for amending or revising the fundamental law, parliamentarians mounted a series of attempted constitutional reform to rectify the imbalance in legislative-executive relations by reconfiguring power-sharing arrangements between the two branches.[20] As previously mentioned, the first modest attempt to amend the new constitution was in reaction to the outbreak of the first Chechen war in the mid-1990s. The next attempt used the presidential election campaign of 1996 as a highly visible venue in which to publicize proposals for constitutional change. The third effort in 1997 was the most effectively organized attempt, reflecting the elite's serious concerns about Yeltsin's physical infirmities and prospective longevity.

As discussed earlier, the 1998 economic crisis provided the window of opportunity for the subsequent reform attempt, which was backed by a very strong parliamentary consensus and was highly focused in its specific proposals for constitutional revision. Had it not been for the last-minute pullout of one of the principal parliamentary factions and the collapse of negotiations, that fourth attempt might well have achieved significant changes to the constitution. The final concerted effort to bring about constitutional reform under Yeltsin occurred in the context of the 1999 parliamentary election campaign. The idea of amending the constitution came to life again as a major campaign issue supported by nearly every party and faction. Even the prospective candidates for the expected June 2000 presidential election to choose Yeltsin's successor weighed in to support the issue. With one exception, all of the putative presidential nominees agreed that reforming the constitution was an issue whose time had come.

The exception was Vladimir Putin, the prime minister, whom Yeltsin had already chosen as the man he wanted to succeed him. In one way or another, President Yeltsin had effectively blocked or deflected all previous attempts at constitutional reform. He had consistently argued that it was premature to consider changing a still relatively new constitution, and especially since it had helped restore political calm and stability to Russian public life. Obviously, embedded within Yeltsin's opposition was his personal interest in avoiding any moves that would diminish his "authority." As the president's first minister, Putin was therefore understandably cautious, offering only lukewarm and somewhat ambiguous support for constitutional reform. Then, abruptly on 31 December 1999, the constitutional revision question became moot after President Yeltsin's surprise resignation as public preoccupation suddenly shifted to the impending critical test for the still-emerging democratic polity, the first transfer of presidential power.

And so Yeltsin quietly but dramatically left the scene. Long depicted as a "soft" authoritarian or a superpresident, in retrospect, he was in fact "no Fujimori" as Eugene Huskey wrote in 1996 with reference to the then Peruvian strongman.[21] In reality, Yeltsin had been subject to constitutionally empowered, legislative constraints as well as to judicial checks on his actual use of power. In addition, as previously noted, he never fully exploited his enormous constitutional authority, and not infrequently exercised political self-restraint as well. Perhaps Yeltsin intuitively understood that constitutions "do not govern by text alone."[22]

For Yeltsin, a pronounced preference for stability over change, or civic peace in lieu of systematic reform, was the core political value of his regime. His was a strategy of equilibrium politics—stay to the middle, avoid the extremes, and accommodate shifting elite and mass differences of opinion. However, Yeltsin's policy of stability came with attendant costs for democratic political development. Rather than putting his shoulder to the further institutionalization of the polity, the president relied on a personalized style of governing through ad hoc bargaining and negotiation, in particular with the provincial governments of the far-flung Russian Federation.[23]

Thus, despite vast institutional resources, the Russian presidency under Yeltsin was weak with consequent negative effects on state building and rule-of-law development. Longer-term institution building suffered as well, resulting in an ineffective central government verging on a loose confederation of mini-states. Law reform lagged, leaving large gaps in the legal fabric, some of which in the late 1990s were still being patched with heavily amended soviet-era legislation. Finally, as laws, decrees, and even high court decisions were increasingly disregarded or evaded by powerful business oligarchs as well as willful provincial chief executives, the process of policy execution was infrequently characterized by implementation failure.

Putin's Policy Responses to Yeltsin's Legacies

Yeltsin's positive legacy to Russia is indisputable. He left a working democratic constitution, an evolving separation of powers doctrine, a largely privatized economy, and a system of regular and reasonably fair elections. However, Yeltsin also bequeathed to his successor fundamental problems potentially subversive of further democratic development, to wit, a weak state as well as chronic legal indiscipline, especially among "runaway field administrators" in the provinces.[24] Putin's policies have been an attempt to respond to these problems.

Yeltsin's Negative Legacy

For Vladimir Putin upon winning the presidency in his own right in early 2000, the most compelling problem of his predecessor's negative legacy was the situation of Russia's runaway provinces. After years of Yeltsin's ad hoc concessions through power-sharing treaties and other deals in order to buy a fragile stability and maintain an uneasy civic peace in center-periphery relations, the federation was in disarray. Plagued by separatist tendencies, the federal relationship was steadily becoming a loose and poorly operating confederation of republics and regions. Legally and constitutionally, this meant the fundamental law of many federation subjects contravened the Russian Constitution by including proclamations of sovereignty, assertions of the right to nullify federal laws, and claims to the status of a subject of international law. In financial terms, provincial separatism manifested itself in diverse ways, including retaining the lion's share of tax revenues collected, withholding levies intended for the central treasury, and generally misallocating federal budget funds.

For Putin, these problems were ultimately rooted in conditions of the weak and ineffective central state and the concomitant poor and erratic legal discipline. Specifically, he inherited an extractive capacity characterized by opaque and conflicting rules with low taxpayer compliance, revenue shortfalls, and much-needed but long-delayed tax law reform only belatedly getting underway. The state's regulative capability in turn was marked by uncertainty and indeterminate effects absent post-soviet codes on criminal and civil procedure and on land and labor which had still not been enacted, as well as yawning gaps in statutory legislation, especially on the economy and joint federal-provincial jurisdiction.

Administrative capacity was in no better shape, plagued by breakdowns and unevenly dispersed inequities, the result of regional and local diversion of program funds, co-optation of federal personnel, and problems of policy implementation in the regions and republics. Finally, as he came into office, Putin was particularly concerned with Russia's inadequate and often inefficient adjudicative capacity, a consequence of underfunded and overloaded courts.[25] He found criminal adjudication frequently marred by long pretrial detentions, while the execution of the civil judgments was persistently slow and often delayed.[26]

Putin's Policy Responses

Putin's policy rationale in response to the received liabilities of the Yeltsin years was that an effective state and a reliable legal system are necessary conditions for further development of a durable democracy and a viable market system in Russia. To this end, the broad themes or metapolicies of his program were to strengthen the state and accelerate rule-of-law development. The latter theme entailed stepping up the pace of post-soviet law reform, including providing new impetus and greater funding for judicial institution building, as well as reinforcing implementation discipline for law, decrees, and court decisions.

Putin's overarching metapolitical emphasis on intensified state building, or in Western conceptual language, "bringing the state back in," involved reasserting federal executive authority over the runaway provinces, and establishing a single, unified legal space within the Russian Federation. The legal instruments to carry out these objectives included his May 2000 presidential decree creating seven federal districts led by powerful presidential envoys, and several new laws which restructured the Federation Council, and gave the president power to remove from office regional or republican chief executives and legislators who persisted in flagrantly defying the federal constitution and laws. These new policies and laws, however, were not without controversy.[27]

Constitutional Quandary: Implementation Versus Reform

Putin's specific policies to carry out his larger objectives evoked sharp debate and opened a conceptual divide among the Russian political elite. The quandary was over whether the president's extensive reform of federal relations constituted implementation of heretofore underutilized constitutional authority as he argued, or if it represented systemic changes in the polity requiring the more politically arduous and legally complex route of constitutional amendment which his critics claimed. In effect, the issue of constitutional revision, which had dogged his predecessor and had never gone away, reemerged to confront President Putin. How eventually the current debate is resolved will no doubt effect the longer term legitimacy and efficacy of the president's program, as well as the extent of compliance or resistance to it.

Putin's Case for Constitutional Implementation

Politically, Putin understandably sought to avoid the time-consuming and difficult path of revising the constitution which, depending on the scope, would require ratification by either two-thirds of the federation subjects or a nationwide referendum. Hence, he asserted the legal rationale that the 1993 constitution had not been fully implemented (i.e., much of the mandated enabling legislation had still not been enacted by 2000), and, in addition, that certain powers granted to the chief executive had been underutilized. Neither claim was unfounded.

Specifically, Putin and his advisors defended his package of legal policies by reference to relevant clauses of the constitution.[28] His decree on the seven super envoys was based on Yeltsin's antecedent presidential representative system (Art. 83.j), as well as on the constitution's "power vertical" clause (Art. 77.2). Putin's law restructuring the upper house rested on the distinction in the dual clause on the Federal Assembly, calling for "forming" (*poriadok formirovaniia*) the Federation Council while electing (*poriadok vyborov*) the State Duma (Art. 96.2). Finally, the president justified his new legal power providing for federal sanctions against provincial officials engaging in unlawful actions on the basis of a cluster of constitutional clauses—the rarely used presidential authority to suspend unconstitutional provincial executive acts (Art. 85.2) along with the clause declaring the president the guarantor of the constitution (Art. 80.2), and a subparagraph of Article 71.d establishing exclusive federal authority over the organization of subnational governments in the Russian Federation.

The Critics' Arguments for Constitutional Reform

Putin's critics were some of the more influential republican presidents and regional governors who in their capacity as senators in the old Federation Council faced eviction from the upper house. Simultaneously, as provincial chief executives, they perceived the potential threat to their local power in the president's sanctions law. Politically, they sought to buy time through extended negotiation within the framework of a constitutional convention to be called for the purpose of drafting a new federal charter. In that arena, they hoped to be able to protect gains obtained through bilateral, power-sharing treaties negotiated with Yeltsin, as well as to defend the sovereignty claims in their provincial constitutions and regional charters, by constitutionalizing both in a new or substantially revised Russian Constitution. Toward this end, the upper house attempted to promote passage of the necessary enabling legislation, a long-pending draft Federal Constitutional Law on the Constitutional Assembly, but without success.

The legal rationale of the president's critics was on firmer ground. Basically, they argued that Putin's federal reform policies, which dramatically altered the existing correlation of forces between center and periphery by means of decrees and laws, were unconstitutional. Systemic changes of such scale and breadth, the critics insisted, could only be accomplished through fundamental constitutional revision. In essence, they rejected "constitutional revolution by stealth."[29]

Their constitutional claims were essentially arrayed against Putin's May decree and the law empowering him to remove elected officials from office. The critics' particular objection to the May decree was the president's grant of authority to his special envoys to bring republican constitutions and regional charters on the one hand, and provincial legislation on the other, into compliance with the constitution and laws of the Russian Federation. In defense of their laws, the governors and presidents pointed out that the constitution's "Joint Jurisdiction" clause of fourteen parts which had been intended to sort out the respective jurisdictions of the national and subnational governments remained mostly unimplemented absent the mandated federal enabling statutes (Art. 72). Therefore, their reasoning went, the longstanding legal vacuum in center-periphery relations had been filled through bilateral treaty negotiations and local legislation, in theory a not unreasonable position to which the president subsequently responded by actively promoting enactment of the necessary defining legislation.

Putin's critics also challenged the sanctions law, considered especially offensive by provincial politicians, with other constitutional arguments. These included the citizens' fundamental right to elect their political leaders (Art. 32.2), as well as the elective principle implied within the constitution's clause on organizing provincial governments (Art. 71.1). Both of these constitutionally based claims, the critics argued, trumped the federal assertion of power to dismiss provincial chief executives and dissolve regional assemblies.

Resistance to Federal
Restructuring and Compromise

Behind the constitutional debate and a pending petition to the Constitutional Court by a leading presidential critic, provincial resistance to Putin's federal restructuring program was growing. Various strong governors and well-entrenched republican presidents contested, filibustered, and delayed the presidential envoys' harmonization campaign to bring provincial fundamental laws into conformity with the federal constitution. Other leaders hectored, harassed, and stalled various aspects of the legal standardization program to bring local legislation into compliance with federal law. A few bold provincial executives even objected to the federal government's reassertion of its right to unilaterally appoint local officials of branch federal agencies throughout the federation.

For the most part, Putin's envoys had successes in their mission to recapture the runaway federation subjects and create a unified, national legal order in spite of the resistance. Still, Putin, no doubt with the 2004 presidential election in mind, took note of the resistance and showed a willingness to make strategic compromises in certain areas to pacify the provincial barons. These included supporting an amendment to the law on term limits for governors and presidents, allowing certain executives to seek reelection beyond a second term. On the issue of federal personnel appointments in the provinces, concessions were made to consult the chief executive involved, especially on key law enforcement appointments. Finally, Putin established a commission to demarcate federal and subnational jurisdictions and propose the necessary legislation to give content and effect to the constitution's "Joint Jurisdiction" clause.

Conclusion

In various ways, President Putin demonstrated political flexibility without threatening the essential integrity of his core program to strengthen the Russian state and restore legal discipline.

As a result, the central state is stronger, and the law more predictable and transparent if not sufficiently equitable to satisfy rule-of-law standards. Putin continues to pursue these objectives toward the ultimate goal of building a more effective, democratic state and creating a comprehensive rule-of-law society in Russia. What tests lie ahead for Russia and whether the country will stumble again or attain its goal remain questions for the future. Meanwhile, democratization in Russia continues as a work in progress.

CHAPTER EIGHT

Democracy and Counterinsurgency in Central Asia

GREGORY GLEASON

In this study of democratization in Central Asia, Gregory Gleason examines the relationship between pro forma institutional change and the survival of traditional authoritarian patterns of behavior rooted deeply in civil societies that, even during the soviet era, combined elements of modernity with traditional practices. He concludes that the post-communist states of the region are not functioning democracies in the dual sense that authoritarian presidents, themselves former high-level officials of the communist era, have clung to power, and that viable civil societies and party systems have not emerged to reign in their control. Paradoxically, he argues that one of the greatest threats to any prospect of real democratization comes from insurgency movements that would create Islamic states to replace the secular pseudo-democracies that have emerged as a consequence of the disintegration of the Soviet Union.

Prior to the outbreak of the Afghanistan conflict in the autumn of 2001, an increase in insurgency throughout Central Asia was imperiling the modest gains of a decade of national consolidation in the states of Central Asia. Confronted by growing religious and political extremism, terrorism, and national separatism, the governments of the region redoubled security measures, imposed new constraints upon domestic political opposition, and weakened their resolve to carry out the processes of modern governance in accordance with international standards. The governments' counterinsurgency measures had a goal of neutralizing terrorists and bandits, but the efforts cast a wide net, ensnaring legitimate critics and opponents as well as many innocent victims. Civil rights activists and proponents of good governance practices in the region found themselves confronting governments that were increasingly inflexible and hostile to differences of opinion and approach.

The terrorist attack on the United States in September 2001 transformed the situation in Central Asia. Enormous effort on the part of the American-led coalition against terrorism in Afghanistan began shaping a new security terrain for the entire West Asian region. The problems of political extremism, terrorism, drug trafficking, and lawlessness that were imperiling normalization in the Central Asian states suddenly drew the attention of the entire world community. New prospects appeared on the horizon for restoring the momentum of the democratizing processes that followed the fall of communism.

How promising are these democratic prospects? What institutional bases are there for the promotion of democratic change in the countries of Central Asia? What features of local political and cultural institutions may serve to strengthen these processes? What features may weaken or threaten them? In this chapter, we respond to these questions by surveying the first decade of transition in Central Asia in broad compass.

A Decade of Independence

If measured in absolute terms, progress toward democracy in all the Central Asian states during the first decade of independence has been modest. Prior to the breakup of the USSR, leaders of the communist party governed the Central Asian region as a whole. Each of the Central Asian republics was administratively managed by a local communist party organization in conjunction with the USSR's economic ministries. These institutions were subordinated to Moscow-based all-union organizations. The independent countries that emerged in Central Asia from the breakup of the USSR—Kazakhstan, Kyrgyzstan, Tajikistan, Turkmenistan, and Uzbekistan—were conceived during the soviet period. None of these "republics" ever existed as an independent state prior to the soviet period. They were artificial creations, products of the soviet Marxist theory of economic and political development for underdeveloped regions. During the soviet period these "socialist republics" were not countries at all, but regions managed by Moscow political authorities. Little republic-to-republic interaction took place. Interaction among the

Central Asian republics was routinely managed by and through Moscow. Furthermore, despite the religious, cultural, and linguistic traditions these republics shared with the countries of the Middle East, China, and West Asia, the Central Asian region was physically separated from the rest of the world by nearly impassible southern and eastern soviet frontiers and by decades of northward-oriented infrastructure development.[1]

When independence came to the Central Asian countries, the soviet-era leadership embraced it with enthusiasm. The opportunities for democratic progress were substantial. Initially the reform trends were clearly oriented in the right direction. Each of the republics' communist party leaders—quickly donning robes of nationalist protectors of the interests of the newly independent states—spoke out in favor of the establishment of secular, democratic independent governments, market economic relations, and foreign relations recognizing international standards.[2] Kazakhstan's Nursultan Nazarbaev was the most forthright of the leaders in this regard, explaining to his colleagues and fellow citizens that the rejection of communism and the adoption of international standards were "merely common sense."[3]

The countries became members of major multilateral international organizations, joining the United Nations, the World Bank, and the International Monetary Fund in 1992.[4] Kazakhstan, Kyrgyzstan, Uzbekistan, Tajikistan, and Turkmenistan all joined the European Bank for Reconstruction and Development in 1992. Kazakhstan, Kyrgyzstan, Tajikistan, and Uzbekistan joined the Asian Development Bank. The countries engaged in the process of accession to the World Trade Organization (Kyrgyzstan in December 1998 would become the first post-soviet country to enter the WTO). Each of the countries began making progress in establishing national sovereignty and transforming the political institutions of the communist period. Kazakhstan and Kyrgyzstan made notable progress in specific areas toward adopting international standards of good governance, eventually adopting tax laws and civil codes that were considered to be among the best of the post-communist world. Uzbekistan, despite a continuing inability to liberalize prices and adjust its currency to international practice, strove energetically to develop a commercially oriented welfare state. Tajikistan, torn by war and internal divisions, clearly moved in the direction of national reconciliation following a series of cease-fire agreements with the opposition and then, in June 1997, the signing of a peace accord and a pact for national reconciliation. Even Turkmenistan, the least successful in making the psychological transition of an open, modern society, made some headway in attempting to harmonize its laws with international practice.

Today as we reflect on a decade of independence, the initial glow of democratic promise for the countries of Central Asia has faded considerably.

Important elements of economic and structural reform have been put in place, but true democratic reform has proved elusive. After a decade of independence, "presidents" governed all the states of Central Asia.[5] All the countries had institutionalized this practice by establishing "presidential" systems, giving the leaders the power to rule by decree with the force of "constitutional law." In all the cases these were leaders who came from the former soviet *apparat* or high rungs of the soviet establishment. While all of the countries had conducted elections, none of the governments can be said to have fully conformed to international standards for free and fair elections. Three of the governments had former communist leaders who extended their mandate in extra-constitutional ways. None of the governments had what could be described as an independent judiciary. None of the governments established a functioning legislature with true powers of the purse. Even in the most open and liberal of the countries—Kazakhstan and Kyrgyzstan—the parliaments had been routed by presidential decree.[6]

In terms of internationally accepted assessments of democratic development, the Central Asian societies have not realized their full potential. The benchmark criteria for measuring democratic progress used by Freedom House rank the Central Asian countries as the lowest of the transition countries.[7] The annual Human Rights reports of the U.S. State Department underscore the authoritarian nature of government in all the societies.[8] Nor can the Central Asian states be said to pass key institutional tests of democratic reform. When asked whether a situation has developed in which "the government can be changed by elections as opposed to one where elections are changed by the government," the answer is no.[9] When asked whether a situation has developed in which "none of the major political actors, parties, or organized interests, forces, or institutions consider that there is any alternative to democratic processes to gain power, and . . . no political institution or group has a claim to veto the action of democratically elected decision makers," the answer is no.[10] When asked whether "the institutional arrangements . . . a façade behind which patrimonial rulers at the center, in the regions, and in other sectors, continue to claim absolute authority over their subjects, or has constitutional democracy in fact begun to tame *vlast*," the answer is the former.[11]

Democratic State Reform, Islamic Insurgency, and Counterinsurgency

There is little agreement regarding what constitutes democratic change in the Central Asian societies.[12] There is even some disagreement over whether the

East European model of change is appropriate in the circumstances of Central Asia.[13] The inability of the Central Asian societies to move as quickly as desirable toward democratic functioning is a reflection of both the insufficiency of the model of democratic change and the incapacity of the societies to carry out the necessary structural changes to implement the model.[14] The insufficiency of the model and the inability of the states to implement it have created a number of distortions in democratic practice in Central Asia. First, the creation of democratic institutions without democratic process has produced "show-case" institutions and a version of what some have called "Potemkin democracy." The institutions and procedures appear to be in place, but do not appear to function. In the most recent presidential election in Uzbekistan, the incumbent president, Islam Karimov, had such an overwhelming advantage that even his only registered opponent, Abdulkhafiz Dzhalalov, publicly announced that he too would vote for the incumbent.[15]

Second, the inherent tension between the sequencing of democratic and market-oriented change has strengthened the hand of despots seeking pretexts for harsh policies. The success of privatization and market change in Central Asia, as in many other transitional contexts, has had the effect of disenfranchising large sectors of the country economically and socially while at the same time giving them the ballot to express their resentment at the cause of their immiseration.[16] To stave off criticism, the leaders have thus marginalized the electoral process to a state not unlike that of electoral practice in the former USSR.

Third, that democratic change which has taken place has been top-down in origin, orientation, and effect. The anticorruption campaign in Kazakhstan, for instance, is managed by the National Security Service; the human rights committee in Tajikistan is essentially managed by the Ministry of Justice; and the most influential NGOs in Uzbekistan are those belonging to a relatively small list of government approved and sponsored organizations.

Fourth, the states of Central Asia exist in a security environment as well as in a development environment. Security considerations often took precedence in decisions regarding development strategies.[17] Kazakhstan, as heir to a substantial portion of the USSR nuclear weapons capability at the time of independence, had certain advantages in its diplomatic interactions with European and North American countries. Uzbekistan and Tajikistan, however, inherited the legacies of lawlessness and underdevelopment that resulted from a decade-long civil war in Afghanistan. As the Central Asian states began to respond to the conditions and constraints of transition, reflecting their leadership priorities and cultural priorities, exploiting their comparative economic advantages, and conscious of guarding their newfound independence in an insecure regional context, they adopted significantly different development strategies.

These contextual aspects of the transition to democracy in Central Asia have played crucial roles in limiting the progress of reform. But in the late 1990s, a new and more formidable challenge to democratic reform arose. This period witnessed a progressive intensification of political conflict that threatens to undermine what little progress that has taken place. The swelling pressures of political insurgency in Central Asia came to threaten even the limited gains of the past decade. A confluence of potent religious ideologies and economic interests in Central Asia was fueling implacable opposition to the authoritarian but secular, post-communist governments. The three legs of this triangle were nationalist-based separatism, Islamic antisecularism, and the drive to control markets in Central Asia, particularly the lucrative drug trade. Beset by fears of terrorism, organized crime, migration, and the loss of political control, the governments of the region struggled to re-impose control over their borders and order over their domestic societies. Borders were reinforced, trade was interrupted, and the movement of people was halted across many of the Central Asian borders. Uzbekistan, the country at the center of the storm, began mining the more difficult to regiment parts of its borders in summer 2000. The highly regimented border with Tajikistan was periodically closed. Air service between Tajikistan's capital, Dushanbe, and Uzbekistan's capital, Tashkent, was reopened in summer 2000 for the first time since 1993. But service was again cancelled a short time later by Uzbekistan, citing fears of terrorism.

The call to jihad—a Moslem holy war—in Central Asia is an extension of the conflicts of the Afghanistan civil war. Over the past few years the cultural confrontations that emerged from the war have became intertwined with Russia's imbroglio in Chechnya and, more recently, with the separatist movement in Xinjiang-Uigur Autonomous Republic of China. The Central Asian states themselves underwent a series of insurgency shocks. The antigovernment uprising in Hujand, Tajikistan, in November 1998 dramatized that the conflicts of the Tajikistan war had not been fully resolved by the Tajikistan peace accord and reconciliation process. Just three months later, Uzbekistan was shaken by terrorist bombings in Tashkent in February 1999. The Kyrgyzstan's hostage crisis in the Fergana Valley in August 1999 drew Kyrgyzstan into the situation. In August 2000 a new hostage crisis in Kyrgyzstan refocused attention on the country's vulnerability. In September, an irregular military force had penetrated into Uzbekistan within one hundred kilometers from the capital. In early 2001 the Central Asian capitals were rife with speculation.

In evaluating the implications of Central Asia's insurgency politics for democratic change, it is important to recognize crucial differences among the states and regions of Central Asia. In the following sections of this chapter, we review the countries from the point of view of their internal dynamics. Each of the countries offers a distinctive portrait consisting of its unique politics, economics, and culture. Later, we reassemble this picture in terms of the interaction of the states.

Kazakhstan and Globalization

Significant progress toward establishing a policy environment conducive to globalization and integration in world markets was made by Kazakhstan in the early years of independence. Kazakhstan was host to the December 1991 conference of former communist party officials that produced the "Alma-Ata Declaration," the legal instrument that brought about the end of the USSR. The Alma-Ata Declaration also established the loose coordinating community called the Commonwealth of Independent States (CIS). Kazakhstan was thus symbolically the resting place of communism and the birthplace of the postcommunist order. Kazakhstan's president, Nursultan Nazarbaev, had previously been a promoter of democratic change within the former USSR and, when the transition came, identified the new Kazakhstan government with the pro-market, democratic reform at an early point. At the Coordinating Conference on Assistance to the New Independent States that took place in Washington in January 1992, U.S. president George Bush noted that "in Central Asia, President Nazarbaev . . . [is] . . . leading the fight for reform."[18] Soon after independence, Kazakhstan's capital, Almaty, became the home for the largest international diplomatic community in Eurasia east of Moscow and west of Beijing.

The Kazakhstan government made coordinated efforts to link security and economic development. Kazakhstan signed the Helsinki Accord, the Strategic Arms Reduction Treaty (START-II), and the Lisbon Protocol in May 1992. Kazakhstan signed the Conventional Armed Forces in Europe Treaty (CFE) in June 1992. Both the START and the CFE treaties were ratified by the Kazakhstan parliament in July 1992. In December 1993, Kazakhstan ratified the nuclear Non-Proliferation Treaty (NPT). The Democratic Partnership Charter signed in Washington in February 1994 and the NATO Partnership for Peace agreement of December 1994 formalized international assurances of regional security cooperation. In December 1994, Great Britain, the United States, and Russia offered Kazakhstan joint comprehensive guarantees of security. The government of China later joined this agreement.

Kazakhstan took steps to integrate into the international community of nations, joining the United Nations in March 1992. Kazakhstan joined the World Bank, the International Monetary Fund (IMF), the Asian Development Bank (ADB), and the European Bank for Reconstruction and Development (EBRD). Kazakhstan started the process of accession to the World Trade Organization (WTO). Kazakhstan initiated a series of bilateral discussions that led to bilateral and regional trade agreements. Kazakhstan was the initiator of the CIS Customs Union, an organization that attempted to implement the goals of the CIS founding documents by maintaining a "common economic space" throughout the former USSR. Kazakhstan was the initiator of the discussions that led to the Cholpon-Ata Regional Cooperation Agreement of April 1994 that pledged Kazakhstan, Kyrgyzstan, and Uzbekistan to observing the principle of maintaining transparent, open borders to facilitate trade and cooperation.

Kazakhstan adopted a tradable currency in November 1993, liberalized prices, and started privatization of major sectors of the economy including industry, telecommunications, and energy. Kazakhstan lifted virtually all subsidies on consumer goods in September 1994 and phased out many industrial subsidies before the end of the year. Kazakhstan commenced the process of balancing the public and private sectors with a series of major reductions in force of public employees and privatization of state-owned public service facilities. Kazakhstan moved quickly to establish a reasonably stable legal and regulatory structure for commerce and civil rights. Kazakhstan adopted a progressive Civil Code, establishing the framework for commercial transactions and property rights. Kazakhstan adopted a modern banking system, a securities exchange system, bankruptcy legislation, and a system of public utilities management. Kazakhstan established the framework for a new system of government fiscal management, with a modern system for managing public external debt, a new tax code, and a new system of tax administration.

During 1994 Kazakhstan experienced very high inflation rates, although this stabilized in 1995. During 1995–1996, the expansion program under Premier Akezhan Kazhegeldin was producing good results, but by 1997 the Asian crisis shook commodity prices, forcing the price of oil down by nearly 40 percent and nonferrous metal prices down by margins as high as 40 percent. Inflation rose again in 1998 in association with the Russian financial collapse. Kazakhstan's high degree of reliance on Russian Federation buyers for oil, gas, and metals meant that the 1998 financial crisis in Russia had immediate impact on Kazakhstan's foreign sales. Given that oil and metals constitute roughly 60 percent of Kazakhstan's exports, the country's terms of trade deteriorated substantially and quickly. In response, Kazakhstan authorities initially tightened fiscal policies in mid-1998, restraining government spending and borrowing but relaxing these policies again as presidential elections approached in January 1999. In the wake of the Russian financial crisis, the Kazakhstan National Bank increased interest rates to avert hyperinflation. In April 1999 the government shifted from the existing monetary policy that allowed the government to peg the currency to the U.S. dollar to restrain wide fluctuations to a floating exchange rate. This presumably would allow the currency markets to equilibrate more quickly. Despite these economic setbacks, Nazarbaev and his government continued to maintain support for post-communist reform. At the critical juncture following the collapse of financial markets in Russia, when some Central Asian politicians were arguing for the adoption of a neo-mercantilist Asian path, Nazarbaev held firm to the reform programs, pledging "to continue the promising advances toward an independent, open and free market economy."[19]

Nursultan Nazarbaev has been criticized for attempting to monopolize political power.[20] The Kazakhstan government has been criticized for the way in which Nazarbaev's leading opponent in the January 1999 presidential election, Akezhan Kazhegeldin, was excluded from participation in the election.[21] The Kazakhstan government has been criticized for failing to curb rent-seeking behavior of minor officials and for failing to create a policy environment that faithfully implements the strong legal and regulatory framework that is on the books. Kazakhstan ranked eighty four on the Transparency International Corruption Perception Index, a ranking better than that of neighboring Uzbekistan but not far removed from countries with notorious levels of corruption such as Uganda and Pakistan.[22] Nazarbaev himself has been accused of giving in to clanism and family relations that could lead to consequences similar to those experienced by the Suharto regime in Indonesia.

Kyrgyzstan on the Reform Path

Kygyzstan is a country that upon independence immediately adopted a neo-liberal approach to the problems of transition. In foreign trade liberalization efforts, Kyrgyzstan's record of achievement has been unmatched. Kyrgyzstan was the first ex-soviet country to follow the advice of the international donor community and withdraw from the ruble zone. It was the first Central Asian country to adopt a Western-style civil code, a modern legal and regulatory framework, to liberalize prices, to overhaul its financial and banking system, to privatize large industrial facilities, and to adopt a relatively open, competitive political system.[23] In 1998 a change in the constitution made

Kyrgyzstan one of the first post-ovate countries to sanction private owner-ship of land.

To promote foreign invest the Kyrgyzstan government established the Committee on Foreign Investments (Goskominvest). The Committee served as an ombudsman to assist foreign investors by providing information and business assistance, simplifying visas and permits, and helping with registra-tion, licensing, and customs procedures. A comprehensive foreign investment law was adopted in September 1997. The law broke new ground in the CIS in serving as regulatory foundation for creating an attractive policy environ-ment for foreign investment in the country. Reflecting its enthusiasm for entering the international trading system, Kyrgystan in December 1998 became the first CIS country to join the World Trade Organization.

Kyrgyzstan was initially relatively unconcerned about security issues, leaving these questions to its more powerful neighbors, Kazakhstan and Uzbekistan. Security issues reemerged with the onset of the Tajikistan war, but Kyrgyzstan's commitment of peacekeeping troops in Tajikistan was merely symbolic and was soon withdrawn. Security problems reemerged in summer 1999 with a hostage crisis that focused attention on the potential for destabilization throughout the entire Central Asian region. Coordination with Uzbekistan, Russia, and other outside actors brought the hostage crisis to a conclusion, but the problems of religious extremism, terrorism, and law-lessness remained.[24]

However, Kyrgyzstan's limited resource endowment and trade depend-ence constrained its real progress.[25] Like the other post-communist states, the Kyrgyzstan economy underwent severe economic contraction in 1993–1995. Kyrgyzstan began to rebound from the post-soviet economic depression before the other CIS countries, showing economic growth as early as 1996. The government budget deficit as a proportion of GDP was cut in half dur-ing the period 1995 through 1997.

Kyrgyzstan introduced the most determined, pro-reform policies in the Central Asian region, perhaps in the entire CIS. Largely thanks to the efforts of its pro-reform president, Askar Akaev, Kyrgyzstan's pro-reform posture quickly made the country the *Wunderkind* of the international donor com-munity. But the promised benefits of rising prosperity remained elusive for the majority of the country's citizens. For the first five years of independence per capita assistance dollars in Kyrgyzstan far exceeded levels in other Eurasian countries. Were it not for foreign aid, Kyrgyzstan's domestic reform efforts might not have been politically sustainable. This fact reinforces the necessity for the Kyrgyzstan government to maintain its neo-liberal orientation.

Petro-Dollars and Sultanism in Turkmenistan

Turkmenistan was a largely underdeveloped socialist republic during the soviet period. With the exception of the natural gas industry, the minimal economic activity that existed in Turkmenistan was maintained by soviet central subsidies. Industry unrelated to the gas and oil complex was generally not commercially viable. The country's specialization in cotton production was based upon massive irrigation subsidies that promoted highly inefficient and environmentally damaging agriculture. As soon as soviet-era subsidies came to an end, most of the nonsubsistence agriculture and non-gas related industry immediately became insolvent.

With an estimated 2.7 trillion cubic meters in natural gas reserves and additional potential reserves estimated at 14 trillion cubic meters, Turkmenistan is the second-largest natural gas producer in the former Soviet Union and the fourth-largest producer in the world. Yet the country's source of gas revenue provided the basis not for broad-based prosperity but for an intense, highly personalistic nationalism revolving around the country's soviet-era communist party boss, Saparmurad Niyazov. Niyazov adopted an assertive posture of national self-reliance based on its gas and oil wealth that he termed the policy of Turkmenistan's "positive neutrality." In practice, the policy meant three things. First, Turkmenistan sought to maintain as much distance as possible from Russia without giving up the big Russian gas market and, most of all, without giving up access to Western gas markets that for the first decade of independence Russia continued to control. Second, it meant wary policies of self-interest with Turkmenistan's southern neighbors. Third, it meant drawing into Turkmenistan foreign investment and foreign commercial debt to the greatest extent possible in order to revitalize the gas-related industry and build a Kuwait-style emirate in Turkmenistan.

In 1998 Turkmenistan produced 13,284 million cubic meters of gas, down from 17,322 million cubic meters in 1997. Turkmenistan produced 6,280 thousand tons of oil in 1998, down from 4,481 thousand tons in 1997. Turkmenistan's gas industry is not limited by capacity. Turkmenistan can expand the output of natural gas with the turn of a valve. The constraints on production arise from the physical transport capacity. In late 1997, Turkmenistan began exporting gas to Iran through a newly completed pipeline. The Turkmenistan government has also sought to develop new pipelines for access to external gas markets. The Turkmenistan government has lobbied hard for international cooperation in the construction of a gas pipeline across the Caspian, through Azerbaijan, Georgia, and the Turkish port of Ceyhan to Western consumers.

Turkmenistan's hydrocarbon resources offer great long-term potential for economic development. But, if past management practice is any indicator of future practices, it also implies certain developmental vulnerabilities. Turkmenistan was an early beneficiary of price liberalization after the disintegration of the USSR. This enabled Turkmenistan to charge world market prices for the gas it supplied to its former soviet-era customers in Ukraine, Georgia, Russia, and other countries. On the other hand, the existing transportation infrastructure made Turkmenistan dependent upon customers in countries that were not in a position to pay. Accordingly, gas was supplied sporadically on credits that exceeded the consumers' ability to pay. A large proportion of Turkmenistan's gas sales were conducted on an inefficient barter basis. This led to serious problems of external arrears and led to a declining gas output. The total of arrears—mainly to Armenia, Azerbaijan, Georgia, and Ukraine—rose to $1.2 billion and the Turkmenistan government interrupted some gas exports in 1997, greatly exacerbating political tensions in the region. Following complex negotiations involving trading partners, governments, commercial banks, and international organizations, many of the debts were rescheduled and the Turkmenistan government resumed gas exports.

While the oil and gas sectors account for a large proportion of foreign currency earnings, they produce incomes that are restricted to a relatively small circle and form only a small portion of overall employment. Agriculture and animal husbandry, in contrast, account for about 20 percent of GDP and more than 60 percent of overall employment.[26] Turkmenistan is among the top-ten cotton producers worldwide. The production of cotton increased in 1999 to 1,200,000 tons, up from 707,000 tons in 1998 and from 630,000 tons in 1997. In an effort to establish food self-sufficiency, Turkmenistan subsidized wheat production leading to an increase to 1,240 thousand tons, up from 655,000 tons in 1997.

Despite some economic gains in recent years, much of Turkmenistan's population (48 percent by World Bank estimates) is living below the poverty level.[27] The government has adopted populist policies to support the social safety net. Since 1992 the government has subsidized housing and related utilities (e.g., electricity, water, gas, sanitation, heating, and hot water) virtually free and subsidizing key consumer goods (e.g., bread, flour, and baby food). According to social indicators, however, the safety net is far from sound. Local gas and water supplies, while without cost to the consumers, are frequently interrupted. The country's infant mortality rate (39.6 per 1,000 live births) is among the highest in the region and life expectancy (63.9 years) is among the lowest in the former USSR. The average family size is 5.6. The 1998 GDP per capita is estimated to be $640.

The international development community has not been satisfied with Turkmenistan's progress toward the adoption of democratic norms of policy and practice. In April 2000 the EBRD took the unprecedented step of suspending its public sector lending programs to Turkmenistan on the basis of the government's unwillingness to implement agreed-upon structural reforms.[28] Turkmenistan's economic development in the years ahead rests upon the country's ability to break out of the cycle of excessive government controls and crony capitalism toward a modern economy based upon international standards.

Uzbekistan's "Asian Path"

Shortly after the collapse of the USSR, Uzbekistan was widely referred to as "the last redoubt of communism" (*kommunisticheskii zapovednik*).[29] Uzbekistan's strong-handed leader, Islam Karimov, only a few years ago a dutiful communist, quickly became an enthusiastic champion of an independent political path and an Uzbek cultural renewal.[30] In ways reminiscent of the actions of Turkey's Kemal Ataturk, Karimov engineered a determined national consolidation. Government, economics, culture—the entire spectrum of policy arenas—were subsumed into the drive to "recover" Uzbekistan. The Russian language, uniformly prevalent just a few years ago, was quickly replaced by the Uzbek language. The neo-mercantilist Uzbekistan government aggressively sought diplomatic and commercial ties with a host of countries.

In Uzbekistan the political leadership played the key role in the determination of policy. When independence took place the existing power structures reconstituted themselves as an independent government. A political opposition did emerge upon independence, but the leading faction of beneficiaries of the old soviet system used their established influence to quickly brush the opposition aside. The new constitution adopted in December 1992 merely institutionalized the existing political system. The government publicly emphasized the symbolism of Central Asian traditions of strong but benign leadership.

During the first decade of independence, politics has been far from pluralistic or competitive in Uzbekistan. The political process is carefully monitored and controlled. Restrictions on the electoral registration process make it possible for the government to exercise a determining influence on the pre-selection of candidates. In theory, the judiciary is independent. In practice, however, the capacity of the judiciary to function as an independent branch of government is limited. While the constitution describes the legislature as the highest organ of power, in fact the country has a unitary, "presidential form of government." In reality, the branches are not coequal or balanced; the executive branch is dominant in virtually all matters. The Uzbekistan government's record on human rights is considered to be negative by most international human rights organizations.[31] Rights to speech, assembly, and religion are circumscribed by the government. There are documented cases in which the security forces have arbitrarily arrested or detained human rights activists, religious activists, and ethnic group activists on false charges.

At the time of independence, the Uzbek economy was more diversified than the economies of the other four Central Asian states. It included agriculture, light industry, heavy industry and important branches in primary commodities. Following the disintegration of the Soviet Union, Uzbekistan's economy was insulated from much of the economic decline that afflicted other former soviet states due to its labor-intensive economy based on agriculture and mineral extraction. The Uzbekistan government embraced the idea of market-based commercial relations, announcing that the country would be "pro-business."[32] Rapid growth in 1992–1995 in oil and gas production allowed Uzbekistan to eliminate oil imports and increase gas exports. Uzbekistan shifted some of its crop acreage from cotton to grains to boost food self-sufficiency.

While these were positive outcomes, they resulted in delaying the structural reforms that Uzbekistan's neighbors, particularly Kazakhstan and Kyrgyzstan, implemented.[33] Many elements of the soviet system were quickly rejected in Uzbekistan. But at the same time many elements of the soviet-era administrative system merely were replaced by an indigenous, state-controlled administrative system that was itself top-heavy and stultifying. In the years to follow, the Uzbekistan government pursued foreign economic policies that stressed a gradual, step-by-step approach to the adoption of macroeconomic reform and market-oriented structural reforms. This conservative transition strategy emphasized establishing self-sufficiency in energy and food grains, exporting primary commodities, particularly cotton and gold, and creating an internally oriented services market.

In September 1996, in connection with a shortfall in foreign reserves, the Uzbekistan Ministry of Finance imposed a system of import contract registration. The goal of the system was to ensure that scarce foreign currency was used primarily to import capital rather than buy consumer goods, particularly luxury goods and items. However, in practice the system severely limited the availability of foreign exchange for all sectors of the economy and retarded economic activity. In subsequent years the Ministry of Finance periodically acted to make the system yet more rigorous as foreign currency reserves continued to dwindle. An overvalued currency also can be expected to lead to the depletion of foreign reserves, which, in turn, can bring about pressures for severe import restrictions and, eventually, the collapse of the free trade policy.[34] Uzbekistan should be encouraging foreign trade for these reasons. Yet in recent years trade between Uzbekistan and its neighbors has contracted sharply. Trade with Kazakhstan shrank from $393 million in 1997 to only $233 million in 1999. Similarly, trade with Kyrgyzstan dropped from $103 million in 1996 to only $43 million in 1999.[35]

An overvalued currency tends to channel trade into narrow and more easily managed sectors. It thus may appear to offer a solution to capital flight. However, there are great efficiency losses associated with currency overvaluation. It requires strict regulation of financial transactions, imposing a heavy burden of monitor and sanctions. Well-connected parties with access to cheap, government-financed foreign exchange and import licenses benefit greatly from this situation. These parties can be expected to lobby to maintain the situation despite great efficiency losses and the corresponding damage to the public interest. The bureaucratic burden of maintaining strict currency controls can be expensive and it unavoidably creates an unfavorable climate for trade. A policy of overvaluation creates a rationale for extending police sanctions even to the extent of replacing the goal of public safety with that of regulating private behavior. It can give rise to an incentive structure in which private parties have an interest in avoiding or evading the legal framework through various forms of side payments and inducements.

Since medieval times in certain oasis cities of Central Asia government positions were sold rather than earned. This was economically rational because government positions carry high prestige and an official can earn an income to pay his superiors by levying "extra" axes, fines, and service fees. In Central Asian cities this was considered a standard practice. Such practices are alive today. They continue and constitute a drain upon the efficiency and equity of government. As one observer noted, "At almost every level of government, 'extra' rates and tariffs are set for otherwise free services, and no query can be resolved without under-the-table cash. Structures supposedly created to cope with corruption exist only to eliminate the undesirables."[36] Use of children for agricultural labor—long a source of external criticism of the soviet economic system—has intensified in the decade since the collapse of communism.[37]

The Uzbekistan government's extensive counterinsurgency campaign has contributed to increased dominance of Uzbekistan's public decision making by the executive branch of government since 1998. Uzbekistan, sharing borders with war-torn Afghanistan and Tajikistan, is the target of terrorist organizations such as the Islamic Movement of Uzbekistan, a group that has claimed responsibility for terrorist attacks and has announced that its goal is to forcibly overthrow the Uzbekistan government. The government's counterinsurgency campaign has involved a sweeping crackdown on terrorist groups.[38] A Helsinki Human Rights Watch report issued in March 2000 documents physical mistreatment of defenders by police, and law enforcement agencies' use of psychological harassment, including prolonged solitary confinement, public denunciation, intimidating, and intrusive police surveillance, and threats of arrest.[39] The counterinsurgency campaign has cast a wide net that also ensnared the regime's legitimate critics as well as numerous innocent victims. Numerous cases were reported by international human rights organizations of violations of human rights and Uzbekistan civil law at the hands of Uzbekistan law enforcement authorities.

War and Reconstruction in Tajikistan

Tajikistan is a small, poor, resource-rich, landlocked country in one of the most inaccessible parts of Asia. The country's mountainous terrain and inadequate transportation and communication infrastructure are key factors in the nine years of severe economic contraction that have taken place since national independence in 1991. The civil strife that immediately followed independence resulted in further deterioration of systems of transportation and communication and contributed to the interruption of normal trade relations with Tajikistan's immediate neighbors.[40] As much as 40 percent of the country's population was directly affected by the civil strife. As many as 50,000 people lost their lives, 600,000 were displaced, and 60,000 fled to neighboring countries.[41] Thousands of women were widowed and tens of thousands of children were orphaned. The ravages of war on Tajikistan were compounded by a series of natural calamities that beset the country, including torrential rains, floods, and earthquakes. Floods destroyed and damaged thousands of homes, buildings, bridges, and public structures.

Physically remote and economically isolated from its neighbors by fears of the spread of political instability, Tajikistan's social and economic indicators cascaded downward in the post-independence period.[42] In 1996 the Tajikistan government adopted a reform strategy promoted by the International Monetary

Fund and the World Bank. The key elements of the strategy included establishing monetary and fiscal discipline, price liberalization and stabilization, and improving resource utilization. The Tajikistan government adopted a policy concentrating on achieving six basic objectives: national reconciliation, macroeconomic stability, poverty reduction, providing basic services, rehabilitating infrastructure, and promoting human resource development. The gradual economic stabilization that followed upon the resumption of normality gave rise to a new optimism for Tajikistan's economic recovery and post-conflict development prospects. In June 1997 the opposing civil war factions reached a peace settlement that, over the past three years, has ushered in a period of reconciliation and reconstruction.

The smallest and most constrained of the countries of the Eurasian region is Tajikistan. While it would have been classified as a lower-middle-income economy in the former soviet period, Tajikistan has become one of the world's poorest countries.[43] It is probable that Tajikistan would have moved decisively in the direction of structural reform initially if the country had not fallen prey to an internal contest for power in the first year of independence. The contest plunged the country into civil war.[44] The war resulted in a blockade of Tajikistan by its neighbors, further compressing the already collapsing Tajikistan economy. The modest level of civil normality that was maintained in Tajikistan was largely a result of the presence of foreign peace-keeping forces. Tajikistan's economy today is based primarily on subsistence agriculture, foreign assistance from donor organizations, barter relations with neighbors, and the commercial export of a few commodities. As much as 80 percent of Tajikistan's foreign exchange earnings result from sales of three commodities: aluminum, cotton, and illegal drugs. The metals and drugs sales are sources of revenue that, under Tajikistan's current conditions, have negligible or negative social welfare effects.

The events that precipitated the Tajikistan war took place in April and May 1992, but the underlying causes of the civil conflict are lodged in territorial and ethnic identities that long predate the soviet period. Prior to the soviet takeover of Tajikistan, no single authority ruled the peoples of Tajikistan's rugged mountains and fertile agricultural valleys. The form of government established under the USSR brought a unified rule to the region but never succeeded in disestablishing traditional regional and clan-based loyalties. The territorial division of Central Asia during the soviet period had long-enduring implications.[45] Democraticization and economic reform in the core regions of the USSR in the late 1980s brought greater self-rule to the outlying regions. In Tajikistan, this was manifested primarily in a resurgence of local territorialism rather than national self-determination.

During the soviet period Tajikistan's primary trading relations were structured around the import of manufactured and consumer goods from the north and the export of primary commodities, particularly aluminum and cotton, to northern markets in the former Soviet Union.[46] Trade was channeled through a small number of corridors, all of which passed through the former Soviet republic of Uzbekistan. Civil strife in Tajikistan interrupted shipping routes through Uzbekistan in 1992. These routes have not been reestablished for normal commercial purposes. Tajikistan's easternmost border with the People's Republic of China previously offered no commercial access to foreign markets. Tajikistan's southern border with Afghanistan has not been used for normal commercial purposes since the outbreak of the Afghanistan war in 1979. Only three major paved roads, each of which has high mountain passes making them unsuitable for most commercial traffic, traverse Tajikistan's northern border with Kyrgyzstan. The northern and southern sections of the country are linked by rail by only one rail line, which traverses Uzbekistan's territory.

The linkage between Tajikistan's foreign policy and its domestic democratization is direct. Prior to national independence a number of political parties came into existence, but during the period of civil conflict the government banned the leading opposition parties.[47] In June 1997 the government reached an accommodation with key opposition leaders, signing a peace accord and establishing a process of national reconciliation. In a national referendum in 26 September 1999 Tajikistan voters approved key changes in Tajikistan's constitution, including an extension of the presidential term of office from five to seven years and changes in the structure of the national parliament. The presidential election of November 1999 returned Imomali Rakhmonov to power. In December 1999 the Tajikistan government allowed the opposition parties to register. Parliamentary elections in February and March 2000 satisfied the reintegration schedule of the peace accord and the Commission on National Reconciliation, having satisfied its mandate, was shut down. These events, all of which took place with continuous support of the United Nations, the major foreign powers, and the major international financial institutions, reflect the close relationship between Tajikistan's interest in maintaining international standards of the international community and the changes in democratic structure and process.

Tajikistan and Russia have a special diplomatic relationship based upon three factors: long association, mutual objectives, and strategic dependency.[48] When President Imomali Rakhmonov observed in November 1999 that Tajikistan had a permanent relationship with Russia and considered Russia to be its most reliable strategic partner, he was acknowledging that the small, remote and poverty-stricken nation sees itself as having few options outside of maintaining close ties with its northern former "elder brother."[49] Why is Russia involved in Tajikistan? Russia shares no common border with Tajikistan, the once sizable Russian population largely has abandoned the country, and there is little in Tajikistan of commercial value to Russia.[50] Yet Russia is by far the largest foreign influence in the country, having maintained troops in the country continuously and having loaned Tajikistan between 1992 and 1999 more than the IMF, WB, EBRD, and ADB combined.[51]

Roots of Insurgency: Afghanistan, Tajikistan, and the Islamic Opposition

The Central Asian portions of the southern border of the former USSR were inherited from the tsarist empire, products of the nineteenth-century great power competition between Russia and Britain. The 1,200 km-long southern border of Tajikistan with Afghanistan is defined for most of its length by the Pani (Pandzh) River. Recent events in Afghanistan may be traced to the political succession that took place when the forty-year rule of Afghanistan's Zahir Shah came to an end in July 1973 at the time of the military coup by the former prime minister, Muhammad Daoud. Five years later, in April 1978, Daoud was overthrown in a coup organized by the Marxist People's Democratic Party of Afghanistan (PDPA). Although Marxist in orientation, the PDPA was anxious to move out of the sphere of influence of Moscow. After the assassination of the PDPA's leader, Nur Muhammad Taraki, in September 1979, the Soviet Union, concerned about the turn of events in neighboring Iran and the possible loss of an allied country on its sensitive southern border, responded by invading Afghanistan to establish a puppet government.

The Soviet Union sought to carry out a socialist-style "progressive" reform in Afghanistan. But the outcome was other than the USSR expected and desired; soviet occupation provoked fierce opposition, galvanizing the various regional and ethnic factions into unified opposition against the Kabul-based government. Afghanistan's seven main factions united in the *jihad* against the occupation. Invoking long-standing tradition of guerilla warfare against foreign invaders, the Mujahedeen fighters sought and received assistance from the outside world. Western powers, led by the United States, were anxious to see the USSR's aims for territorial expansion contained by an indigenous opposition. The U.S. Congress provided security aid to the Mujahedeen. Most of the assistance was funneled through Pakistan, particularly to the opposition encampments filled with Afghan refugees in Pakistan's northeastern province. Afghanistan proved to be an intractable conflict for the USSR. It was surely an important factor in the dissension that swept soviet society in the 1980s, leading to the disintegration of the country. After years of futile conflict, the Soviet Union resolved in 1986 to withdraw. The April 1988 Geneva accord devoted to demilitarization specified a date of 15 February 1989 for withdrawal of soviet troops.

The soviet leadership had initially expected that victory would be swift and sure in Afghanistan. The USSR opposed efforts early on by the UN to mediate a withdrawal of soviet troops. The United States initially pushed for a negotiated settlement, but fully expected that the USSR would not withdraw because the core interest of the USSR in occupying Afghanistan was not capture of the country but the capture of a route to a warm seaport for the soviet navy. Consequently, the United States publicly supported efforts to negotiate a withdrawal, but privately concentrated its real focus on aiding Pakistan in its support of the Mujahedeen opposition.[52] When the ovate government first became serious about the withdrawal from Afghanistan there was still an expectation that the withdrawal could be conducted "with honor" and that the soviet-installed government, or some government that was not in the end inimical to the USSR, could be stabilized. The United States, however, found the continuation of pro-soviet government in Afghanistan to be unacceptable, although little serious contemplation was given to what alternatives might exist. The United States clung to the position that a peace agreement would require that restrictions be placed on all foreign arms supplies to Afghanistan. The rationale was that this would be necessary in order to keep the Soviet Union from surreptitiously supplying friendly forces within the country even after it had withdrawn. By late summer 1987 the soviet government had made a decision to withdraw from Afghanistan even if it meant losing face and abandoning efforts to prop up the Kabul government.

As soviet troops withdrew from the country, the soviet-installed government in Afghanistan, headed by Muhammad Najibullah, who had led the country since 1986, sought to maintain rule after the expulsion of soviet troops. The seven leading parties of the Mujahedeen opposition immediately banned together to form Afghan Interim Government and displace the Najibullah government. Mujahedeen coalition was not immediately successful. It took three years before the alliance captured Kabul in April 1992. During the conflict, political control was fragmented among regionally and ethnically based war-era military chieftains. Ideological and ethnic divisions among the leaders of the wartime coalition reemerged after the fall of Kabul, as the commanders turned on one another in a contest for the ultimate control of the government. The contest quickly turned back to the instruments of war.

In the wake of the disastrous fighting among the Afghanistan factions, a new force emerged. In 1994 a coalition of Mujahedeen forces calling itself the Taliban took up arms to cleanse the country from the corruption and internal strife of the post-conflict competition among warlords. The Taliban was born as a movement in the northwestern province of Pakistan during the early 1990s. Capturing Kandahar in November 1994 and Herat in September 1995, the Taliban fighters pushed through southern and eastern Afghanistan, uniting the primarily ethnic Pashtu areas under strict Islamic rule. The Taliban succeeded in capturing Kabul in September 1996, ousting the government of Burhanuddin Rabbani and establishing Taliban supreme leader Mullah Mohammad Omar in power.

The Taliban leaders refused to negotiate and compromise with the Afghanistan regional warlords and gained rapid popularity in Afghanistan. They captured the city of Kandahar and then went on, in 1996, to capture Kabul. They claimed that their goal was to establish the world's most pure Islamic state, banning frivolities like television, music, and cinema. They proclaimed a campaign against official corruption. Their attempts to eradicate crime have been reinforced by the introduction of Islamic law, including public executions and amputations. They soon adopted regulations forbidding girls from going to school and women from working.

Opposition to the Taliban remained active, however, particularly in the northern and eastern part of the country. Commander Abdul Rashid Dostam's National Islamic Movement, consisting heavily of ethnic Uzbeks, controlled several north-central provinces. Commander Ahmad Shah Masood controlled the ethnic Tajik majority areas of the northeast.[53] The so-called Northern Alliance consists of former Mujaheddin forces which were generally united against the soviet invasion through the mid-1980s but which struggled against one another after the soviet withdrawal until again uniting in response to the Taliban. The Northern Alliance supports the internationally recognized government of Afghanistan led by President Burhanuddin Rabbani. It is composed primarily of Tajiks, Uzbeks, and some other smaller groups, and has had support in one form or another from the Central Asia governments, Russia, the United States, and Iran.

Given the illegitimate conditions under which the Taliban gained power and established political control, the UN and other international organizations were unwilling to recognize the Taliban as the legitimate government of Afghanistan, deferring decision on diplomatic credentials. The Organization of the Islamic Conference left the Afghan seat vacant until the question of legitimacy could be resolved. Major world governments and international organizations instituted sanctions against the Taliban.

All U.S. personnel at the U.S. Embassy in Kabul were evacuated in 1989, and no other diplomatic mission represents U.S. interests or provides consular services. President Clinton signed an executive order imposing financial and commercial sanctions against the Taliban in Afghanistan, a faction that currently exercises de facto control over much of the country, for their support of Osama bin Laden and his terrorist network. On 7 December 2000, the United States and Russia introduced a new sanctions resolution against the Taliban for their refusal to comply with earlier (1999) United Nations Security Council Resolution 1267, demanding that Taliban authorities turn indicted terrorist Osama bin Laden over to a country where he can be brought to justice. Bin Laden had been allied with the most fundamentalist leaders of the Mujahedeen Afghan resistance, particularly Gulbuddin Hekmatyar, the head of the group called the Islamic Party. After the fall of the soviet-backed government, Hekmatyar briefly became Afghanistan prime minister and sought to capture Kabul in an effort to dislodge more moderate Mujahedeen leaders. Hekmatyar denounced the United States and backed Iraq during the Persian Gulf War in 1991, as did bin Laden. On 20 August 1998, U.S. war fighters attacked a terrorist camp under the direction of bin Laden. The U.S. government imposed sanctions on Afghanistan in July 1999. In October 1999, the UN Security Council demanded that the Taliban surrender bin Laden.[54] The United Nations imposed sanctions on Afghanistan in November 1999.

During 1999 and 2000 the Taliban gradually extended its control northward, eventually ousting Masood's troops and capturing the city of Taloqan in September 2000.[55] After the defeat of the opposition and the fall of the northern Afghanistan provinces, the Taliban exercised authority virtually throughout the entire country. Taliban representatives immediately appealed for diplomatic recognition from the international community. The conflict moved into a new phase in early 2000 as the Taliban sought to establish diplomatic recognition as the legitimate government of Afghanistan.[56]

After the Taliban gained control in Afghanistan there was a steady escalation in the challenges to political authority in Central Asia. The hostage taking, coup attempts, and marauding detachments of armed irregulars that had grown almost commonplace in parts of war-torn Tajikistan—the small but strategically placed country bordering China and Afghanistan—spilled out into the other countries of Central Asia in late 1998. An assassination attempt on the life of Uzbekistan's president, Islam Karimov, in early 1999 signaled a new stage in Central Asia's post-independence politics. The regime's political opponents shifted from subversion to armed confrontation. With inspiration drawn from Afghanistan's Taliban, and with arms financed, at least in part, from revenues derived from Central Asia's rapidly expanding traffic in opium, a relatively small group of terrorists were distorting the prospects for democratic change throughout Central Asia.

The terrorist actions dramatized to all the governments of the region that they shared the diplomatic goal of containing disorder and lawlessness. Gradually a consensus formed that a syndrome of lawlessness involving political opposition, radical religious doctrine, weapons, and illegal activities, principally gun running and narcotics trafficking, was drawing the countries of the region into common peril. As Kyrgyzstan's president Askar Akaev put it, the traffic in drugs and weapons had become "problem Number One" for Kyrgyzstan.[57] According to a recent report of the UN Office for Drug Control and Crime Prevention, in 1998 the expansion of poppy cultivation in Afghanistan was particularly evident in the northern part of the country, which, the report pointed out, could "result in a further preferred use of Central Asia as a transit zone for opium and heroin trafficking."[58] True to the pattern of development of many Latin American countries where a situation of high production and low indigenous use eventually gave way to a situation of high production and high indigenous use, the countries of West Asia have also witnessed a rise in local use despite the low profits that the depressed economies of the countries can support.[59]

Kazakhstan president Nursultan Nazarbaev warned that drugs, terrorism, and scarce water resources were the main threats to stability in Central Asia.[60] Russian defense minister Igor Sergeyev, during his visit to Astana in March 2000, said, "An analysis of the military-political situation in this region suggests that the Central Asian states are in the vanguard of the struggle against international terrorism and religious extremism."[61] Russia's view was that the war in Chechnya, terrorist acts in Russia and in Uzbekistan, and hostage taking in Kyrgyzstan all had links to Islamic extremism that leads back to training camps in Afghanistan. Sergei Yastrzhembsky, Russian president Putin's national security advisor, stated in June 2000 that Russia was considering preventive air strikes on sites in Afghanistan.[62]

The passage of UN Security Council Resolution 1333 in November 2000 constituted a new stage in international cooperation to pull the countries of Eurasia together.[63] The United States and Russia, former rivals in the confrontation over Afghanistan, now stood united in countering the threat of terrorism and lawlessness that was the legacy of that war.

Uzbekistan at the Center

Uzbekistan is the focus of the terrorist activity, and control over the Tashkent government is clearly the prize in the competition. Karimov has used subtle methods in the past. He succeeded in co-opting many proponents of the pre-independence nationalist Birlik (Unity) movement by first isolating and hounding its leaders while simultaneously inviting Birlik's young, talented activists into his own soviet-based, but cosmetically reconstituted, "nationalist Uzbek" government. Uzbekistan's policy is the key to the calculus of forces in the region. What steps can the Uzbekistan government take to neutralize the terrorist opposition without risking further deterioration in regional trade and cooperation regime and without giving into a wholesale assault on the political and regional diversity within its own society?

First, Uzbekistan's previous posture has led it to increasingly policies of autarky and self-reliance. These policies reflect a choice on the part of Karimov to break with the soviet-era domination by Moscow and to retool for a world outside the neo-colonialism of the former soviet space, what is now referred to as the Commonwealth of Independent States. The go-it-alone policies may have been understandable in the heady days of national independence. But in a world of globalization, no country is an island. Uzbekistan should seek to gain reentrance by stepping back from the self-reliance of the first decade and seek to dialogue with the outside world. The expectations of the first decade of independence have not borne the expected fruit. In terms of aggregate measures, post-communist economic growth has been restored in Uzbekistan and other Central Asian states, but at great costs to the social cohesion of the societies. The soviet system championed an egalitarianism of paupers. The Central Asian post-soviet states tend to champion an elitism of the politically connected. Both are built upon bad economics. But the former is hardly more stable and durable than the other. Among democracies, publics may have greater or lesser capacity to endure social inequality and economic calamity. Central Asians no doubt have substantial resilience to endure economic austerity. But this should not be expected to last forever. Democracy eventually builds a market economy, based upon voluntary and fair relationships or democracy will fail.

Second, Uzbekistan has begun a counterinsurgency campaign that runs the risk of being counterproductive. Uzbekistan should draw a sharp distinction between legitimate political disagreement and political extremism. Once this distinction is drawn, it should become the measure for acceptable disagreement. Extremists benefit if the government does things that are self-defeating. Chasing individual terrorists is emotionally satisfying and makes for good press, but it hardly constitutes diplomatic thinking by grand design.

Third, Uzbekistan has adopted trans-border policies that threaten to hobble the state's economic development. Uzbekistan should reverse the trend of the past two years in terms of its border arrangements. The country should seek to harness the benefits of globalization while protecting its security. The key is not to build strong states in the traditional sense, but to build strong societies and capable states. Only strong societies can endure the powerful forces of globalization. Only strong states can promote globalization.

Fourth is the problem of "the new security" in the environment of the twenty-first century. The key to Central Asia's future is not to be found in a new level of ideological management of society, but in an opening up of new opportunities for trade, communication, and the visibility of international standards and conditions. In a more globalized, more transparent Uzbekistan, violations of best practice and civil rights will be more visible to the outside world. Only new opportunities will ensconce a new generation in the expectation that commitment to self and society are not incompatible and that Central Asia can experience sustained growth and development with equity and dignity. The doctrines of terrorists can only be truly overcome by the desire of the people of Uzbekistan to live better.

CHAPTER NINE

Institutionalizing Electoral Democracy in Post-Communist States

JACK BIELASIAK

Jack Bielasiak addresses the critically important question of the development of political parties, examining their creation in the new democracies of Eastern Europe and the former Soviet Union in relation to the civil societies within which they function and the formal institutions of government which they affect. He observes that party development is uneven over the twenty-seven post-communist nations, with party systems generally better developed in Eastern Europe than in the states that emerged from the breakup of the Soviet Union. He attributes this uneven pattern of development to features inherent in both the institutional structures and civil societies of these diverse nations. In terms of institutional structures, while the formal requirements for enfranchisement and the threshold vote level that parties must attain to obtain seats in the legislature have remained relatively stable, the large number of parties and the ease with which existing parties disband and new parties form has compromised the creation of stable party systems. In terms of civil society, the at-best nascent development of non-party groups to represent elements of the community, the continuing reliance on informal "networks of power," and the tendency to personalize political leadership at the highest levels also have retarded the development of party systems.

How robust are the emerging democracies of post-communism? There is widespread consensus that strong party systems are necessary for the consolidation of modern, representative democracies, yet substantial disagreement exists as to the parties' abilities to evolve into institutionalized party regimes providing representation to citizens' preferences. The contention centers on whether the emergent party and electoral structures in East Europe (EE) and the former Soviet Union (FSU) are well defined and crystallized, or volatile and rudimentary. For some observers, the building of an institutionalized party system is a drawn-out and difficult process defined by substantial uncertainty and chaos.[1] For others, political parties are able to provide representation to the electorate from the beginning of democratization, and establish a well-entrenched competitive party regime.[2]

Theories of Party Regime Formation

The debate is bolstered by empirical evidence on both sides. The claim for the rapid emergence of democratic party systems rests primarily on individual-level data from extensive surveys of the EE and FSU publics, which find that the electorate is well aware of its socioeconomic and political interests, distinguishes between party positions on issues, and identifies parties that best represent its preferences.[3] The congruence between citizen and party positions gives way to voting behavior that crystallizes into a stable party regime. In contrast, studies looking at systemic-level electoral behavior or institutional structures reveal considerable volatility for party preferences across elections. The focus here is on an excessive number of political competitors that presents voters with too much political "noise," so that choices are difficult and fleeting.[4] The result constitutes a highly unstable party edifice, defined by unsteady political actors, fickle electorates, and uncertain competition.

These respective understandings on the breakdown of communism and the transition to democracy form the basis for the "tabula rasa" and "structure" views of post-communist development.[5] The first account sees a weak political society created by the disintegration of communism and conditioned by an open political marketplace subject to extensive raiding by political entrepreneurs,[6] by major dislocations and uncertainties,[7] by multiple and complex tasks in (re)creating markets, cultures, and polities,[8] by an "antipolitics" bias against party competition,[9] and by the absence of intermediary associations and social capital.[10] Together the chaotic socioeconomic and political conditions, the unprecedented opportunities for political mobilization by ambitious actors, and weak civil societies that fail to bind citizens to interest structures, are formidable impediments to the conversion of social cleavages into salient political identities that produce informed choices. The formation and consolidation of a well-structured party regime cannot take shape under these circumstances.

The response from the "structured" position is aimed at demonstrating the rapid translation of social, economic, and culture cleavages into salient political interests expressed in party politics. The premise is that the citizens' and the elites' cognitive understandings of the post-communist transformations are sufficient to enable political mobilization around well-defined competitive axes reflected in party positions and supports.[11] The tendency toward rapid consolidation is reinforced by the electoral game, so that winning or losing defines the viability of political competitors. Elections act as a filter that forces political entrepreneurs to recognize the realities of victory or defeat.[12] These outcomes ensure a streamlining of political actors on the political supply side, rendering choices more informed and manageable. Together the cleavages' saliency and the electoral filter are sufficient sorting devices to enable the institutionalization of political parties in a stable democratic regime.

Underpinning the tabula rasa and structured perspectives is the view that a consistent party regime is necessary to guarantee the democratization of the post-communist states. The debate is not about whether parties have assumed a critical role in the democratic practices of EE and the FSU. In large part, this is taken for granted. What is at stake is whether the party regime of post-communism has been sufficiently institutionalized to provide effective competition and to engage the citizenry in the democratic process, so as to assure the sustainability of political democracy. In short, the institutionalization of the party system is an essential expression of the democratic project.

Electoral Democracy

For those reasons, the focus here is on the institutional arrangements that facilitate political competition and popular participation. As such, the approach takes a deliberately narrow perspective on the issue of democratization. The exclusive concern with electoral democracy has its costs, for it presents the danger of "electorism," that is, the assumption that the presence of elections and parties is sufficient for the flourishing of democracy.[13] Such a view undervalues other dimensions associated with the building of free societies. Instead, the path can lead to "delegative"[14] or "illiberal"[15] forms of democracy. Nonetheless, there are strong theoretical reasons to consider this limited version of democracy.[16]

Political democracy rests primarily on institutional foundations that enable universal participatory and free competitive practices, articulated best by Dahl's understanding of polyarchy.[17] This perspective emphasizes a competitive environment that assures equal access to diverse political actors. While the factors that lead to democracy are significant, the polyarchy approach is not as vested with economic, social, and cultural preconditions necessary for the successful transition to democracy as the "prerequisites of democracy" school.[18] It also focuses less on "substantive democracy's" concerns with social and economic outcomes that can produce reserved domains or brownout areas that diminish democracy.[19]

The polyarchy view is concerned foremost with the citizenry's access to the democratic process, the extent of competition in the political realm, and the representation of citizens' preferences in public decision making. The consolidation of open participation and competition is an essential step in the pursuit of more extensive forms of democracy that extend beyond electoral boundaries.[20] Robert Dahl's empirical democratic theory, while falling within the scope of a minimum definition of democracy, goes beyond the Schumpterian minimalist definition that understands democracy as elite competition for the popular vote that ensures an alteration in power.[21] Polyarchy is predicated on the existence of fair, consistent rules and political rights that underpin universal participation and free competition.[22]

The question before us is whether the formation of party regimes in the post-communist states has been sufficiently stable and institutionalized to safeguard the politics of choice envisaged by electoral democracy. This brings us back to the earlier consideration about the sustainability of well-defined patterns of political competition and participation, as in the structured view of post-communism, or the failure to create steadfast norms and behaviors among voters and parties, as in the tabula rasa view. Empirical assessments fall primarily on three basic systemic properties of electoral democracy: the rules for political engagement, the effectiveness of party contestation, and the extent of popular participation in the electoral process. Throughout, the emphasis is on the stability or fluidity of these features, to discern the extent to which the democratic process remains inchoate and variant or crystallized and constant, that is, the degree of institutionalization in the components parts of democratic party regimes—rules, competition, and participation.[23]

The first measure looks to the reliability of rules that govern party competition and political behavior. Stability of electoral democracy rests on consistent regulations in the electoral environment, especially in the way votes are configured to establish political representation.[24] Extensive or frequent alterations in rules are bound to disrupt the positions and strategies of voters and political entrepreneurs, and lead to uncertainty about future payoffs in the political game. Changes in rules disturb voting habits and party calculations that are bound to undermine the consolidation of nascent democratic practices.

The second measure concerns the stability of political contestation, as evident by the number of political parties engaged in the political process and by electoral volatility, that is, the consistency of popular support across elections. Some students of emerging democracies have stressed the relative high fluidity of the new party systems, characterized by an unusually high number of political competitors that appear or disappear, and contribute to extensive vote swings between elections.[25] In contrast, the claim for effective political competition rests on a steady stream of political actors whose political placement is understandable to the voters, resulting in less volatile behavior.

The third measure concentrates on access to and representation in the party regimes. The extent of participation in the electoral process is a validation of the new party systems, allowing significant shares of the citizenry to "buy into" the representation offered by the emerging parties. The assumption is that greater engagement in electoral choice enhances governmental response to a wider circle of constituencies, providing for inclusiveness in the political process.[26] Especially in new democracies, where large sectors of the population were excluded previously from influence, participation in political life is an important indicator of the democratic opening. While other avenues of participation are available, the exercise of the right to vote and choose is fundamental for democratic success.

The empirical data for measures of electoral rule, political competition, and public participation are based on the elections since the collapse of communism in Eastern Europe in 1989 and the dismemberment of Yugoslavia and the Soviet Union in 1991. Some transitions that led to clear authoritarian outcomes are excluded from the study. The analysis takes a comparative approach that places the evidence on the post-communist party regimes in the broader context of emerging democracies. The evaluation of change in regulations, contestation, and participation in EE and the FSU can be enhanced by a baseline comparison with other democratic endeavors. However, the practice of measuring developments in the new democracies against the standard of mature democracies in the West is flawed, for it naturally produces evidence of greater fluidity and instability in the former. A more fruitful approach is to compare systemic developments along analogous periods in the establishment of democratic politics, that is, in the initial stages of democratization in postwar Western Europe, Southern Europe, and Latin America. To further enhance the comparative dimension, I differentiate the post-communist sample into regional configurations that facilitate a more nuanced analysis. Regional clusters are also useful as reflections of prior regime types and transition modes, elements that have been identified as critical explanatory variables for the stabilization of democratization in former communist states.[27]

Reforming Electoral Rules

Consistent rules foster party stabilization by reinforcing the expected mechanical effects of the vote to seat conversion and the psychological expectations of voters and politicians.[28] In contrast, changes in rules alter the allocation of votes into seats, and disturb the expected utility payoffs for political parties. This shortens the time horizon for the behavior of political entrepreneurs who are less willing to commit to the negotiations and accommodations made necessary by steadfast rules of "the only game in town."[29] Changes in electoral regulations have a propensity to destabilize the system, but the question is which reforms are sufficiently powerful to alter the political process by eliciting new patterns of competition that undermine the stability of the party regime.

Studies of democracies have shown that the most salient variables for the electoral rules-party systems linkage are electoral formula, district magnitude, legal threshold, and assembly size.[30] Change in electoral formula between single member district (SMD) and proportional representation (PR) has even led to the formulation of a law that associates plurality elections with a two-party system and PR list elections with multipartism.[31] No doubt, shifts in formula do alter the contours of competition and the choices provided to voters. On the other dimensions, Lijphart has argued that a variance of 20 percent in district magnitude, legal threshold, or assembly size has a similarly meaningful impact, in effect establishing a new electoral system that undermines the institutionalization of rules that drive stable behavior.[32]

The evidence on innovation in these properties of the electoral systems during the emergent phase of new democracies reveals that the post-communist reforms do not diverge significantly from the other cases of democratization (see table 1). If anything, for the most significant change, that of the electoral formula, the alterations are less frequent in the EE and the FSU countries than in the other regions (.37 versus .45 average). In all the regional subgroups, there are cases of the adaptation of new formulas, but these are

Table 1. Electoral Rule Changes (N) in Emerging Democracies

Country	Electoral Formula	District Size[a]	Threshold	Assembly Size
Postwar West Europe				
Austria (1945–56)	0	0	0	0
France (1945–56)	1	1	0	1
Germany (1949–57)	0	2	1	0[b]
Italy (1946–58)	1	1	1	2
Region total	2	4	2	3
Region average	.5	1	.5	.75
Southern Europe				
Greece (1974–85)	1	0	1	0
Portugal (1975–87)	0	0	0	0
Spain (1977–89)	0	0	0	0
Region total	1	0	1	0
Region average	.3	0	.3	0
Latin America				
Argentina (1983–93)	0	NA	0	1
Bolivia (1979–93)	1	0	0	1
Brazil (1982–90)	0	NA	NA	2
Paraguay (1983–93)	1	NA	0	2
Region total	2	—	0	6
Region average	.5	0	1.5	
East Central Europe				
Czech R. (1990–98)	0	0	0	0
Hungary (1990–98)	0	0	1	0
Poland (1991–97)	1	1	1	0
Slovakia (1990–98)	0	1	2	0
Region total	1	2	4	0
Region average	.25	.5	1	0
Southeast Europe				
Albania (1991–97)	2	2	2	2
Bulgaria (1990–97)	1	1	0	1
Romania (1990–00)	0	1	1	1
Region total	3	4	3	4
Region average	1	1.3	1	1.3

Table 1 continued on next page

Table 1 (continued)

Country	Electoral Formula	District Size[a]	Threshold	Assembly Size
Former Yugoslavia				
Croatia (1992–00)	1	1	2	2
Macedonia (1994–98)	0	0	0	0
Slovenia (1992–00)	0	0	0	0
Region total	1	1	2	2
Region average	.33	.33	.66	.66
Baltic States				
Estonia (1992–99)	0	1	0	0
Latvia (1993–98)	0	0	1	0
Lithuania (1992–00)	0	0	1	0
Region total	0	1	2	0
Region average	0	.33	.66	0
FSU Europe				
Moldova (1994–01)	0	0	1	1
Russia (1993–99)	0	0	0	0
Ukraine (1994–98)	1	0	0	0
Region total	1	0	1	1
Region average	.33	0	.33	.33

[a]To avoid a duplicate count, changes in district size due to electoral formula changes are not counted.

[b]The assembly size in Germany can vary with the size and distribution of the compensation vote tiers.

SOURCES: Calculations from data in Inter-Parliamentary Union, *Chronicle of Parliamentary Elections* (Geneva: Annuals), and on line at www.ipu.org; IFES, *Election Law Compendium of Central and Eastern Europe* (Kyiv, 1995); Mark P. Jones, "A Guide to the Electoral Systems of the Americas," *Electoral Studies* 14 (March 1995); and Arend Lijphart, *Electoral Systems and Party Systems* (Oxford: Oxford University Press, 1994).

infrequent. The ability to reconstruct the electoral process by modifying its most fundamental institutional arrangement is not pursued extensively by the democratizing states of the postwar era, regardless of time or place.

For the other features of the electoral laws as well, the former communist states do not show a more experimental mode than their counterparts in earlier democratization phases, although more regional variation is apparent here. Reforms in district size occur most often in the West European states and Southeast Europe, while Latin American and Southeast European countries adjust assembly size most frequently. For the post-communist sample as a whole, many of the adjustments in both these electoral features do not reach the 20 percent significance criterion. While assembly size is reduced in several countries, the meaningful alterations are in Albania's downsizing from 250 to 140 seats between the 1991 and 1992 election, and the Bulgarian shift from the 400 seats grand constituent assembly in 1990 to a 240 working legislature in 1991.[33] The significant adjustments in district magnitude are more frequent, as evident in changes in Poland in 1993, Albania in the mid-1990s, Croatia in 1995, and Slovakia in 1998—although no discernable pattern in terms of reducing or increasing district magnitude is evident. Overall, these changes do not suggest that the manipulation of electoral regulations is meant to favor large parties over small ones, or diminish the chances for proportional representation within the party system.[34]

The intended effects are clearer in regard to the legal vote threshold necessary for party entry into parliament. This is the most utilized election law adjustment among the EE and FSU polities, and is more frequent than equivalent changes in Western Europe, Southern Europe, and Latin America (table 1). In this instance, reform is always in the direction of higher thresholds, with the single exception of the reduction from 4 percent to 2 percent in Albania for the 1997 election. Elsewhere, the minimum vote requirement has moved to a relatively high legal barrier of 5 percent, and even reached 6 percent for a single party in the 2001 election in Moldova, with higher threshold in place for coalitions. Of the various institutional components that make up the electoral system, the threshold for parliamentary representation is the most amenable to change. And it has important consequences, for it initiates a greater hurdle to gain legislative representation. The numerous increases in the legal barrier are evidently a response to the continuing proliferation of political actors, in an attempt to curb the fragmentation of the party system. Higher minimums are intended to eliminate from the legislative arena small, often more extremist political parties, and in that way stabilize electoral democracy.

With the exception of the threshold increases, the laws that govern electoral behavior have been largely institutionalized in the post-communist states. True, major changes in electoral rules did take place in EE and the FSU in the phase immediately preceding the founding elections in the region. The natural course in the transition from authoritarian to democratic politics is to introduce new rules for the founding elections, but in several post-communist instances a major revision of electoral contest took place prior to the collapse of the communist regimes.[35] These electoral contests—the breakaway elections —took place in Poland in 1989 and in 1990 in many of the republics of the disintegrating Soviet and Yugoslav federations. The rules for the breakaway elections were basically the already existing electoral laws, now open to contestation by alternative candidates and movements. As such, they took place under an SMD majority runoff formula that signified both continuity with past practices and strategic considerations by communist politicians. Faced for the first time with meaningful opposition, the latter favored district level contests as a means to enhance their organizational resources and individual candidacies rather than rely on the "communist" party label, since personal name identification and patron-client resources are considered more worthy in local districts than nationwide lists.

Despite these strategic calculations by the communist elite, the rules of the breakaway elections did not offer much salvation to the ruling parties. Instead, the open contests provided impetus for the new anticommunist, often nationalist, coalitions to usher in a new political era. Among the changes was a push for revisions of the codes that would govern the next round of political contests, that is, the fully democratic, founding elections. At this juncture, the old SMD formula was jettisoned off in favor of incorporating the proportional representation principle, either as part of a mixed system that combined both SMD and PR tiers, for example, in Croatia, Lithuania, and Russia, or as pure PR systems, for example, in Poland, Estonia, and Moldova.[36] The shift to PR reflected a preference by new political elites, who sought to gain access to the legislative arena through a more open electoral mechanism, one that emphasized proportionality rather than winner-take-all contests. From that point on, revisions in the electoral formula have consistently favored PR, without a single instance of an opposite reform from PR to SMD. For example, these reforms involved the abandonment of mixed electoral structures to full PR in Bulgaria in 1991 and Croatia in 2000, and from SMD majority runoff to hybrid SMD and PR systems in the Ukraine and Macedonia in 1998.

The pattern of change reveals contrary impulses in the two dominant reform practices, the formula and threshold features. Formula alterations systematically favor better representation of political actors by opening up the process, while the increases in the legal threshold have the effect of restricting representation by limiting party entry into parliament. The explanation for this reform dynamic lies in the sequencing of the two innovation types. In the early phase of democratization, the diminished power of the communist elite provided opportunity for rival political players to demand representation in the governing process and to push for the abandonment of the winner-take-all system. The explosion of political competition during the opening phase of post-communist politics then produced multiple contenders that contributed to unstable party politics and brought about the increases in the legal threshold to stream down the chaotic political scene in many EE and FSU cases. In other instances, for example, Croatia, the dominance of the HDZ hegemonic political movement held sway for a prolonged period of time, and postponed the revision of the electoral formula until its disintegration on the eve of the 2000 election.

While subregional variations in rule changes are apparent, these are driven primarily by extensive experimentation in a particular country. Thus, at first glance, the most frequent alteration in electoral codes appears in the Balkan region, in the former Yugoslavia and neighboring countries, an apparent reflection of greater instability in the region. But much of this variance is accounted for by innovations in Albania and Croatia, although the causal relationship between rule transformation and the political environment is uncertain.[37] For example, do the chaotic conditions in Albania afford opportunities for political actors to engage in rule manipulation to gain political advantage, or are frequent changes symptomatic of efforts to find a stable political outcome? In Croatia, during the dominance of the HDZ, reforms in district magnitude and the threshold fit the presumption of a hegemonic movement's attempts to restrict political access. But a similar tendency takes shape in countries with a more pluralistic political regime, as in the increases in threshold evident in Poland, Hungary, Latvia, or Lithuania. The same reform, for example, threshold alteration, may be intended to maintain the political dominance of the predominant party, as in the early years in Romania, Slovakia, and Croatia, or to curb the anarchistic fragmentation of the political space, as in Poland and the Baltic countries.

What, then, is the evidence about the institutionalization of electoral rules to stabilize politics in post-communism? The temporal implementation over the past decade and the comparison with previous periods of democratic construction reveal that the rules for democratic governance have been in place without too much disruption and experimentation. The primary adjustments in the electoral codes of EE and the FSU are at the very start of democratization, during the breakdown of the communist regimes and the construction of competitive politics. This is the pattern for the most important property of electoral systems, the electoral formula, which is in place prior to the conduct of the founding elections in all but three cases. Attempts to fine-tune electoral rules in the other domains persist over a longer period of time, although most concerted efforts are found in the initial democratic phase, while the other "significant" adjustments are restricted primarily to raising the voting threshold.

The impulse to experimentation with electoral codes is not any more extensive in the post-communist world than in the previous episodes of democratization in Western Europe, Southern Europe, or Latin America (table 1). While the frequency of increases in the legal bar may be more prevalent in the former communist states, adjustments in assembly size occur more often in the other regions. On the electoral formula, the dimension with the most likely impact on political behavior, the ex-communist states tend to be less prone to change than the earlier democratizing cases. On balance, then, there is a strong tendency toward the early institutionalization of electoral regulations in the post-communist polities. The evidence supports the contention that it is difficult to engage in electoral engineering after initial systemic conditions are in place. Once the EE and FSU states abandoned the electoral practices associated with the communist regime, moving away from the SMD competitive elections in the waning days of communism toward full or hybrid PR systems during the foundation of democracy, the capacity to reform rules declined.

At least on the evidence concerning the institutional arrangements associated with electoral democracy, the *tabula rasa* perspective of inchoate systems is not warranted. Instead, we can point to a more mature and structured regulatory environment. On this measure, the post-communist states are as likely to move rapidly to the structuring of democracies than earlier episodes of post-authoritarian transitions. Whether the stability of electoral codes translates into stable behavior that fosters enduring democratic practices is an issue that requires analysis of the opportunities for political competition and participation in the emerging democracies of post-communism.

Effective Political Competition

The stability of the electoral process is predicated on a "clear structure of competition" that demarcates party positions that afford meaningful choices to the electorate and provides opportunities for diverse inputs into the legislative agenda.[38] The structure view sees the rapid conversion of social cleavages into salient political identities that create a strong foundation for citizens' steady identification and support for preferred political parties. In this perception, the competitive framework is indeed consistent and crystallized. The contrasting *tabula rasa* argument looks to an institutional framework that is open and weak, defined by parties that lack clear identities and constituencies, and is prone to fusion and fission that cause confusion among the voting public. The result is a proliferation of political actors in the new democracies that render voting patterns highly volatile and unpredictable. In the first image, the structure of competition is effective due to well-delineated cleavages built around a limited number of political actors; in the second image, the routinization of voter preferences is far from complete, so that numerous political contenders continue to mobilize support, contributing to major shifts in voting profiles from election to election.

To assess the effectiveness of competition in the emerging party structures, I concentrate on standard evaluations of party systems: the effective number of political actors and electoral volatility. Stability of party regimes is defined in part by the number of functioning political actors, for it configures the political space and the placement of parties along that space, in turn, defining choices for the electorate. A study of West European systems found that a greater number of contending parties reduces the distance between them on ideological and policy positions, facilitating more frequent vote switching. A survey of Latin American systems reached a similar view, so that more parties contributed to more intensive polarization, rendering democratic politics more difficult.[39] At the very least, then, the number of effective parties is an indicator of political fragmentation that has strong bearing on the institutionalization of party regimes. The measure of "effective number of parties" uses the Laakso and Taagepera formula: $N = 1/\Sigma \, p_i^2$ where N is the effective number of parties and p_i is the fractional share of votes for the i-th party.

The second measure of the institutionalization of party competition relies on the Pederson index of electoral volatility, which concentrates on changes in the voting share for parties in consecutive elections. The premise is that stability of party systems is associated with voting that is consistent over time rather than subject to significant swings in the electorate's preferences, contributing to an inchoate structure of winners and losers that undermines the overall stability of political democracy. The standard evaluation of volatility is calculated as $V = \frac{1}{2}\Sigma \, |v_{p,t} - v_{p,t-1}|$ where $v_{p,t}$ stands for the percentage of the vote obtained by a party at election t, and $v_{p,t-1}$ for the percentage in the previous election.

The evidence on both the effective number of political parties and electoral volatility in EE and the FSU is that institutionalization is more precarious in the post-communist setting than in earlier episodes of transition from authoritarianism to democracy (see table 4). The effective number of electoral parties (ENEP) in the former communist states is consistently high among virtually all the party systems (tables 2 and 3). The ENEP for thirty-five out of

Table 2. Elections in Eastern Europe: Unicameral or Lower Chambers

Country	Election Date	% Voter Turnout	No. Party Lists in Election	No. Party Lists in Assembly >1 mbr	VOL. %	ENEP
Albania	1991	98.9	11	3		2.15
	1992	91.5	11	4	28.8	2.20
	1996	89.9	24	5	7.8	2.80
	1997	72.6	23	7	34.7	2.87
Bulgaria	1990	90.6	37	5		2.75
	1991	83.9	41	3	13.8	4.19
	1994	75.2	48	5	17.5	3.87
	1997	67.5	na	5	22.8	2.99
Croatia	1990	84.5	36+	2		
	1992	75.6	15	7	16.9	4.26
	1995	68.8	28	8	10.6	3.79
	2000	69.3	55	9	23.1	4.08
Czech Rep.	1990[a]	96.8	22	4		3.18
	1992[a]	85.1	41	8	12.5	7.69
	1996	76.3	16	6	18.5	5.33
	1998	73.9	13	5	7.4	4.73
Hungary	1990	65.1	54	6		6.76
	1994	68.9	34	6	26.4 PR	5.54
	1998	56.3	26	6	28.5 PR	4.30
Macedonia	1994	77.3	38	5		
	1998	72.9	28** 17 *	6	44.5	5.06
Poland	1991	43.2	111	17		14.69
	1993	54.0	35	7	26.8	9.81
	1997	47.9	21	6	22.3	4.55
Romania	1990	86.2	73	11		2.25
	1992	76.3	83	7	25.5	7.04
	1996	76.0	NA	6	12.4	6.10
	2000	65.3	80	6	21.0	5.24
Slovakia	1990[a]	95.4	22	7		5.76
	1992[a]	84.7	41	5	17.9	4.22
	1994	75.4	18	7	13.3	5.37
	1998	84.2	NA	6	20.1	5.36
Slovenia	1992	85.9	25	8	18.4	8.40
	1996	73.7	24	7	25.4	6.34
	2000	69.9	16	8	22.1	5.10

[a]Refers to the Czechoslovak Republic, but the results are for the Czech and Slovak National Councils.

*PR tier   **SMD tier

SOURCE: IPU, *Chronicle of Parliamentary Elections and Developments* (Geneva, 1990 to 1997 annuals) and on line www.ipu.org; Rose, Munro, and Mackie (1998); and election notes in *Electoral Studies*.

Table 3. Elections in the Former Soviet Union: Unicameral or Lower Chambers

Country	Election Date	% Voter Turnout	No. Party Lists in Election	No. Party Lists in Assembly >1 mbr	VOL. %	ENEP
Estonia	1992	67.8	38	7		8.88
	1995	69.5	30	7	28.4	5.93
	1999	57.4	12	7	23.4	6.90
Latvia	1993	89.9	28	8		6.04
	1995	72.6	26	9	33.5	9.62
	1998	71.0	21	6	24.5	7.03
Lithuania	1992	75.3	25* 22*	7		3.83
	1996	52.9	27** 25*	7	28.9	7.20
	2000	58.63	16*	8	49.6	5.58
Moldova	1994	79.3	13	4		3.85
	1998	69.2	15	4	36.6	5.79
	2001	70.0	17	3	36.5	3.54
Russia	1993	54.3	13^	9		7.58* 3.23**
	1995	64.4	43*	12	42.5	10.68* 6.10**
	1999	61.7	26*	8	52.1	6.80*
Ukraine	1994	75.8	28	10	NA	NA
	1998	70.8	30*	14	NA	10.78*

*PR tier only   **SMD tier only

SOURCE: IPU, *Chronicle of Parliamentary Elections and Developments* (Geneva, 1990 to 1997 annuals) and on line at www.ipu.org; Rose, Munro, and Mackie (1998); and election notes in *Electoral Studies.*

the forty-nine elections held during this time is above 4.0, and within this number eighteen have an ENEP higher than 6.0. Countries that are subject to the most intense competition in terms of the average number of political actors are Poland (9.6), Russia (8.3), Latvia (7.5), Estonia (7.2), and Slovenia (6.6). On the opposite end, there are virtually no states in the proximity of a two-party structure, with Albania (2.5), Bulgaria (3.6), and Croatia (3.8) exhibiting the lowest average ENEP. In the first two states, a competitive axis defined by the heirs of the ruling communist party and the opposition movement prevailed for much of the decade, thereby limiting the number of entrants into the political contest. In Bulgaria, this was altered by the formation of an important political grouping for the June 2001 election, the

National Movement Simeon the Second, resulting in an ENEP increase at the start of the millennium. In Croatia, the predominance of the HDZ faced by a splintered opposition produced an ENEP above 4.0 in the first half of the decade, but was reduced after the opposition formed an electoral alliance against the HDZ in the 2000 election.

Most post-communist party structures are defined by high multipartism. The average ENEP for twelve out of the sixteen cases is above the 5.0 "high" mark used in the classification of party systems.[40] The large number of active political actors constitutes an important indicator of a propensity toward more intense and inefficient competition, facilitating conditions of "extreme pluralism" that undermine stability and consolidation.[41] While such a political outcome depends also on other factors, mainly on an ideological dimension that is not available in the study of post-communist states, there are systemic properties evident that contribute to such "extreme" tendencies, for example, the actual number of active parties in electoral competition, as well as comparisons to previous democratization episodes.

The comparative factor accentuates the differences between the ex-communist and other emerging party systems: 5.7 to 3.8 average ENEP respectively, with the five post-communist subregions ranging from 3.7 to 6.7 ENEP. The most extensive multipartism in the earlier transitions occurs in France (4.8), Spain (3.8), and Brazil (6.7), conditions that are surpassed by many EE and FSU countries (table 4). No doubt, the number of actors involved in the democratic process in the aftermath of communism has led to the formation of a more fractionalized political space than the initial experiences with democratization in Western Europe, Southern Europe, and Latin America.

The evident proliferation of political parties is further evident in the extreme high number of electoral lists competing in the EE and FSU elections (tables 2 and 3). The structure of political completion has become wide open to new entrants after the collapse of the communist regimes, attracting political entrepreneurs representing a wide array of contending ideologies, issues, ambitions, and histories. The competitive drive has been facilitated by relaxed entry requirements that allowed the formation of a multitude of parties attempting to capture a share of the electorate after its release from the monopolistic constraints of communism. The result has been a veritable rush into the electoral process, at times involving dozens of party lists on the ballot. The Polish case of 1991 is no doubt a primary example of excessive political appetites, with 111 different party lists contesting for entry into the Sejm. The extent of contestation, and the resultant large number of lists (29) actually entering parliament, contributed to a chaotic situation. The response was a political effort that culminated in successful electoral engineering that established disincentives for competition, and reduced significantly the number of entrants for the 1993 election.[42] Still, in many of the post-communist states, electoral contests are characterized by a high number of party entries throughout the decade of democratization. This factor may be at the root of a current wave of efforts in several EE and FSU states to institute new requirements for party registration, financing, and voter petitioning that would create more effective barriers to entry into the party regime and foreclose the prevailing ease of access.

The trend over the democratic decade does show evidence of an electoral win-lose funnel that has curbed the number of competing parties in many of the party regimes, but by no means all. In most cases, the founding elections attracted a large number of contenders that diminished in subsequent elections, a response to the failure of small, uncompetitive parties to attract support. In addition, new electoral procedures, that is, higher thresholds, discouraged potential contestants. In these circumstances, the ability of parties to present themselves at the voting booth declined, as in Hungary, the Czech Republic, Poland, Slovenia, and the Baltic states. However, other countries evidence an opposing path than leads to an increase in the number of electoral lists competing for voters' support. This is the case in conditions of an initial regime-opposition dominant hold on electoral contestation or in conditions of a strong nationalist movement dominating politics; the unraveling of these movements provides the political opportunity structure for the mobilization of new political forces that enter the political arena in the guise of new political parties. This pattern is present in Albania, Bulgaria, and Croatia.[43] In Russia, the political and legal maneuvering in the 1993 election is responsible for the suppressed number of competitors at the time, and the subsequent increase in the 1995 contest.[44]

In short, a dual track is evident in the post-communist world. In some countries the party system has become less cluttered with supplicants for legislative representation, and the tendency is toward more manageable competitive entry. In other cases, entry to the party systems has actually opened up over the past decade. In many post-communist party regimes, the number of lists presenting themselves to the voters remains high, so the actual empirical range is from a high of eighty in Romania to a low of twelve in Estonia for the round of elections at the end of the millennium.

As concerns the prevailing multipartism in the effective number of political parties, the temporal trend is mixed as well, although a more marked difference exists between the FSU and EE (tables 2 and 3). In the latter, the ENEP after the founding elections declines in all but Albania and Slovakia, and the 2001 election in Bulgaria—a fact explained by the political crises in these countries that draw public support away from dominant incumbent forces to political challengers, giving way to a higher ENEP. In the rest of EE, the competitive potential represented by the effective number of electoral parties diminished. Again the most dramatic shift occurs in Poland, from the pure PR 1991 highly fractured party regime (14.7 ENEP) to the more moderate party system in the 1997 election (4.5 ENEP), reflecting strategic responses by party leaders to experiences of electoral defeat and new regulatory incentives. Among the soviet successor states, there is more vacillation over time but the ENEP throughout most of the region for the round of elections at the end of the 1990s is among the highest for the entire post-communist period, for example, 6.8 in Russia, 7.0 in Latvia, and 10.8 in the Ukraine.

In general, throughout EE and FSU the temporal trend does not indicate a sufficient tampering of voting contestation among numerous party contenders (see tables 2 and 3). The result is a high number of effective parties for most of the decade, a condition of political fragmentation that remains unusually high even by the world standards of previous democratization experiences. The question, then, is whether the more fractured political environment permeated by numerous contenders for political representation contributes to more extreme electoral volatility in the post-communist states.

There are a number of significant trends in the data on volatility, in relation to the post-communist universe and in comparison to other democratizing regions. For example, a distinction occurs between the countries of EE and the soviet successor states, exemplified by average volatility of 23 percent over the decade for the former bloc and 32 percent for the former republics (table 4). The distinction between the soviet and EE patterns can be located in two features of their political history. First, the longer and more controlling soviet regime eradicated attachments between its citizens and alternative political expressions to a greater extent than some EE states with "softer" political regimes and more articulate political opposition. Second, the post-soviet transitions appear more turbulent, generating a greater tendency of voters to express dissatisfaction with the incumbents by supporting opposition or new political parties. The first path is clearly visible at various elections in the Baltic states, where the electorate time and time again switched support away from government parties to opposition movements, either in the form of ex-communist, populist, conservative, or nationalist forces. In the Russian case, the extreme volatility is due to the appearance of "parties of power" prior to the 1999 election that attained 37 percent of the voters' support, and together with other new political formations attracted 45 percent of the vote in 1999. Thus dissatisfaction with incumbent policymakers and the appearance of fresh political entities provided opportunities for high volatility in the post-soviet states.

Volatility is more contained for the East Central and Southeast European states. In part, the index is once more reflective of the early political dominance of the umbrella or nationalist movements, as in Slovakia (17.1 volatility) or Croatia (18.1). In both cases, the crisis around these political expressions produced more fragmented political interactions that result in higher volatility in the latest round of elections than in the two previous cycles (table 2). The most stable voting among the former communist countries is in the Czech Republic, with a 13 percent average volatility that compares well with cases from the other periods of emerging democracies. Except for this case, all other post-communist party systems are subject to high volatility (above 20 percent) during the latest round of elections. Over time, during the three or four elections cycles since 1989, little decline in volatility has taken place in EE and the FSU. Despite the fluctuations evident from election to election, the average volatility in the first cycle of the EE states was 20 percent (n = 8) in the early 1990s and stands at 25 percent (n = 7) after the third cycle at the beginning of the millennium. The same pattern characterizes the Baltic republics (32 percent average volatility) and Moldova (36 percent), although Lithuania and Russia evidence an increase in volatility between the early and the late 1990s, with around 50 percent volatility in the latest election (table 3).

The extent of volatility in the electoral cycles of the post-communist states remains high after a decade of democratization. In that respect, there are some important distinctions between these emerging party regimes and the earlier democratizing pathways in Europe. The postwar Western European and the Southern European transitions show an average electoral changeover during the first decade of their democratization of 11 percent and 16 percent respectively—with Austria and Portugal as the most stable party systems, and Italy and Spain as the least consistent in these two waves of democratization (table 4). Still, the most fluid vote in these Western cases compares favorably with the extent of volatility in the third wave of democratization in Latin America and the post-communist world, whose average index of volatility is 26 percent and 28 percent for each region. In brief, the volatility within the party regimes of the latest democracies is twice that of the earlier ones.

The West and South European countries were able to stabilize faster and more extensively than the third wave democracies, as evident by both the comparative indices for ENEP and volatility across the different regions and

Table 4. Electoral Performance in Emerging Democracies

	V/VAP (%)	IEP Vol. (%)		ENEP	N Elects.	Period
Postwar Europe						
Austria	82.9	0.815	7.1	2.6	4	45–56
France	72.6	0.693	10.4	4.8	4	45–51
Germany	82.9	0.754	13.9	3.5	4	49–61
Italy	91.6	0.857	14.1	3.9	4	46–58
	82.5	**0.780**	**11.4**	**3.7**		
Southern Europe						
Greece	84.2	0.810	18.4	2.9	4	74–85
Portugal	87.3	0.802	8.7	3.5	4	75–80
Spain	77.1	0.715	21.9	3.8	4	77–86
	82.9	**0.776**	**16.3**	**3.4**		
Latin America						
Argentina	80.9	NA	12.7	3.2	6	83–93
Bolivia	56.3	0.506	33.0	4.7	4	79–93
Brazil	76.2	NA	40.9	6.7	2	86–90
Paraguay	52.8	NA	25.8	2.1	2	89–93
Chile	83.9	NA	15.8		2	89–93
	73.9	**0.505***	**25.6**	**4.2**		
East Central Europe						
Czech Rep.	82.8	0.694	12.8	5.2	4	90–98
Hungary	68.4	0.579	27.4	5.5	3	90–98
Poland	48.4	0.374	24.6	9.6	3	91–97
Slovakia	85.2	0.735	17.1	5.2	4	90–98
	71.2	**0.596**	**20.5**	**6.4**		
Southeast Europe						
Albania	85.3	0.803	23.8	2.5	4	91–97
Bulgaria	81.6	0.699	18.0	3.4	4	90–97
Romania	76.8	0.599	19.6	5.1	4	90–00
	81.2	**0.700**	**20.5**	**3.7**		
Former Republics of Yugoslavia						
Croatia	75.4	0.629	16.9	4.0	3	92–00
Macedonia	72.6	0.681	44.5	5.0	2	94–98
Slovenia	78.5	0.660	22.0	6.6	3	92–00
	75.5	**0.657**	**27.8**	**5.2**		
Baltic States						
Estonia	44.2	0.384	25.9	7.2	3	92–99
Latvia	52.2	0.454	29.0	7.5	3	93–98
Lithuania	57.9	0.432	39.2	5.5	3	92–00
	51.4	**0.423**	**31.4**	**6.7**		

Table 4 (continued)

	V/VAP (%)	IEP Vol. (%)		ENEP	N Elects.	Period
FSU Europe						
Moldova	58.5	0.433	36.5	4.4	3	94–01
Russia	57.9	0.401	47.3	8.3	3	93–99
Ukraine	70.8	0.543	NA	NA	2	94–98
	62.4	**0.459**	**41.9**	**6.4**		

*Average for Bolivia, Colombia, Ecuador, Peru, and Venezuela (Centellas, 2000).

Country	Election Date	V/VAP (%)	Blank V (%)	Excluded V (%)	1EP
Estonia	1992	40.9	1.5	14.6	0.344
	1995	48.8	0.9	12.7	0.422
	1999	42.8	1.6	8.4	0.386
		44.2	**1.3**	**11.9**	**0.384**
Latvia	1993	57.7	1.5	10.6	0.508
	1995	50.6	1.0	12.1	0.440
	1998	48.2	2.7	11.5	0.415
		52.2	**1.7**	**11.4**	**0.454**
Lithuania	1992	70.2	3.1	14.1	0.584
	1996	50.0	4.9	32.7	0.320
	2000	53.5	4.4	23.5	0.391
		57.9	**4.1**	**23.4**	**0.432**
Moldova	1994	64.1	5.0	18.1	0.499
	1998	57.0	3.4	23.6	0.421
	2001	54.4	2.5	28.4	0.380
		58.5	**3.9**	**23.4**	**0.433**
Russia	1993	51.8	6.8	12.9	0.420
	1995	62.8	1.9	49.5	0.311
	1999	59.1	2.0	18.7	0.471
		57.9	**3.6**	**27.0**	**0.401**
Ukraine	1994	73.4	6.3	5.3	0.651
	1998	68.1	3.1	34.2	0.434
		70.8	**4.7**	**19.8**	**0.543**

time periods.[45] In the post-communist political environment, an open marketplace has persisted from election to election, with numerous parties still involved in the competitive quest for electoral support. In many instances, the transformation of party regimes remains significant as new political parties appear, old ones disintegrate, and the remaining party competitors are subject to drastic shifts in voter support. This is often tied to the difficulties associated with the economic transformation to market and the social dislocations entailed by it. Yet such swings in the vote profile are made possible precisely because the impact of policy costs is not diffused by a strong party system, in which identities and constituencies are tied and loyal to specific political parties. Rather, voters are free to select among several contending parties and often turn minor support for larger backing, or vice versa. For that very reason, party regime institutionalization in the former communist states is a more precarious and drawn-out process than in the other instances of emerging democracies.

In figure 1, plotting ENEP and volatility of all the democratic electoral experiences in the postwar period, the point is reinforced. Nearly all the post-communist countries are located above an ENEP "high" index of five, and situated in a volatility measure that extends beyond 15 percent. This contrasts with the position of the West European states located at the lower end of both indices. The Latin American cases are more spread out, with Brazil and Bolivia closer to the EE and FSU norm and Argentina to the Western one. Within the post-communist sample, the successor soviet states are subject to more extensive fragmentation (ENEP) and fluidity (volatility index) than their counterparts in East Europe. Even so, for all post-communist countries the consolidation of party competition along clear lines and actors is elusive. The lack of stabilization is bound to be detrimental to the institutionalization of the party regimes in these newly democratizing states. The volatility rates remain among the highest in all democratizing electoral systems, comparable to the Latin American situation, and the party fragmentation indicators are consistently among the highest for all emerging party structures, including the Latin American transitions. So even in comparison to the earlier democratic episodes, the former communists systems continue to be characterized by greater fractionalization and volatility.

Effective Political Participation

A basic right associated with the democratic opening centers around the population's ability to fully participate in the political process. Restrictions to

Figure 1. Average Volatility and ENEP in Emerging Party Systems

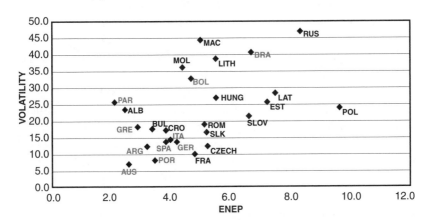

engagement in politics under authoritarian regimes give way to the premise that all citizens have an equal right and ability to exercise their political options. The very definition of electoral democracy rests on this fundamental right, guaranteed by universal franchise and institutional procedures of representation.[46] This of course does not signify that voting turnout is equated with democracy; free political competition assured by civil guarantees is necessary for meaningful participation, and other nonvoting forms of participation are important venues for democratic expression.

Yet political participation can be an important indicator of the quality of democracy, insofar as it delineates the inclusiveness of political practices and the accountability of the government. Mass participation at the very least defines the social and political groups that engage in the "minimal" practice of politics, and that need to be taken into account by an elite interested in political longevity. On the other hand, electoral democracy is diminished when hurdles are imposed on members of the polity in the exercise of their franchise, contributing to the exclusion of citizens from the democratic endeavor. Most importantly, political democracy is dependent on citizen participation to express political preferences. Citizens excluded from the process render the democratic principle of representative governance less complete. This does not mean that polities with low rates of participation in electoral politics are nondemocratic; the right to nonparticipation may well be as important as the right to take part in politics. Rather the issue evolves around the ability of emerging party regimes to assure the broad representation of the citizenry as a means to foster the acceptance of democratic institutions and procedures, so as to facilitate the consolidation of the democratic system.

Extensive participation facilitates the routinization of political rules, legitimizes the regime of representation formed by party choices, and ensures the inclusiveness of the democratic process.[47]

While broad political participation is the ideal of democracy, the practice often falls short of intent. The problem is to discern whether the shortfall is the result of impediments placed by the institutional mechanisms of the new democracies, other social practices, or political preferences. This is especially the case during the current third wave of democracy, when the dominant ideological norm around the globe creates extensive pressures for the semblance of electoral democracy. Politicians everywhere are well cognizant of the requirements to appear democratic and provide citizens with universal franchise. Thus electoral codes may contain provisions for equal access to the vote for all members of the polity, while informal practices can undermine the universality principle by imposing specific citizen qualifications or demanding educational achievements. While it is often difficult to differentiate between voluntary and imposed exclusion from the practices of electoral democracy, the extent of political inclusiveness can be operationalized to provide a sense of "effective participation" in democracy. This approach is given additional credence by the fact that proportional representation systems have been the overwhelming choice of the EE and FSU states, attempting to provide access and representation to most of their citizens.

To gauge the extent of participation in the political democracies of the post-communist era, I rely on several indicators and a cumulative index of participation developed in the context of the Latin American democratizations.[48] Citizen participation is first assessed in terms of voter turnout, but as a ratio of the adult voting population (V/VAP) rather than registered voters —precisely because we are interested in determining if a significant portion of the population is unable to participate due to difficulties in the registration phase. If registration presents barriers due to language or literacy requirements, this will surface in the proportion of the adult population deprived of the franchise. Second, citizens who cast unmarked or spoiled ballots may well be committed to the institutional framework of democracy, but either are unfamiliar with the proper procedures to cast valid votes or engage in deliberate nullification due to disapproval of the political choices. In either case, blank and null votes (B) are invalidated in the final tally, so that the voters are unrepresented in the emerging party regimes. Invalid votes embody preferences that are not well represented in the party system. A decline in the share of invalid votes signifies more effective representation, better identification with political parties, and consolidation of the party system. Invalid votes are measured as the ratio of bland and null votes over the total vote cast for each election. Third, the share of the vote for parties that compete in the election process but fail to attain the sufficient minimum for representation in the legislative arena is "wasted" as an effective expression of political leverage and collective preferences. Supporters for these extra parliamentary parties are effectively disfranchised from the primary decision-making institution, and are deprived of an important voice in policy deliberations. While other avenues for political engagement may be open, the foreclosure of deliberation in the legislative agenda is an important deprivation of political engagement that is likely to affect voters' standing vis-à-vis the party regime. Consolidation of electoral and party systems is in part a strategic learning process that allows voters and politicians to better differentiate between winners and losers and shift support to expected utility by casting votes for parties likely to offer representation. Excluded vote (E) is measured as the ratio of votes for unrepresented parties over the total vote for all political parties.

A composite index of effective participation (IEP) consists of the three indicators of political engagement, that is, IEP = V/VAP x (1-B) x (1-E), ranging from zero (voters are deprived of participation) to one (full citizen participation).[49] Greater inclusiveness, as evident in higher V/VAP but lower invalid and excluded votes, is an indication of citizens' acceptance of the electoral mechanism and the party system, whereas large disenfranchisement either through registration or wasted votes makes for less effective participation in the choices offered by the party regime.

There is an obvious demarcation in access to politics between the earlier waves of democracy in Western Europe and Southern Europe and the third wave democratization in Latin American and EE and FSU (table 4). The electorate in the Western part of the European continent has a very high participation rate, evident in an IEP of .780, followed by the former communist states at .567 and Latin American states at .505. The experience of the latter is especially revealing, for elections in these states are often compulsory but large sectors of the voting age population are restricted in their ability to register due to literacy and other requirements.[50] In addition, many of these countries are also plagued by a high percentage of invalid votes, so that on average about half of the eligible population is unable or unwilling to take part in the system. In contrast, in the European countries in the prior wave of democratization, the ability of the population to engage in the political process and find representation in the party system is evident from the very beginning. The pattern cuts across all the indicators of effective participation, across all the cases in West Europe, and is sustained for most of the initial experience with democracy. Italy and Austria are the most "effective" participatory states, with consistently close to 90 percent of the voting age population taking part in the elections (except for Austria's low 67 percent in the first postwar general contest), and with fewer than 3 percent wasted votes in the elections of the 1940s and the 1950s. Among these countries, France and Spain are at the low end of participation in electoral democracy, driven primarily by lower V/VAP turnout but not by blank or excluded votes. This configuration suggests that while large proportions of the population are denied or self-select out of participation, among those who do take part in political democracy there is a high commitment to the process (relatively few spoiled ballots) and at least in France a high sense of validation through votes for parties attaining parliamentary voice (excluded vote of less than 1 percent). In Spain, the excluded vote (4 percent to 6 percent) is the highest for the region, a reflection of support for small regional and minority parties.

While it is possible to speak of high effective participation in West and South Europe, and low effective participation for Latin America, the experience of the post-communist states is more diverse. In one striking manner, the empirical evidence is counterintuitive: the IEP is highest for the Southeastern states (.692), followed by the former republics of Yugoslavia (.657). The countries of Central Europe, where democracy is more entrenched, display less comprehensive access to the existing party regime (.596). The causes behind these trends can be traced to the initially high stakes politics in many of the Balkan cases, producing extensive popular mobilization that found an outlet in electoral politics as well as other forms of political expression. For the first two election cycles, the countries in this region demonstrate unusually high electoral engagement, whether measured by the ratio of voters to the adult population (V/VAP) or to registered rolls (compare tables 2 and 5). This initial commitment to electoral politics declines significantly in most of these countries during the decade of democratization; the sharpest decline, from mid 90 percent V/VAP to mid 60 percent V/VAP, occurs in Bulgaria and Albania, and a similar but less precipitous decline is evident in Romania and Slovenia. In Croatia and Macedonia a much lower initial level of engagement is sustained over time. Here the pattern demonstrates that the heightened interest in politics produced by the disintegration of the communist regime stands out as an unusual phenomenon that is restricted to the first taste of democratic politics, but cannot be upheld after the return to "normal" politics.

The index of effective participation in all democratization regimes is lowest among the soviet successor states. Not surprisingly, given the longstanding difficulties concerning the position of the Russian population among the newly independent nations of the Baltic, the levels of effective participation in the region fall below the .500 mark—so that over half the eligible

Table 5. Effective Participation in Post-Communist States

Country	Election Date	V/VAP (%)	Blank V (%)	Excluded V (%)	1EP
Albania	1991	98.9		4.4	0.945
	1992	89.2		1.8	0.876
	1996	89.5		9.4	0.811
	1997	63.4		8.8	0.578
		85.3		**6.1**	**0.803**
Bulgaria	1990	94.0	3.0	2.7	0.887
	1991	84.5	2.7	24.9	0.617
	1994	81.1	1.2	15.6	0.676
	1997	66.9	0.8	7.6	0.613
		81.6	**1.9**	**12.7**	**0.699**
Croatia	1992	74.9	4.7	15.9	0.600
	1995	72.2	3.3	11.0	0.621
	2000	79.2	1.7	14.7	0.664
		75.4	**3.2**	**13.9**	**0.629**
Czech Rep.	1990	93.1	1.4	18.8	0.745
	1992	83.8	1.7	19.2	0.666
	1996	77.6	0.6	10.6	0.690
	1998	76.7	0.4	11.4	0.677
		82.8	**1.0**	**15.0**	**0.694**
Hungary	1990	75.9	3.5	15.9	0.616
	1994	69.4	1.6	12.6	0.597
	1998	59.9	1.2	11.4	0.524
		68.4	**2.1**	**13.3**	**0.579**
Macedonia	1994	71.2	5.9	NA	
	1998	74.0	2.5	5.6	0.681
		72.6	**4.2**		
Poland	1991	44.4	5.6	7.1	0.389
	1993	52.0	4.3	35.1	0.323
	1997	48.8	3.9	12.4	0.411
		48.4	**4.6**	**18.2**	**0.374**
Romania	1990	83.5	6.5	4.9	0.742
	1992	76.2	12.7	19.1	0.538
	1996	78.2	6.5	17.6	0.602
	2000	69.1	6.2	21.0	0.512
		76.8	**8.0**	**15.7**	**0.599**
Slovkia	1990	93.1	1.4	7.8	0.846
	1992	83.8	1.7	23.6	0.629
	1994	75.9	1.6	13.1	0.649
	1998	88.0	1.7	5.8	0.815
		85.2	**1.6**	**12.6**	**0.735**
Slovenia	1992	85.5	7.0	17.7	0.654
	1996	75.5	5.9	11.4	0.629
	2000	74.6	3.3	3.7	0.695
		78.5	**5.4**	**10.9**	**0.660**

population lacks a voice in the representation system created by the new party regimes. This condition is created by disparities in registration opportunities and significant levels of excluded vote. In Estonia and Latvia there is a large differential between voter turnout as recorded by V/Registration versus V/VAP, confirming the apparent failure of the Russian population to register and take part in the politics of choice.[51] The discrepancy between the two measures declines with succeeding elections in Estonia, from a 27 percent differential in 1992 to one of 15 percent in 1999, evidence of rectification in the adult age population gaining access to the political process—either as a result of population shifts in favor of the majority or the integration of the Russian population into mainstream Estonian politics. Once they enter the system, voters accept the political process, for few cast null or blank ballots, although a higher percentage (from 8 percent to 13 percent) vote for political parties unable to clear the minimum threshold for participation in parliamentary deliberations. In this way, a significant proportion of the voting public exercises a voice that in subsequently muted.

In the other successor states of the Soviet Union, effective participation is also problematic. In Russia (IEP at .401) this is driven by low popular entry into electoral politics. And once engaged, a significant portion of the vote is "wasted" by opting for parties unable to attain parliamentary representation. The evidence on the 1993 election confirms the political turbulence of the times, expressed in low V/VAP turnout as well as a substantial number of spoiled and excluded votes. At the time, some contending parties were precluded by legal action from participation in the election, and a factor that may well explain the low V/VAP turnout and the unusually high number (6.8 percent) of invalid ballots, since supporters of the banned parties had an incentive to express their dissatisfaction about the choices offered by the existing "legal" party regime. The ban also contributed to a lower excluded vote than in subsequent Russian elections, since part of this potential vote is reflected in the lower turnout and higher invalid vote. When the party system is reopened to all contenders for the 1995 election, expanding the lists from thirteen to forty-three in the proportional representation tier, effective participation declines even further, to one of the lowest indices (.311) for all democratizing cases. In 1995, however, this is due to the excessive fragmentation of the vote among many contending parties, producing a hyper exclusion vote (49.5 percent). As a result, about half of the voting public in the Russian PR election fails to translate its voting preference into a legislative "voice." Beyond the four parties able to meet the 5 percent minimum threshold requirement, the vote is dispersed along the entire political spectrum, testifying to the fractionalization of the party system. Four years later, for the 1999 vote, the party regime is streamlined in favor of the "parties of power" reducing substantially the excluded vote, to 18 percent, bringing the IEP to .471, that is, an effective participation shift from about a third to a half of the voting age population.

The Ukrainian path is similarly characterized by low effective participation, yet defined less by the failure to engage in the electoral process (V/VAP average of 71 percent). Rather the system is plagued by substantial numbers of spoiled ballots and excluded votes. In this instance as well, the population's ability to find representative recourse in the party system is curtailed; in the latest 1998 election a third of the vote was dispersed among too many parties. Once more, the extreme fractionalization of the party space contributes to a highly ineffective mode of participation. However, some remedy for this pattern is available in the Russian and Ukrainian cases in the other tier of the mixed electoral system, since voters may be able to back individual candidates in single member districts that provide them with representation.

This form of corrective is not available for states with full PR elections. Poland is a good example of a highly competitive party system that is plagued by an "effective participation" measure (.374 average) that is among the lowest in the post-communist states. In large part, this reflects the problem with party fragmentation, the dispersal of vote among numerous political actors, and the resulting wasted vote. This amounted to 35 percent in the 1993 election, when many parties on the right failed to clear the newly instituted minimum 5 percent requirement for parliamentary entry, and as a result left their electorate without effective means in legislative policy deliberations. The lesson of the 1993 debacle for the right was rectified in some measure by the formation of a coalition (AWS) under the umbrella of the Solidarity trade union, which allowed AWS to emerge as the new dominant political force in the 1997 election and improve effective participation for the voting public. Nonetheless, despite the political realignments, IEP remains low in Poland (.411). Party system fractionalization remains a problem, as evident in the disintegration of the AWS coalition and other political parties, and the regrouping and formation of new parties (e.g., Citizens' Platform) in preparation for the fall 2001 election. This chaotic party scene, with constant realignment of the major political players, may well contribute to political confusion that is expressed in greater reluctance to take part in the electoral process. It is also the case that the high level of political mobilization in Poland prior to the collapse of communism attuned the public to other forms of political expression that tend to devalue electoral politics. For that reason, levels of turnout have been consistently low in Polish elections, particularly so in parliamentary contests where the fragmentation of the party regime reinforces confusion and disengagement.

Low effective participation is evident in many post-communist states, to a degree that is often more visible than in the prior democratization experiences of Europe and Latin America—an artifact of the institutional provisions of the post-communist electoral democracies and the entry of an extensive, even excessive, number of players in the new democracies of EE and FSU. The profiles of individual countries are part of a more general pattern that places most of the post-communist states at the low end of effective participation, leaving out substantial portions of their populations from taking an active role in the choices provided by electoral democracy. Even when involved, many preferences of voters are "wasted" on party choices that fail to enter in a meaningful way the policy arena. The combination of electoral mechanisms and fragmented party regimes contributes to the disjuncture between the post-communist and prior experiences with political democracy (table 4). The primary factor responsible for the difference is the excluded vote: the highest share for the non-communist systems, in Germany in the 1950s and Spain and Portugal in the 1970s, ranges around 5 percent to 7 percent, a percentage that would place these cases at the low end of the excluded vote in the post-communist countries. Among the latter, there often occurs a hyper exclusion that reaches well over 30 percent of the vote at various elections, culminating in national exclusion averages above 20 percent. A similar, but not as acute difference is visible in the patterns of null and blank votes among several former communist states, which in general surpass spoiled ballots in the voting experiences of West and Southern Europe. Taken together, the V/VAP turnout, blank vote, and excluded vote measures provide for political participation in post-communist states that is not well wedded to a party regime able to command substantial support among the electorate. Instead, it suggests that whatever the sharpness of social cleavages, their political saliency remains dispersed among numerous competing political actors, contributing to a large share of "wasted" votes.

These measures of effective participation argue for weak institutionalization of party regimes in the post-communist world. If the consolidation of electoral democracy depends on widespread access, acceptance, and representation of political choices, then the democratizing experience of the EE and FSU states lags behind that of the earlier Western phase of democratic building. In many respects, the post-communist pathway to the stabilization of democratic practices is akin to the Latin American road to democracy. As in the data on the effective number of political parties and electoral volatility, the third wave exhibits patterns of effective participation that are more problematic than the earlier movements toward democracy. In much of EE and FSU, more people remain either (self-) disfranchised from the electoral opportunities afforded by the post-authoritarian political process, or take part in the process without establishing a stake in the structures of representation developed by the new party regimes. The reason may be traced precisely to less entrenched party systems, often subject to convulsions produced by the appearance of new political actors and characterized by swings in support across the political space and the legislative alley. The result is a political fragmentation enhanced by multipartism and low effective participation. In these circumstances the rapid turnover of parties and voters across the democratic landscape is the "natural" state of democratization, producing a slower and more tortuous path to the institutionalization of party regimes.

Conclusion

After a decade of constituting new electoral and party systems, the democratization efforts in EE and FSU have produced conditions that are neither as fragile as the *tabula rasa* prediction, nor as solid as the structured affirmation. Electoral democracies embedded in a well-defined culture of competition and mode of participation have evolved in the post-communist context, but continue to be based on party regimes that experience profound changes in the structures of contestation and representation. The path to consolidation in these emerging democracies is more drawn out and more precarious than in the earlier democratization experiences of Western and Southern Europe. Instead, the post-communist democratic edifice is more akin to the third wave democratization evident in the Latin American context.

All the democratic pathways, from the postwar West to the post-communist East, have been successful at the electoral engineering of competitive regulations. In most states of EE and the FSU, the rules associated with the "only game in town" have been institutionalized early in the transition from authoritarian to democratic politics. After the initial shift away from the majority, single-member district formula to proportional representation codes, few systemic revisions have taken place in the rules that govern political competition. True, adjustments in the other features of the electoral convention have been in evidence, but most have failed to be of sufficient significance to alter the incentive structure for the behavior of party leaders and the voting public. The one measure that has been subject to greater experimentation is the threshold for party entry into the legislative arena, with sequential increases that do affect the strategic behavior of political actors. The intent here is to curb the extensive fragmentation of the electoral party system by reducing its impact on the parliamentary party structure. These efforts do not undermine significantly the widespread stability of electoral regulations, which have been in place since the second-generation elections throughout most of the post-communist period. In the regulatory context, the consolidation of electoral democracies can be ascertained.

Is the institutionalization of competitive regulations a steppingstone in the consolidation of party regimes defined by regular patterns of competition and representation? The usual expectation is that consistent rules are necessary to guide the behavior of political entrepreneurs and voters, resulting in steady patterns of electoral choices and entrenched party systems. While rule institutionalization may well be a necessity, it is apparently not a sufficient condition. In the West European and Southern European transitions, stable regulations and stable party politics proceeded apace, although this was not the case in the Latin American democratizations, where the consistency of electoral codes continued to produce inchoate party structures. The post-communist experience with democracy is closer to the Latin American variant than the earlier European ones.

The evidence on the development of democratic party regimes in EE and the FSU confronts higher than usual multipartism and volatility. On the latter measure, voting support for political parties from election to election varies significantly in most cases. Volatility rates that are among the highest of all transitions confirm the continuing indeterminacy of voting preferences, at least as expressed for specific political parties. The proclivity to high volatility is no doubt facilitated by the multipartism permeating the post-communist party systems, indicated by both the unusually large number of competitors entering the electoral arena and the high number of "effective parties" able to attract measurable support from the voting public. In this regard, the condition of the post-communist political space is more fragmented than any prior transition, even that of Latin American party systems. While there is a downward trend over time in the number of electoral lists and the effective number of parties competing in EE and the FSU, fragmentation and multipartism remain prevalent.

Similar trends are also responsible for much of the "ineffective participation" shaping democratic representation in many former communist states. Faced by a wide array of political competitors and high volatility in the preference structure, many voters seem to tune out the political "noise" and refrain from political participation. Even among those sectors of the electorate that exercise their mandate, a significant proportion is left out of the representative framework by casting votes for "excluded parties," diluting their voice in the legislative arena. As a result, the inclusive nature of the electoral regimes constructed over the past decade is undermined. This too casts a shadow on the achievements of electoral democracy and preempts the consolidation of party regimes fully representative of the people's choice. Yet here as well, there is a consistent movement away from the earlier exclusion and waste, so that sequential win-lose outcomes affect not only the institutional makeup of the party system but also contribute to public learning that defines institutional choices in favor of better representation. In this manner, inclusion on the participatory dimension of party regimes moves forward, and in that sense helps to foster a more structured environment in the nascent political democracies of East Europe and the former Soviet Union.

Overall, the evidence points out the *tabula rasa* claim that despite persistent cleavages in society and public awareness of party identities, institutional factors such as party structures are critical influences on the competitive process and the public's commitment to political democracy. The significant number of political competitors, the fractured political space, and the major shifts in voting patterns render more precarious the path to the institutionalization of party regimes under post-communism. The electorates may well be aware of their interests and the predominant cleavages in society, but the heritage of weak political identities faced by a diversified party system undermines the institutional connections between parties and voters, reducing opportunities for the rapid consolidation of the party regime.

In this way, the future of the post-communist party systems appears to resemble more the development of the third wave Latin American experience than the prior democratization episodes in Western Europe and Southern Europe. In large part, this may be driven by the nature of the political parties that compete in and the electoral regulations that govern electoral democracy in the latest transitions. For the latter, the evidence is generally of stability in the election codes and other rules of competition; but such a pattern may in fact "institutionalize" mechanisms that facilitate the participation of new political players in the electoral game. Thus low barriers for entry into the process, through minimal requirements of support or financial backing, that were instituted at the dawn of democratization may in fact perpetuate the multipartism, fragmentation, and volatility of the system even as electoral democracies mature.

There is evidence of such a pattern in the constant reconfiguration of the political space through the appearance, merger, and dissolution of political parties in many of the EE and FSU countries. This speaks to the nature of political actors in the new democracies, which reflect less the traditional mass political organizations with strong constituencies and local activism than new types of formations. These tend to be more like movement or cartel parties that are less organized, less hierarchical, and less tied to constituencies, that is, parties that are not as strictly bound to administrative or membership constraints. This allows for greater political entrepreneurship, culminating in extensive party reconstruction throughout the decade, evident in the latest wave of elections. Prominent recent examples include the unraveling of prominent parties, as the Freedom Union and Solidarity Electoral Action in Poland before the 2001 election or the appearance of completely new political movements just prior to electoral contests, as Unity in Russia or the Movement for Simeon II in Bulgaria, which were able to attract a vast plurality of voters' support. Such developments demonstrate the continuing malleability of the institutional structure of the party regimes in the post-communist democratization, which hinders stabilization and consolidation even in the face of the winners and losers produced by the electoral funnel. There are some cases where the electoral filter gave shape to clear and seemingly permanent winners, most clearly evident in Hungary and the Czech Republic, that have contributed to the coalescence of the party system. In most other countries, notably in Southeast Europe and the soviet successor states, the party regimes continue to be defined by chaotic political circumstances that provide opportunities for entrepreneurs to reshape or form anew political parties that define the multipartism and fractionalization of the political space and the volatility of the political trend. In these circumstances, the institutionalization of party systems in the nascent political democracies of post-communism continues to be a slowly evolving process that lags behind the consolidation evident in prior democratic projects.

CHAPTER TEN

A Decade of Nonnationalism?

Regime Change As Surrogate for Identity Change

RAYMOND TARAS

Raymond Taras examines another important element of civil society—the crea-tion of a sense of national identity in Russia—and its implications for the for-mation of democratic institutions and state building. He argues that the development of a sense of Russian identity and of an accepted definition of what constitutes the "community" that was to be the new Russian Federation was an especially difficult task because of the multiethnic nature of both the old soviet state and the new Russian entity, itself to be known by the ethnically neutral term "Rossiiskaia" rather than by the ethnic label "Russkaia." Gorbachev's demo-cratic revolution further complicated the task by failing to obtain support for a new union treaty and by animating separatist forces before democratic institu-tions could take firm root. Both shortcomings have compromised the democratic project in post-communist Russia. In many ways, Taras avers, Russia is a state without a nation. While the present conflicting interpretations of what it means to be Russian has made it difficult for Russian nationalists to capture political power, it has also given rise to a new form of imperialism within the Russian Federation based upon exploitation of uneven economic development among the many entities that make up that federation and the substitution of authoritar-ian rule from the center.

There are two arguments to this chapter. First, since the soviet collapse in 1991, Russian politics have been noteworthy for the inability of nationalist movements and their leaders to gain formal power, even though they have exerted significant influence in the State Duma and on the two presidents of the federation. Second, Gorbachev's failure to obtain sufficient support for a new union treaty not only undermined the USSR but also the democratic project as well. There has been regime change in Russia, to be sure, but it has largely entailed incorporating the traditional, imperial style of rule into a new institutional framework.

The geniality of this approach is that it has made the need to redefine Russian national identity—an otherwise difficult and conflictual task—superfluous. In her incisive study of Latvia's road to independence, Rasma Karklins described three types of ethnopolitical identities: the ethnic community proper, the territorial state, and the political regime. She argued: "Although many theorists ask what economic, social, or other factors promote or assuage ethnic assertiveness, few examine the links between types of political regimes and types of ethnic politics. The Soviet experience suggests that regime type is crucial to whether nations want to identify with an established multinational state or seek to form new states."[1] This chapter contends that the case of post-soviet Russia demonstrates how regime change, in conjunction with territorial state reconfiguring, can dispel excessive nationalist introspection about how the ethnic community is to be defined.

Karklins' analysis underscored the diverse reasons behind the assault on the soviet system, but it sees the primary struggle as having focused on regime change which in turn impacted ethnopolitics. She asked: "Does it matter whether a multinational state—be it the former USSR or another state—is ruled autocratically or democratically, and if so how?" One of her chief arguments was that a democracy could not be reconciled with an ethnic control system. Adopting her logic, we suggest that because post-Gorbachev Russia has been ruled autocratically (though in a substantively different way from Soviet authoritarianism); the ethnic control system has been overhauled but retained. Within the Russian Federation, therefore, identity politics have taken on new discursive forms but have preserved the old content, which centers on the Russian imperial idea.

Empire as Russian— Not Russian Nationalist—Idea

The collapse of the USSR bewildered soviet specialists and compelled them to reflect upon the nature of the system constructed by Lenin and Stalin.

Victor Zaslavsky, for one, could not hold back his astonishment: "The sudden dissolution of the Soviet Union in 1991 was one of the most unusual events in world history; it is probably the only case of a superpower and its empire collapsing in peacetime, and seemingly for largely internal reasons."[2] A key question for him and others was whether the Soviet Union simply represented a new ideological variant of old Russian imperialism or really set the stage for internationalism that communist leaders in the fifteen soviet republics insisted was the objective. Some experts argued that the USSR had never been an empire in the classical sense: "it was the dream of creating a state from an empire that separated soviet-type imperialism from that practiced by traditional empires."[3] From this perspective, the USSR represented a concerted effort to overcome both the nationalisms of constituent peoples and the internationalism that Marxist ideologues had foisted on skeptical soviet leaders.

Since the 1990s, historical revisionism has cast the USSR as an empire like all others. One group of scholars described how "even from those commentators who during the late 1980s were uneasy about labeling the Soviet Union 'an empire,' a historical revisionism is now underway in which, in light of the USSR's collapse along multiethnic lines, the Soviet Union is busily being reinvented as empire."[4] This perspective has been favored by some of the former soviet republics that are apprehensive about President Vladimir Putin's long-term goals: "for many in the borderland states, having experienced 'imperial disintegration,' the question on the agenda is now one of 'potential imperial [Russian] reconstruction.'" Depicting the USSR as empire, therefore, has political uses in the post-soviet landscape: "through the construction of the 'other' as 'empire,' we can begin to comprehend how the borderland states' interpretations of their previous and current relations with the Soviet Union help structure the idea of empire as a continuing and uninterrupted Russian project."[5]

The notion of *federal colonialism* has been introduced to capture the former relationship between the Soviet center and the fourteen non-Russian "borderland republics." The argument is that the Soviet Union contained features of both federalism and colonialism: "while sovereignty resided with the center rather than in the ethnorepublics, the particular nature of the soviet federation ensured that nation-building took place at both the ethnorepublic and all-union levels."[6] Although Moscow opposed any de facto rights to self-determination by the republics, neither did it embark on a consistent, uniform policy of cultural standardization in the ethnorepublics: "one of the major paradoxes of the soviet empire was that it provided the social space for nation-building at the ethnoregional scale."[7] The policy of indigenization or nativization (*korenizatsiia*) of communist elites served as an affirmative action program for non-Russian leaders. Zaslavsky went so far as to claim: "From its very inception, soviet federalism fostered the policy of preferential treatment of the representatives of local nationalities within their own terri- tories."[8] Terry Martin provided extensive evidence in support of the view that throughout the 1920s and 1930s the Bolshevik government systematically promoted national consciousness among the non-Russian minorities and even created statist institutions for them.[9] Admittedly the union republics "were not all treated uniformly by the center, nor in turn were relations between the ethnorepublics and the center predicated on similarity."[10] Conversely, the strength of nationalist mobilization differed from one Soviet republic to another,[11] a trend that was still discernable in the twenty-one republics created within the Russian Federation. If the Soviet Union was depicted as having been at most imperial, not imperialist, the same seemed to apply to the successor Russian state.[12]

The cascading nationalism in the soviet republics in the late 1980s owed much, paradoxically then, to the Kremlin's empathetic view of national affilia- tion that was clearly at odds with the professed goal of creating an all-union nation, or *sovietskii narod*. Nationalities specialist and policy advisor Valery Tishkov regretted this fact. He emphasized how an "important element of soviet-style ethnonationalism is viewing a nation as a homogeneous body, a kind of collective individual with common blood and soul, primordial rights, and a single will. Over the course of many decades, this vision of an ethno- nation acquired deep emotional and political legitimacy."[13] Inevitably, when the soviet center weakened such "subnations," indoctrinated with soviet ideology, demanded the status of nations and, quickly thereafter, nation- states. As a result, soviet policy on nationalities self-destructed.

One ancillary feature about the Soviet Union distinguishing it from other empires was the discrediting of the nationalism of the imperial people itself. As early as 1923, even before Lenin's death, a resolution of the Communist Party Congress stated that once Russian nationalism had been eliminated, other nationalisms would lose their *raison d'être* and also wither away. The reasoning was that the Russian "other" would have been removed from the political topography. This argument was reiterated at the 1930 party congress. In the intervening period, "The soviet state embarked on a major effort of social engineering aimed at creating the cultural infrastructure of national communities that were at a very early stage of development. New nations were established, given languages, alphabets, cultures and so on, but under the strict control of the communist party."[14] To be sure, in 1938 Russian became a com- pulsory language throughout the Soviet Union, and in the war years references to Russia's past imperial greatness were a common motif. As Ronald Suny wrote: "The imperial aspects of the soviet system became clearer in the 1930s as Stalin moved steadily away from the more radical aspects of *korenizatsiia* and gave a much more positive valence to Russian language and culture."[15]

But after Stalin's death in 1953 cultural nationalist tendencies among non-Russian peoples began to reappear. Linguistic choice in educational institutions was reinstituted under Leonid Brezhnev and ethnic republics were not unduly harassed if they stuck to the tried-and-true formula of "socialist in form, nationalist in content." Some commentary went so far as to claim that the USSR did not just treat non-Russian nations well, it even built new nations. In describing the ironies of soviet history, Suny reported that "a principal one must be that a radical socialist elite that proclaimed an internationalist agenda . . . in fact ended up by making nations within its own political body."[16]

Not surprisingly, when in the 1980s Russians had to face rising criticism of their supposedly deceitful commitment to *faux* multiculturalism, a backlash was inevitable. The reaction was first evidenced on the cultural plain, in the works of the village prose writers in the 1970s. In politics, the reaction was evidenced in the version of Russian nationalism propagated by Boris Yeltsin, dramatized by his ostentatious resignation from the federal communist party in July 1990. While he attributed his departure to distaste for soviet authoritarianism in its jazzed-up Gorbachev guise, he quickly perceived the advantages of being an ethnic entrepreneur. As Igor Zevelev reported, "Russians emerged from the USSR as an incomplete nation with a surprisingly low level of national consciousness and lack of a mass-based national movement."[17] This was what Yeltsin set out to redress.

If the USSR had been a Russian empire in disguise and state socialism the ordering principles undergirding Russian nationalism, then many of its features had begun to infuriate more traditional Russian nationalists. The soviet project became the target when Russians sensed that they no longer were treated equitably. On the eve of soviet collapse, then, Russian nationalists began raising the ethnic justice question. Why were small or backward soviet republics receiving more than their fair share of the dwindling pool of resources? Why were their cultural practices, most notably in Central Asia, *bakshish,* excepted from communist social engineering? Furthermore, Russian nationalists condemned what they saw as the predatory behavior of many non-Russians: "Why do Estonians and Latvians, Armenians and Georgians, enjoy higher standards of living than we do?" Average Russians felt that ethnic mafias carried out a disproportionate amount of the country's criminal activity. The ethnic *kto kovo* question—who was taking advantage of whom—became highly salient.

In explaining the nationalist mobilization of Russians, Mark Beissinger suggested that "the construction of a modern Russian identity could occur only on the basis of the deconstruction of the symbiosis between Russian and soviet imperial identities."[18] Roman Szporluk observed how Russians "were used to being 'the leading nation' in the USSR, but they were also an object of manipulation and a victim of political manipulation—their identity made and remade by the party."[19] An underlying assumption in such arguments was that regime change for Russians would largely make redundant the need for a change in national identity. The logic went that redefining the Russian state as democratic, as Yeltsin was to do, could help mitigate a national identity crisis.

A Decade of Imperial Rebuilding?

Has an empire arisen on the ashes of a preceding one? Was the imperial idea truly banished with the end of the communist system? These questions have sparked a lively debate among scholars and policy makers alike since 1991. From the perspective of Moscow, the answer is clearly no to the first question. But from the periphery, in the north Caucasus among Chechens and their neighbors, and further away among Buryats and Tuvans in East Asia, the answer is just as clearly yes. For a dominant nation's rule can be a minority nation's subjugation and, conversely, several nations' subjugation may become another nation's empire.

The debate might best be framed as whether Russia can extricate itself from empire. As one writer put it, "the Soviet Union is so damned big that it has too many common homes for the comfort of its many neighbors."[20] In a more metaphorical formulation, writer Alexander Solzhenitsyn asked: "Should we be struggling for warm seas far away, or ensuring that warmth rather than enmity flows between citizens?"[21]

Empires may be ruled over using military force, but they can also be controlled employing soft power, for example, economic resources. Russia of the 1990s used the two strategies in tandem to keep the "near abroad" just that. Whether this leads to the conclusion that Yeltsin's Russia behaved imperiously toward its national minorities and its far-flung regions is debatable. Certainly when important differences about important issues emerge, Moscow has imposed its own preferences. As an important example, 60 percent of voters in the non-ethnic (that is, Russian) regions of the Russian Federation voted in favor of adopting a new constitution in the December 1993 referendum; but only a minority (48 percent) endorsed it in the ethnic (non-Russian) republics. Other questions were raised about the validity of the referendum, of course, but the constitution was nevertheless enacted. The bottom line was that the Kremlin got its way, notwithstanding the lack of enthusiasm for the federal constitution among non-Russians.

Today a discussion of empires may seem anachronistic, and references to a Russian imperium almost appear to be a bad joke. But let us consider Alexander Motyl's proposition: "although imperialism may belong to the past, empire may belong to the future."[22] True, the emergence of empires through land acquisition is now improbable. But the author contends that "although the international sources of empire may have declined in importance, the internal sources are not only present, but, arguably, have assumed greater salience."[23] The two principal internal processes that can lead to empire are differentiation resulting from uneven modernization, and the substitution of dictatorship for democracy in multinational states. Postsoviet Russia may embody a mix of these two variants. It is a fact that "today, for the first time in centuries, ethnic Russians represent a significant majority of the state they live in eighty percent instead of fifty percent."[24] But even if its borders have been redrawn, Russia can still be thought of as an empire for one of two very different reasons: it has not developed into a nation-state with a problem-free national identity and is still marked by socioeconomic differences between the core and the periphery; alternatively, it constitutes a multinational state, but the core rules over the periphery in an authoritarian manner.

Discussions of empire invariably touch on colonialism. In the view of some specialists, the communist system was an instrument "enabling Russia to resist successfully that liquidation of colonialism carried out elsewhere in the world."[25] A radical proposition would be that Yeltsin-style democracy served as an instrument masking and simultaneously facilitating Russia's transition from soviet republic to Russian empire. Although the body of evidence is not one-sided enough to support this proposition, it is nevertheless revealing that since its independence at the end of 1991 the Russian Federation has been viewed as a renewed threat to both the newly independent states neighboring it and the "submerged nations," or national minorities, within Russia. It was Yeltsin's use of the mantra of democracy that helped deflect charges of nationalist restoration under his presidency.[26]

There are many who believe that Yeltsin acted sincerely in dismantling not just the structure of the soviet empire but the foundations of a possible Russian one. French sovietologist Helene Carrere d'Encausse rose to the defense of the new Russia and suggested, "The idea of the cost of the empire led to the slogan 'Russia out of the empire,' which became very popular in the early 1990s. . . . In the new Russia, the Russian mind is no longer an imperial mind; on the contrary, the Russian population is largely, if not unanimously, convinced that the progress of the nation and the progress of the empire would be difficult to reconcile."[27] Leon Aron credited Yeltsin with this makeover: "Yeltsin is the first Russian leader who has not expanded, or at least strengthened, the domestic empire. . . . Yeltsin has reversed a 400-year-old political tradition in which the Russian national idea was identical with the Russian imperial idea."[28]

But how other nations view Russia may be the most important signpost indicating whether it retains imperial ambitions. Beissinger pointed to "the widespread perception throughout the region that, in spite of the collapse of the Soviet Union, the empire lives on."[29] Further, "perceptions of empire, a longing for empire, and a discourse of empire remain characteristic features of post-soviet politics."[30] As a result, "in the fractious realm of Russian domestic politics, one clear consensus among groups of all persuasions is that Russia should remain one of the world's 'Great Powers.'"[31] Roman Szporluk asserted that "just as in the case of the tsarist empire and the Soviet Union, modern Russia cannot behave simply as though it is the nation-state of the Russians. Whether that makes it imperialist is another question."[32] Significant, too, is the widespread perception among Russians themselves—including both elites and masses—who live in regions of the Federation that Moscow has behaved like an imperial center. Bo Petersson commented: "it is striking how frequently it is the center, Moscow, that is being Othered. It is the center that is scapegoated and blamed for all ills that have befallen the country and the regions, and it is the center that is seen as continuously scheming to worsen the situation even more."[33] From this general skepticism about how Russian governance has changed we can at a minimum infer that imperial habits die hard.

If Russia's imperial status has diminished, then, its imperial identity may persist. A factor that has contributed to this process is the strengthening of Russia's collective "Other"—the West—and the West's reticence to grant Russia recognition as a great power still.[34] Instead, Russia's marginal status has been underscored as NATO enlarged in 1998, Serbia was attacked in 1999, ex-soviet republics in Central Asia were persuaded to make air bases available to the American military in 2001, the G-7 kept Yeltsin and Putin on the outside whenever crucial policy questions came up, and the IMF compiled a school-like report card on Russia's economic behavior. What has been seen as the West's humiliating treatment of Russia has caused imperial identity not to recede but to revive. The carte blanche given by Russian elites and masses to President Putin since 2000 is the best evidence of this.

Ilya Prizel summarized the debate about empire: "Some feel that Russia will not be able to retain its truncated integrity without at least a partial resurrection of the empire, while others believe that the demise of the empire has had a liberating effect on Russia that will allow it to become a normal nation pursuing its own national interest rather than imperial demands."[35] Prizel clearly found the first approach to be the more influential: "the ideal of Russia as a superior civilization and a transcendent empire with a universal mission has remained. Indeed, a Russian national identity without this vision has yet to emerge. Were the Russians to establish such a concept of national identity, it would allow Russia to make peace with itself and the international system."[36] This is a pious wish, and it is far from certain that a thoroughly de-imperialized Russia would usher in an era of peace for Russians and their neighbors.

The crisis of Russian identity needs to be contextualized. It is interconnected with the more general post-communist crisis of statehood. As Judy Batt has written, many issues bearing on nationalities, like the status of minorities, are "inseparable from the fundamental questions that the majority nation itself has to resolve concerning its own identity, its relation to the state, and the state's place in Europe and the wider international order."[37] Especially given a weak state, weak central authority, and weak democracy, Russian identity has been suffering from a profound existential crisis. That is why drawing attention to both change in regime identity (even if it has not been as sweeping as has been made out) and continuity of imperial identity (even though how "continuous" it has been is tenuous) is such an important exercise.

Discourse on Russian Identity

Since the late 1980s a variety of discourses on Russian identity has appeared. In the words of cultural theorist Svetlana Boym, "There is still, in present-day Russia, a great urge to find a single, all-embracing narrative—national, religious, historic, political, or aesthetic—to recover the single dramatic plot with devils and angels, black and white swans, hangmen and victims, that would explain Russia's Past, Present, and Future."[38] The undertaking has been of great importance to political leaders seeking popular legitimacy and electoral support—party names such as "Unity," "Our Home is Russia," "Great Power," and "Fatherland" testify to the attention paid to the "all-embracing narrative." But identity discourse has also been of great concern to historians, philosophers, and writers.

The political discourse promoted by the Yeltsin administration was statist and emphasized that the Russian homeland was now the Russian Federation and nothing beyond it. However, two empire-restoring, irredentist discourses emerged, one from the political right, the other from the left. The first highlighted the need for reuniting historic Russian lands settled centuries ago by Russians, principally, Ukraine, Belarus, northern Kazakhstan, and parts of Estonia. The rightist nationalist discourse centered on the reconstruction of the former tsarist empire. The second invoked the goal of a reconstituted soviet homeland and argued, "As the motherland of socialism, Russia is the advanced point of exemplarity."[39] It followed from this that the mission of the Russian nation was to bind together other peoples into a common destiny.

There have been many other understandings of identity that have been advanced in recent years, of course. One relatively influential approach accepted the idea of a Russian nation that subsumed its diaspora, but simultaneously insisted that the Russian Federation was the natural Russian homeland. This pragmatic, legalistic approach was favored for a time by the Yeltsin administration: "by offering extra-territorial citizenship to all those who have a connection—ethnic or historic—to the Russian homeland, Russia has attempted to redefine the nation while at the same time acknowledging the inviolability of the borderland states' sovereign spaces. The regime has therefore attempted to create a Russian nation without restoring the homeland-empire."[40] When Yeltsin launched the war on Chechnya in 1994, it became clear that such a seemingly liberal discourse on identity did not exclude an aggressive practical side.

What these different discourses on identity have in common are grounding in alternative visions of borders and borderlands. Perhaps the most celebrated, if not necessarily influential discourse on non-soviet Russian imperial identity has been Eurasianism. It consists of a remarkably diverse set of characteristics. Russian philosopher Lev Gumilev stressed its ethnographic dimension: "Eurasia is not merely a huge continent; it contains in its center a super ethnos bearing the same name."[41] Eurasia is part of a tripod that includes the Muslim world to the south and the Germanic-Latin world to the west. It is the latter—the West—that poses the greater threat to Eurasia. The Eurasian idea asserts that "if Russia is to preserve its cultural heritage; it must maintain a culturally non-threatening union with the Turkic people or face a cultural annihilation inflicted by the West . . . Since, according to many statists, Russians cannot exist as Russians outside a Russian state, making a multinational Russian state across Eurasia is vital to the survival of Russians as a people."[42]

A bewildering political characteristic of Eurasianism has been identified by Andrei Tsygankov. "Unlike Western realists who emphasize nation-states as key players of international politics, Eurasianists argue in favor of empires as the key units of action."[43] Unlike other contemporary narratives of Russian identity, this one begins with the claim that a Eurasian Russia must be at least the size of the USSR and perhaps even greater. Like other discourses, Eurasianism has separate strands. "Modernizers offer the restoration of the Soviet Union under the name of the Eurasian empire to maintain geopolitical balances and international stability."[44] By contrast, in order to contain American imperialism, the main threat to Russia, Europe, and Asia, "expansionists advocate a further imperial expansion of Russia beyond the borders of the former Soviet Union."[45]

Russian politics has been affected by the bizarre ideas of the Eurasianists, if only indirectly. Russia's neo-communists share a common cause and seem natural partners in a political coalition with this group.[46] Novelist and politician Alexander Prokhanov was a key figure in the effort to forge an opposition bloc to Yeltsin and worked with communist party head Gennady Zyuganov to develop a "patriotic" front based loosely on Eurasian ideas. In Prokhanov's newspaper *Den* (renamed *Zavtra* in 1993), Alexander Dugin established himself as the leading theoretician of neo-Eurasianism.[47] His vision of world history was one of perpetual conflict between "the order of Eurasianists" and "the order of Atlanticists." Accordingly, "the Germans and Russians have embodied the Indo-European ideal of rooted, spiritual, Aryan Eurasianism in more recent history; the Jews, British, and Americans, the rootless, materialistic, commercial Atlanticist idea."[48] For Dugin, with both Islam and a spiritually revived Europe as allies, "Russia's long-term task is to unite the anti-Atlanticist, antimondialist forces of Eurasia in a new imperial alliance. . . . Dugin's envisioned continental imperial alliance will span the Eurasian landmass from Dublin to Vladivostok, with Moscow ('the third Rome') serving as the continental capital."[49]

Such versions of Eurasianism fly in the face of much of Russian public opinion. The general cultural orientation of Russians is toward Europe.[50] A stigma is attached, especially by better-educated Russians, to the "Asiatic" element in Russian society. Solzhenitsyn cited other reasons for rejecting a Eurasian identity: Russia had to "free itself of great-power thinking and imperial delusions. The time has come for an uncompromising choice between an empire . . . and the spiritual and physical salvation of our own people."[51] By "our own people" he meant the European subjects of the tsarist empire.

Let us examine one last type of identity that gained currency before Putin became president. It was based on a "Russia of regions" and was heralded as a realistic solution to the problems of centrifugalism and identity loss in the Russian Federation. The risks associated with devolution of power to regions, the argument went, would be worth taking if Russian identity overall were strengthened. Cultural theorist Ulf Hedetoft reflected upon a model of partial convergence between national identity and regional cultures in which the latter "identify with the nation, but in the sense that they see themselves as the best, highest, most particular manifestations of national identity, thus partly appropriating this identity for themselves, whilst (in most cases) still recognizing the rightful belongingness of other regions to the national sphere."[52] The weakness of the Russian center would, under this model, be compensated for by regionalism as a vessel of the national identity. Putin's recentralization of power has made this discourse moot.[53]

Is the Russian idea, even if extensively reinterpreted for the new century, fated to exclude liberal virtues and democratic processes? We have been reviewing arguments indicating how embedded the imperial idea is in the historical construct of Russia. But for analytic purposes it may be valuable to decouple the often-interchanged notions of imperial identity and authoritarian nationalism. While recognizing that peoples forcibly subjected to either care little for such conceptual nitpicking, by making this distinction we may be able to tease out implications for Russia's future political system.

Michael Billig has written that "nations often do not typically have a single history, but there are competing tales to be told. In Britain, the same people will speak about the national past using conservative and liberal tales."[54] So too in Russia, a conservative national tale can describe Russian nationalism and the rise of a greater Russia, and a liberal civic narrative can invoke the construction of a harmonious multinational empire where Russian nationalism is checked. This multinational state could be cast as an empire, of course, but it would be described as a successfully organized empire, like the contemporary United States, Britain, or South Africa. Imperial identity understood this way could then be more easily reconciled with the practice of democracy.

Institutions, the Imperial Past, and Russia's Democratic Quotient

Neither Yeltsin nor Mikhail Gorbachev before him was willing to cut through the Gordian knot of nationalism that would have allowed for a deeper democratization process to be set in motion. Each was concerned that nationalists at the head of diverse ethnic groups living across the country would make use of the opportunity opened up by democracy to declare sovereignty and independence. In turn, statehood for republics and autonomous republics would provide grounds for leaders to slam the door on democratization. The logic was that national self-determination *was* democracy and needed no further iteration. The irony was that Gorbachev and Yeltsin's fear of anarchy resulting from deeper democratization caused them to behave in precisely the way that they posited ethnic entrepreneurs of republics and autonomies would behave: they began to reinforce central management of democratic processes (which is a *non sequitor*) while basking in the self-determination they believed they had brought their nations.

Gorbachev's resignation speech in December 1991, for example, contained a final plea for the preservation of the union. Yeltsin's resignation speech in December 1999 contained greater vanity. After stating that he was handing power over to Prime Minister Putin, he remarked: "I have always had confidence in the amazing wisdom of Russian citizens. Therefore, I have no doubt what choice you will make at the end of March 2000" in the presidential elections. Each leader stressed the virtue of continuity with his rule. Yet neither of these leaders had succeeded in brokering a renegotiated federalism among subjects of their federations. To the end Gorbachev continued to insist on a union of at least twelve Soviet republics. In the midst of a brutal attack on the Chechen population, Yeltsin continued to maintain the inviolability of Russian Federation borders. Intractability on their visions of state unity, borders, and identity made antidemocrats out of them.

A salient question for democracy in Russia is, then, whether a negotiated pact concluded by central and republic leaders on distribution of powers would have more efficiently promoted democratic construction in the USSR or, subsequently, the Russian Federation while protecting the integrity of the federation. Alone, such a pact would not have guaranteed genuine political pluralism, the process of deriving political outcomes from the play of impartial rules, and other defining features of democracy. Many other factors affecting democratic development were involved: the subject and parochial political cultures in existence, the authoritarian instincts of leaders like Gorbachev and Yeltsin, the strength of antidemocratic forces, the inexperience of political party formation, elections, rule of law, and other institutional prerequisites for democracy. But let us nevertheless speculate about how the nonexistence of a nationalities pact negotiated by subjects of the federation weakened the process of democratization.

For Gorbachev the problem was that he obtained only tactical support for his new union treaty which was approved in the April 1991 referendum held in only nine of the fifteen republics. To be sure, the political resources

that were shifting out of his hands during the transition phase would probably have made any pact that he concluded insignificant. The soviet leader
implicitly recognized that the referendum had still left everything on the table
when he promised to leave the aspiring secessionists with the option to
"decide for themselves what they need and what kind of society they want to
have."[55] In sum, agreement on a transitional pact in 1991, with Gorbachev
serving as the central actor, would not have guaranteed that the soviet
nationality question was resolved and that it was safe to proceed and build
democratic institutions and promote democratic processes.

Apart from actors and their resources, the role played by political institutions and the structured patterns of interaction they produce needs to be
examined. After all, key actors, their resources, and preferences are in large
measure structured by a state's "normal" institutional configuration, which
in the case of Russia really signified the seventy-year-old system of communist rule. Institutions engender sets of expectations about the payoffs and
overheads of particular actions, but when they are brought into question so
are the benefits and costs.[56]

Institutions derive their power from regularity, that is, repeated recourse
to and use of them by political actors. When this configuration comes under
attack as during an elite or mass bid for regime change, and when politics
therefore become abnormal, the existing rules of the game and even the
informal constraints on political behavior are undermined.[57] The moment
the possibility of change of a rule is suggested, the institution represented by
that rule is weakened. This is most dramatically illustrated by the fate of the
Soviet Union itself; once the terms and rules of the union were put into
question, the USSR itself was seriously destabilized. By contrast, the learning
curve for Yeltsin convinced him not to tamper with overarching rules
because doing precisely that had led to the demise of his predecessor.
Another example of how putting rules into doubt can produce a billiard-ball
effect is the fate of the soviet parliament. By 1990, in the words of Tishkov, it
had "*de facto* acquired the expression of an assembly of nations."[58] Again,
Yeltsin sought to avoid making the same mistake by weakening the influence
of the non-Russian bloc of deputies in the legislature. With the Putin presidency, ethnic republic and Russian regional representatives in parliament
were placed even more firmly under the control of the Kremlin.

When the probability of a rule change becomes high, even inevitable,
then the political game that it underpins is brought into question. Political
actors will no longer predicate their actions on the basis of rules that they
realize are disintegrating. Gorbachev's error was to do just that; Yeltsin's forte
was to make sure that basic rules—such as those governing the institutional

form that relations among nations—were not in a state of flux. Gorbachev was leader when transition began. At the CPSU Congress, meeting in July 1990 for what turned out to be the last time, the Central Committee, Politburo and, ultimately, General Secretary were successively delegitimized as sources of authority. Constraints on soviet republic leaders, like the need to consult with the Kremlin before deciding on policy initiatives, vanished when Gorbachev came to be viewed as a lame duck, in great part discredited by Yeltsin's call in 1990–1991 for a complete rewriting of rules governing center-republic relations. Yeltsin's famous exhortation was for the subjects of the federation to take as many powers as they could swallow. The result was that no institutions were left to structure the transition. How the transition was to proceed came down to a contest between Gorbachev and Yeltsin, one that proved to be one-sided given the shift in their respective resource bases.

From 1991 to 1999, post-communist rulers headed by Yeltsin acquired new resources, began to write new rules, and set up new constraints. The two Russian invasions of Chechnya were the primary example of the emergent rule on nationalities. By contrast, no better example of the failure of rule making applying to post-soviet nations can be found than the pathetic fate of the Commonwealth of Independent States. Clearly, at the turn of the twenty-first century many rules and constraints remained either ineffective or elusive, and the Putin administration assigned itself the mission of tightening rules and constraints whenever they were too loose and liberal.

The institutionalist framework that we have outlined for studying the nationalities question can suggest the extent to which the nature of soviet disintegration had an impact on the character of post-soviet democratization. What is clear from our general analysis is that at a time of crisis, transition, and change, political outcomes were not reducible to actors' immediate preferences. Even if they were murky, rapidly changing, and/or one-time-only (as during perestroika), rules of the game during the transition period shaped the method of play employed by political actors and the eventual outcomes. The transition may not have been directly structured by institutions or by expectations resulting from repeated games, but it nonetheless was extensively structured by a series of one-time-only games.[59]

Why, we may ask, did Gorbachev and the communist elite allow such single-play games to be held if they seemed to threaten their power and positions? The answer lies in the sequencing and timing of the games: each game resulted in a redistribution of power. Thus, acquiescing to political pluralism after seven decades of one-party rule changed the nature of the game, as well as the weight and distribution of political resources. The patronage embedded in the nomenklatura system, which fashioned the hierarchical relationship between central and regional elites, became obsolete. In these circumstances, an even quasi-competitive election, or indeed any election that produced a political arena for discrediting incumbent forces, changed the game decisively. As Juan Linz and Alfred Stepan reminded us in this context, "elections can create agendas, can create actors, can reconstruct identities, help legitimate and delegitimate claims to obedience, and create power."[60]

Under conditions of what can be termed electoral populism, new political possibilities arose in Russia. The emergence of a new political opportunity structure favoring out-groups (more precisely, the most outsider of the insider group of which Yeltsin was the best representative) took on crucial significance. Positioning and sequencing became overriding political imperatives, for taking the initiative and becoming the first to embark on constitutional and electoral innovations was likely to determine which political actors would become dominant with what relative strength.

The institutionalist perspective holds that with repeated plays actors learn what the implication of a given resource in a political game will be. But in a new or changing game they must guess, and some leaders arrive at better educated guesses than others. In Gorbachev's case, he repeatedly guessed wrongly in the conditions of uncertainty prevailing in the second half of the 1980s. He sided with democrats too early in the game, as at the January 1987 Central Committee plenum recommending democratization. Then he joined up with unreconstructed communists when their position had been lethally weakened, as at the March 1990 Congress of People's Deputies where he was chosen to head a strong presidency (a hastily created soviet institution that had little legitimacy in any political arena). As this chapter has argued, Gorbachev was also repeatedly wrong on the nationalities question. His mistake was in what Paul Goble characterized as "running against the republics" after 1985.[61] The inconsequential September 1989 Central Committee plenum on nationalities and the largely symbolic March 1991 referendum on the union treaty were good illustrations of this.

Gorbachev's numerous mistaken guesses made under conditions of uncertainty had the effect of redistributing advantages and disadvantages in unintended ways. Thus he crippled the hitherto dominant actor, the communist party leadership of which he was a member, and promoted new players to prominence, in particular the nationalist elites of the republics. By avoiding confrontations with or altogether ignoring them, he effectively lost all influence on the nationalist upsurge in the republics. Similarly, his exclusion or diminution of key political actors at various junctures—above all Yeltsin but also the respected democratic Andrei Sakharov—lost him stewardship over the process of democracy. Russia's democratic quotient may never have been very high. How could it be without the foundations of a civil society, a state firmly governed by the rule of law, and a system of checks and balances between branches of government? But the result of single-play games under Gorbachev further stacked the odds against a full democratic breakthrough.

Conclusion

Unlike Poland or Hungary, transition in the soviet case did not involve either a unified reform-oriented elite or an extrication pact for communist incumbents. The consequence in the short term was bickering over rules, power struggles, coup d'êtats (like in August 1991 to preserve the USSR and in October 1993 to preserve Yeltsin's oligarchy) and, in the arena of nationalities politics, sovereignty games played by Russia's regions. All of this seriously destabilized the emergent political system and led from the outset to a flawed democratization process.

The nature of transition scarred Russian democracy, but so did nearly a decade of rule by Yeltsin. True, the regime change that was gradually instituted in the 1990s provided Russia with a remade political identity that, on the surface, appropriated the trappings of democracy. Furthermore, the traditional imperial style of rule in the country was retained with slight modifications. For those best placed to judge—nations neighboring Russia—imperial identity had not been dispelled and under Putin, if anything, it has been fanned. At the individual level these changes meant little. As Stephen White observed, early in the new century "Russians were sick of experiments, bitter about the failures of their political class, and desperate for the first time in their lives to 'live normally'—whatever the regime might choose to call itself."[62] The novelty of a democratic regime identity had worn thin, and the reversion to a more understandable identity based on Russia's imperial greatness was once again becoming an appealing, visceral alternative.

CHAPTER ELEVEN

Consolidation As a Work in Progress

DONALD R. KELLEY

As the participants in the Fulbright Institute conference quickly concluded when they assembled to consider the fate of democracy in Eastern Europe and the former Soviet Union a decade after the fall of communism, the passage of ten years was at best an incomplete benchmark to assess the consolidation of democratic regimes. Some things were clear. A decade had permitted certain conclusions to be reached about the institutional features of virtually all of the successor regimes, and there was clear agreement that while a minority of the nations had clearly succeeded in consolidating democratic regimes, the vast majority had either failed or were still somewhere in an uneasy transition from authoritarian to democratic rule. That said, certain conclusions emerged from the discussions, some expressing our agreement on what now seemed certain about the transition and what remained to be decided, and some reflecting certain themes that appeared repeatedly in our discussions.

What We Are Sure Of . . .

Certain verities emerged from our discussions. Most obvious was the universally shared view that, whatever the future might hold, there would be no return to the communist regimes of the past. While "reverse waves," as

Huntington terms them, might occur, they would not recreate the communist regimes, implemented through an interlocking party and state and characterized by a centrally planned economy. In that sense, both the doctrine of socialism-cum-communism and the institutional forms of the Leninist party-state are in the garbage heap of history. To be sure, much of the past survives in other forms; that said, it survives in different institutional forms, sometimes inimical to the democratic project, but sometimes easing the transition to whatever passes for democracy in these new nations.

Although the overall assessment of the consolidation of democratic rule must be negative for all but about a third of the post-communist nations, there are bright spots, at least in terms of the trends that may be noted. Without question, those nations which began the post-communist era with democracy in name only remain essentially authoritarian states; no seemingly democratic constitutions or professed adherence to democratic norms obviates the reality that nearly dictatorial regimes have taken up where the Leninist party-state left off. It is also true that executive leadership, usually embodied in a strong presidency, has gained in power over the last decade in most post-communist nations. Even if democratically elected in competitive races, such executives already typically possessed strong constitutionally mandated powers and exercised broad influence even beyond these legal norms. But as noted in a number of the chapters above, even strong presidents typically operate within a framework of political realities that hedges their powers, if only out of the need to avoid confrontation with the legislature. Even if one acknowledges the growing strength of such presidencies, it is far from certain that—within limits—the trend automatically compromises the further consolidation of democratic rule, especially if it is linked to the difficult but necessary task of state building as a prerequisite for the emergence of competent government. One may lament the growing power of the Russian presidency under Putin, for example; taken in perspective, however, it may be preferable to the on-again, off-again confrontational style of Boris Yeltsin and a necessary phase in the creation of a law-governed society. As the phrase "within limits" suggests, however, there are certain boundaries that cannot be crossed without injury to democratic rule. The extension of presidential terms by referenda as has occurred in Central Asia, and the creation of Lukashenka's dictatorial presidency clearly cross the line. In some cases, especially regarding the media, Putin maneuvers dangerously close to the mark. But his efforts to bring order to the party systems probably will not endow Unity with unchallenged dominance at the polls, especially in legislative elections, and his attacks on the Yeltsin-era oligarchs can only help to shift increasing power into the hands of legitimately elected officials. And in one sense, there is good news: three of the region's once most objectionable authoritarian states—Serbia (and, by implication, Yugoslavia), Croatia, and Slovakia—have moved strikingly toward greater democracy, largely as a consequence of the failure of hypernationalism and the persistence of democratic opposition forces.

It is also reasonably certain that the military will not play the role of a Praetorian guard, as once feared. Much of that fear had been misplaced given the party's tight control over the military during the years of communist rule. It stemmed as much from the assumption that the military might remain the only organized force in an otherwise disintegrating society, or that it might inherit the mantle of nationalism as from concern that its monopoly of armed force would tempt it to stage a "colonels' revolt." Reality has been quite different. While the military has remained one of the mainstays of the political right, arguing for social discipline condemning real or imagined foreign encroachments, it has hardly become a viable political force in its own right. Political leaders of both the right and the left have seized nationalism as their own, depriving the military of its ability to wave the flag in defense of traditional values. Economic realities also have taken their toll. Vast cuts in spending, an end to conscription, and corruption within the military have lowered its visibility and prestige within society. In a very real sense, the military's main battle has been for survival, not for political power.

The same cannot be said of the former soviet-era security forces, which have survived quite nicely in all but the most liberal democracies of Eastern Europe. To be sure, their impact varies from nation to nation. In the pseudo-democracies of Central Asia or Belarus, they remain active in conducting surveillance on and in some cases outright suppressing opposition forces. It is more difficult to access their impact in Russia and Ukraine, where they are important instruments in the hands of strong presidents and the "parties of power." That said, however, it must be noted that even the most unreformed *chekist* operates within a different political milieu, his or her activities hedged by the realities of imperfect political competition and a multitude of countervailing forces.

It is also reasonably safe to conclude that attempts to consolidate power through the creation of an "ethnic state" are destined to ultimate failure, although they may possess brief and tumultuous trajectories. The problem lies both in linking the notions of ethnic and national identity—nation states per se rarely corresponded to geographic boundaries, especially in this part of the world—and with the political and economic costs that attend any attempt to create the sort of militant ethnic identity that is the prerequisite for such regimes. This is not to argue that nationalism may not become an important and legitimate defining force in a new sense of communal identity, itself a necessary prerequisite to democratic rule. Indeed, Ray Taras argues convincingly that the absence of such consensus in the Russian case has been an impediment to the democratic experiment and a temptation to resurrect the notion of imperial rule as an important marker of self-identity. But it is to argue that an exaggerated sense of national or ethnic identity will substantially undermine efforts to establish democratic constraints on executive power and obviate attempts to codify minority rights and/or procedural constraints through the rule of law. Moreover, such exaggerated ethno-nationalism breeds conflict—largely its intent in the first place, especially to justify authoritarian rule in the face of alleged challenge to the power or very survival of the dominant group—and such conflicts, however popular at the first, exact terrible costs in terms of the suppression of opposition groups, domestic violence and civil war, and ostracism and potentially even sanctions from the international community. The bright spot in the argument, at least so far among the former communist states, is that the worst examples of such ethno-nationalist authoritarianism have eventually yielded to a combination of domestic and international pressures to institute democratic rule.

It also seems virtually certain that the commitment to the creation of a market economy cannot be reversed. This is not to argue, of course, that capitalism will not take different forms reflecting the diversity of post-communist experiences, or that pure market economies will be any more in evidence than in the rest of the global capitalist world. But it is to assert that two shibboleths of the old order have departed forever. The first is that, in the final analysis, the state bears responsibility both for the fate of the economy and for the well-being of its individual citizens; while the state is still expected to play a role, it is now perceived as regulatory rather than directive in nature. Although political leadership will be held responsible for the economy, as in any democracy, they have surrendered institutional control. Indeed, it may convincingly be argued that because of the incomplete creation of regulatory mechanisms, the leaders of the vast majority of post-communist nations now have less control over their economies than do their counterparts in long-established democracies, where regulatory mechanisms and safety nets have evolved over time.

The second shibboleth to be surrendered is the notion of relative economic isolation from the global economy. To be sure, even during the last decades of communist rule, the nations of Eastern Europe established closer economic ties with the capitalist world and the Soviet Union ventured into global the market, albeit it predominantly as a supplier of energy and raw materials. That said, it remained true through the 1980s that the Soviet

Union attempted to integrate the socialist nations into a viable—or perhaps merely defensive—economic entity dominated by Moscow, luring Eastern Europe with cheap energy prices and providing thinly veiled assistance to the less developed economies of Central Asia. Whatever the cost-benefit mix, the relationship ended with the fall of communism and the limited success of efforts to create de facto free trade areas within the former soviet bloc. Now all must engage, with varying degrees of success, the broader world economy, liberated from the constraints that Moscow imposed until the early 1990s but also shorn of the grudgingly acknowledged benefits that came from the relationship.

It also is clear that most of the nations that overthrew communist rule have unambiguously embraced—or more correctly, re-embraced—their European identity in ways that go well beyond closer economic ties. The much-discussed and overly feared debate in Russian political and intellectual circles on the nation's European or Eurasian identity is not new, nor is it likely to be any more quickly decided in the twenty-first century than it was in the nineteenth. The more extreme rhetoric aside, the issue turns more on whether the new Russia will engage Europe as just another essentially European nation or as a nation with a mixed European and Asiatic heritage. What is not in dispute is the need to engage an increasingly unified and powerful Europe. The argument is not about separatism, but about the terms of engagement, must as the British after World War II had to make the painful and occasionally disruptive choice about its divided loyalties to the continent or the commonwealth. Even those nations on the periphery of Europe—the Caucasus, for example—have cast their lot with closer ties to the European community, and those further afield in Central Asia have embraced efforts to form a broader sense of regional identity or to forge ties with Europe and the broader global community. The point—not a small one—is that the once central affinity to bind solely to the Russian core of the former soviet empire for economic and cultural as well as political reasons is now a thing of the past.

And What We Are Uncertain About . . .

In other areas, a decade of the post-communist experiment has revealed no clear answers. For many of the nations examined in this study, the jury is still out on the essential question—has democracy been consolidated—at least if we interpret democracy in the conventional sense that includes both formal institutions and the wide assortment of supportive social entities and psychological dispositions that seem necessary for its long-term survival. In that sense, the only "consolidated" nations seem to lie at the extremes of the continuum. Few would argue against the conclusion that East European nations such as the Czech Republic, Poland, or Hungary or the former Baltic republics of the Soviet Union have "made it" as full-fledged democracies. And few would shrink from the opposite conclusion that others such as the former Central Asian republics have taken a course that seems certain not to result in bona fide democratic rule. In this sense, they have "consolidated" their fate as post-communist nations. But for the "middle third," as Valerie Bunce has termed them, the trajectory remains unclear. To be sure, all have perfectly valid democratic constitutions, hold elections, and evidence the other trappings of democracy, at least in the formal sense. But it can also be argued that these nations are beset by contradictory trends, sometimes presenting evidence of the painfully slow movement toward more democratic norms—the peaceful transfer of power in Russia, for example, or a more dramatic transfer of control in Yugoslavia—but also sometimes moving seemingly in the other direction—more stringent control over the media in Russia, or attempts to drive smaller political parties from the playing field. In truth, sometimes it is simply impossible to call the play in terms of its impact on the consolidation of democratic rule. For example, do Putin's efforts to strengthen the presidency and the central administration constitute a step backward, especially in terms of the centralization of power, or are they a necessary step in the creation of state mechanisms that are competent to enforce the rules of the game of democratic politics? Clearly arguments can be made in either direction, and without a crystal ball—or the certainty of historical determinism that once guided the Soviet Union's musing about its future—it is difficult to categorize these developments with certainty.

While we are certain that a proper civil society must be created if democracy is to survive in the long run, we are far less sure about what form it must take in the post-communist world and how to assess progress toward its creation. Some things do seem certain. Whatever institutional form it takes, it must strike a balance between representing the diversity of society and finding a degree of consensus that permits stable governments to form. In most democracies, this balance eventually emerges through the interplay of the party and interest group systems, which institutionalize the diverse interests of the society and define some commonly accepted rules, written or unwritten, that stabilize their interaction among them and with the formal institutions of government. But in the post-communist context, both elements are still in the formative stage. As Jack Bielasiak has noted, the creation of stable party systems has lagged behind the advent of formal institutions. How many parties is enough, and how many are too many, at least in terms of the creation of a stable and yet representative democracy? The persistence of informal networks as described by Michael Urban is further evidence of the incomplete development of secondary associations that would routinize the interaction between individual citizens and the larger institutional context. Moreover, the rules of the game have been in flux in many of the post-communist democracies. While the formal requirements of winning office are clearly stated—although subject to manipulation—the unwritten norms vary greatly from country to country and from election to election, especially to the extent that they fail to inform and give structure to the tactical choices of would-be democrats who are simply trying to play the game to their advantage under conditions of uncertainty.

But other things are even less certain about the creation of a viable civil society. What role should the state play in encouraging its formation? While virtually all observers agree that the state should not create civil society—at least in the sense that it takes the initiative in creating parties and intermediate association—it is less clear how far the state must go to establish conditions favorable for the emergence of such entities. For example, the creation of a presidential party nested within an otherwise competitive party system may be acceptable, while the formation of such a party that drives all others from the playing field is not. Similarly, state initiatives to create a legal order that facilitates the emergence of a pluralistic civil society, especially the creation of secondary associations other than parties, or efforts to encourage coalition formation with an otherwise cacophonous diversity of multiple actors may actually help in the creation of a stable democracy, while state efforts to stage-manage and control such organizations may choke off the emergence of an independent civil society. As before, our ambiguity lies mostly within the "middle third" of post-communist nations. Those in the top third in which the last decade has witnessed the creation of nearly consolidated democracies will have little difficulty in maintaining a viable and independent civil society, and those in the bottom third have little hope for its creation, having engineered a post-communist state corporatism of their own in which the state openly manages associational activity. It is in the middle third, where formal democratic institutions are out of synchronization with incomplete civil societies, where the ambiguity persists.

We also remain uncertain about the extent to which the congruence between political and other social organizations envisioned by Harry Eckstein can or will be created within post-communist systems—or how important it is in the short run for the democratic project. While there is a credible argument to be made that such congruence is supportive of democratic rule in the long run—that is, that in established democracies, the presence of democratic norms and practices in nonpolitical settings contributes to the maintenance of democratic political forms—it is far less certain that it is a *necessary* condition for the creation of new democracies, especially where cultural norms historically lie far off the mark. We simply do not know the appropriate threshold values, that is, how much congruence is necessary before nonpolitical norms can play an important role in political life, or conversely, how much formal and institutionalized manifestations of democratic rule are dependent upon norms in other walks of life.

Most uncertain of all is the generational issue. While we are reasonably sure that the fondness the old order witnessed among older citizens socialized into the communist order and enamored of its tendency to provide a predictable, if uninspiring sense of social and economic security will pass with time, we are far less certain about what the next generation thinks about democracy and the market economy. To be sure, the polls have proven to be hopeful, at least in the sense that they reveal a philosophical commitment to democracy and a sense that the average citizen generally perceives his/her life to be less controlled by government interference. But there are two worrisome realities. The first speaks to the sense that respondents may be simply registering their ability to cope with change; the New Russia Barometer seems to suggest that a sort of "revolution of declining expectations" may account for the higher level of acceptance of the post-communist reality. While this may diminish pressure for political and economic institutions to perform at a higher level in the short run, it can hardly assure their continued acceptance over a prolonged period of time. The second worrisome reality speaks to what may be going on in the minds of the new political and economic elites who have prospered in the post-communist world. In a very cynical sense, they have accepted democracy and a market economy because they have figured out how to turn it to their advantage; thus their acceptance is tactical, and by that token, it may, as the old saying goes, be a mile wide and an inch deep. Learned behavior may not yet be habituated behavior, and how long it will take for the former to become the latter is a threshold we cannot yet know with certainty.

Recurring Themes

Certainties and uncertainties aside, there are some common themes that have emerged in our discussion of the post-communist experience. While our intellectual modesty compels us to acknowledge that they may simply flow from our limited and repetitive vision, the more likely explanation is that the last decade has indeed witnessed common experiences that characterize the transition from communist one-party rule to the diverse modalities of democratic rule that now exist.

The first commonly shared theme emphasizes the juxtaposition—a Marxist would describe it as a "contradiction"—of similarity and diversity. While all of the twenty-seven post-communist nations have adopted formal democratic institutions that share many common structural features, the diversity of the real world manifestations of democratic rule is incredibly eclectic. As noted before, nineteen have created mixed presidential/parliamentary systems, and the remainder have cobbled together institutional systems closer to the purely parliamentary model. That said, we can never venture far from the realization that, as a number of the contributions to this volume have demonstrated, history and culture matter in ways that transform the process of democratization in ways consistent with the nation's past and with its sense of self-identity and destiny. A nation's experiences before and/or during communist rule have left their marks, as did the trajectory across which each nation shed that rule in the late 1980s or early 1990s. Having rejected the proffered and standardized model of a future communist society, each nation rediscovered its history and culture, adding to them whatever seemed relevant to the reanimation of its separate identity and whatever explained away the ill-considered side trip down the Leninist path and legitimated the political forces that rose from the ashes of communist rule. And in most nations, the reemergence of the national "self" raised as many questions as it answered: who and what are we in this modern world, European, Asiatic, or some mixture of the two; what is our historical and cultural relationship to the West, the East, or the South; are we imperial or colonial, beneficiary or victim of our own history and the actions of our neighbors; are we "one" or "many," at least in terms of cultural identities within the formal boundaries of our nation?

Another recurring theme was state building, and in some cases, nation building as well. Both are more than just the creation of formal institutions and the delineation of geographic boundaries. In a modern state, they form the core of both the creation of an effective political order and the definition of national self-identity. As a number of contributors have observed, in many ways the communist experience entailed strong elements of state and nation building. With the exception of those states in which power remained in the hands of newly professed democrats drawn from the old *nomenklatura*, the immediate post-communist experience witnessed what has been termed the "shrinkage" of the state, that is, a striking diminution of the capability of once-strong states to perform the necessary functions of government. While such shrinkage was in some ways a liberating experience—few objected to a reduction in the omnipresence of an Orwellian state—it also manifested negative consequences for efforts to establish a viable democratic order and market economy. In the absence of rules and/or the capability to enforce what few rules existed, the weak states stood idly by as entrepreneurial politicians fashioned a leader-centered form of democratic rule and both *nomenklatura* capitalists and the newly empowered oligarchs created a sort of lawless, cowboy capitalism.

The tide of the argument seems now to have turned. While there remains serious concern about limiting those powers of the state that may encroach on democratic rule—the "controlling *vlast*" argument articulated most directly by Thomas Remington—there is nonetheless the recognition that the state must be empowered to create the necessary preconditions for the maintenance of democratic procedures and the creation of a viable civil society needed to sustain democratic rule and a market economy in the long run. The idea that viable democracies require viable states is now accepted, at least insofar as it refers to the creation of a proper legal framework for political and economic life, the creation of a sense of a law-governed society, and the perception that the state is both neutral and capable of enforcing whatever rules of the game are commonly accepted. To be sure, the balance between state empowerment and controlling the power of the state is difficult to find, but that can be as true for long-standing democracies as for newly created ones. The point is that state building, understood in terms of creating competent institutional structures, is now accepted as the necessary counterpoint to limiting the power of the state, once again creating a dynamic tension that must be accepted if democracy is to be consolidated.

The largely unintended consequences of soviet-era efforts at nation building also profoundly affected the nature of the post-communist democratic experiment. Paradoxically, the pro forma federal nature of both the Soviet Union and Yugoslavia preserved, and in some cases actually created, a sense of national identity. Boundaries were marked that persist virtually unaltered, national labels were applied (or invented), soviet internal documents carried a statement of ethnic identity, and perceptions of entitlement and victimization were lodged in the minds of the diverse peoples of multiethnic states. To be sure, we can never know how deeply the sense of *soviet* identity took root even in the best of times; to the extent that the Soviet Union offered its peoples a sense of membership in a larger and more powerful state, or to the degree that its chiliastic promise of a communist utopia mesmerized those who hoped for a better life, or to the measure that the

USSR promised a job, housing, food, and a reasonable degree of social security, then it is at least arguable that being a part of the *sovietskii narod* (the soviet people) was an acceptable compromise with one's original sense of ethnic or national identity. It can hardly be accidental, however, that the rebirth of nationalist sentiments occurred simultaneously with the palpable decline in the system's ability to provide both material succor and hope for the future. In Yugoslavia, the sense of Yugoslav nationalism had never taken root, even in the best of time, and was further compromised after Tito's death by the absence of strong federal leadership, the growth of Serbian nationalism, and overall economic malaise.

Another unintended impact of efforts at nation building came through the creation of the viable counter-elites who emerged at the end of the communist era to lead the newly independent nations. Especially in the Soviet Union, many of the political leaders of these autonomy-cum-independence movements came from within the middle to upper levels of the *nomenklatura* itself who had risen to prominence on a regional basis precisely because the federal nature of the system and the regime's propensity to promote what it considered to be loyal local talent to positions of authority at the republic level. This is not to argue, of course, that legitimate pro-independence leaders would not have emerged from other sources; this was typically the case in Eastern Europe or the Baltic states, where trade union officials, religious leaders, or intellectuals stepped up to face the challenge. But it is to observe that the emergence of such *nomenklatura* nationalists/democrats affected both the fall of the communist regimes and the nature of the new democracies. If, on the one hand, we can legitimately (and cynically) note the opportunistic nature of their conversion to democracy and national values, then we must grudgingly admit that their continued rule perhaps provided a sense of continuity through the first phases of the transition. To be sure, for some the transformation was in name only; especially in Central Asia, little changed except the labels and the texts to be quoted to legitimate the exercise of unchallenged power. But for others, the transformation was more genuine, albeit filled with internal contradictions confusing to both their own citizens and outside observers.

Soviet-era institutions created under the guise of federalism also provided a useful mechanism to facilitate the advent of democratic rule. Simply put, the formal institutions of government already existed at the subnational level, ready to be captured by the *nomenklatura* democrats or others who would turn them to their purpose. In broad strokes, the pattern usually first began with inroads into or perhaps the outright takeover of the republic legislature and perhaps its counterparts in the major cities. This usually occurred simultaneously with the disintegration of the monopoly rule of the local communist party. The last step in the process was the creation of a new executive presidency to replace the de facto leadership of the republic communist party first secretary. The point is that there already existed a structure that everyone knew and understood; you know which institutions could now be captured now that democratic reforms offered real choices, you knew how to form political organizations that could compete for power, and you eventually figured out how to create the sort of strong executive leadership that had been exercised by the local communist party first secretary.

Paradoxically, the Russians themselves may have experienced one of the most difficult and contradictory efforts at nation building. The problem lay not with boundaries or institutions—although, except for a brief period during Khrushchev's rule, there was no separate Russian communist party organization—but with the less tangible questions of perceived identity and role. Without doubt, the Russian Federation is the most ethnically diverse of all of the post-soviet states, and maintaining the formal federal structure encourages the sort of dualism that characterized the soviet era. From the historical perspective, what it meant to be *Russian* within the *soviet* empire was never clear; were we senior partners and elder brothers whose wealth and experience entitled us to be a role model for the "lesser" nations, or were our interests ignored and our resources diverted by a central, all-union leadership intent on currying the favor of the non-Russian peoples? The contradictory truth was that both perceptions existed simultaneously, both within the leadership and among the common folk, and it undoubtedly persists today within the *Rossiiskaia* (unlike *Russkaia,* this form implies no ethnic identity) *Federatsiia.* And the real problem, as Ray Taras points out, was that answering this key question had little to do with the creation of democratic institutions. The two issues—and in some ways the two constituencies—were at best unconnected and at worst in conflict.

Another recurring theme was the notion of "stakeholders" in the new political and economic order. By "stakeholder," we refer to someone who has a perceived interest in the success of the democratic institutions and the market economy. Two caveats are in order, however, before we further explore this concept. The first is tied to the qualifying term "perceived"; whatever the objective conditions that might be apparent to an outside observer, the important consideration is whether citizens see themselves as beneficiaries of the new system, and the time frame within which they make such a calculation. Even if the short-term benefits are questionable, the new democracies and market economies can survive in the long run if voters and consumers think that things will improve with time. Conversely, even the best of times can do little to consolidate the new order if voters and consumers are distracted by other issues—civil wars, ethnic conflicts, or disputes with one's neighbors, for example—that divert their attention away from the performance of political and economic institutions.

The second caveat attaches to the measure of "success," which is highly subjective and idiosyncratic. If it means that the newly created political and economic institutions must perform at the level of their long-established counterparts in other nations, then the standard of judgment is set impossibly high, at least in the short run. But if it means that success may be proclaimed if the present is measurably better than the past—or soon will be, if one applies a somewhat longer time frame—then the task is far less daunting. Less government interference certainly is preferable to its omnipresence under the old order, even if it still plays a more directing role than in established democracies; economic growth and spreading prosperity are to be valued over the stagnation of the past, even if significant pockets of poverty remain; and political empowerment at the polls certainly is better than the single-candidate sham elections of the past, even if the party system is less than stable and the politicians themselves less than pure democrats. The point is that to the extent that the political and economic revolutions of the last decade are seen as "works in progress," it is easier for the participants in this ongoing process to perceive themselves as already having, or in the near future, developing a stake in the eventual success of the democratic project.

It is also important to realize that such "stakes" may be highly specific to different elements of the society. For the new political and economic elites, whether created by the selective conversion of former members of the *nomenklatura* or by the emergence of new entrepreneurial elements, acceptance that they have a significant stake in the new order will depend upon their perception of a manageable "ladder of success" to political and economic power and the acquisition of "equity" in terms of real and social capital in the new system. By "ladder of success," we refer to the new elite(s) ability to comprehend and to become meaningful players in the competition for political and economic power. The "ladder" in this sense pertains to the ability to climb to the top of the pile of competing forces; to know the formal and informal rules of how the game is played, and to be able to play it with some degree of success; to accept and to manage the ambiguities of what democratic theorists term "bounded uncertainty"; and/or to understand and manipulate the vagaries of continuing oligarchic rule. And "equity" in this sense refers both to an ownership of and/or control over the privatized resources of the market economy and to control or to influence the "social capital"—experts, campaign advisors, qualified managers, and those who shape public opinion—needed to acquire or to maintain preeminent status at the top of the ladder of success. As a number of the contributors to this volume have argued, the acquisition of this stake by both the survivors of the old order and by the new political activists who have emerged since the fall of communism may be the most important factor in explaining why imperfect democracies have tended to "stick," to use Valerie Bunce's term, or why potential elites have been so anxious to try their hand at the new post-communist politics in the hope of climbing the ladder as have their counterparts elsewhere. The long-term implications aside, in the short run the ability of such elites to make democratic institutions (however imperfect) or market economies (however inequitable) work to their advantage may be necessary to the very survival of the new order.

Another, less institutionalized, sense of "stakeholding" is also apparent and perhaps even necessary in the newly crafted post-communist democracies. It is the sense of belonging to, and thus having a real stake in the success of, the sort of informal networks that exist at two different levels of many of these new political orders. At the top, such networks constitute the informal mechanisms that are made necessary by the incomplete (or more charitably, the nascent) development of political parties and associational groups. To be sure, to the extent that these networks substitute for or inhibit the development of such entities, they delay the consolidation of viable democracies whose operation depends upon what might be termed the vertical integration of supportive formal and informal institutions. But in the short run, they may be necessary for the survival of not yet fully institutionalized systems, and the price to be paid may be an acceptable trade-off for the survival of an as-yet imperfect democracy. At lower levels, the sort of coping networks described by Michael Urban also develop a significant clientele of "stakeholders," at least in the sense that they are used by friends and cohorts as ways of dealing with a complex, potentially hostile (or at the least, indifferent), and under-institutionalized milieu within which everyone must function on a day-to-day basis. His warning that the development of these linkages may substitute for the creation of formal associations and other entities is well taken. But in the short run their existence may fill in some of the gaps of the new social and economic order and actually diminish the demands made on formal government institutions, a salutary situation if one considers the reduced capacity of the state itself.

Notes

CHAPTER TWO
The Complexity of Democratic Consolidation
Donald R. Kelley

1. Andreas Schedler, "What Is Democratic Consolidation?" *Journal of Democracy* 9, 2 (April 1998): 92.

2. Juan J. Linz and Alfred Stepan, "Toward Consolidated Democracies," *Journal of Democracy* 7, 2 (April 1996): 16.

3. David Collier and Steven Levitsky, "Democracy with Adjectives: Conceptual Innovation in Comparative Research," *World Politics* 29 (April 1997): 430–51.

4. Joseph Schumpeter, *Capitalism, Socialism, and Democracy* (London: Allen and Unwin, 1943), 269.

5. Robert A. Dahl, *Polyarchy: Participation and Opposition* (New Haven, Conn.: Yale University Press, 1971), and *Dilemmas of Pluralist Democracy* (New Haven, Conn.: Yale University Press, 1982).

6. Samuel P. Huntington, *The Third Wave: Democratization in the Late Twentieth Century* (Norman: University of Oklahoma Press, 1991), 280–316.

7. Schedler, "What Is Democratic Consolidaton?" 90–91.

8. Larry Diamond, "Is the Third Wave Over?" *Journal of Democracy* 7, 3 (July 1996): 23–24.

9. Gabriel Almond and Sidney Verba, *The Civic Culture: Political Attitudes and Democracy in Five Nations* (Princeton, N.J.: Princeton University Press, 1963), 13–14.

10. Gabriel Almond, "Comparative Political Systems," *Journal of Politics* 18, 3 (August 1956): 37.

11. Giuseppe DiPalma, *To Craft Democracies: An Essay on Democratic Transitions* (Berkeley: University of California Press, 1990).

12. Harry Eckstein, "Congruence Theory Explained," in Harry Eckstein, Frederic J. Fleron Jr., Erik P. Hoffmann, and William M. Reisinger, eds., *Can Democracy Take Root in Post-Soviet Russia: Explorations in State-Society Relations* (Lantham, Md.: Rowman and Littlefield, 1998), 3–33.

13. Ibid., 4.

14. Ibid., 28.

15. Larry Diamond, "Toward Democratic Consolidation," *Journal of Democracy* 5, 3 (July 1994): 5.

16. Ibid., 7

17. Ibid., 15.

18. Peter L. Berger, "The Uncertain Triumph of Democratic Capitalism," *Journal of Democracy* 3, 3 (July 1992): 7–16.

19. Adam Przeworski, Michael Alvarez, Jose Antonio Cheibub, and Fernando Limongi, "What Makes Democracy Endure?" *Journal of Democracy* 7, 1 (January 1996): 39–55.

20. Seymour Martin Lipset, "The Centrality of Political Culture," in Larry Diamond and Marc Plattner, eds., *The Global Resurgence of Democracy* (Baltimore, Md.: Johns Hopkins University Press, 1993), 134–37; and *Political Man: The Social Basis of Politics* (Baltimore, Md.: Johns Hopkins University Press, 1981).

21. Przeworski et al., "What Makes Democracy Endure?" 40.

22. Ibid., 41–42.

23. Ibid., 45.

24. Ibid., 47–49; and Juan J. Linz, "Presidential or Parliamentary Democracy: Does It Make a Difference?" in Juan J. Linz and Arturo Valenzuela, eds., *The Failure of Presidential Democracy* (Baltimore, Md.: Johns Hopkins University Press, 1994), 73–74.

25. Ezra Suleiman, "Presidentialism and Political Stability in France," in Linz and Valenzuela, *Failure of Presidential Democracy*, 137–62.

CHAPTER THREE

Comparative Democratization:
Lessons from the Post-Socialist Experience

Valerie Bunce

1. The phrase is taken from Samuel Huntington, though at the time of his writing he did not include the communist world or Africa. See *The Third Wave: Democratization in the Late Twentieth Century* (Norman: University of Oklahoma Press, 1991).

2. See, for example, the preconditions discussed by Barrington Moore, *Social Origins of Dictatorship and Democracy: Lord and Peasant in the Making of the Modern World* (Boston: Beacon Press, 1966); Brian Downing, *The Military Revolution and Political Change: Origins of Democracy and Autocracy in Early Modern Europe* (Princeton, N.J.: Princeton University Press, 1992).

3. Andrew Janos, *East Central Europe in the Modern World: The Politics of the Borderlands from Pre- to Post-communism* (Stanford, Conn.: Stanford University Press, 2000); Ralf Dahrendorf, *Society and Democracy in Germany* (Garden City, N.Y.: Doubleday, 1967).

4. See, especially, Jeffrey Herbst, *States and Power in Africa: Comparative Lessons in Authority and Control* (Princeton, N.J.: Princeton University Press, 2000).

5. See Valerie Bunce, "The Political Economy of Post-socialism," *Slavic Review* 58 (December 1999); Vladimir Popov, "Explaining the Magnitude of the Transformational Recession," unpublished manuscript, Moscow, 1999; Vladimir Popov, "The Political Economy of Growth in Russia," Program on New Approaches to Russian Security, no. 17, Davis Center, Harvard University.

6. The fall of production throughout the region, for example, has been far greater than that registered by countries during the Great Depression. See Bela Greskovits, *The Political Economy of Protest and Patience* (Budapest: Central European University Press, 1998).

7. Popov, "The Political Economy." Also see Bela Greskovits, "The Unveiled Periphery: Backwardness under Post-communism," Unpublished manuscript, Central European University, 2000; Timothy Frye, "The Perils of Polarization: Economic Performance in the Post-Communist World," Paper presented at the annual meeting of the American Political Science Association, San Francisco, 30 August–2 September 2001; Herbert Kitschelt, "Post-Communist Economic Reform: Causal Mechanisms and Comcomitant Properties," Paper presented at the annual meeting of the American Political Science Association, San Francisco, 30 August–2 September 2001.

8. For further elaborations of political diversity, see Karen Dawisha and Stephen Deets, "The Divine Comedy of Post-Communist Elections," Department of Government and Center for the Study of Post-socialist Societies, the University of Maryland, 1999.

9. "The Comparative Survey of Freedom," *Freedom Review* 28 (1998).

10. Philip Roeder, "The Triumph of Authoritarianism in Post-Soviet Regimes," Paper presented at the annual meeting of the American Political Science Association, Boston, 3–6 September 1999.

11. See Douglas Dion, "Evidence and Inference in the Comparative Case Study," *Comparative Politics* 30 (1998).

12. Bunce, "The Political Economy"; M. Steven Fish, "Democratization's Prerequisites," *Post-Soviet Affairs* 14 (1998): 212–47.

13. M. Steven Fish, "Reversal and Erosion of Democracy in the Post-communist World," Paper presented at the annual meeting of the American Political Science Association, Boston, 1998; Stephen Hanson and Jeffrey Kopstein, "The Weimar/Russia Comparison, " *Post-Soviet Affairs* 13 (1997): 252–83.

14. Valerie Bunce, "Sequencing Political and Economic Reforms," in John Hardt and Richard Kaufman, eds., *East-Central European Economies in Transition* (Washington, D.C.: U.S. Congress, 1994), 46–63; M. Steven Fish, "The Determinants of Economic Reform in the Post-communist World," *East European Politics and Societies* 12 (1998): 31–78; Valerie Bunce, "Democratization and Economic Reform," *Annual Review of Political Science* (Beverly Hills, Calif.: Sage, 2001). For a cautionary note on interpreting this relationship, see Andrew Barnes and Marcus Kurtz, "Ten Years of Post-communist Transitions? Does

Economic Liberalization Lead to Democratization?" Paper presented at the annual meeting of the Midwest Political Science Association, 27–30 April 2000.

15. Mark Beissinger, *The Tides of Nationalism: Order, Event and Collapse of the Soviet State* (Cambridge: Cambridge University Press, 2001).

16. Valerie Bunce, *Subversive Institutions: The Design and the Destruction of Socialism and the State* (Cambridge: Cambridge University Press, 1999).

17. An observation also made by Terry Lynn Karl for Latin America. See "The Hybrid Regimes of Central America," *Journal of Democracy* 6 (1995): 72–86.

18. Valerie Bunce, "The Return of the Left and the Future of Democracy in Eastern and Central Europe," in Birol Yesilada, ed., *Political Parties: Essays in Honor of Samuel Eldersveld* (Ann Arbor: University of Michigan Press, 1999), 151–76.

19. Terry Lynn Karl, "Dilemmas of Democratization in Latin America," *Comparative Politics* 23 (1990): 1–22.

20. I have borrowed this phrase from Charles King. See *The Moldovans: Romania, Russia and the Politics of Culture* (Hoover/Stanford: Hoover Institution Press, 2000). Also see "Post-Post-communism: Transition, Comparison and the End of 'Eastern Europe,'" *World Politics* 53 (October 2000): 143–72.

21. A point made very well by Herbert Kitschelt and Edmund Malesky. See "Constitutional Design and Post-communist Economic Reform," Paper presented at the Midwest Political Science Conference, Chicago, 28 April 2000.

22. Janos, *East Central Europe, in the Modern World.*

23. Ibid.; Jeffrey Kopstein and David Reilly, "Explaining the Why of the Why: On Fish's *Determinents* of Economic Reform in the Post-communist World," *East European Politics and Societies* 13 (1999): 613–24.

24. Ibid.

25. See, especially, Karl, "Dilemmas." For a more thorough-going critique of these arguments, see Valerie Bunce, "Comparative Democratization: Big and Bounded Generalizations," *Comparative Political Studies* 33, 6–7 (August–September 2000): 703–34.

26. This point is elaborated in Valerie Bunce, "Comparative Democratization: Big and Bounded Generalizations."

27. As Nancy Bermeo summarizes and then challenges in her forthcoming book. See *Ordinary People in Extraordinary Times: The Citizenry and the Collapse of Democracy* (Princeton, N.J.: Princeton University Press, 2001). Also see Sheri Berman, "Civil Society and the Collapse of the Weimar Republic," *World Politics* 49 (1997): 401–29; David Becker, "Beyond Democratic Consolidation," *Journal of Democracy* 10 (1999): 138–51.

28. See *On Democracy* (New Haven, Conn.: Yale University Press, 1998).

29. Adam Przeworski and Fernando Limongi, "Modernization: Facts and Theories," *World Politics* 49 (1997): 155–84.

30. See, for example, the quotations by Vladimir Putin cited by John Lloyd in the *Globe and Mail,* 28 June 2000, reprinted in *Johnson's Russia List,* no. 4387, 6 July 2000.

31. "Winners Take All: The Politics of Partial Reform in Postcommunist Transitions," *World Politics* 50 (1998): 203–34.

32. This is precisely the argument presented by Daniel Treisman and Andrei Shlaifer in *Without a Map: Political Tactics and Economic Reform in Russia* (Cambridge, Mass.: MIT Press, 2000).

33. *Socialism, Capitalism, Transformation* (Budapest: Central European University, 1995).

34. See, especially, Giuseppe DiPalma, *To Craft Democracies: An Essay on Democratic Transitions* (Berkeley: University of California Press, 1990). Also see Guillermo O'Donnell, Philippe C. Schmitter, and Laurence Whitehead, eds., *Transitions from Authoritarian Rule,* 4 vols. (Baltimore, Md.: Johns Hopkins University Press, 1986).

35. A useful discussion of the place of proximate versus distal influences on democratization can be found in Herbert Kitschelt, "Review Essay: Structure and Process-Driven Explanations of Regime Change," *American Political Science Review* 86 (1992): 1028–34.

36. Brian Loveman, "Protected Democracies and Military Guardianship: Political Transitions in Latin America, 1978–1993," *Journal of Inter-American Studies and World Affairs* 36 (1994): 105–89.

37. There is also growing interest in this variable in Latin America, largely as a result of growing concerns about one aspect: rule of law. See Guillermo O'Donnell, "Delegative Democracy," *Journal of Democracy* 5 (1994): 55–69, and O'Donnell, "Horizontal Accountability in New Democracies," *Journal of Democracy* 9 (1998): 112–26.

38. See, especially, Herbst, *States and Power in Africa.*

39. See, especially, Kathryn Stoner-Weiss, "Central Weakness and Provincial Autonomy: Observations on the Devolution Process in Russia," *Post-Soviet Affairs* 15 (1999). Also see Steven L. Solnick, "Russia on the Edge," *East European Constitutional Review* 7 (Fall 1998); Kathryn Stoner-Weiss, *Local Heroes: The Political Economy of Russian Regional Governance* (Princeton, N.J.: Princeton University Press, 1997); Russell Bova, "Democratization and the Crisis of the Russian State," in Gordon B. Smith, ed., *State-Building in Russia: The Yeltsin Legacy and the Challenge of the Future* (Armonk, N.Y.: M. E. Sharpe, 1999); Alfred Stepan, "Russian Federalism in Comparative Perspective," *Post-Soviet Affairs* 16 (April–June 2000): 133–76.

40. As Anatol Lieven has argued, Chechnya testifies to the weakness of the Russian state. See *Chechnya: Tombstone of Russian Power* (New Haven, Conn.: Yale University Press, 1998).

41. See, especially, Popov, "The Political Economy." For some other insightful

discussions of Russian economic difficulties, see David Woodruff, *Money Unmade: Barter and the Fate of Russian Capitalism* (Ithaca, N.Y.: Cornell University Press, 1999); Shlaifer and Treisman, *Without a Map;* Joseph Stiglitz, "What I Learned at the World Economic Crisis," *New Republic,* 17 April 2000; Brian Pinto, Vladimir Drebentsov and Alexander Morozov, "Non-Payments Cycle in Russia Suffocates Economic Growth—Proposal of World Bank Economists," *Transition: Newsletter about Reforming Economies,* World Bank/William Davidson Institute, 10, 6 (December 1999): 1–5; Jacquest Sapir, "Russia's Crash of August 1998: Diagnosis and Prescription," *Post-Soviet Affairs* 15, 1 (1999): 1–36.

42. My thanks to Ashutosh Varshney for pointing this out. See Katherine Belmont and Ashutosh Varshney, "Nationalism and Secession: Comparing India and Sri Lanka," Paper presented at the conference on Powersharing and Peacemaking, La Jolla, 8–9 December 2000.

43. See Valerie Bunce, *Subversive Institutions.*

44. The phrase is drawn from Bernard Silberman. See *Cages of Reason: The Rise of the RationasState in France, Japan, the United States and Great Britain* (Chicago: University of Chicago Press, 1993).

45. See Valerie Bunce, "Stalinism and the Management of Uncertainty," in Gyorgy Szoboszlai, ed., *The Transition to Democracy in Hungary* (Budapest: Hungarian Institute of Political Science/Hungarian Academy of Sciences, 1991).

46. Michael Mann, *The Sources of Social Power* (Cambridge: Polity Press, 1993).

47. This discussion of the nation and nationalism is based upon a number of sources. See Bunce, *Subversive Institutions;* Benedict Anderson, *Imagined Communities: Reflections on the Origins and Spread of Nationalism* (London: Verso, 1991); Eric Hobsbawm, *Nations and Nationalism since 1780: Programme, Myth, Reality,* 2nd ed. (Cambridge: Cambridge University Press, 1992); Crawford Young, "The Dialectics of Cultural Pluralism: Concepts and Reality," in Crawford Young, ed., *The Rising Tide of Cultural Pluralism: The Nation-State at Bay?* (Madison: University of Wisconsin Press, 1993), 245–78.

48. Michael Hechter, *Containing Nationalism* (Oxford: Oxford University Press, 2000).

49. See, especially, Sidney Tarrow, *Power in Movement* (Cambridge: Cambridge University Press, 1994). For evidence about the decline of ethnic conflict, see Ted Robert Gurr, *Minorities at Risk* (Washington, D.C.: U.S. Institute of Peace, 2000).

50. "Post-Post-communism: Transition, Comparison, and the End of 'Eastern Europe,'" *World Politics* 53 (October 2000): 143–72.

51. This has been analyzed most systematically by Mark Beissinger. See *The Tides of Nationalism: Order, Event and the Collapse of the Soviet State* (Cambridge: Cambridge University Press, 2002).

52. See, especially, Yitzhak Brudney, *Reinventing Russia: Russian Nationalism and the Soviet State, 1953–1991* (Cambridge, Mass.: Harvard University Press, 1998). Also see Veljko Vujacic, "Historical Legacies, Nationalist Mobilization and Political Outcomes in Russia and Serbia: A Weberian View," *Theory and Society* 25 (December 1996): 763–801. For a discussion of the relationship between Western influence, on the one hand, and the costs of economic reform and the power of illiberal nationalists in Russia, see Stephen Shenfield, "Foreign Assistance as Genocide: The Crisis in Russia, the IMF, and Interethnic Relations," in Milton Esman and Ronald Herring, eds., *Carrots, Sticks and Ethnic Conflict: Rethinking Development Assistance* (Ann Arbor: University of Michigan Press, 2001).

53. "Transitions to Democracy: Toward a Dynamic Model," *Comparative Politics* 2 (1970): 337–63.

CHAPTER FOUR

A Decade of Change but Not Much Progress: How Russians Are Coping

Richard Rose

1. Richard Rose, *A Decade of New Russia Barometer Surveys* (Glasgow: University of Strathclyde Studies in Public Policy, 2001).

2. Iver B. Neumann, *Russia and the Idea of Europe* (London: Routledge, 1996).

3. Vladimir Putin, *First Person* (London: Hutchinson, 2000).

4. Edward Keenan, "Muscovite Political Folkways," *Russian Review* 45 (1986): 115–81.

5. Valerie Bunce, *Subversive Institutions: The Design and the Destruction of the State* (Cambridge: Cambridge University Press, 1999).

6. Giuseppe DiPalma, *To Craft Democracies: An Essay in Democratic Transitions* (Berekley: University of California Press, 1990).

7. Paul Pierson, "Increasing Returns, Path Dependence, and the Study of Politics," *American Political Science Review* 94, 2 (2000): 251–68.

8. Arthur H. Miller and Thomas F. Klobucar, *American Journal of Political Science* 44, 4 (2000): 667–85.

9. Archie Brown, "The Brezhnev Era, 1964–82," in Archie Brown, M. Kaser, and G. S. Smith, eds., *The Cambridge Encyclopedia of Russia and the Former Soviet Union* (Cambridge: Cambridge University Press, 1994), 122–25.

10. Jan Winiecki, *The Distorted World of Soviet-Type Economics* (London: Routledge, 1988); Philip G. Roeder, *Red Sunset: The Failure of Soviet Politics* (Princeton, N.J.: Princeton University Press, 1993).

11. Irene A. Boutenko and Kirill Razlogov, *Recent Social Trends in Russia, 1960–1995* (Montreal: McGill Queen's University Press, 1997); Barbara Anderson and Brian D. Silver, "Sex Differentials in Mortality in the Soviet

Union," *Population Studies* 40 (1986): 191–214; F. Meslé, V. Shkolnikov, and J. Vallin, "Mortality by Cause in the USSR in 1970–1987: The Reconstruction of Time Series," *European Journal of Population* 8 (1992): 281–308.

12. Rudolf Andorka, Tamás Kolosi, Richard Rose, and György Vukovich, eds., *A Society Transformed: Hungary in Time-Space Perspective* (Budapest: Central European University Press, 1999), 188.

13. Isaiah Berlin, *Two Concepts of Liberty: An Inaugural Lecture* (Oxford: Clarendon Press, 1958); Richard Rose, "Freedom as a Fundamental Value," *International Social Science Journal* 145 (1995): 457–71.

14. Gabriel Almond and Sidney Verba, *The Civic Culture* (Princeton, N.J.: Princeton University Press, 1963); Robert D. Putnam, *Making Democracy Work* (Princeton, N.J.: Princeton University Press, 1993).

15. Juan J. Linz, *Totalitarian and Authoritarian Regimes* (Boulder, Colo.: Lynne Rienner, 2000).

16. David Braybrooke and C. E. Lindblom, *A Strategy of Decision* (New York: Free Press, 1963).

17. Richard Rose, "Adaptation, Resilience and Destitution: Alternative Responses to Transition in the Ukraine," *Problems of Post-Communism* 42, 6 (1995): 52–61.

18. Alena V. Ledeneva, *Russia's Economy of Favours* (Cambridge: Cambridge University Press, 1998).

19. Gregory Grossman, "The Second Economy of the USSR," *Problems of Communism* 26, 5 (1977); A. Katsenelinboigen, "Coloured Markets in the Soviet Union," *Soviet Studies* 29, 1 (1977): 62–85.

20. Richard Rose, "Contradictions between Micro- and Macro-Economic Goals in Post-Communist Societies," *Europe-Asia Studies* 45, 3 (1993): 419–44.

21. Richard Rose, "What Is the Demand for Price Stability in Post-Communist Countries?" *Problems of Post-Communism* 45, 2 (1998): 43–50.

22. European Bank for Reconstruction and Development (ERBD), *Transition Report Update* (London: ERBD, 2001).

23. Joseph A. Schumpeter, *Capitalism, Socialism and Democracy,* 4th ed. (London: Allen and Unwin, 1952).

24. Larry Diamond, *Developing Democracy: Toward Consolidation* (Baltimore, Md.: Johns Hopkins University Press, 1999).

25. Putin, *First Person,* 214.

26. Richard Rose and Doh Chull Shin, "Democratization Backwards: The Problem of Third-Wave Democracies," *British Journal of Political Science* 31, 2 (2001): 331–54.

27. Adam Przeworski, *Sustainable Democracy* (New York: Cambridge University Press, 1995).

28. Richard Rose, Neil Munro, and Stephen White, "Voting in a Floating Party System: The 1999 Duma Election," *Europe-Asia Studies* 53, 3 (2001): 419–43.

CHAPTER FIVE
Taming *Vlast:* Institutional Development in Post-Communist Russia
Thomas F. Remington

1. On strategic behavior by U.S. Supreme Court justices, see Lee Epstein and Jack Knight, *The Choices Justices Make* (Washington, D.C.: CQ Press, 1998); William N. Eskridge Jr., "Overriding Supreme Court Statutory Interpretation Decisions," *Yale Law Journal* 101, 2 (1991); William N. Eskridge Jr., "Reneging on History? Playing the Court/Congress/President Civil Rights Game," *California Law Review* 79, 3 (1991): 613–84.

2. Stephen White, Richard Rose, and Ian McAllister, *How Russia Votes* (Chatham, N.J.: Chatham House, 1997), 270.

3. On the turn of scholarly attention to the quality of government after the transition, see Herbert Kitschelt, Zdenka Mansfeldova, Radoslaw Markowski, and Gabor Toka, *Post-Communist Party Systems: Competition, Representation, and Inter-Party Cooperation* (Cambridge: Cambridge University Press, 1999), 383. For overviews of the application of theories of democratization to the post-communist experience, see Valerie Bunce, "Comparative Democratization: Big and Bounded Generalizations," *Comparative Political Studies* 33, 6/7 (2000): 703–34, and her essay in this volume.

4. On the "low-level equilibrium trap" that post-communist politics can fall into as a result of the ratcheting downward of both popular expectations of government and the quality of government services provided, see Richard Rose, William Mishler, and Christian Haepfer, *Democracy and Its Alternatives: Understanding Post-Communist Societies* (Baltimore, Md.: Johns Hopkins University Press, 1998).

5. Kitchelt et al. argue that the predominance of patronage-based parties (parties that avoid policy commitments and stay in power by providing career and material benefits to their clients, as opposed to programmatic parties, characteristic of more highly developed politics) in the post-soviet countries and in southeast Europe can be explained by the legacy of their pre-transition regime and society, where the political opposition was neither well organized nor programmatic.

6. World Bank, *World Development Report, 1997: The State in a Changing World* (New York: Oxford University Press, 1997).

7. See, for example, Joel Hellman, "Constitutions and Economic Reform in the Postcommunist Transitions," *East European Constitutional Review* 5 (winter 1996): 46–56; Joel Hellman, "Winners Take All: The Politics of Partial Reform in Post-communist Transitions," *World Politics* 50, 1 (1998): 203–34; Andrei Shleifer and Daniel Treisman, *Without a Map: Political Tactics and Economic Reform in Russia* (Cambridge, Mass.: MIT Press, 2000); Joel S. Hellman, Geraint

Jones, and Daniel Kaufman, *"Seize the State, Sieze the Day": State Capture, Corruption, and Influence in Transition* (Washington, D.C.: World Bank Institute, 2000); World Bank. *Anticorruption in Transition: A Contribution to the Policy Debates* (Washington, D.C.: World Bank Institute, 2000); Stephan Haggard and Matthew D. McCubbins, eds., *Presidents, Parliaments, and Policy* (Cambridge: Cambridge University Press, 2002).

8. Dani Rodrik, *The New Global Economy and Developing Countries: Making Openness Work* (Policy Essay, No. 24), Overseas Development Council (1999); "Development Strategies for the Next Century," paper prepared for conference on "Developing Economics in the 21st Century," Institute for Developing Economies, January 2000.

9. Valerie Bunce, *Subversive Institutions: The Design and the Destruction of Socialism and the State* (Cambridge: Cambridge University Press, 1999); Philip G. Roeder, *Red Sunset: The Failure of Soviet Politics* (Princeton, N.J.: Princeton University Press, 1993).

10. John H. Aldrich, *Why Parties? The Origin and Transformation of Political Parties in America* (Chicago: University of Chicago Press, 1995), 24–35.

11. Adam Przeworski, *Democracy and the Market: Political and Economic Reforms in Eastern Europe and Latin America* (Cambridge: Cambridge University Press, 1991).

12. James D. Fearon, "Electoral Accountability and the Control of Politicians: Selecting Good Types versus Sanctioning Poor Performance," in Adam Przeworski, Susan C. Stokes, and Bernard Manin, eds., *Democracy, Accountability, and Representation* (Cambridge: Cambridge University Press, 1999), 55–97.

13. Kitschelt et al., 80–97. Kitschelt and his co-authors depict spatially several types of representation relations between parties and their supporters, including both "mandate" and "trustee" types of representation.

14. Susan C. Stokes, "What Do Policy Switches Tell Us about Democracy?" in Przeworski, Stokes, and Manin, eds., *Democracy, Accountability, and Representation,* 98–130.

15. John Dunn, "Situating Democratic Political Accountability," in Przeworski, Stokes, and Manin, eds., *Democracy, Accountability, and Representation,* 333–34.

16. Dunn, "Situating Democratic Political Accountability," 337–41.

17. Guillermo O'Donnell, "Horizontal Accountability in New Democracies," *Journal of Democracy* 9, 3 (1998): 112–26.

18. Robert A. Dahl, *Dilemmas of Pluralist Democracy: Autonomy vs. Control* (New Haven, Conn.: Yale University Press, 1982).

19. Technically, policy reverts to the "reversionary point." This point is developed further below.

20. Article 10 reads: "State power in the Russian Federation is exercised on the

basis of the separation of legislative, executive and judicial powers. Bodies of legislative, executive and judicial power are independent."

21. Timothy Frye, "A Politics of Institutional Choice: Post-Communist Presidencies," *Comparative Political Studies* 30, 5 (October 1997): 523–52.

22. Matthew Soberg Shugart and Stephan Haggard, "Institutions and Public Policy in Presidential Systems," in Haggard and McCubbins, *Presidents, Parliaments, and Policy,* 72–73.

23. According to a January 2001 public opinion survey by VTsIOM, Russia's major survey research organization, only 26 percent of the public regards the Duma as playing a very large or large role in Russian affairs, while 38 percent consider its role small or very small. By comparison, the president's role is rated as large by 58 percent of respondents. However, the previous summer, only 19 percent considered the Duma's role large and 46 percent small, so that there may be a trend toward considering the Duma more influential. See L. A. Sedov, "Obshchestvennoe mneie v ianvarie 2001: roman naroda s vlast' iu prodolzhaet-sia," VTsIOM report, 8 February 2001, posted to the Polit.ru website on 9 February 2001.

24. For instance, M. Steven Fish, "The Executive Deception: Superpresidentialism and the Degradation of Russian Politics," in Valerie Sperling, ed., *Building the Russian State: Institutional Crisis and the Quest for Democratic Governance* (Boulder, Colo.: Westview, 2000), 177–92; also M. Steven Fish, "When More Is Less: Super Executive Power and Political Underdevelopment in Russia," in Victoria Bonnell and George W. Breslauer, *Russia in the New Century: Stability or Disorder?* (Boulder, Colo.: Westview, 2001), 15–34.

25. For instance, Robert Sharlet, "Russia's Second Constitutional Court: Politics, Law, and Stability," in Bonnell and Breslauer, *Russia in the New Century,* 59–77; Michael McFaul, *Russia's Troubled Transition from Communism to Democracy: Institutional Change during Revolutionary Transformations* (Ithaca, N.Y.: Cornell University Press, forthcoming).

26. Boris Yeltsin, *Midnight Diaries,* trans. Catherine A. Fitzpatrick (New York: Public Affairs, 2000), 23–24.

27. George W. Breslauer, "Personalism Versus Proceduralism: Boris Yeltsin and the Institutional Fragility of the Russian System," in Bonnell and Breslauer, *Russia in the New Century,* 35–58.

28. Georgii Sataroy et al., *Epokha Yel'tsnia; orcherki politicheskoi istorii* (Moscow: Vagrius, 2001), 384.

29. The term "veto bargaining" is Charles Cameron's and refers to his argument about the strategic implications of the veto power possessed by IS presidents. Charles M. Cameron, *Veto Bargaining: Presidents and the Politics of Negative Power* (Cambridge: Cambridge University Press, 2000).

30. This follows Thomas F. Remington, "The Evolution of Executive-Legislative Relations in Russia since 1993," *Slavic Review* 59, 3 (2000): 499–520.

31. Note that the Russian constitution does not restrict parliament from introducing any bills or amendments; the president has no "exclusive" or "gate-keeping" authority, other than the stipulation that the government submit the budget. (Shugart and Haggard note that some Latin American presidents have this right, but they also incorrectly assign it to the Russian president. Cf. "Institutions and Public Policy in Presidential Systems," 80.)

32. Under a ruling by the Constitutional Court in April 1996, the president may use his decree power to "fill a gap" in existing legislation, even in cases where the constitution requires a law. See *Sobranie zakonodatel'stva Rossiiskoi Federstii,* no. 19, 6, May 1996, item 2320, ruling of 30 April, pp. 4950–60, at p. 4953. The majority of the court held that: "The president is made the guarantor of the Constitution of the Russian Federation and ensures the coordinated functioning and cooperation of the organs of state power. As a result of that, the issuing by him of ukazy that fill gaps in the legal regulation of questions demanding a legislative solution does not contradict the Constitution of the Russian Federation so long as such ukazy do not contradict the Constitution of the Russian Federation and federal laws, and their action is limited in time until such time as corresponding legislative acts are adopted." Recently, however, one of the judges of the court offered the qualification that the president could not use this power when the legislation required was a constitutional law. (The issue arose in connection with President Putin's use of decree power to put new words into effect for the newly adopted national anthem. Putin's haste in doing so was motivated by the presumed need to ensure that the anthem would have words when it was played on New Year's Eve on nationwide television. In the event, the Duma was hardly likely to challenge Putin in court over the matter.) See *Segodnia,* December 29, 2000.

33. *Segodnia,* 8 July 1994.

34. *Segodnia,* 19 July 1994.

35. *Segodnia,* 19 July 1994.

36. Satarov et al., *Epokha Yel'tsina,* 419.

37. RFE/RL Newsline, 25 June 1997; *Segodnia,* 25 June 1997; *Segodnia,* 26 June 1997.

38. On the necessity of compromise with the Duma to get some sort of budget law through, even a wildly irresponsible and unrealistic one; see Satarov et al., *Epokha Yel'tsina,* 440–41.

39. Thomas F. Remington, Steven S. Smith, and Moshe Haspel, "Decrees, Laws, and Inter-Branch Relations in the Russian Federation," *Post-Soviet Affairs* 14, 4 (1998): 319.

40. See the article published on the website Polit.ru of 26 January 2001, from *Vedomosti,* of 25 January 2001, by Natal'ia Neimysheva and Natal'ia Melikova, entitled "Zemliu vse zhe budut prodavat.'" The article was prompted by the Duma's passage in first reading of legislation giving legal force to Chapter 17 of

the Civil Code, which specifically authorizes the buying and selling of land. It quotes the director of marketing of the real estate agency Inkoei Sidorenkov, as declaring: "What happened is the prelude to a revolution in the market for land parcels, exurban real estate, and elite housing. A person who invests money in land and construction of a home must be certain that he is buying it legally, and that no problems with the land will arise."

41. Satarov et al., *Epokha Yel'tsina,* 426.

42. Ibid., 489, 503.

43. Keneth R. Mayer, *With the Stroke of a Pen: Executive Orders and Presidential Power* (Princeton, N.J.: Princeton University Press, 2001).

44. Satarov et al., *Epokha Yel'tsina,* 427.

45. Ibid.

46. As President Putin did in August 2001. The new commission was to set the rates charged for electric power, railroad haulage, heating, electricity transmission, housing and utilities services, ports and terminals services, and the transportation of oil and gas.

47. The number of published normative decrees per year has been running at about 200, although there are probably many more unpublished normative decrees. The great majority of normative decrees concern minor administrative matters, such as name changes for federal agencies and the official coat of arms to be assigned to a particular department. A growing number of decrees rescind previous decrees that have been superseded by legislation. In contrast, in the period from January 1994 through December 1999, that is, the entire terms of the first and second Dumas, the Duma passed 1500 laws, or 250 per year.

48. The famous "trophy art" case established this obligation. Yeltsin had argued that as "guarantor of the constitution" he could refuse to sign bills he deemed illegal, but the Constitutional Court ruled otherwise, requiring the president to sign a bill where parliament had duly overridden his veto. See: Postanovleine Konstitutsionnogo suda Rossiiskoi Fedreasii, "Po delu o razreshenii spora mezhdu Sovetom Federastii I Prezidentom Rossiiskoi Federatsii, mezhdu Gosurdarstvennoi Dumoi I Prezidentom Rossiiskoi Federastii ob obiazannosti Prezidenta Rossiiskoi Federatsii podpisat' priniatyi Federal'nyi zakon 'O kul'turnykh tsennostiakh, peremeschchennykh v Soiuz SSR v resul'tate Vtoroi mirovoi voiny I nakhodiashchikhsia na territorii Rossiiskoi Federatsii," *Sobranie Zakonodatel'stva Rossiiskoi Federatsii* 16 (20 April 1998): 3624–30.

49. As Kieth Krehbiel has shown, the veto power allows the president to move policy in his direction up to the position of the two-thirds' veto pivot, that is, the legislator whose position is such that two-thirds of the legislators are located on the side away from the president's position, and only one-third to the president's side of him. As long as that legislator's position still falls short of the point at which the chamber as a whole—that is, median legislator—prefers the status quo to the bill, the president and legislature can agree to the bill. See

Keith Krehbiel, *Pivotal Politics: A Theory of U.S. Lawmaking* (Chicago: University of Chicago Press, 1998).

50. The logic of the deputies' calculations when electoral utility becomes distinct from policy utility, as in the case in a system where parliament can be dismissed, has been analyzed by John Huber. See John D. Huber, *Rationalizing Parliament: Legislative Institutions and Party Politics in France* (Cambridge: Cambridge University Press, 1996); also John D. Huber, "The Vote of Confidence in Parliamentary Democracies," *American Political Science Review* 90, 2 (1996): 269–82.

51. The final approved draft of the 1993 constitution omitted language that had been in earlier Kremlin-drafted versions that would have permitted the president to dissolve the Duma not only if it failed to confirm his nominee for prime minister, but also in the event that there was a "crisis of state power" that could not be resolved otherwise. The president's right of dissolution was thus far more narrowly specified in the final text.

52. Steven S. Smith and Thomas F. Remington, *The Politics of Institutional Choice: Formation of the Russian State Duma* (Princeton, N.J.: Princeton University Press, 2001).

53. Moshe Haspel reports that most committee recommendations to adopt and to reject packages of amendments are accepted on the floor the first time they come up (73.7 percent of the sets that committees recommended for acceptance; 70.5 percent of the sets of amendments recommended for rejection). Individual deputies may demand that some particular amendment be voted on separately and the chair generally puts such motions to a vote, but only 10.6 percent of the amendments that committees wanted to reject are passed on the floor. Haspel also finds that the more balanced the partisan makeup of a committee, the greater its success in winning approval on the floor which it has voted out, in part because members themselves are more likely to support their committees' products in plenary session. Moshe Haspel, "Committees in the Russian State Duma: Continuity and Change in Comparative Perspective," *Journal of Legislative Studies* 4, 1 (spring 1998): 199–201.

54. On the existence of cycling majorities in the RSFSR Congress and Supreme Soviet, see Jo Andrews, *Legislative Instability* (Cambridge: Cambridge University Press, forthcoming). On the comparison of the Duma with its predecessor parliaments, see Thomas F. Remington, *The Russian Parliament: Institutional Evolution in a Transitional Regime, 1989–1999* (New Haven, Conn.: Yale University Press, 2001).

55. The problem is that most factions are disciplined because their members share common ideological outlooks, and therefore find it hard to persuade their members to support ideologically unpalatable positions. See Thomas F. Remington, "Coalition Politics in the New Duma," in Vicki L. Hesli and William

Reisinger, eds., *The 1999–2000 Elections in Russia: Their Impact and Legacy* (Cambridge: Cambridge University Press, forthcoming).

56. John M. Carey and Matthew S. Shugart, eds., *Executive Decree Authority* (Cambridge: Cambridge University Press, 1998); Matthew S. Shugart and John M. Carey, *Presidents and Assemblies: Constitutional Design and Electoral Dynamics* (Cambridge: Cambridge University Press, 1992).

57. Cf. Rick Wilson, "Transitional Governance in the United States: Lessons from the First Federal Congress," *Legislative Studies Quarterly* 24, 4 (1999): 543–68.

58. This law had a peculiar history. As a constitutional law, it had to be passed by two hundred votes in the Duma, which is also the margin needed to override a presidential veto. It passed both chambers by constitutional majorities but Yeltsin vetoed it in May 1997. Both chambers overrode his veto in summer 1997 and sent it back. Yeltsin returned it to the Duma without review, a practice of dubious constitutional validity which Yeltsin occasionally used when he claimed to find procedural irregularities in its passage. The parliament then appealed to the Constitutional Court to demand that Yeltsin sign the law since his veto had been overridden. Yeltsin then retreated and agreed to sign the law if the parliament promised to make certain modifications. The Duma's chairman promised that the amendments would be made. Yeltsin then signed the law, in December 1997, and the Duma then made the requested amendments.

59. Article 77, paragraph (1), provides that: "The system of bodies of state power of the republics, krays, oblasts, cities of federal significance, the autonomous oblast and autonomous okrugs as established by the components of the Russian Federation independently in accordance with the fundamentals of the constitutional system of the Russian Federation and the general principles of the organization of representative and executive bodies of state power established by federal law."

60. However, parliament and president have softened the blow quite a bit, exempting from this law those governors whose second term began before October 1999. Currently president and parliament are discussing yet another set of amendments that would tighten the rules again and restrict the number of regional governors who can run for a third or fourth term.

61. Article 75, para. 3, of the constitution stipulates: "The system of taxes levied for the federal budget and the general principles of taxation and levies in the Russian Federation are established by federal law." Since there already was a legislative basis for taxation, the president could not act to "fill a gap" by decree, and so has had to win Duma consent to tax reform.

62. Article 118, para. 2: (3) The judicial system of the Russian Federation is established by the constitution of the Russian Federation and by federal constitutional law.

63. A crucial element in Charles Cameron's model of veto bargaining is the uncertainty the U.S. Congress faces in knowing whether the president will veto

a bill, and the uncertainty that both Congress and the president face about whether Congress can override the veto.

64. In 1999 the court struck down a few provisions of the bill, but upheld the rest as constitutional. The parliament in 2000 passed a new version of the bill that met the court's objections.

65. *Gosudarstvennaia Duma: Steogramma zasedanii. Biulleten'* 78 (526). 21 February 2001 (Moscow: Izdanie Gosudarstvennoi Dumy), 38.

66. The decision was issued on June 25, 2001.

67. Polit.ru, 24 January 2001.

68. Thomas F. Remington, *The Russian Parliament: Institutional Evolution in a Transitional Regime* (New Haven, Conn.: Yale University Press, 2001).

69. Chapter 17 provided that "persons holding a land parcel as property have the right to sell it, give it as a gift, give it as security, or rent out and dispose of it in another way insofar as the given lands have not been removed from circulation or been limited in circulation on the basis of law." As a concession to the agrarians, when the Civil Code was passed in 1994, the Duma agreed to a transitional provision which froze the validity of Chapter 17. One legislative strategy for the liberals was therefore to bypass the attempt to draft a Land Code, and instead to unfreeze Chapter 17, and then pass implementing legislation defining how the right to land could be exercised.

CHAPTER SIX
Social Relations and Political Practices in Post-Communist Russia

Michael Urban

1. Katherine Verdery, *What Was Socialism, and What Comes Next?* (Princeton, N.J.: Princeton University Press, 1996), 205.

2. On the late-soviet period, see: T. H. Rigby and B. Harasymiw, eds., *Leadership Selection and Patron-Client Relations in the USSR and Yugoslavia* (London: Allen and Unwin, 1983); Michael Urban, *An Algebra of Soviet Power: Elite Circulation in the Belorussian Republic, 1966–1986* (Cambridge: Cambridge University Press, 1989); John Willerton, *Patronage and Politics in the USSR* (New York: Cambridge University Press, 1992); Joel Moses, "Regional Cohorts and Political Mobility in the USSR: The Case of Dnepropetrovsk," *Soviet Union* 3 (pt. 1, 1976): 63–89. Studies addressing clientelism in earlier periods of Soviet history include T. H. Rigby, "Early Provincial Cliques and the Rise of Stalin," *Soviet Studies* 33 (January 1981): 3–28; Graeme Gill, *The Origins of the Stalinist Political System* (Cambridge: Cambridge University Press, 1990); and Gerald Easter, *Reconstructing the State: Personal Networks and Elite Identity in Soviet Russia* (Cambridge: Cambridge University Press, 2000).

3. William DiFranceisco and Zvi Gitelman, "Soviet Political Culture and 'Covert Participation' in Policy Implementation," *American Political Science Review* 78 (September 1984): 603–21; Don Van Atta, "Why There Is No Taylorism in the USSR," *Comparative Politics* 18 (April 1986): 327–37; Lewis Siegelbaum, "Soviet Norm Determination in Theory and Practice, 1917–1941," *Soviet Studies* 36 (January 1984): 45–68; Michael Urban, "Local Soviets and Popular Needs: Where the Official Ideology Meets Everyday Life," S. White and A. Pravda, eds., *Ideology and Soviet Politics* (London: Macmillan, 1987), 136–58; idem, "Conceptualizing Political Power in the USSR: Patterns of Binding and Bonding," *Studies in Comparative Communism* 18 (winter 1985): 207–26.

4. Norbert Elias, *The Civilizing Process, Vol. I: The History of Manners* (New York: Pantheon, 1978).

5. Susan Rose-Ackerman, *Corruption: A Study of Political Economy* (New York: Academic Press, 1978), 9 (italics in original).

6. Frederico Varese, "Pervasive Corruption," A. Ledeneva and M. Kurkchiyan, eds., *Economic Crime in Russia* (The Hague: Kluwer Law International, 1999), 99–111, esp. 111.

7. Charles Tilly, "Epilogue: Now Where?" G. Steinmetz, ed., *State/Culture: State Formation after the Cultural Turn* (Ithaca, N.Y.: Cornell University Press, 1999), 407–19.

8. James Alexander, *Political Culture in Post-Communist Russia: Formlessness and Recreation in a Traumatic Transition* (New York: St. Martin's Press, 2000), esp. 83–117.

9. George Breslauer, "Personalism Versus Proceduralism: Boris Yeltsin and the Institutional Fragility of the Russian System," V. Bonnell and G. Breslauer, eds., *Russia in the New Century: Stability or Disorder?* (Boulder, Colo.: Westview, 2001), 35–58.

10. Georgi Derluguian, "The Russian Neo-Cossacks: Militant Provincials in the Geoculture of Clashing Civilizations," J. Guidry et al., eds., *Globalizations and Social Movements: Culture, Power and the Transnational Public Sphere* (Ann Arbor: University of Michigan Press, 2000), 288–314.

11. *Inter alia:* Norbert Elias, *The Civilizing Process, Vol. II: Power and Civility* (New York: Pantheon, 1982); Fernand Braudel, *The Wheels of Commerce* (New York: Harper and Row, 1984); Joel Migdal, *Strong Societies and Weak States* (Princeton, N.J.: Princeton University Press, 1988); Charles Tilly, *Coercion, Capital and European States, A.D. 990–1992* (Oxford: Blackwell, 1990); Marc Raeff, *The Well-Ordered Police State* (New Haven, Conn.: Yale University Press, 1983).

12. James Scott, *Seeing Like a State: How Certain Schemes to Improve the Human Condition Have Failed* (New Haven, Conn.: Yale University Press, 1998).

13. Pierre Bourdieu, "Rethinking the State: Genesis and Structure of the Bureaucratic Field," Steinmetz, ed., *State/Culture*, 53–75.

14. Karl Marx and Frederick Engels, *Selected Works* (Moscow: Progress, 1968), 31.

15. Timothy Mitchell, "Society, Economy and the State Effect," Steinmetz, ed., *State/Culture,* 76–97; esp. 77.

16. Michel Foucault, *Discipline and Punish: The Birth of the Prison* (New York: Pantheon, 1977).

17. Mitchell, "Society, Economy and the State Effect," 89.

18. Ibid., 83–87.

19. Nancy Ries, *Russian Talk: Culture and Conversation during Perestroika* (Ithaca, N.Y.: Cornell University Press, 1997); Dale Pesmen, *Russian and Soul: An Exploration* (Ithaca, N.Y.: Cornell University Press, 2000).

20. M. N. Afanas'ev, *Klientelizm i rossisskaya gosudarstvennost,* 2nd ed. (Moscow: Moskovskii obshchestvennyi nauchnyi fond, 2000), 421–425.

21. David Woodruff, *Money Unmade: Barter and the Fate of Russian Capitalism* (Ithaca, N.Y.: Cornell University Press, 1999). See also Vladimir Chorniy, "Russia: Multiple Financial Systems and Implications for Economic Crime," Ledeneva and Kurkchiyan, eds., *Economic Crime in Russia,* 223–36; Peter Rutland, "Introduction: Business and the State in Russia," in his *Business and the State in Contemporary Russia* (Boulder, Colo.: Westview, 2001), 1–32, esp. 2.

22. Vladimir Volkov, *The Monopoly of Force: Violent Entrepreneurship and State Formation in Russia, 1987–2000* (unpublished manuscript); Kathryn Hendley, Peter Murrell, and Randi Ryterman, "Law, Relations and Private Enforcement: Transaction Strategies of Russian Enterprises," *Europe-Asia Studies* 52, 4 (June 2000): 627–56.

23. Neil Robinson, "The Economy and the Prospectus for Anti-democratic Development in Russia," *Europe-Asia Studies* 52, 8 (December 2000): 1391–1416, esp. 1406.

24. M. Steven Fish, "The Executive Deception: Superpresidentialism and the Degradation of Russian Politics," V. Sperling, ed., *Building the Russian State: Institutional Crisis and the Quest for Democratic Governance* (Boulder, Colo.: Westview, 2000), 177–92; idem, "When More Is Less: Superexecutive Power and Political Underdevelopment in Russia," Bonnell and Breslauer, eds., *Russia in the New Century,* 15–34; Breslauer, "Personalism Versus Proceduralism," ibid., 35–58.

25. Richard Sakwa, "State and Society in Post-Communist Russia," N. Robinson, ed., *Institutions and Political Change in Russia* (New York: St. Martin's Press, 2000), 192–211.

26. Nicolas Hayoz and Victor Sergeyev, "Social Networks in Russian Politics," (unpublished manuscript, Moscow, 2001).

27. Steven Solnick, *Stealing the State: Control and Collapse in Soviet Institutions* (Cambridge, Mass.: Harvard University Press, 1998); Simon Johnson and Heidi Knoll, "Managerial Strategies for Spontaneous

Privatization," *Soviet Economy* 7 (October–December 1991): 281–316; Simon Clarke, "Privatization and the Development of Capitalism in Russia," in S. Clarke et al., eds., *What about the Workers? Workers and the Transition to Capitalism in Russia* (London: Verso, 1993), 199–241; Darrell Slider, "Privatization in Russia's Regions," *Post-Soviet Affairs* 10 (October–December 1994): 367–96; Pekka Sutela, "Insider Privatization in Russia: Speculations on Systematic Change," *Europe-Asia Studies* 46, 3 (May 1994): 417–35; Michael McFaul, "State, Power, Institutional Change and the Politics of Privatization in Russia," *World Politics* 47 (January 1995): 210–43.

28. Peter Reddaway and Dmitri Glinski, *The Tragedy of Russia's Reforms: Market Bolshevism against Democracy* (Washington, D.C.: U.S. Institute of Peace Press, 2001); Stefan Hedlund, *Russia's "Market" Economy: A Bad Case of Predatory Capitalism* (London: UCL Press, 1999); Vladimir Tikhonov, "The Second Collapse of the Soviet Economy: Myths and Realities of the Russian Reform," *Europe-Asia Studies* 52, 2 (March 2000): 207–36.

29. Michael Burawoy and Kathryn Hendley, "Between *Perestroika* and Privatization: Divided Strategies and Political Crisis in a Soviet Enterprise," *Soviet Studies* 44, 3 (May 1992): 371–402.

30. David Stark, "Recombinant Property in East European Capitalism," G. Grabner and D. Stark, eds., *Restructuring Networks in Post-Socialism* (Oxford: Oxford University Press, 1997), 35–69. See also: David Stark and Lazlo Bruszt, *Postsocialist Pathways: Transforming Politics and Property in East Central Europe* (Cambridge: Cambridge University Press, 1998); Aydir Hayri and Gerald McDermott, "The Network Properties of Corporate Governance and Industrial Restructuring," *Industrial and Corporate Change* 7, 1 (1998): 153–93.

31. Andras Sajo, "Corruption, Clientelism, and the Future of the Constitutional State in Eastern Europe," *East European Constitutional Review* 7 (spring 1998): 37–46.

32. Paul Khlebnikov, *Godfather of the Kremlin: Boris Berezovsky and the Looting of Russia* (New York: Harcourt, 2000).

33. Caroline Humphrey, "Traders, 'Disorder,' and Citizenship in Provincial Russia," M. Burawoy and K. Verdery, eds., *Uncertain Transition: Ethnographies of Change in the Postsocialist World* (Lanham, Md.: Rowman and Littlefield, 1999), 21.

34. Michael Urban, "Post-Soviet Political Discourse and the Creation of Political Communities," A. Schonle and A. Mandelker, eds., *Lotman and Cultural Studies: Encounters and Extensions* (Bloomington: Indiana University Press, forthcoming).

35. Alexei Yurchak, "Heteronymous Business," Paper presented at the Mellon Conference "Entrepreneurs, Entrepreneurialism, and Democracy in Communist and Post-Communist Societies, University of California, Berkeley, 19–20 May 2000, 13.

36. Alena Ledeneva, "Introduction: Economic Crime and the New Russian Economy," Ledeneva and Kurkchiyan, eds., *Economic Crime in Russia,* 10.

37. M. N. Afanas'ev reports survey findings that show the proportion of Russians regarding personalistic ties as the best way to get along in life increasing from 74 to 84 percent over the course of the 1990s. See his *Klientelizm i rossiiskaya gosudarstvennost,* 9.

38. Rutland, "Introduction . . ." to his *Business and the State in Contemporary Russia,* 17–25; Reddaway and Glinski, *The Tragedy of Russia's Reforms,* esp., 463, 478–79.

39. Victor Sergeyev, *The Wild East: Crime and Lawlessness in Post-Communist Russia* (Armonk, N.Y.: M. E. Sharpe, 1998), 80–87.

40. G. V. Golosov and Yu. D. Shevchenko, "Sotsial'nye seti i elektoral'noe povedenie," G. Golosov and E. Yu. Meleshkina, eds., *Politicheskaya sotsiologiya i sovremennaya rossiiskaya politika* (St. Petersburg: Boreiprint, 2000), 100–125; Michael Urban and Vladimir Gel'man, "The Development of Political Parties in Russia," B. Parrot and K. Dawisha, eds., *Democratic Changes and Authoritarian Reactions in Russia, Ukraine, Belarus and Moldova* (Cambridge: Cambridge University Press, 1997), 175–219; Daniel Treisman, "Dollars and Democratization: The Role and Power of Money in Russia's Transitional Elections," *Comparative Politics* 31 (October 1998): 1–21; esp. 16–17.

41. Nonna Barkhatova, "Russian Small Business, Authorities and the State," *Europe-Asia Studies* 52, 4 (June 2000): 657–76; Michael Urban, *The Rebirth of Politics in Russia* (Cambridge: Cambridge University Press, 1997), 305–6; Afanas'ev, *Klientelizm . . . ,* 287–92.

42. A recent book traces historically different "patterns of regional development" —some initiated prior to the advent of the Soviet system—that persist in modified form in the present. Although the patterns vary in important ways, they all tend to converge in patrimonial authoritarianism that joins together their respective power networks. See S. Ryzhenkov, G. Lyukhterhandt-Mikhaleva, and A. Kuz'min (eds.), *Politika i kul'tura v rossiiskoi provintsii* (Moscow: Letnii sad, 2000).

43. James Hughes, Peter John, and Gwendolyn Sasse, "From Plan to Network: Urban Elites and the Postcommunist Organizational State in Russia," *European Journal of Political Research* 41, 3 (2002): 395–420.

44. Marie Mendras, "How Regional Elites Preserve Their Power," *Post-Soviet Affairs* 15 (October–December 1999): 295–311, esp. 303; Vladimir Gel'man, "Regime Transition, Uncertainty and Prospects for Democratization: The Politics of Russia's Regions in Comparative Perspective," *Europe-Asia Studies* 51, 6 (September 1999): 939–56.

45. Burawoy and Hendley, "Between Perestroika and Privatization."

46. Vladimir Gel'man, *Transformatsiya v Rossii: politicheskii rezhim i*

demokraticheskaya oppozitsiya (Moscow: Moskovskii obshchestvennyi nauchnyi fond, 1999), 73.

47. Rostislav Turovskii, "Sil'nyi tsentr—sil'nye regiony?" *NG-Stsenarii*, 3 (14 March 2001), 2.

48. Mary McAuley, *Russia's Politics of Uncertainty* (Cambridge: Cambridge University Press, 1997).

49. Turovskii, "Sil'nyi tsentr—sil'nye regiony?"

50. Mendras, "How Regional Elites Preserve Their Power," 307.

51. Grigorii Golosov, "Gubernatory i partiinaya politika," *Pro et Contra* 5 (winter 2000) (electronic version).

52. Gel'man, *Transformatsiya v Rossii*, 157; Urban and Gel'man, "The Development of Political Parties in Russia," Parrot and Dawisha, eds., *Democratic Changes and Authoritarian Reactions . . .* , 175–219.

53. Fish, "When More Is Less," Bonnell and Breslauer, eds., *Russia in the New Century*, 25–26 (italics in original).

54. For an account of the phenomenon during the elections to the State Duma following El'tsin's coup d'état and the institution of a new set of rules regarding the right to rule itself, see Michael Urban, "December 1993 as a Replication of Late-Soviet Electoral Practices," *Post-Soviet Affairs* 10 (April–June 1994): 127–58.

55. Sergeyev, *The Wild East*, 41–53.

56. Leonid Fituni, "Economic Crime in the Context of Transition to a Market Economy," Ledeneva and Kurkchiyan, eds., *Economic Crime in Russia*, 18.

57. *Johnson's Russia List* (17 March 2001), recirculating an item from the Russian Information Agency.

58. According to the ratings composed by Transparency International in 1997, Russia appeared at the bottom of the list of states abiding by the rule of law, wedged between Pakistan and Columbia. Cited in Donatella della Porta and Alberto Vannucci, *Corrupt Exchanges: Actors, Resources and Mechanisms of Political Corruption* (New York: Aldine de Gruyter, 1999), 6. Transparency International's ratings of corrupt states in 2001 placed Russia in the same position, occupying the slot between Pakistan and Ecuador. *Nezavisimaya gazeta* (29 June 2001).

59. Volkov, *The Monopoly of Force*.

60. Alena Ledeneva, *Russia's Economy of Favours: Blat, Networking and Informal Exchange* (Cambridge: Cambridge University Press, 1998), Ledeneva, "Introduction . . ." Ledeneva and Kurkchiyan, eds., *Economic Crime in Russia*, 8.

61. Heiko Pleines, "Large-scale Corruption and Rent-seeking in the Russian Banking Sector," Ledeneva and Kurkchiyan, eds., *Economic Crime in Russia*, 191–207.

62. Sergei Guk, "Dirty Money and White Collars," WPS Monitoring Agency (www.wps.ru/e_index.html).

63. RFE/RL Newsline, 5, 1, Part 1, 6 June 2001.

64. Cited by Leonid Fituni, "Economic Crime in the Context of Transition . . ." Ledeneva and Kurkchiyan, eds., *Economic Crime in Russia,* 29–30.

65. Louise Shelley, "Is the Russian State Coping with Organized Crime and Corruption?" Sperling, eds., *Building the Russian State,* 107.

66. Sergei Peregudov, "The Oligarchical Model of Russian Corporatism," Archie Brown, ed., *Contemporary Russian Politics, Politics: A Reader* (Oxford: Oxford University Press, 2001), 259–68.

67. Mikhail Fradkov interviewed by Viktor Kuz'min, *Nezavisimaya gazeta* (31 May 2001), 1, 4.

68. Vladimir Chorniy, "Russia: Multiple Financial Systems and Implications for Economic Crime," Ledeneva and Kurkchiyan, eds., *Economic Crime in Russia,* 226–27.

69. Eva Busse, "The Embeddedness of Tax Evasion in Russia," ibid., 129–46.

70. Shelley, "Is the Russian State Coping . . . ?" Sperling, eds., *Building the Russian State,* 107–8.

71. Afanas'ev, *Klientelizm . . . ,* 182–205.

72. Donald Jensen, "How Russia Is Ruled," Rutland, ed., *Business and the State in Contemporary Russia,* 36.

73. Reddaway and Glinski, *The Tragedy of Russia's Reforms,* 485.

74. Ibid., 607; Shelley, "Is the Russian State Coping . . . ?," Sperling, ed., *Building the Russian State,* 106; Paul Khlebnikov, *Godfather in the Kremlin,* 296–97.

75. *Inter alia:* S. Frederick Starr, "Soviet Union: A Civil Society," *Foreign Policy* 70 (spring 1989): 26–41; Gail Lapidus, "State and Society: Toward the Emergence of Civil Society in the Soviet Union," A. Dallin and G. Lapidus, eds., *The Soviet System in Crisis* (Boulder, Colo.: Westview, 1991), 130–50; Russell Bova, "Political Dynamics of the Post-Communist Transition: A Comparative Perspective," *World Politics* 44 (October 1991): 117, 134; Marcia Wiegle and Jim Butterfield, "Civil Society in Reforming Communist Regimes: The Logic of Emergence," *Comparative Politics* 25 (October 1992): 1–23; Vladimir Tismaneanu, *Reinventing Politics* (New York: Free Press, 1992).

76. D. Rueschemeyer et al., eds., *Participation and Democracy East and West: Comparisons and Interpretations* (Armonk, N.Y.: M. E. Sharpe, 1998).

77. William Smirnov, "Democratization in Russia: Achievements and Problems," Brown, ed., *Contemporary Russian Politics,* 520.

78. The official figures for the percentage of the population living below this line in late 1998 were 41.2 percent. See Reddaway and Glinski, *The Tragedy of Russia's Reforms,* 620.

79. Marc Howard, *Demobilized Societies: The Weakness of Civil Society in Postcommunist Europe* (Cambridge: Cambridge University Press, 2003).

80. Bela Greskovits, *The Political Economy of Protest and Patience* (Budapest: Central European University Press, 1998).

81. Marina Kurkchiyan, "The Transformation of the Second Economy into the Informal Economy," Ledeneva and Kurkchiyan, eds. *Economic Crime in Russia,* 83–97; Afanas'ev, *Klientelizm . . . ,* 166–71, 281.

82. Michael Burawoy, Pavel Krotov, and Tatyana Lytkina, "Domestic Involution: How Women Organize Survival in a North Russian City," Bonnell and Breslauer, eds., *Russia in the New Century,* 232–33.

83. Ledeneva, *Russia's Economy of Favours,* 192–206; Burawoy, Krotov, and Lytkina, "Domestic Involution," Bonnell and Breslauer, eds., *Russia in the New Century,* 231–61.

84. Svetlana Barsukova, "Tenevoi i fiktivnyi rynki truda v sovremennoi Rossii," *Pro and Contra* 5 (winter 2000) (electronic version).

85. Even in the case of business transactions among firms, the personal dimension operates decisively. According to one study, about half of these transactions are accomplished via friendship networks in which mutual obligations are sustained while, in the remainder, trust is low and defaults on obligations are frequent. Hendley, Murrell, and Ryterman, "Law, Relationship and Private Enforcement . . ." 638.

86. Oleg Kharkhordin, *The Collective and the Individual in Russia: A Study of Practices* (Berkeley: University of California Press, 1999).

87. Oleg Kharkhordin and Theodore Gerber, "Russian Directors' Business Ethic: A Study of Industrial Enterprises in St. Petersburg, 1993," *Europe-Asia Studies* 46, 7 (October 1994): 1075–1108.

88. Richard Ericson, "The Russian Economy since Independence," G. Lapidus, ed., *The New Russia: Troubled Transformation* (Boulder, Colo.: Westview, 1995), 37, 44; Sergei Khrushchev, "The Political Economy of Russia's Regional Fragmentation," D. Blum, ed., *Russia's Future: Consolidation or Disintegration?* (Boulder, Colo.: Westview, 1994), 92–93.

89. Sarah Ashwin, *Russian Workers: The Anatomy of Patience* (New York: St. Martin's, 1999).

90. Risto Alapuro and Markuu Lonkila, "Networks, Identity and (In) Action: A Comparison between Russian and Finnish Teachers," *European Societies* 2, 1 (2000): 65–90.

91. Yuliya Shevchenko, "Mezhdu grazhdanskim obshchestvom i autoritarnym gosudarstvom (O pol'ze politicheskikh partii v Rossii)," *Pro et Contra,* 5 (winter 2000) (electronic version).

92. Cited in Gel'man, *Transformatsiya v Rossii,* 51.

93. For an example, see Igor Klyamkin and Lilia Shevtsova, "The Tactical

Origins of Russia's New Political Institutions," Brown, ed., *Contemporary Russian Politics,* 14–16.

94. Peter Reddaway, "Will Putin Be Able to Consolidate Power?" in *Post-Soviet Affairs* 17 (January–March 2001): 23–44.

95. Yulia Latynina, "How the FSB Is Faring in Business," *Moscow Times* (25 April 2001) (*Johnson's Russia List,* 25 April 2001).

96. Eugene Huskey, "Overcoming the Yeltsin Legacy: Vladimir Putin and Russian Political Reform," Brown, ed., *Contemporary Russian Politics,* 82–96.

97. Nikolai Petrov, "Consolidating the Centralized State, Weakening Democracy and the Federal System," *Russian Regional Report* 6, 23 (19 June 2001): 4.

98. Dmitrii Ol'shanskii, "Dezintegratsiya: Novye simptomy staroi bolezni, *Pro et Contra,* 5 (winter 2000) (electronic version). For a concise summary of the major appointment made by Putin during the government reshuffle of spring 2001, and their apparent network associations, see Marina Volkova and Vladislav Kuz'michev, "Kadrovaya strategiya prezidenta—pyat':chetryre v pol'zu 'staroi' komandy," *Nezavisimaya gazeta* (19 June 2001), 1, 3.

99. Volkov, *The Monopoly of Force;* Vadim Radaev, "Corruption and Violence of Russian Business in the Late 1990s," Ledeneva and Kurkchiyan, eds., *Economic Crime in Russia,* 63–82, esp. 78–79.

100. Afanas'ev, *Klientelizm i rossiiskaya gosudarstvennost,* 267–68, 292–97.

CHAPTER SEVEN

Russia in the Middle: State Building and the Rule of Law

Robert Sharlet

1. Valerie Bunce's term. See her "Comparative Democratization: Lessons from the Post-Socialist Experience," in this volume.

2. Harry Eckstein, "Congruence Theory Explained," in Harry Eckstein, Frederic J. Fleron Jr., Erik P. Hoffmann, and William M. Reisinger, *Can Democracy Take Root in Post-Soviet Russia?* (Lanham, Md.: Rowman and Littlefield, 1998), 4.

3. The state-building framework that follows is drawn from Stephen Holmes, "Cultural Legacies or State Collapse?" in Michael Mandelbaum, ed., *Post-Communism* (New York: Council on Foreign Relations, 1996), ch. 1.

4. See Gordon B. Smith, *Reforming the Russian Legal System* (Cambridge: Cambridge University Press, 1996), esp. ch. 5 and 7–9; and Robert Sharlet, "Constitutional Implementation and State Building: Progress and Problems of Law Reform in Russia," in Gordon B. Smith, ed., *State-Building in Russia* (Armonk, N.Y.: M. E. Sharpe, 1999), ch. 4.

5. See Andrea Stevenson Sanjian, "State-Society Relations and the Evolution of Social Policy in Russia," in Smith, ed., *State-Building in Russia,* ch. 8.

6. See Peter H. Solomon Jr. and Todd S. Fogelsong, *Courts and Transition in Russia: The Challenge of Judicial Reform* (Boulder, Colo.: Westview, 2000).

7. For an account of the First Republic, see John Lowenhardt, *The Reincarnation of Russia: Struggling with the Legacy of Communism, 1990–1994* (Durham, N.C.: Duke University Press, 1995), 126–42. Although they do not agree with my conclusions on avoiding a return to authoritarianism, see the extensive discussion in Peter Reddaway and Dmitri Glinski, *The Tragedy of Russia's Reforms: Market Bolshevism against Democracy* (Washington, D.C.: U.S. Institute of Peace, 2001), ch. 7. For an analysis of the constitutional issues in the crisis of the First Republic and ensuing interregnum, see also Robert Sharlet, "Russian Constitutional Crisis: Law and Politics under Yeltsin," *Post-Soviet Affairs* 9, 4 (1993): 314–36.

8. See Kathryn Stoner-Weiss, "The Russian Central State in Crisis: Center and Periphery in the Post-Soviet Era," in Zoltan Barany and Robert G. Moser, eds., *Russian Politics: Challenges of Democratization* (Cambridge: Cambridge University Press, 2001), esp. 111–18 and 132–34; and Steven Solnick, "Is the Center Too Weak or Too Strong in the Russian Federation?" in Valerie Sperling, ed., *Building the Russian State* (Boulder, Colo.: Westview, 2000), esp. 141–45.

9. See Anatol Lieven, *Chechnya: Tombstone of Russian Power* (New Haven, Conn.: Yale University Press, 1998).

10. I discussed the paradox more fully in Robert Sharlet, "Reinventing the Russian State," *John Marshall Law Review* 28, 4 (1995): esp. 781–86; and in Sharlet, "Transitional Constitutionalism: Politics and Law in the Second Russian Republic," *Wisconsin International Law Journal* 14, 3 (1996): 514–20.

11. The Federal Constitutional Law on the Ombudsman was eventually passed in 1997. For the text, see E. M. Koveshnikov, comp., *Khrestomatiia po rossiiskomu konstitutsionnomu pravu* (Moscow, RF: Izdat. NORMA, 2001), 171–79.

12. For a brief discussion of the *Chechen case,* see Herman Schwartz, *The Struggle for Constitutional Justice in Post-Communist Europe* (Chicago: University of Chicago Press, 2000), 147–49. For an analysis of the second Constitutional Court's subsequent development, see Robert Sharlet, "Russia's Second Constitutional Court: Politics, Law, and Stability," in Victoria E. Bonnell and George W. Breslauer, eds., *Russia in the New Century: Stability or Disorder?* (Boulder, Colo.: Westview, 2001), ch. 4.

13. For accounts of the lead-up events and the August crisis itself, see Leon Aron, *Yeltsin: A Revolutionary Life* (New York: St. Martin's Press, 2000), 680–85; and Reddaway and Glinski, *The Tragedy of Russia's Reforms,* 595–603.

14. For a discussion of the political maneuvers and constitutional issues in the August crisis, see Robert Sharlet, "Russian Constitutional Change: An Opportunity Missed," *Demokratizatsiya* 7, 3 (1999): 437–47.

15. For a brief discussion of the 2000 presidential election, see Thomas F. Remington, *Politics in Russia,* 2nd ed. (New York: Longman, 2001), 184–85.

16. For a discussion of the strategic incentives, see Thomas F. Remington, "Taming *Vlast:* Institutional Development in Post-communist Russia," in this volume.

17. See Michael McFaul's careful analysis of Russia's system-learning process during the Second Republic in his *Russia's Unfinished Revolution: Political Change from Gorbachev to Putin* (Ithaca, N.Y.: Cornell University Press, 2001), esp. 354–59 and 363–67.

18. This contrarian evaluation of the Yeltsin presidency is well argued in Eugene Huskey, *Presidential Power in Russia* (Armonk, N.Y.: M. E. Sharpe, 1999), esp. ch. 8.

19. See Robert Sharlet, "The New Russian Constitution and Its Political Impact," *Problems of Post-Communism* 42, 5 (1995): 3–4.

20. The various attempts to revise the Constitution are closely examined in Robert Sharlet, "The Politics of Constitutional Amendment in Russia," *Post-Soviet Affairs* 13, 3 (1997): 197–227; Sharlet, "Russian Constitutional Change: An Opportunity Missed," *Demokratizatsiya* 7, 3 (1999): 437–47; and Sharlet, "Russian Constitutional Change: Proposed Power-Sharing Models," in Roger Clark, Ferdinand Feldbrugge, and Stanislaw Pomorski, eds., *International and National Law in Russia and Eastern Europe: Essays in Honor of George Ginsburgs* (The Hague, The Netherlands: Martinus Nijhoff, 2001), 361–72.

21. Eugene Huskey, "Democracy and Institutional Design in Russia," *Demokratizatsiya* 4, 4 (1996): 467.

22. Louis Fisher, *Constitutional Dialogues: Interpretation as Political Process* (Princeton, N.J.: Princeton University Press, 1988), 11.

23. See George Breslauer, "Personalism Versus Proceduralism: Boris Yeltsin and the Institutional Fragility of the Russian System," in Bonnell and Breslauer, eds., *Russia in the New Century: Stability or Disorder?* ch. 3.

24. The phrase is Herbert Kaufman's. See his "The Collapse of Ancient States and Civilizations as an Organizational Problem," in Norman Yoffee and George L. Cowgill, eds., *The Collapse of Ancient States and Civilizations* (Tucson: University of Arizona Press, 1988), 227–29.

25. For a Constitutional Court justice's critical evaluation of Russia's adjudicative capacity, see Gadis Gadzhiev, "Sud'ia ne dolzhen iskhodit' iz togo, chto zakon—eto vsegda pravo," *Strana.Ru* (1 November 2000) at www.strana.ru.

26. See Peter L. Kahn, "Agency Design and Agency Mission in the Russian Bailiffs Service: Enforcement of Civil Judgments in the Former Socialist Countries," *Post-Soviet Affairs* (forthcoming).

27. For an extensive discussion of Putin's policy responses, see Robert Sharlet, "Putin and the Politics of Law in Russia," *Post-Soviet Affairs* 17, 3 (2001): 195–234.

28. See *Konstitutsiia Rossiiskoi Federatsii/The Constitution of the Russian Federation* (Moscow: Iuridicheskaia literatura, 1994).

29. Eugene Huskey's phrase. See his "The New Russian Prefects: Presidential Representatives in the Center-Periphery Struggle," in Archie Brown and Lilia Shevtsova, eds., *Gorbachev, Yeltsin, and Putin: Political Leadership in the Russian Transition* (New York: Carnegie Endowment, 2001).

CHAPTER EIGHT
Democracy and Counterinsurgency in Central Asia
Gregory Gleason

1. For background on Central Asia, see William Fierman, *Soviet Central Asia: The Failed Transformation* (Boulder, Colo.: Westview, 1991); Denis Sinor, *The Cambridge History of Early Inner Asia* (Cambridge: Cambridge University Press, 1990); Ahmed Rashid, *The Resurgence of Central Asia: Islam or Nationalism?* (Karachi: Oxford University Press, 1994); Dilip Hiro, *Between Marx and Muhammad: The Changing Face of Central Asia* (London: Harper Collins Publishers, 1994); Roald Z. Sagdeev and Susan Eisenhower, eds., *Central Asia: Conflict, Resolution and Change* (Chevy Chase: CPSS Press, 1995); Mehrdad Haghayeghi, *Islam and Politics in Central Asia* (New York: St. Martin's Press, 1995); Shireen T. Hunter and Marie Bennigsen Broxup, *Central Asia since Independence* (Westport, Conn.: Praeger Publishers, 1996); R. D. McChesney, *Central Asia: Foundations of Change* (Princeton, N.J.: Darwin Press, 1996); Gregory Gleason, *Central Asia: Discovering Independence* (Boulder, Colo.: Westview, 1997); Lena Jonson, *Russia and Central Asia: A New Web of Relations* (London: The Royal Institute of International Affairs, 1998); Olivier Roy, *The New Central Asia: The Creation of Nations* (New York: New York University Press, 2000).

2. At independence, all the countries of the Central Asian region subscribed to the general principles of the international community, namely the sovereign equality of states; the right of noninterference in domestic affairs of the sovereign state; territorial integrity of the state; the obligation to abide by international agreements; the principle of the peaceful settlement of disputes; and the obligation to engage in international cooperation consistent with national interests.

3. See Nazarbaev's speech to the Kazak SSR Supreme Soviet, 10 December 1991, "Vybor—Tsvilizovannoe Demokratichskoe Obshchestvo," *Pyat' let nezavisimosti* (Almaty, Kazakhstan, 1996), 19–24.

4. Tajikistan joined the World Bank and the IMF in 1993. Tajikistan joined the Asian Development Bank in March 1998. Turkmenistan joined the ADB in 2000.

5. Nursultan Nazarbaev, president of Kazakhstan, is a former first secretary of the Kazakhstan republic communist party organization. Islam Karimov, president of Uzbekistan, is a former first secretary of the Uzbekistan republic

communist party organization. Saparmurad Niyazov, president of Turkmenistan, is a former first secretary of the Turkmenistan republic communist
party organization. Emomali Rahmonov, president of Tajikistan, is a former
Kuliab region communist party official. His predecessor as president, Rakhmon
Nabiev, who died under mysterious circumstances in May 1993, was a former
first secretary of the Tajikistan republic communist party organization. Among
the Central Asian presidents, only the president of Kyrgyzstan, Askar Akaev,
does not belong to the former party *nomenklatura,* although in some respects
even Akaev, a physicist who trained in Leningrad and who served briefly as the
president of the Kyrgyzstan Academy of Sciences, can also be considered a
member of the soviet elite.

6. For additional background on government and governance in these countries, see Amnesty International, *Annual Report 2000* (New York: AI, 2000);
Committee to Protect Journalists, *Attacks on the Press in 1999* (New York: CPJ,
2000); Freedom House, "Freedom in the World 1998–1999" (New York:
Freedom House, 2000); *U.S. Department of State Report on Human Rights
Practices for 2000,* Bureau of Democracy, Human Rights, and Labor (February
2001).

7. The Freedom House Annual Surveys measure progress toward democratic
ideals on a seven-point scale for political rights and for civil liberties (with 1
representing the most free and 7 the least free). Changes in countries' scores
from year to year are monitored via annual surveys. The political rights measurement addresses the degree of free and fair elections, competitive political
parties, opposition with an important role and power, freedom from domination by a powerful group (e.g., military, foreign power, totalitarian parties), and
participation by minority groups. The civil liberties measurement addresses the
degree to which there is a free and independent media; freedom of discussion,
assembly, and demonstration; freedom of political organization; equality under
the law; protection from political terror, unjustified imprisonment, and torture;
free trade unions, professional and private organizations; freedom of religion;
personal social freedoms; equality of opportunity; and freedom from extreme
government corruption.

8. The U.S. Department of State is instructed by Congress annually to prepare a report on the observance of international standards of human rights in
all the major countries of the world. The opening lines of the Human Rights
Reports on the Central Asian countries suggest the overall character of the
appraisal. Kazakhstan—"The Constitution of Kazakhstan concentrates power
in the presidency. President Nursultan Nazarbayev is the dominant political figure." Kyrgyzstan—"Although the 1993 Constitution defines the form of government as a democratic republic, President Askar Akayev dominates the
Government." Tajikistan—"Tajikistan is ruled by an authoritarian regime that
has established some nominally democratic institutions." Turkmenistan—

"Turkmenistan, a one-party state dominated by its president and his closest advisers, continues to exercise power in a Soviet-era authoritarian style despite Constitutional provisions nominally establishing a democratic system." Uzbekistan—"Uzbekistan is an authoritarian state with limited civil rights." See the U.S. Department of State Report on Human Rights Practices for 2000 (Released by the Bureau of Democracy, Human Rights, and Labor, February 2001).

9. Bernard Lewis, "A Historical Overview," *Journal of Democracy* 72 (1996): 53.

10. Juan J. Linz, "Transitions to Democracy," *Washington Quarterly* 13 (1990): 156.

11. Thomas F. Remington, "Taming *Vlast:* Institutional Development in Postcommunist Russia." Paper prepared for the Fulbright Institute Conference on International Affairs, University of Arkansas, 5–6 April 2001, 3.

12. The model of the idealized democracy includes the establishment and protection of the functioning institutions of democracy. This includes formal institutions that provide for responsiveness, representation, and public accountability. This has usually been interpreted to mean a three-branched government of executive, legislative, and judicial powers, balanced through formal legal constraints stipulated in a written constitution and buttressed by widespread public support for the underlying principles and objectives of government. The pillars of this form of democracy include the rule of law and the fabric of a civil society. The rule of law emphasizes a simple and transparent legal framework that protects human rights as absolute rights, that sustains an enabling environment for business and private interactions, and that provides for dispute resolution through the protection of the independence of the judiciary. Civil society emphasizes the preeminent position of the rights of the individual. In civil society the power of government flows from the aggregate public interest. The authorities and prerogatives of government are determined by the delegation of authority to the government by the people. The government is empowered to act as the agent of the people, to protect, secure, and advance private aims.

13. A recent USAID program notes that while the rapid structural reform model has been highly successful in Central Europe, particularly Poland, there is ample evidence that successful Central Asian development strategies should differ considerably. The USAID strategy document notes that the Central Asian states gained independence as a consequence of the disintegration of the USSR. They have no history of independent existence, they have historically been isolated, have less than a decade of experience in national self-development, and are situated in a highly competitive international context. The report concludes that in Central Asia a longer-term approach is needed. It should be an approach that builds upon popular knowledge and contributes to the public demand and political will for pluralistic economic and political change within government,

business, and professional sectors, and among the citizenry. *USAID's Assistance Strategy for Central Asia 2001–2005* (Almaty: U.S. Agency for International Development, July 2000), 3.

14. On the impact of the domestic politics of transition, see Russell Bova, "The Political Dynamics of the Post-Communist Transition: A Comparative Perspective," *World Politics* 44, 1 (October 1991): 114–21; Paul Kubicek, "Regionalism, Nationalism, and Realpolitik in Central Asia," *Europe-Asia Studies* 49, 4 (1997): 637–65.

15. The Organization for Security and Cooperation in Europe (OSCE), one of the main bodies upholding democratic practices and human rights on the continent, had earlier refused to observe the 9 January 2000 presidential election, seeking not to dignify the process with formal presence. Shortly after the election, Najmiddin Komilov, the head of Uzbekistan's Central Electoral Commission, announced that nearly 92 percent of the voters favored President Islam Karimov. The U.S. government ridiculed this outcome at a Press Conference of 12 January 1999, at which U.S. State Department spokesman James Rubin summarized that "The Government of Uzbekistan refused to register truly independent, opposition parties, nor did it permit members of these parties to run for president. The sole candidate permitted to oppose President Karimov was a public supporter of Karimov's policies and leadership, and was quoted during the campaign as stating he himself intended to vote for Karimov." (http://secretary.state.gov/www/briefings/statements/2000/ps000112a.html)

16. For an exploration of this thesis, see Adam Przeworski et al., *Sustainable Democracy* (Cambridge: Cambridge University Press, 1995).

17. On Central Asian security considerations, see Ali Banuazizi and Myron Weiner, eds., *The New Geopolitics of Central Asia and Its Borderlands* (Bloomington: Indiana University Press, 1994); William E. Odom, *Commonwealth or Empire? Russia, Central Asia and the Transcaucasus* (Indianapolis, Ind.: Hudson Institute, 1996); Martha Brill Olcott, *Central Asia's New States: Independence, Foreign Policy, and Regional Security* (Washington, D.C.: U.S. Institute of Peace, 1996); Hafeez Malik, ed., *Central Asia: Its Strategic Importance and Future Prospects* (New York: St. Martin's Press, 1996); Karen Dawisha and Bruce Parrott, eds., *Conflict, Cleavage, and Change in Central Asia and the Caucasus* (Cambridge: Cambridge University Press, 1997); John Anderson, *The International Politics of Central Asia* (Manchester: Manchester University Press, 1997); Boris Rumer and Stanislav Zhukov, eds., *Central Asia: The Challenges of Independence* (Armonk, N.Y.: M. E. Sharpe, 1998); Hooman Peimani, *Regional Security and the Future of Central Asia* (Boulder, Colo.: Praeger Publishers, 1998); Gary K. Bertsch, Cassady B. Craft, and Scott A. Jones, eds., *Crossroads and Conflict: Security and Foreign Policy in the Caucasus and Central Asia* (New York: Routledge, 1999); Robert E. Ebel and Rajan Menon,

eds., *Energy and Conflict in Central Asia and the Caucasus* (New York: Rowman and Littlefield, 2000); Sherman W. Garnett, Alexander G. Rahr, and Koji Watanabe, *The New Central Asia: In Search of Stability* (Washington, D.C.: Trilateral Commission, 2000).

18. *Dispatch* (Washington, D.C.: U.S. Department of State) 3, No. 4 (27 January 1992): 57–60, at 57.

19. See N. Nazarbaev, "Address of the President of the Republic of Kazakhstan to the People of Kazakhstan: On the Situation in the Country and Major Directions of Domestic and Foreign Policy: Democratization, Economic and Political Reform for the New Century," *Panorama* 38 (2 October 1998): 1. Nazarbaev's rhetorical commitment to democracy and a market-oriented economy has remained virtually constant through the years of his rule. In this regard, compare the ideals expressed in his speeches collected in *Five Years of Independence* (Almaty: Kazakhstan, 1996) or program for the future expressed in *Kazakhstan-2030: Prosperity, Security and Ever-Growing Welfare of all the Kazakhstanis* (Almaty: Ylim, 1997) with Islam Karimov's justification of authoritarianism in his Uzbekistan on the *Threshold of the Twenty-first Century* (New York: St. Martin's Press, 1998).

20. Akezhan Kazhegeldin, "Shattered Image: Misconceptions of Democracy and Capitalism in Kazakhstan," *Harvard International Review* 22 (winter/spring 2000); Hugh Pope and David Cloud, "Struggle in Kazakhstan Is the Apparent Spark for U.S. Investigation," *Wall Street Journal* (5 July 2000).

21. Kazakhstan's 1999 elections were criticized by the U.S. State Department, the Organization for Security and Cooperation in Europe, and Freedom House. During the early stages of the 1999 presidential campaign in Kazakhstan, then U.S. vice president Al Gore personally phoned Kazakhstan president Nazarbaev to object to the disqualification of Akezhan Kazhegeldin as a candidate in the Kazakhstan presidential elections. See Steve LeVine, "Caspian Logic: Democracy? Sure, Sure. Now Buy Our Oil," *New York Times*, 3 January 1999. Nazarbaev waived aside such objections. The OSCE Office for Democratic Institutions and Human Rights (ODIHR) sent a mission to Kazakhstan from 16 to 20 November 1998 to assess the pre-election situation in the country. The mission expressed serious doubts that the principles for democratic elections, as formulated in OSCE commitments, would be met by the 10 January 1999 presidential election. Accordingly, the ODIHR Press Release of 3 December 1998 stated, "The ODIHR believes that the Government of Kazakhstan should postpone the election to allow for adequate preparations to ensure a demo-cratic election." ODIHR Press Release No. 4/98, "Kazak Elections Not Meeting OSCE Commitments." Russian prime minister Evgenii Primakov met with Kazakh officials in Astana on 22 December to sign agreements on bilateral rela-tions. Primakov was quoted in the press as saying, "We support the [incum-bent] president of Kazakhstan," and adding that "Russia is not one of those

governments that is trying to pry into the internal affairs of Kazakhstan," ITAR-TASS as reported in *RFE/RL Newsline,* 23 December 1998.

22. Transparency International Press Release, Berlin (26 October 1999).

23. For an analysis of the challenges of independence and democratization in Kyrgyzstan, see Jeremy Bransten, "Kyrgyzstan: A Democracy Only for the Rich," *RFE/RL Newsday,* 14 October 1997; John Anderson, *Kyrgyzstan: Central Asia's Island of Democracy?* (London: Harwood Academic Publishers, 1999).

24. "Tajik Militants Take Kyrgyz Officials Hostage," RFE/*RL Newsline,* 10 August 1999.

25. "Kyrgyz Republic—Recent Economic Developments," International Monetary Fund Staff Country Report, No. 99/31 (5 May 1999).

26. These figures are from World Bank country profiles. Also see Peter R. Craumer, "Agricultural Change, Labor Supply, and Rural Out-Migration in Soviet Central Asia," in Robert A. Lewis, ed., *Geographic Perspectives on Soviet Central Asia* (London: Routledge, 1994), 132–80.

27. "Turkmenistan: Recent Economic Developments," International Monetary Fund Staff Country Report, No. 99/140 (10 December 1999).

28. "EBRD Cuts Turkmen Loans, Slams Political System," *Reuters,* 18 April 2000.

29. C (pseudonym), "One Man Rule in Uzbekistan: A Perspective from within the Regime," *Demokratizatsiya* 1, 4 (1993): 44–55.

30. Islam Karimov's justification of authoritarianism is presented in his *Uzbekistan on the Threshold of the Twenty-first Century* (New York: St. Martin's Press, 1998). Some scholars have seen intimations of democratization in the Karimov government's policies. Frederick Starr argued in the pages of *Foreign Affairs* in early 1996 the Kazakhstan may have won accolades for its democratic rhetoric and for relinquishing its soviet-era nuclear weapons, but that in fact Uzbekistan showed greater promise of promoting enduring reform and stability in the region. Starr viewed Kazakhstan's prospects for reform as dimmed by its ethnic and territorial divisions, by the absence of a strong scientific intelligentsia, by the weakness of local administrative institutions, and by an underdeveloped industrial base. Starr saw in Uzbekistan a candidate for a regional stabilizer as the most likely for fending off Russian and Iranian great power stratagems in the region. And he saw in Uzbekistan the first tentative indications of a model that could be adopted to move the other newly emergent societies of Central Asia moved toward international standards of governance and economic functioning. Starr asserted that despite Uzbekistan's "flirtations with Middle Eastern and Asian models of authoritarianism," the country was developing the groundwork for a civil society. S. Frederick Starr, "Making Eurasia Stable," *Foreign Affairs* (January–February, 1996): 80–92.

31. Commission on Security and Cooperation in Europe, *Human Rights and Democratization in Uzbekistan and Turkmenistan* (Washington, D.C.: U.S.

Government Printing Office, 2000). Also see "Straightening Out the Brains of One Hundred: Discriminatory Political Dismissals in Uzbekistan," *Helsinki Watch* (April 1993): 5, 7; Wendy Sloane, "Uzbekistan Cracks Down on Human Rights Activists," *Christian Science Monitor* (24 May 1994): 7.

32. S. Frederick Starr, "Making Eurasia Stable," *Foreign Affairs* (January–February 1996): 80–92.

33. "Republic of Uzbekistan: Recent Economic Developments," International Monetary Fund Staff Country Report, No. 00/36 (29 March 2000).

34. "IMF Pressures Uzbekistan to Make Currency Convertible," *RFE/RL Newsline,* 29 June 2000.

35. Calculated from Table 37, Uzbekistan: Direction of Trade with Traditional Trading Partners by Country, 1996–97. "Uzbekistan: Recent Economic Developments," International Monetary Fund Staff Country Report, No. 00/36 (March 2000): 74.

36. Mikhail Degtiar, "Clans, Cotton and Currency," *Central Asian Times* 2, 41 (84) 12 October 2000.

37. Ibid.

38. Helsinki Human Rights Watch, "Leaving No Witnesses: Uzbekistan's Campaign against Rights Defenders," March 2000.

39. Ibid.

40. On the events leading up to the Tajikistan civil war, see Shahram Akbarzadeh, "Why Did Nationalism Fail in Tajikistan?" *Europe-Asia Studies* 48, 7 (1996): 1105–29.

41. "UNHCR report on Tajikistan, January 1993–March 1996," United Nations High Commissioner on Refugees, May 1996, 4. Also see "Return to Tajikistan, Continued Regional and Ethnic Tensions," *Human Rights Watch/Helsinki* (HRW/H) 7, 9 (May 1995): 4–7.

42. Gregory Gleason, "Foreign Policy Dimensions of Tajikistan's Transportation Policy," *Central Asian Monitor* 6 (2000): 13–19.

43. "Republic of Tajikistan: Recent Economic Developments," International Monetary Fund Staff Country Report, No. 00/27 (March 2000).

44. Mohammad-Reza Djalili, Frederic Grare, and Shirin Akiner, *Tajikistan: The Trials of Independence* (London: St. Martin's Press, 1997).

45. Tajik and Uzbek populations in Central Asia have historically been intertwined. At the time of the territorial division of Central Asia into republics, of a total population of 1,100,000 ethnic Tajiks in Central Asia, only about 300,000 found themselves within the newly established state of Tajikistan. The gerrymandering of borders is "explained by the desire of the Uzbeks to have the historically important cities of Bukhara and Samarqand as part of Uzbekistan, despite the fact that for centuries the majority of the cities' population was Tajik. This was a matter of prestige rather than a political necessity, for, when the Russians conquered Central Asia in the second half of the nineteenth

century; they made Tashkent the political, administrative, and cultural center of Russian Turkistan, replacing cities of Bukhara and Samarqand, which had been regional centers for centuries." Sergei Gretsky, "Civil War in Tajikistan: Causes, Developments and Prospects for Peace," in Roald Z. Sagdeev and Susan Eisenhower, eds., *Central Asia: Conflict, Resolution, and Change* (Washington, D.C.: Center for Political and Strategic Studies, 1995).

46. For background on the soviet period in Tajikistan, see Teresa Rakowska-Harmstone, *Russia and Nationalism in Central Asia: The Case of Tajikistan* (Baltimore, Md.: Johns Hopkins University Press, 1970).

47. During the period of civil conflict the registration of the Islamic Renaissance party, the Rastohez National Movement, the Lali Badakhshan Movement, and the Democratic party was suspended. A faction of the Democratic party was registered in 1995. In December 1999 the Tajikistan government allowed the remaining opposition parties to register.

48. Gregory Gleason, "Why Russia Is in Tajikistan," *Comparative Strategy* 20, 1 (2001): 77–89.

49. *RFE/RL Newsline,* 17 November 1999.

50. Gleason, "Why Russia Is in Tajikistan."

51. "Republic of Tajikistan: Recent Economic Developments," International Monetary Fund Staff Country Report, No. 00/27 (March 2000). Table 46. Tajikistan External Debt.

52. David B. Ottaway, "CIA Removes Afghan Rebel Aid Director: Handling of Program Was Criticized on Hill," *Washington Post,* 2 September 1989; Henry Bradsher, *Afghanistan and the Soviet Union* (Durham, N.C.: Duke University Press); Zalmay Khalilzad, "Soviet American Cooperation in Afghanistan," in Mark N. Katz, ed., *Soviet American Conflict Resolution in the Third World* (Washington, D.C.: U.S. Institute of Peace, 1991), 67–94.

53. Masood is leader of the Jumbesh-e Melli-ye Islami-ye Afghanistan.

54. Resolution 1267 (1999) of 15 October 1999.

55. "Taliban Capture Key Northern City after Heavy Fighting," *Associated Press,* 7 September 2000.

56. Shortly after the capture of Taloqan, Turkmenistan president Niyazov dispatched Special Envoy Boris Shikhmuradov to Islamabad to initiate a dialogue with Pakistan officials on political recognition for the Taliban government. Raja Asghar, "Pakistan Backs Turkmenistan's Afghan Peace Move," *Reuters,* 31 August 2000.

57. *RFE/RL Newsline,* 15 December 1998.

58. United Nations, *Global Illicit Drug Trends* (New York, 1999), 20.

59. See Barry Bearak, "Adding to Pakistan's Misery, a Heroin Epidemic," *New York Times,* 19 April 2000, A1.

60. "Drugs, Terrorism, Water Threaten Central Asia, Says Nazarbayev," Reuters, 25 February 2000.

61. "Russian Defense Minister Predicts Instability In Central Asia," Interfax News Agency, 29 March 2000.

62. Vladimir Mukhin, "Taliban Threat Sees Uneasy Alliance on Uzbek Border," *Russia Journal* 3, 25 (68) 1 July 2000.

63. During late March 2000 George Tenet, director of the U.S. Central Intelligence Agency visited the Central Asian capitals of Astana and Tashkent. Somewhat later, in early April 2000, Louis Freeh, director of the U.S. Federal Bureau of Investigation, visited Tashkent for discussions on cooperation in the fight against crime and terrorism. U.S. secretary of state Madeleine Albright made an official visit to Central Asia (14–20 April 2000), stopping in Astana and Tashkent. General Anthony Zinni, Commander in Chief (CINC) of the U.S. Army Central Command visited the region in May 2000. The U.S. Department of State hosted a regional Central Asian Counter-terrorism Conference, 13–15 June 2000 in Washington. The conference focused on means for strengthened counter-terrorism cooperation and efforts to combat other trans-border threats, underscoring the proposition that national strategies needed to be based on the rule of law and respect for human rights if they were to succeed as long-term efforts to curtail support for terrorism. Stephen Sestanovich, former Ambassador at Large and Special Adviser to Secretary of State for the New Independent States, visited Central Asia in July 2000. See also the discussion of the geopolitical signficance of Central Asia in CIA, *Global Trends 2015: A Dialogue about the Future with Nongovernment Experts* (Washington, D.C.: Central Intelligence Agency, 2001). (*http://www.cia.gov/cia/publications/ global-trends2015/globaltrends2015.pdf*). Also see Charles Fairbanks, C. Richard Nelson, S. Frederick Starr, and Kenneth Weisbrode, *The Strategic Assessment of Central Asia* (Washington, D.C.: Central Asia and Caucasus Institute, January 2001). (*http://www.acus.org/Publications/policypapers/internationalsecurity/Central%20 Eurasia.pdf*); International Crisis Group, *Central Asia: Islamicist Mobilization and Regional Security* (Brussels: ICG, March 2001). (*http://www.intl-crisisgroup.org/projects/showreport.cfm?reportid=245*)

CHAPTER NINE
Institutionalizing Electoral Democracy in Post-Communist States
Jack Bielasiak

1. Peter Mair, *Party System Change: Approaches and Interpretations* (Oxford: Clarendon Press, 1997); Scott Mainwaring and Timothy Scully, eds., *Building Democratic Institutions: Party Systems in Latin America* (Stanford, Conn.: Stanford University Press, 1995).

2. Goldie Shabad and K. M. Slomcznski, "Political Identities in the Initial Phase of Systemic Transformation in Poland: A Test of the Tabula Rasa Hypothesis," *Comparative Political Studies* 32, 6 (1999): 690–723.

3. Arthur Miller, Gwen Erb, William Reisinger, and Vicki Hesli, "Emerging Party Systems in Post-Soviet Societies: Fact or Fiction," *Journal of Politics* 62, 2 (2000): 455–90.

4. Mair, *Party System Change*; Petr Kopecky, "Developing Party Organizations in East Central Europe: What Kind of Party Is Likely to Emerge?" *Party Politics* 1, 4 (1995): 515–34.

5. Jack Bielasiak, "Substance and Process in the Development of Party Systems in East Central Europe," *Communist and Post-Communist Studies* 30, 1 (1997): 23–44.

6. Mair, *Party System Change*; Peter Mair, "Electoral Markets and Stable States," in M. Moran and W. Wright, eds., *The Market and the State: Studies in Interdependence* (New York: St. Martin's Press, 1991).

7. Valerie Bunce and Maria Csanadi, "Uncertainty in the Transition: Post-Communism in Hungary," *East European Politics and Society* 7, 2 (1993): 240–75.

8. Claus Offe, "Capitalism by Democratic Design? Democratic Theory Facing the Triple Transition in East Central Europe," *Social Research* 58, 4 (1991): 865–902.

9. Elizabeth Kiss, "Democracy without Parties?" *Dissent* (spring 1992): 226–31.

10. Andrzej Rychard, *Reforms, Adaptation, and Breakthrough* (Warsaw: IFIS, 1993).

11. Herbert Kitschelt, "The Formation of Party Systems in East Central Europe," *Politics and Society* 20, 1 (1992): 7–50; Geoffrey Evans and Stephen Whitefield, "Identifying the Basis of Party Competition in Eastern Europe," *British Journal of Political Science* 23, 4 (1993): 531–48; Gabor Toka, "Parties and Electoral Choices in East Central Europe," in Paul Lewis and Geoffrey Pridham, eds., *Stabilizing Fragile Democracies* (London: Routledge, 1996); Shabad and Slomczynski, "Political Identities"; Miller et al., "Emerging Party Systems."

12. Attial Agh, "The Hungarian Party System and Party Theory in the Transition of Central Europe," *Journal of Theoretical Politics* 6, 2 (1994): 217–38; Paul Lewis, "Democratization and Party Development in Eastern Europe," *Democratization* 1, 3 (1994): 391–405; David M. Olson, "Party Formation and Party System Consolidation in the New Democracies of Central Europe," *Political Studies* 46 (1998): 432–64.

13. Terry Lynn Karl, "Dilemmas of Democratization in Latin America," *Comparative Politics* 23, 1 (1990): 1–21.

14. Guillermo O'Donnell, "Delegative Democracy," *Journal of Politics*, 5, 1 (1994).

15. Farred Zakaria, "The Rise of Illiberal Democracy," *Foreign Affairs* 76, 6 (1997).

16. David Altman and Anibal Perez Linan, "Assessing the Quality of Democracy: Freedom, Competitiveness, and Participation in eighteen Latin American Countries," Working Paper, University of Notre Dame, 1999; Muguel Centellas, "The Consolidation of Polyarchy in Bolivia," Paper presented at the Midwest Political Science Convention, Chicago, Illinois, 2000.

17. Robert Dahl, *Polyarchy: Participation and Opposition* (New Haven, Conn.: Yale University Press, 1971).

18. Seymour Martin Lipset, "Some Social Prerequisites of Democracy: Economic Development and Political Legitimacy," *American Political Science Review* 53, 1 (1971): 69–105; Adam Przeworski, Michael E. Alvarez, Joseph Antonio Cheibub, and Fernando Limongi, *Democracy and Development: Political Institutions and Well-Being in the World, 1950–1990* (Cambridge: Cambridge University Press, 2000).

19. Samuel Valenzuela, "Democratic Consolidation in Post-Transitional Settings: Notion, Process, and Facilitating Conditions," in Scott Mainwaring, Guillermo O'Donnell, and Samuel Valenzuela, eds., *Issues in Democratic Consolidation: The New South American Democracies in Comparative Perspective* (Notre Dame: University of Notre Dame Press, 1992); Guillermo O'Donnell, "On the State, Democratization, and Some Conceptual Problems: A Latin American View with Glances at Some Postcommunist Countries," *World Development* 21 (1993): 1355–69.

20. Centellas, "The Consolidation of Polyarchy in Bolivia."

21. Joseph A. Schumpeter, *Capitalism, Socialism and Democracy* (New York: Harper and Row, 1976).

22. Dahl, *Polyarchy.*

23. Mair, *Party System Change;* Scott Mainwaring, "Party Systems in the Third Wave," *Journal of Democracy* 9, 2 (1998): 67–82.

24. Gary Cox, *Making Votes Count* (Cambridge: Cambridge University Press, 1997); Arend Lijphard, *Electoral Systems and Party Systems* (Oxford: Oxford University Press, 1994).

25. Mair, *Party System Change.*

26. Centellas, "The Consolidation of Polyarchy in Bolivia."

27. Kitschelt, "The Formation of Party Systems in East Central Europe."

28. Maurice Duverger, *Political Parties: Their Organization and Activity in the Modern State* (New York: Wiley, 1954).

29. Juan J. Linz and Alfred Stepan, *Problems of Democratic Transition and Consolidation* (Baltimore, Md.: Johns Hopkins University Press, 1996).

30. Rein Taageper and Matthew Sogberg Shugart, *Seats and Votes* (New Haven, Conn.: Yale University Press, 1989); Lijphard, *Electoral Systems;* Cox, *Making Votes Count.*

31. Duverger, *Political Parties.*

32. Lijphard, *Electoral Systems.*

33. Kimmo Kuusela, "The Founding Electoral Systems in Eastern Europe," in Geoffrey Pridham and Tatu Vahnanen, *Democratization in Eastern Europe* (New York: Routledge, 1994).

34. Jack Bielasiak, "The Institutionalization of Electoral and Party Systems in Postcommunist States," *Comparative Politics,* forthcoming.

35. Ibid.

36. Inter-Parliamentary Union, *Annuals* from 1990 to 1999, *Chronicle of Parliamentary Elections and Developments* (Geneva: IPU and on-line at www.ipu.org).

37. Leonard J. Cohen, "Embattled Democracy: Postcommunist Croatia in Transition," in Karen Dawisha and Bruce Parrott, eds., *Politics, Power and the Struggle for Democracy in South-East Europe* (Cambridge: Cambridge University Press, 1997); Nicholas Pano, "The Process of Democratization in Albania, in Dawisha and Parrott, eds., *Politics, Power and the Struggle for Democracy.*

38. Mair, *Party System Change.*

39. Mainwaring and Scully, *Building Democratic Institutions.*

40. Markku Laakso and Rein Taagerpera, "Effective Number of Parties: A Measure with Application to West Europe," *Comparative Political Studies* 12 (1979): 3–27.

41. Giovanni Sartori, *Parties and Party Systems* (Cambridge: Cambridge University Press, 1976); Jean Blondel, "Party Systems and Patterns of Government in Western Democracies," *Canadian Journal of Political Science* 10, 3 (1968): 180–203.

42. Francis Millard, "The Polish Parliamentary Elections of October 1991," *Soviet Studies* 44, 5 (1992): 837–55; Francis Millard, "The Shaping of the Polish Party System," *East European Politics and Society* 8, 3 (1994): 295–314.

43. Pano, "The Process of Democratization in Albania"; John Bell, "Democratization and Political Participation in Postcommunist Bulgaria," in Dawisha and Parrott, *Power, Politics and the Struggle;* Cohen, "Embattled Democracy."

44. Stephen White, Richard Rose, and Ian McAllister, *How Russia Votes* (Chatham, N.J.: Chatham House, 1997).

45. Stefano Bartolini and Peter Mair, *Identity, Competition, and Electoral Availability* (Cambridge: Cambridge University Press, 1990); Leonardo Morlin, *Democracy between Consolidation and Crisis: Parties, Groups, and Citizens in Southern Europe* (Oxford: Oxford University Press, 1998).

46. Robert Dahl, *Dilemmas of Pluralist Democracy: Autonomy vs. Control* (New Haven, Conn.: Yale University Press, 1982).

47. Centellas, "Polyarchy."

48. Altman and Perez Linan, "Assessing the Quality;" Centellas, "The Consolidation" and "Polyarchy."

49. Centellas, "Polyarchy."

50. Lawrence LeDuc, Richard G. Niemi, and Pippa Norris, eds., *Comparing Democracies: Elections and Voting in Global Perspective* (Thousand Oaks, Calif.: Sage, 1996).

51. Toivo Raun, "Democratization and Political Development in Estonia," in Dawisha and Parrott, *The Consolidation of Democracy in East Central Europe* (Cambridge: Cambridge University Press, 1997); Vello Pettai and Marcus Kreuzer, "Party Politics in the Baltic States: Social Basis and Institutional Context," *East European Politics and Society* 13, 1 (1999): 148–89.

CHAPTER TEN
A Decade of Nonnationalism?: Regime Change as Surrogate for Identity Change

Raymond Taras

1. Rasma Karklins, *Ethnopolitics and Transition to Democracy: The Collapse of the USSR and Latvia* (Washington, D.C.: Woodrow Wilson Center Press, 1994), 152.

2. Victor Zaslavsky, "The Soviet Union," in Karen Barkey and Mark von Hagen, eds., *After Empire: Multiethnic Societies and Nation-Building—The Soviet Union and the Russian, Ottoman, and Habsburg Empires* (Boulder, Colo.: Westview, 1997), 73.

3. Mark B. Beissinger, "Elites and Ethnic Identities in Soviet and Post-Soviet Politics," in Alexander J. Motyl, ed., *The Post-Soviet Nations: Perspectives on the Demise of the USSR* (New York: Columbia University Press, 1992), 162.

4. Graham Smith, Vivien Law, Andrew Wilson, Annette Bohr, and Edward Allworth, *Nation-building in the Post-Soviet Borderlands: The Politics of National Identities* (Cambridge: Cambridge University Press, 1998), 3.

5. Ibid., 9.

6. Ibid., 4.

7. Ibid., 5–6.

8. Victor Zaslavsky, "Nationalism and Democratic Transition in Postcommunist Societies," *Daedalus* 121, 2 (spring 1992): 101.

9. Terry Martin, *The Affirmative Action Empire: Nations and Nationalism in the Soviet Union, 1923–1939* (Ithaca, N.Y.: Cornell University Press, 2001).

10. Smith et al., *Nation-building in the Post-Soviet Borderlands*, 7.

11. See Ian Bremmer and Ray Taras, eds., *New States, New Politics: Building the Post-Soviet Nations* (Cambridge: Cambridge University Press, 1997).

12. For example, Dmitry Gorenburg, "Nationalism for the Masses: Popular Support for Nationalism in Russia's Ethnic Republics," *Europe-Asia Studies* 53, 1 (January 2001): 73–104.

13. Valery Tishkov, *Ethnicity, Nationalism and Conflict in and after the Soviet Union: The Mind Aflame* (London: Sage, 1997), 233.

14. George Schopflin, "The Communist Experience and Nationhood," in Andre Gerrits and Nanci Adler, eds., *Vampires Unstaked: National Images, Stereotypes and Myths in East Central Europe* (Amsterdam: Royal Netherlands Academy of Arts and Sciences, 1995), 192.

15. Ronald G. Suny, "The Russian Empire," in Barkey and von Hagen, *After Empire,* 152.

16. Suny, "The Russian Empire," 153.

17. Igor Zevelev, *Russia and Its New Diasporas* (Washington, D.C.: U.S. Institute of Peace, 2001), 34.

18. Beissinger, "Elites and Ethnic Identities in Soviet and Post-Soviet Politics," 150.

19. Roman Szporluk, "Introduction: Statehood and Nation Building in Post-Soviet Space," in Szporluk, ed., *National Identity and Ethnicity in Russia and the New States of Eurasia* (Armonk, N.Y.: M. E. Sharpe, 1994), 6.

20. Martin Walker, *Guardian Weekly,* 14 February 1988. Quoted in Gertjan Dijkink, *National Identity and Geopolitical Visions: Maps of Pride and Pain* (London: Routledge, 1996), 98.

21. Dijkink, *National Identity and Geopolitical Visions,* 101.

22. Alexander J. Motyl, "Thinking about Empire," in Barkey and von Hagen, *After Empire,* 28.

23. Motyl, "Thinking about Empire," 25.

24. Andre Liebich, *Les minorites nationales en Europe centrale et orientale* (Geneva: Georg, 1997), 130.

25. Walter Kolarz, "Colonialism: Theory and Practice," in George Gretton, ed., *Communism and Colonialism: Essays by Walter Kolarz* (London: Macmillan, 1964), 23.

26. The argument that Yeltsin appropriated nationalist ideas that deliberately or inadvertently undermined the liberal-democratic movement is made by Yitzhak M. Brudny, *Reinventing Russia: Russian Nationalism and the Soviet State, 1953–1991* (Cambridge, Mass.: Harvard University Press, 2000), 259–65.

27. Helene Carrere d'Encausse, *The Nationality Question in the Soviet Union and Russia* (Oslo: Scandinavian University Press, 1995), 54.

28. Leon Aron, "The Emergent Priorities of Russian Foreign Policy," in Leon Aron and Kenneth Jensen, eds., *The Emergence of Russian Foreign Policy* (Herndon, Va.: U.S. Institute of Peace, 1994), 19.

29. Mark R. Beissinger, "The Persisting Ambiguity of Empire," in *Post-Soviet Affairs* 2, 2 (1995): 149. See also William Odom and Robert Dujarric, *Commonwealth or Empire? Russia, Central Asia and the Transcaucasus* (Indianapolis, Ind.: Hudson Institute, 1995); Uri Ra'anan and Kate Martin, *Russia: A Return to Imperialism?* (New York: St. Martin's Press, 1995).

30. Beissinger, "The Persisting Ambiguity of Empire," 163.

31. P. O'Prey, "Keeping the Peace in the Borderlands of Russia," in William J.

Durch, ed., *UN Peacekeeping, American Policy, and the Uncivil Wars of the 1990s* (New York: St. Martin's Press, 1996), 411.

32. Quoted by Paul Flenley, "From Soviet to Russian Identity: The Origins of Contemporary Russian Nationalism and National Identity," in Brian Jenkins and Spyros A. Sofos, eds., *Nation and Identity in Contemporary Europe* (London: Routledge, 1996), 245.

33. Bo Petersson, *National Self-Images and Regional Identities in Russia* (Aldershot: Ashgate, 2001), 187.

34. For a detailed historical analysis, see Iver B. Neumann, *Russia and the Idea of Europe: A Study in Identity and International Relations* (London: Routledge, 1995).

35. Ilya Prizel, *National Identity and Foreign Policy: Nationalism and Leadership in Poland, Russia, and Ukraine* (Cambridge: Cambridge University Press, 1998), 10.

36. Prizel, *National Identity and Foreign Policy,* 155.

37. Judy Batt, "The Politics of Minority Rights in Post-communist Europe," in Finn Laursen and Soren Riishoj, eds., *The EU and Central Europe: Status and Prospects* (Esbjerg: South Jutland University Press, 1996), 48.

38. Svetlana Boym, *Common Places: Mythologies of Everyday Life in Russia* (Cambridge, Mass.: Harvard University Press, 1994), 228.

39. Smith et al., *Nation-building in the Post-Soviet Borderlands,* 11.

40. Ibid., 13.

41. Lev N. Gumilev, *Ot rusi k rossii: ocherki etnicheskoi istorii* (Moscow: Ekoproc, 1992), 297. Quoted by Prizel, *National Identity and Foreign Policy,* 230.

42. Prizel, *National Identity and Foreign Policy,* 230.

43. Andrei P. Tsygankov, "Hard-line Eurasianism and Russia's Contending Geopolitical Perspectives," *East European Quarterly* 32, 3 (fall 1998): 318.

44. Ibid., 322.

45. Ibid., 323. For the differences between modernizers and expansionists, see Table 1, p. 330.

46. See Veljko Vujacic, "Serving Mother Russia: The Communist Left and Nationalist Right in the Struggle for Power, 1991–1998," in Victoria E. Bonnell and George W. Breslauer, eds., *Russia in the New Century: Stability or Disorder?* (Boulder, Colo.: Westview, 2001), 290–325.

47. Aleksandr Dugin, *Konservativnaya revolutsia* (Moscow: AKIRN, 1994).

48. Quoted in Wayne Allensworth, *The Russian Question: Nationalism, Modernization, and Post-Communist Russia* (Lanham, Md.: Rowman and Littlefield, 1998), 250.

49. Quoted in ibid., 250–51.

50. See David Kerr, "The New Eurasianism: The Rise of Geopolitics in Russia's Foreign Policy," *Europe-Asia Studies* 47, 8 (December 1995): 977–88.

51. Alexander Solzhenitsyn, *Rebuilding Russia* (New York: Farrar, Straus, and Giroux, 1991), 10.

52. Ulf Hedetoft, *Signs of Nations: Studies in the Political Semiotics of Self and Other in Contemporary European Nationalism* (Aldershot: Dartmouth, 1995), 160.

53. See James Hughes, "From Federalization to Recentralization," in Stephen White, Alex Pravda, and Zvi Gitelman, eds., *Developments in Russian Politics,* 5th ed. (Houndmills: Palgrave, 2001), 128–46.

54. Michael Billig, *Banal Nationalism* (London: Sage, 1997), 71.

55. Mikhail S. Gorbachev, "Interview," *Der Spiegel,* 25 March 1991, 175.

56. Adam Przeworski, *Democracy and the Market* (Cambridge: Cambridge University Press, 1991).

57. Douglass C. North, *Institutions, Institutional Change, and Economic Performance* (Cambridge: Cambridge University Press, 1991), 91.

58. Valery Tishkov, "Ob ideye natsiyi," *Obshchestvennye nauki* 4 (1990): 95.

59. Marjorie Castle, "A Successfully Failed Pact? The Polish Political Transition of 1989," Doctoral dissertation, Stanford University, Department of Political Science, 1995, chapter 1.

60. Juan J. Linz and Alfred Stepan, "Political Identities and Electoral Sequences: Spain, the Soviet Union, and Yugoslavia," *Daedalus* 121, 2 (spring 1992): 133.

61. Paul Goble, "Gorbachev and the Soviet Nationality Problem," in Maurice Friedburg and H. Isham, eds., *Soviet Society under Gorbachev* (Armonk, N.Y.: M. E. Sharpe, 1987).

62. Stephen White, "From Communism to Democracy?" in White, Pravda, and Gitelman, *Developments in Russian Politics,* 17.

Contributors

JACK BIELASIAK is Professor of Political Science at Indiana University. He received his Ph.D. from Cornell University and is a specialist on Eastern Europe. He has published in *Communist and Post-Communist Studies, American Political Science Review,* and *East European Quarterly.* He is currently at work on *Polish Politics: Edge of the Abyss.*

VALERIE BUNCE is Professor of Political Science at Cornell University. She received her Ph.D. from the University of Michigan. Her works include *Subversive Institutions: The Design and Destruction of Socialism and the State* and *Do Leaders Matter: Executive Succession and Public Policy under Capitalism and Socialism.*

GREGORY GLEASON is Professor of Political Science at the University of New Mexico. He received his Ph.D. from the University of California, Davis. A specialist in Central Asia, he is the author of *The States of Central Asia: Discovering Independence.*

DONALD R. KELLEY is Professor of Political Science and Director of the Fulbright Institute of International Relations at the University of Arkansas. He received his Ph.D. from Indiana University. His works include *Politics in Russia and the Successor States, Soviet Politics from Brezhnev to Gorbachev,* and *Soviet Politics in the Brezhnev Era.*

THOMAS F. REMINGTON is Professor of Political Science at Emory University. He received his Ph.D. from Yale University. He is author of *The Politics of Institutional Choice: Formation of the Russian State Duma, Politics in Russia,* and *Parliaments in Transition.*

RICHARD ROSE is Director of the Centre for the Study of Public Policy at the University of Strathclyde, and Director of the New Russia Barometer. He received his Ph.D. from Oxford University. Most recently published among his many books are *The Prime Minister in a Shrinking World: The Paradox of Power, International Encyclopedia of Elections, Democracy and Its Alternatives: Understanding Post-Communist Societies,* and *How Russia Votes.*

ROBERT SHARLET is Chauncey Winters Professor of Political Science at Union College. He received his Ph.D. from Indiana University. His books include *Constitutional Politics in Russia, Soviet Constitutional Crisis: From De-Stalinization to Disintegration,* and *Selected Writing on Soviet Law and Marxism.*

RAYMOND TARAS is Professor of Political Science at Tulane University. He received his Ph.D. from the University of Warsaw and is author of *National Identities and Ethnic Movements in Eastern Europe, Post-Communist Presidents, New States, New Politics: Building the Post-Soviet Nations,* and *Consolidating Democracy in Poland.*

MICHAEL URBAN is Professor of Political Science at the University of California, Santa Cruz. He received his Ph.D. from the University of Kansas. His books include *The Rebirth of Politics in Russia, Ideology and System Change in the USSR and Eastern Europe,* and *More Power to the Soviets.*

Index